D1569939

Mining the Summit

Mining the Summit

Colorado's Ten Mile District, 1860–1960

by

**Stanley Dempsey and
James E. Fell, Jr.**

University of Oklahoma Press
Norman and London

By James E. Fell, Jr.

Ores to Metals: The Rocky Mountain Smelting Industry (Lincoln, Nebr., 1980)
Arthur Redman Wilfley: Miner, Inventor, and Entrepreneur (coauth.)
  (Denver, Colo., 1982)
Aurora: Gateway to the Rockies (coauth.) (Evergreen, Colo., 1985)
Mining the Summit: Colorado's Ten Mile District, 1860–1960 (Norman, 1986)

Library of Congress Cataloging-in-Publication Data

Dempsey, Stanley, 1939–
  Mining the summit.

  Bibliography: p.
  Includes index.
  1. Mineral industries—Colorado—History.   I. Fell,
James E., 1944–   II. Title.
HD9506.U63C64   1986   338.2′09788′4   86-40071
ISBN 0-8061-2005-3 (alk. paper)

For Judy

Contents

Illustrations

Maps

Preface

THIS book had its origins in the early 1960s when Stanley Dempsey, then a young attorney, went to work for the Climax Molybdenum Company. His job was to help the firm acquire land in the Ten Mile Mining District north of Leadville, Colorado, and to disincorporate the old towns of Recen and Kokomo. This would pave the way for the expansion of the world's largest molybdenum mine. Aside from the professional objectives at hand, the task sparked Dempsey's interest in Ten Mile's history. Ruins dotted the landscape, and old miners and the descendants of early settlers had fascinating stories to tell. Yet the record itself was unclear. The locale obviously had an intriguing story, for even a cursory survey of past events revealed a bonanza king shot in the midst of a claim dispute, the most eminent of nineteenth-century mining geologists battling a recalcitrant federal bureaucracy, and an introspective inventor quietly developing what would become a world-famous piece of mining machinery. More research revealed a gold rush to gulches buried by snowdrifts in midsummer, a silver stampede in the midst of winter, and a devastating fire that wiped out an entire town in a single night.

The result of this investigation ultimately revealed a mining district that had been a microcosm of the cyclic development characteristic of mining throughout Colorado and much of the West. The first miners came to find gold, but over the years, the episodic production shifted from gold to silver, then to lead and zinc, and finally to molybdenum. This of course reflected the general shift in Colorado's output from precious to base metals, each change accompanied by the larger-scale mobilization of capital and labor, the use of more advanced technology, and the ongoing development of the infrastructure required to support mining. Yet there were differences at Ten Mile. If the modest output of gold and silver, lead and zinc, made it a microcosm of nineteenth century mining, then the massive production of molybdenum in the twentieth century transformed this isolated valley (and adjacent parts of Lake County) into the foremost metal mining area in Colorado and one of the most important in the world.

Although mineral production underscored all phases of the valley's development, the climate and geography also had a profound influence on life. The district was so high above sea level that the short summers, long winters, and frequently inclement weather interfered with mining, hampered communications, disrupted transportation, and made life difficult. Subfreezing temperatures, deep snows, and deadly avalanches created havoc from October to May and beyond, while spring runoffs drowned mines and turned roads into quagmires. And Ten Mile itself, sandwiched between two rugged mountain ranges was so isolated, so remote, that it fostered no permanent settlements except those based on the minerals industry. Even so, Ten Mile's development generally trailed similar events taking place at the great mining center clustered around California Gulch and its successor, the City of Leadville, less than twenty miles away.

No book of this size could have been completed without the assistance of many others, and the authors wish to acknowledge those whose contribution was special. Bud and Sharon Recen offered much encouragement in the early stages of research, and the late Henry Recen's accounts, told in the lobby of the Brown Palace Hotel, were as interesting as they were informative. Both Helen Byron and the late Walter Byron provided considerable assistance. Mr. and Mrs. Cecil Work of Lancaster, Pennsylvania, and Jay E. Niebur of Boulder, Colorado, were very gracious in loaning photographs and offering insights into life in Kokomo. Donald Gelbard of Kalamazoo, Michigan, took time on a sweltering Sunday in August 1981 to point out the Robinson gravesite. Maxine Benson, Colorado State Historian, helped bring author and coauthor together. Mae Jacobs, Muriel Drysdale, and Kenje Ogata typed portions of various drafts, and JoAnn Buck typed the final draft. Many libraries assisted in this project, but particular thanks are due to the Colorado Historical Society, Denver Public Library, Colorado School of Mines, University of Colorado, Western Michigan University, Harvard Business School, Library of Congress, and National Archives.

Lakewood, Colorado   STANLEY DEMPSEY
Louisville, Colorado   JAMES E. FELL, JR.

Mining the Summit

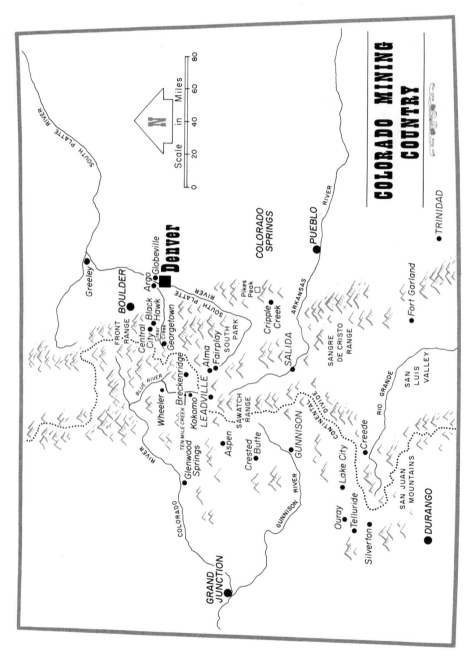

COLORADO MINING COUNTRY

Scale in Miles

0   20   40   60   80

A Ceaseless Stream

THE Ten Mile that James McNulty and other miners saw for the first time in that spring of 1860 must have looked just as it had for decades. It was a high, rugged country deep in the fastness of the Rocky Mountains. Towering peaks, snowcapped most of the year, formed the skyline on every side and dominated the landscape like no other feature. There was some open space, but what little there was consisted of a densely wooded valley some 10,000 feet above sea level. It was from here that the contour of the land rose up sharply into long lines of ridges and peaks, particularly toward the east where jagged spires nearly 14,000 feet high stood like ancient sentinels guarding the approaches below. So rapid was the gain in elevation that these crags delayed the sunrise in the morning, while their smaller, more rounded counterparts across the valley hastened the sunset in the evening. Between the peaks that formed the southern boundary of Ten Mile, there was a low passage known as Arkansas Pass, a name taken from the east fork of the river that rushed away on the other side. And thirteen or so miles away along the northern rim, the valley pressed into a high, rocky defile known as Ten Mile Canyon, which twisted its way a short distance north until it ran into a second canyon that capped it like a T.

Down through the valley flowed a stream known as Ten Mile Creek. It collected its first waters from the runoff on Arkansas Pass, but its real headwaters rushed down from the deep, steep-walled basin, or cirque, on Bartlett Mountain, the light-gray peak shaped like a giant bowl just east of the pass. From here the creek meandered north collecting water that spilled out of the small lakes and tarns or that plunged down through the deep valleys that ancient glaciers had cut in the mountainsides. During the winter the bitter cold in Ten Mile froze the stream into solid ice, and the first blizzards buried it from view until the season played out. In the spring the melting snows turned the creek into a torrent that churned with white water and carried ice, wood, and rocks down pell-mell, but as spring gave way to summer, the surge subsided into a peaceful current that splashed its way north to an eventual rendezvous with Blue River, which rose across the mountains east of Ten Mile. The two streams joined together some ten miles below Breckenridge, and while no one is sure today, it seems likely that Ten Mile Creek drew its name from this happenstance. From the confluence, Blue River meandered north to its own junction with the Colorado River in what was known as Middle Park, and from there the waters flowed on in concert through the mountains and deserts of the West until they emptied into the Pacific Ocean.

Because of the rapid, 4,000-foot gain in elevation, Ten Mile had several different life zones. The valley floor was heavily forested with thick groves of aspen and pine, spruce and fir, along with low shrubs like cinquefoil and juniper. Year round they covered the valley with a deep green carpet. There was only one seasonal change in this. Every fall the aspen leaves dappled the valley with brilliant hues of yellow and orange much as if a wandering artist had dabbed the country with a giant paintbrush. Then for the winter the aspen huddled together like tall gray poles until the arrival of spring turned their branches back into green. Although Ten Mile had few open spaces, those it had were covered with short grasses that, except for a brief green time in the spring, formed a light straw-brown cover that rippled in the winds until the first snows covered them over. And during the short summer season a myriad of blooming flowers graced the fields, forests, and streams with every color. [1]

Forests covered most of Ten Mile up to an altitude of nearly eleven thousand feet, but here the trees took on a gnarled, stunted look, a sign that the lower montane region was at last giving way to the alpine tundra. Here at timberline, life changed abruptly. The high winds, low temperatures, lack of cover, and short growing season put an end to the high forest growth, although shrubs that could stand the exposure managed to form a thick, sometimes impenetrable ground cover that clung to the high slopes for life. There were more open areas, too, and it was here that the low grasses and miniature flowers formed a soft, gentle carpet whose texture broke the severity of the cliffs, spurs, and ridges. The short, though relatively warm, summer months, good water, and brilliant sunshine turned this tundra into a greensward that teemed with hardy wildflowers. Here the tiny forget-me-nots seemed to combine with the intense blue of the Colorado sky and the pure white of the alpine snow to produce a perfect reflection of the lofty surroundings.

Above timberline the open tundra continued upward to the mountain summits. Here, in this arctic climate, the high winds, scarce soil, bitter cold, and scanty water made life ever more marginal. The short grasses and miniature flowers gave way to even hardier grasses, sedges, and cushion plants that eked out a precarious living from season to season. Pale green lichens clung to a hazardous life on the surface of large gray boulders and precipitous rock walls. This inhospitable region of cliffs, crevasses, and gulleys stood out in sharp relief, forming the spectacular profile of crags that could be seen from the valley far below.

No one could say that Ten Mile teemed with wildlife. The weather and altitude made sure of that. Small, adaptable animals like the spruce grouse, ptarmigan, and snowshoe rabbit, or the porcupine, coyote, and red squirrel, all made permanent homes in the lowlands. So, too, did small numbers of beaver. One animal that really found the country to its liking was the ubiquitous red fox, which was particularly obvious in the spring as it chased small rodents across the snowbanks. Larger animals such as the black bear, elk, and mule deer roamed through the woods and grazed in the open spaces, but they were only transients wandering through in search of food, shelter, and safety as the season permitted. Although an occasional grizzly bear chanced into the country to prey upon the small, the weak, or the unlucky, the only large creature that made a permanent home here was the mountain sheep that grazed in the valley, but spent much of its life on the high slopes above timberline. Substantial numbers of cutthroat trout and other fish made their homes in the nooks and crannies of Ten Mile Creek or in the many small lakes and tarns. And far above, golden eagles rode the air currents high over the valley, matching the lofty majesty of the mountains.

The long winters and inclement weather dominated the eternal cycle of seasonal change. The freeze lasted a full eight months, from October through May, and just a few miles away, where records have long been kept, the average yearly temperature was just 33 degrees Fahrenheit, a scant one degree above freezing. The snowstorms began early and stayed late, covering the valley with a deep white carpet, building impassable snowdrifts, and capping the ridges, cliffs, and peaks with a thick white mantle. Sometimes the wind currents blew off this snow in filaments that looked like slender white streams of frigid smoke. The long winter also made its presence known in the spring when the melting snowpack turned trails into quagmires and streams into torrents. Summer days, however, were pleasant, though often interrupted by sudden thunderstorms. Only for a brief time in the fall, in September and October, did stable weather prevail on the landscape, and in that season the crisp, cloudless autumn days always seemed to be a pleasant reward for the persevering who had endured the difficult weather of other seasons.

This geography and climate profoundly influenced the residents of Ten Mile. Small, hardy animals adapted to the environment and stayed year round, but larger ones did little more than use the valley as a high passage to lower, more temperate, and more plentiful climes. The same was true with man. The extremes of climate and terrain were so great that for centuries the people who came here found little to hold them. The hunting was slight, the beaver few, the land unsuited for agriculture. Like the large animals, man from the very earliest times—perhaps ten thousand years ago—was but another traveler through Ten Mile, not an occupant, at least not until the third great shaping force in the region, its mineral resources, offered him something that compelled him to stay. It was this that brought James McNulty and others like him across the summit of Arkansas Pass in that fateful spring of 1860.

The Geology

The geology of Ten Mile is complex. The rugged terrain along the eastern side of the district, including the Ten Mile Range itself, is underlain by rocks of the Precambrian era, meaning that they were formed between 2.5 and 1.5 billion years ago. These rocks are crystalline, composed of feldspars, quartz, and mica; and they are light in color and very hard. But the high terrain that forms the central and western parts of the district is different. It consists of sedimentary rocks formed by ancient seas that covered the region between 225 and 550 million years ago during the Paleozoic era. Then in the relatively recent Tertiary period, beginning some 60 million years ago and lasting to just over 1 million years ago, igneous rocks and related solutions intruded into both the crystalline rocks and the sedimentary rocks, bringing valuable minerals. For the most part these so-called intrusive rocks are light-colored porphyries that were formed into stocks, dikes, and sills. In the tens of thousands of years that followed their formation, the differential erosion of a thick series of such sedimentary rocks and the sills of igneous rocks produced the prominent layering that can be seen here and there, perhaps most noticeably on the slopes of Jacque Mountain, one of the main peaks on the western border of Ten Mile.

Before the beginning of the Paleozoic era, the Precambrian rocks of the Ten Mile Range had been tightly folded, strongly metamorphosed, partially melted, intruded by large bodies of molten granite, fractured, faulted, uplifted tens of thousands of feet, and finally eroded to a nearly planar surface. Then, during the early Paleozoic era, the broad lowland was covered from time to time by shallow seas that left their record in the small patches of limestone, quartzite, and shale found on Chalk Mountain and other sites. During the late Paleozoic, the seas receded. Gypsum evaporite deposits grew in the ephemeral lakes of the basin center. Streams that flowed into the area deposited coarse sediments on the alluvial fans that bordered the basin and the flanks of the neighboring uplifts. The 2,000-foot thickness of the Maroon formation on Jacque Mountain is evidence of this last event.

Ten Mile does not have any rocks of the Mesozoic era, which extended from 180 to 60 million years ago. Nonetheless, beginning at a time near the end of this era, and extending down into the Tertiary era, there was a long period of faulting, uplifting, and eroding, as well as the intrusion of igneous rocks. Brittle crystalline rocks were cracked, and the sedimentary rocks were warped, folded, and faulted. Masses of igneous rocks, predominantly various types of porphyry, were injected into areas of weakness in the existing rock masses. In many places, the porphyries pushed into spaces along the bedding planes in the sedimentary rocks, forming sills. As Tertiary time continued, crustal readjustment and intrusion resulted in the placement of large stocks of porphyry.

In late Tertiary times an uplift took place along the Mosquito fault, which runs from the southern boundary of the district near Climax north for a distance of some thirty-three miles. On the east side of this fault a large block was raised several thousand feet relative to the rocks on the west side. Since then, the glacially sculptured remnants of this block have formed the peaks of the Ten Mile Range.

With the Tertiary period came the formation of the primary deposits of gold, silver, copper, lead, and zinc. Mineralizing solutions emanating from an igneous-hydrothermal system in the area penetrated the rock fissures which had been created by the folding and faulting. At those places where the mineral-bearing solutions came in contact with the limestone, the solutions dissolved and replaced the existing rock atom for atom, forming a replacement deposit. These deposits varied in size. Some were no more than a few feet long and a few inches wide, yet one on Sheep Mountain was 2,000 feet long and thirty feet thick. Lead, zinc, iron, and copper sulfides made up the bulk of what geologists call the economic mineralization, but the sulfides also had some gold and silver associated with them. The ore in all these deposits was generally restricted to the limestone.

Although most of the replacement deposits were rich in base metals, they held relatively little silver and gold. Near the surface, however, portions of many deposits were subjected to thousands of years of weathering. Down to various depths, this constant exposure to the air and water, heat and cold, changed the character of the deposits. The sulfides were oxidized, the upper layers of lead and zinc were removed, and perhaps most important, the gold and silver were concentrated, a process known today as secondary enrichment. These segments became relatively rich in silver and gold.

In addition to replacement deposits Ten Mile also had veins of mineral. They formed in the rock fractures when mineralizing solutions invaded bringing silver, gold, quartz, and sulfides such as pyrite, pyrrhotite, galena, sphalerite, and chalcopyrite. When these solutions solidified into hard rock, they formed true fissure veins. Over the passage of time, oxidation and secondary enrichment also altered these deposits, usually near the surface. Where a vein was reasonably open, however, and where the water level fluctuated, the oxidation extended several hundred feet below the surface. [2]

Besides the vein and replacement deposits, Ten Mile had a third type that formed as a result of weathering, stream erosion, and mechanical concentration. As the vein and replacement deposits oxidized, running water carried away the lighter minerals and those that dissolved. The water also carried off the heavier minerals, but because of their high specific gravity—in other words their high weight relative to that of water—they settled out quickly wherever the velocity of the streams diminished. There they were concentrated into deposits of their own. Gold was by far the most important substance that settled out, and the resulting concentrations, in which gold was mixed together with sand, gravel, and other heavy minerals, became known as placer deposits.

Glaciers also had a profound effect on the landscape, particularly during the most recent period of glaciation that ended about twenty thousand years ago. On the Arkansas River side of Ten Mile there moved a huge mass of ice about fifteen miles long, four thousand feet thick, and covering some twenty square miles. It probably spilled over the edge of the Arkansas Valley, carving out the Arkansas Pass as it went. Ten Mile also had its own glacier. It cut out the cirque on Bartlett Mountain from where it flowed down into the lowlands, one arm extending down the Eagle River Valley and the other down Ten Mile.

The ice age left its mark throughout the district. The U-shaped valley of Clinton Creek is a classic example of glaciation, a place where one can see glacial striations, or in other words, the scratches on the bedrock. The glaciers also made sharp cuts in the slopes of Jacque Mountain, making it easy to see the levels the glacier reached as it pushed its way down the valley. In other places where certain rocks appear to be out of place—older rocks lying on top of younger—glacial action carried them to their present site. Perhaps the most noticeable products of these ice age processes are the spurs and pinnacles of the Ten Mile Range. Even Robinson and Wheeler flats are remnants of the ice age: near the end of that epoch the melting ice formed glacial lakes; as over the years these silted up, sand, gravel, and peat accumulated, and so built up the flats to the levels seen in the late nineteenth century.

From the top of Chalk Mountain, it is easy to visualize the glaciers at the zenith of their development. The sinuous curves of the Arkansas glacier, flowing away to the south as a true river of ice, must have been impressive. And then a short distance away to the east and north the Ten Mile glacier flowed down from Bartlett Mountain to Robinson Flats, where it split into two segments. With its jumbled ice falls glistening in the sun, it must have been equally spectacular. [3]

The Gold Rush

No one will ever know when the first people came to Ten Mile, but it seems likely they appeared about 10,000 years ago. From that time forward Ten Mile was largely a passage on the route from South Park to North Park. And that is what it was when the first written records appeared about 1800. By then the Indians knew it as part of an ancient route, and that it remained, except for some minor beaver trapping, until the end of the 1850s. Then everything changed in sudden fashion, all in response to rumors that had drifted down through the years, rumors that gold could be found in the Rocky Mountains. [4]

As the warm southern winter of 1857 closed down on the dusty streets of Auraria, Georgia, William G. Russell took a notion to look for gold on the high plains near the point where the South Platte River left the mountains on its long journey to the sea. Early the next year Russell, his brothers, and a few other Georgians set out for Kansas Territory. At Fort Leavenworth, they joined a party of Cherokee Indians led by John Beck, who knew Russell from their days in California and who may have found gold on the high plains himself. The combined party, now more than one hundred men strong, trudged across the prairie. Eventually, they reached the South Platte River, then traced it down to a much smaller stream, known as Cherry Creek from the trees that grew along the banks. After pitching their tattered canvas tents, they fell to work on the sands and gravels, and here on the future site of Denver, they found the telltale colors of placer gold. [5]

Every man was exultant, each one thought he had found his El Dorado, and they all tossed hosannas into the hot summer air; but over the next few weeks, the hopes and dreams of sudden wealth turned into frustration and disappointment. Placer mining was backbreaking work, and the placers of Cherry Creek held little gold. Disillusionment grew, and in the fall, with hopes dashed, most of Russell's men began the long trek home. Yet as chance would have it, some weeks before, a trader bound east had arrived on Cherry Creek, where he bartered for a few flakes of the precious metal. The farther he went, the greater the wealth seemed. Once he arrived in the Missouri Valley, the newspapers and outfitters did the rest, and the rush was on.

A fiasco loomed that winter as the first miners arrived at Cherry Creek. A few of these people, however, had been schooled in the mining country of Georgia and California, and they perceived that the gold panned by Russell's men had been washed down from the mountains that framed the western skyline. Even though winter had cast a snowy mantle over the country, a few prospectors decided to take their chances in the mountains in hope of finding the golden treasure before the thousands of fifty-niners they knew would arrive in the spring. And so small parties of gold seekers, even single men, left their camps on the high plains to ascend the partially frozen streams that ran down through the steep gulches, rocky gorges, and narrow canyons of the Front Range. [6]

One of these men was John H. Gregory, a weather-beaten Georgia miner. He struggled up the narrow canyon carved by the Vasquez Fork of the South Platte, a name soon changed to Clear Creek. Gregory eventually took the north fork of this stream, which brought him to a series of high hills timbered with firs. Here, in what is now the town of Black Hawk, Gregory found a rich placer. It was February 1859. Although he nearly perished in a late winter snowstorm, he found shelter in Golden, then returned with several friends to look for the source of the gold. In May, Gregory located the first system of vein gold ever discovered in the Rocky Mountains—the soon-to-be-famous Gregory lode. [7]

Meanwhile, the news of gold on Cherry Creek had created a sensation in the Missouri Valley towns. Thousands of people decided to head west to the mountains. Even though nearly 600 miles of open prairie stretched out from the points of embarcation to the gold region, by early 1859 innumerable "pilgrims" had taken to the trails bound for Pike's

Peak, the majestic landform that was actually several days travel south of the discoveries. Frank Fossett, a later commentator, wrote of "an almost continuous stream of humanity" crossing "an ocean of dust and solitude" on the way to El Dorado. Perhaps it was, as he said, a stampede never before equalled except by the California gold rush ten years before. The discoveries of Russell, Gregory, and others had transformed the country almost overnight. [8]

"Cities" rose everywhere. On the high plains around Cherry Creek, groups of promoters, more interested in selling land than panning gold, platted Montana City, St. Charles, and Auraria, although these villages or plats of villages could hardly be described as anything more than clusters of tattered tents, decrepit tipis, rough-hewn wagons, and dingy log cabins thrown together in a hodgepodge that other promoters soon transformed by legal and other means into Denver City. In the mountains conditions were much the same, if not worse. The towns of Black Hawk and Nevadaville, with Central City in between, rose in the mining country opened by Gregory. And on South Clear Creek the towns of Idaho Springs, Empire, and Georgetown emerged in the valley first prospected by George A. Jackson, another important discoverer.

Not everyone saw the rapid influx of fifty-niners as beneficial or welcome, however. If Frank Fossett spoke for the boomers, then George Bent spoke for the Indians. The son of William Bent and his Cheyenne wife, Owl Woman, the short, darkly complected Bent was the product of the older cultures of the plains. Years later, he remembered the long lines of wagon trains, the bands of riders on horseback, and the small parties on foot that poured in like "a ceaseless stream." He also remembered that the Indians who watched these "mad proceedings" thought the whites were "crazy." But the red men were also alarmed, said Bent, because the fifty-niners invaded their old hunting grounds, drove off the buffalo, and cut down the few trees. Yet the Indians could do nothing because they were "overawed by the great inrush." They had never dreamed there were so many men in the whole white tribe. [9]

By summer so many fifty-niners had crowded into the placers of Clear Creek that latecomers had to push farther west if they hoped to find gold. Some parties trudged over the bare, rugged continental divide west of Clear Creek to prospect along the banks of the Snake and Blue rivers. A few of these men found rich placers in what they named Georgia, French, and Humbug gulches, located on the upper reaches of Blue River, and they founded Breckenridge, a typical mining boomtown, just east of the Ten Mile Range.

Still other parties crossed the mountains to the south. Many groups hauled their hopes and gear into South Park, where they found placer gold in Tarryall Creek and the South Platte River. These discoveries prompted the founding of more towns—Tarryall, Buckskin Joe, and Fairplay. Other parties went even farther west to the Arkansas River, where they prospected in places they called Cache Creek, Missouri Bar, and Lake Creek. These men found gold as well, but they founded no towns, at least not in 1859. [10]

So as that special year wound down to its close, Ten Mile lay quietly in the high country, a place remote, isolated, and generally unvisited except by travelers. So far as anyone knows, the gravels of Ten Mile Creek were laced with gold, but no one had found them. The lodes above were exposed to view, but no one had seen them. An ancient trail snaked down through the timber, but no one had marked the route. Except for a sign here and there, the wilderness solitude was complete.

CHAPTER 1

Resolved by the Claim Holders

ALMOST nothing is known of James McNulty. Nothing of his origins, nothing of his character, nothing of the hopes that drove him on, and nothing of his ultimate fate. Time, it seems, has swallowed him up. Save for the gold rush, he might have disappeared from the record entirely; yet even so, he remains at best an enigma, a shadowy figure moving through the twilight of the historical landscape. Whoever he was, larger events had caught him up, carried him off to the Rocky Mountains, and thrust him down the path of discovery.

McNulty's days in the mountains apparently began in 1859. There is some evidence that like many a would-be miner, he headed west in the first wave of "pilgrims" who engulfed the foothills of the "Snowy Range" about the time that astounding news burst over the high plains—a miner named John Gregory had discovered a rich deposit of placer gold on the North Fork of Clear Creek. Wasting no time at Denver City, or wherever he may have been, McNulty hurried up Clear Creek Canyon to the Gregory Diggings.

The gulch teemed with fifty-niners that summer. They staked out claims along the narrow streams, dug up the gravels, and hammered together the crude sluice boxes that proved far better for capturing gold than pans, cradles, and rockers. Unless he had come from older mining regions such as California or Georgia, it seems likely that McNulty got his first experience that feverish season. The techniques of prospecting and placering were not hard to learn. What was hard, for McNulty and

13

everyone else, was to find a good claim and hold onto it. There was not enough gold-bearing ground for everybody. Prices soared to fantastic heights, speculators did a brisk business, and claim jumpers stood ready to pounce on any land that looked abandoned. Although many miners quit in frustration after a short time, even days, in the diggings, the more determined spilled out into the nearby gulches to search for new placers. The most astute searched for the telltale outcroppings of lode gold where there might be a real bonanza. And as the first mining companies began to open this storehouse of underground treasure, the sharp crack of blasting powder and the monotonous thud of stamps crushing ore echoed across the canyon walls. [1]

And James McNulty? He stayed on North Clear Creek for only that season. By the fall of 1859 the boomers had taken up the good placers, the price of claims remained stratospheric, and a poor man, as McNulty presumably was, could see little future in hanging on. Moreover, the new mining camps had comparatively little shelter—a few log cabins, tents, shacks, and other rude dwellings thrown together in off-hours. Men who had marveled at summer snowstorms justifiably thought that such rough homes might be dangerous places to face the unknown rigors of a mountain winter. Like many a fifty-niner McNulty decided to retreat from the high country. If he had a placer, he sold it. If he toiled with other partners, he took his share. Or if he worked for one of those first mining companies, he asked for his wages. With whatever he earned that summer, he trudged down from the mountains to Denver City.

Now about one year old, Denver was hardly the Queen City of the High Plains that its boosters liked to pretend. To be sure, it was more than the motley collection of tents, shacks, and log cabins clustered haphazardly around Cherry Creek and the South Platte River that it had been the spring before. Denver now had blocks and straight streets, frame structures and business houses, even a few boardwalks and brick buildings. But it was still a hard place. Dust, potholes, and debris—to say nothing of violence—loomed large in town, and there were few amenities to grace the lives of most people who called this "mile-high city" their home. Even so, it offered a tired miner more food and shelter than could any crude mining camp in the mountains. [2]

So into this port in the prairie sea came a host of men. In they came from the forks of Clear Creek, the Blue River diggings, the Arkansas Valley, and from just about everywhere else. And week after week, as they played cards in dim rooms, shivered on the cold windy plain, and whiled away the hours, they talked about gold. Everyone, it seems, had

a story to tell. And just as in 1858, when the grossly exaggerated reports of the Cherry Creek placers touched off the rush, the rumors, unconfirmed reports, and tall tales grew by inference, suggestion, and conjecture into golden treasures. James McNulty must have heard most of
these stories, he may have told a few himself, and no doubt he pondered
his future day by day as he waited for winter to pass, cooped up as he
was in this muddy, cold, and dreary outpost.

As time passed, the reports of gold in the Arkansas Valley surpassed
the others in McNulty's mind. Cache Creek, Kelly's Bar, Lake Creek—
he had never seen them, but prospectors who had gone there the last
summer had all found placer gold. Or so they said. If only he could get
there first this year! The valley was far from Denver, but McNulty may
have reasoned that this might prove advantageous. Few men would risk a
distant journey over the mountains to unknown country, few miners had
been there before, and most, it seemed, had decamped for the winter—
some were right here in Denver. At the first signs of spring McNulty
made his decision to set out for the Arkansas country, and he joined
or put together a party of Irishmen, among whom was John Gibbs of
Brooklyn, New York. [3]

McNulty and his partners were by no means alone. A miner named
Slater assembled a party bound for the Arkansas. So did Horace A. W.
Tabor, a stocky, moustachioed farmer originally from New England, but
more recently from Kansas. There were others as well. So eager were
these companies to get to the river that many left before spring arrived.
And they had luck. The winter was remarkably mild and free of snow,
travel was fast, and a few parties arrived in the valley as early as February. By the time the Tabor, Slater, and McNulty companies reached
Cache Creek, about April 1, they found the best placers taken. After
spending a short time working the icy gravels remaining, the meagre returns convinced them that they had better move on. Undaunted, they
struggled on up the valley, panning here and sluicing there, and probably
failing to appreciate the spectacular scenery in their battle with the
snow, ice, and cold, and in their search for the yellow metal. [4]

Toward the end of April, several men broke off from the Slater Party
to begin prospecting a winding gulch that ran off to the east. They found
the snow deep, but this rarely deterred prospectors in quest of gold. On
April 26 one of these men, the veteran miner Abe Lee, dug through a
drift to paydirt, and perhaps he shouted, "By God, I've got California
here in this pan," as legend says he did. Whatever the truth, California
Gulch it was from then on. The news spread like wildfire through the

other parties struggling upriver. Tabor rushed there on the day of discovery; in came McNulty and Gibbs, and dozens of others; and a day later the miners created the California Mining District to firm up their rights. [5]

As the gold fever mounted over the next few weeks, in rushed hundreds of argonauts. With more discoveries came the formation of new mining districts, and by summer the boomers had staked out claims 100 feet wide for seven miles up and down the gulch. The jerry-built homes that snaked through the woods and brush soon evolved into the towns of Oro City and Sacramento City. They were nothing spectacular even by the rough standards of mining camps, but they offered a modicum of civil government and launched the political career of Horace Tabor. [6]

Yet what really mattered was gold. Some claims were undeniably rich. The Discovery—presumably Lee's—was said to have yielded over $60,000 that summer, the number 5 and 6 claims above about $65,000 each, and the number 1 claim below about $55,000. Tabor and his partner were reputed to have taken out more than $75,000 between them. This was the stuff of dreams. But the pay streak was spotty, and many claims paid little or nothing at all. There were simply too many people and too little good placering ground to satisfy everyone. And among the disappointed, it seems, were James McNulty and John Gibbs. In June, less than two months after Abe Lee had dug through the snows to paydirt, they decided to move on once more. [7]

After loading their gear, McNulty and his comrades retraced the ancient Indian route that led up the east fork of the Arkansas. They must have panned for gold as they trudged along, but they found only colors. Nothing to hold them for long. After a few days, they reached the summit of Arkansas Pass, got their first glimpse of the still-unnamed Ten Mile country below, and began their descent into the valley. The sun set, and they decided to camp for the night at the mouth of the first gulch they came to. It was only a mile or so long with low walls that sloped away much as if someone had scooped out the ground with a giant spoon. But water was abundant, and so were the willows and underbrush that formed a thick cover alongside a stream that tumbled down through the snowdrifts. Altogether, a pleasant space. The next morning, McNulty and company decided to prospect before moving on. And that day they had luck. They found gold in good quantity, and in tribute to James McNulty, they agreed to call this place McNulty Gulch. [8]

The prospectors may have tried to keep their discovery secret, but before long, someone headed back to California Gulch, passed the word, and the rush was on. Miners sold poor claims in a hurry, shoved their gear into packs, and set their course for "McNultee," as one of them wrote. By foot, by horse, and by mule they came, some by themselves, others in groups, some well-equipped, others not so. As many as five hundred men arrived in a single day. The news took longer to work its way around the mountains to the Blue River diggings, but when word arrived, out came more boomers. Miners were now rushing into the valley from two directions, and they were beginning to call it "Ten Mile," probably because they thought the stream running down through the center emptied into Blue River ten miles below Breckenridge. [9]

By late spring McNulty and the others were spending most of their days at the backbreaking toil of placer mining, but very few found the sudden wealth they had hoped or expected. The placers were spotty, and the miners had to strip away much overburden. The deep snow and intense cold, even in June, hampered work still more, and after all this tedious effort, day after day, the miners found pay dirt in the form of coarse gold on only twelve or fourteen claims. These were very rich, however, and some have contended that McNulty Gulch yielded more metal in proportion to its size than any other diggings in the Rockies. The Brooks brothers, who bought McNulty's claim, reportedly took out $15,000 in less than sixty days from only 120 feet of ground. Several other pits but twenty feet square reputedly yielded gold worth anywhere from $10,000 to $30,000. And from that first season McNulty Gulch became renowned for the size of its nuggets. One valued at $475 was for many years thought to be the largest ever found in Colorado. So large a nugget was unusual, but it was not uncommon for miners at McNulty to find others weighing fifty pennyweights. [10]

But most of the boomers had come too late. The first men had taken up nearly all the good placering ground. As early as July, scarcely two months after McNulty's discovery, Mathew Sheriff, a miner from Illinois, wrote in his diary that "McNultee" was a "hard place to get to" and once there he saw "no chance for claims." He went back to California Gulch. [11]

Like Sheriff, most of the latecomers had to move on. Many trudged down the valley, and a few dug out gold in Clinton, Mayflower, Gilpin, and Humbug gulches, all of which resembled McNulty. They were heavily forested, and each had a small creek tumbling down through the woods and brush. But none proved as rich as McNulty. Other treasure seekers who prospected between Ten Mile and Oro City found gold in Bird's Eye, Iowa, and other gulches running down to the Arkansas River. [12]

Despite the gold fever, living conditions in Ten Mile were primitive. At first McNulty and other miners lived in tents and lean-tos. Only later, when they realized it would be some time before the placers gave out, did they build sturdier log cabins. Yet they never developed an orderly townsite. They simply "camped out" on their claims. What emerged in McNulty Gulch was a stringlike community with as many as three thousand miners. The dwellings were rough and unpretentious, but gold became the standard medium of exchange. Musical troupes put in an occasional appearance, itinerant ministers preached in the open air, and bands of musicians enticed weary miners into gambling dens day and night.

Supplies, however, were hard to get: picks, scales, paper, candles, axes, shovels, boots, cans, utensils, knives, nails, saws, guns, bullets— no luxuries—just the things that would keep a man going body and soul. They were scarce because Ten Mile was so hard to reach. The soaring peaks barred direct access from Breckenridge or South Park. Ten Mile Canyon was narrow, steep, and difficult of passage, and any goods coming that way had first to come over Argentine, Boreas, or Loveland Pass, all of them high, windy, and snowy. The best access to Ten Mile was the old trail of the Indians and fur traders, the route over Arkansas Pass, the one followed by McNulty himself. Just by tramping along, the miners turned this passage into a crude "highway" that snaked its way from California Gulch, and by midsummer mule skinners were cursing their teams over the mountains to supply the camps in Ten Mile. Yet there was nothing frequent or regular about the mule trains. The miners had to depend on themselves, particularly for food, and they killed large numbers of deer and mountain sheep. Diets were long on flesh and short on fruits and vegetables. [13]

One of the men who came to sell goods was Scott J. Anthony, a Kansas merchant struck by the gold fever. Early in 1860 he drove a wagon train up the Arkansas River to California Gulch. There he traded, but after a short time, he went on to Ten Mile just as even more exhilarating news broke over the region. [14]

Among the miners in Ten Mile was Henry C. Justice, a man with origins as obscure as James McNulty's. Justice may have been looking for gold, but toward the middle of August, he discovered a silver outcrop on the hill between Gilpin Gulch and McNulty Gulch. The news traveled fast, and miners rushed to the site. Perhaps silver, not gold, would make them rich.

On Monday, August 21, the excited prospectors assembled, as they wrote, "on the divide between McNulty's Gulch and the Arkansas River" to organize a mining district. They called Justice to chair the meeting and Anthony to serve as secretary. That done, they chose Anthony and two others, a committee of three to draw up "laws and rules for the governance of the silver mining region in this vicinity." That day Anthony and his colleagues created a document with thirteen articles, named the deposit the Justice lode, and called the general area the Washoe Mining District, no doubt after the booming silver region in Nevada. Once reassembled, the miners concurred, elected Anthony president of the district, and chose Justice recorder.

These articles accomplished several important objects. They specified the boundaries of the district, the size of claims, the requirements for recording, the mechanism of transfer, and the right of the miners to change these rules if they chose. Altogether, Washoe reflected the standard features of mining district organization. What made it different from others in the Rockies was that it applied to silver, not to gold. [15]

The silver miners now besieged Recorder Justice in their efforts to file claims. Anthony took the number one claim north of the discovery while Justice took the 100 feet that formed the first claim south. On it went. That first day the silver men took up twenty claims to the north and twenty-six to the south. And if Justice hoped to spend more time on his own property, then he was wrong; for three days he had to spend much of his time recording. When the sun set over the peaks on August 24, he had recorded 158 claims north and another 158 south, a total of 316. Individuals like Anthony, Justice, and A. S. Weston, long a minor figure on the Colorado mining scene, took up nearly all the claims, but a few went to partnerships like that of William Clancey and Charles Blake, a couple to firms like David Ogden & Company, and several to persons who took claims side by side to form the property of a mining company. At least one claim went to a woman, Sarah M. Grannis, who took number seventy-seven south of the discovery on August 23. [16]

No sooner had Justice made his discovery, however, than other prospectors began looking for outcrops, and almost immediately a man named Brooks, perhaps one of the brothers who had bought out McNulty, found a silver deposit a short distance away. Miners poured in, named the discovery the Brooks lode, and organized Sulivan's District, which probably took its name from James Sulivan, an obscure man whose name appears here and there in the records of California Gulch. To be president of the district, the miners chose Hugh Strickland, an individual apparently disposed to negotiation and compromise, which was fortunate because the boundaries of Sulivan's District overlapped with Washoe, and almost immediately trouble loomed between rival claimants searching for silver.

To devise a peaceable solution, Justice and Strickland organized committees to investigate the contested ground and propose a settlement. After a conference on September 1, the two groups agreed that miners who had recorded claims with their respective districts would be entitled to them, from separate discoveries the claims should follow the direction of the lodes, and perhaps most important of all, the midway point between the Justice and the Brooks lodes should form the boundary between the two. This agreement apparently satisfied the majority of people in both districts, and peace prevailed. [17]

Even though the miners had settled a potentially violent dispute, they had no means to alter the progression of seasons. The coming of September brought an end to the summer thunderstorms, a more tranquil season set in, and the slender aspen began their autumnal change into brilliant hues of orange and yellow. While many miners continued working their claims, they also began making plans to depart. They knew that Ten Mile offered little shelter and no reliable means of supply. Winter might prove very dangerous. Even though silver had created a sensation, the miners could do little more than pick up float and chip samples for future assay. The placer miners were frozen out. Some years later Daniel Ellis Connor, a miner, hunter, and would-be Confederate soldier who frequented these parts, remembered that July, August, and September "about constitute the mining season on top of the ground in placer and surface diggings." Yet 1860 was exceptional. The mild fall allowed the placer men to keep going into October, when the snow and cold drove them out at last. [18]

Although the silver miners had already formed two mining districts, not until late October did the placer men create one for themselves. Just as the freeze shut down the sluice boxes, a group traveled around the mountains to Breckenridge, the small hamlet that was fast becoming the principal community in the sparsely settled Blue River Valley. There, on October 26, these men organized the McNulty Mining District, drew up its laws, and elected a slate of officers.

Twelve articles defined property rights and spelled out a rough system of law enforcement. One article called for the election of two officers, a president and a recorder, who would have one-year terms. The president would preside at all miners' meetings and serve as a magistrate in other districts; the recorder would keep a record of all meetings, claims, trials, and arbitrations. All claims in the district would be 100 feet square; any miner could hold one by preemption and others by purchase, but every claim had to be recorded and all deeds of transfer properly attested and placed in the district records, which would be regarded as sufficient evidence of ownership.

On went the articles. All trials, whether civil or criminal, would be conducted by a jury of six miners who owned a claim or part of a claim.

A PLAYED-OUT GULCH. McNulty, Mayflower, and other gulches may have looked something like this once the gold boom evaporated in the mid-1860s. Drawn by Frenzeny and Tavernier, and published in *Harper's Weekly,* November 27, 1875.

The rules of such trials would be similar to those in "common justice's courts" and gave the right of appeal to the "justice court of the Blue River judicial district," another extralegal entity like the mining districts themselves. Finally, the document specified that all claims would be good for one year beginning that day; all meetings would require adequate posting; any ten miners could require the president to hold a special meeting; and all the articles could not be amended or repealed until the following July, except by a two-thirds vote of the claim holders. In that first election Albert Mathews was chosen president of the district and C. A. Holman recorder, two men as little known today as James McNulty. [19]

District organization was important. Like other westerners, the people in Ten Mile felt uncertain about the legality of their activity on the public domain, and were anxious to be protected in their possession of valuable mines. Technically, they were trespassers on federally owned land. The United States had not adopted a general mining law, and other public statutes governing settlement and occupation were inappropriate for the conditions encountered in the Rockies.

Mining districts like those in Ten Mile generally accomplished five objectives. They set the size of claims; they enforced the law of use; they maintained inclined locations—the right to mine down a vein if it departed from the boundaries; they required that all claims be recorded; and they insisted on this record as final should disputes arise. Some districts also drew up civil and criminal rules. What is important is that mining camps grew up long before organized government in the traditional sense caught up with the miners. The exigencies of the situation compelled these men to adopt some form of government, and their answer was the mining district. With but a few violent exceptions the miners' rules and the popular courts that enforced them adhered to American constitutional principles as well as notions of fair play. [20]

As the snowstorms swirled through the mountains that winter, a few veteran miners made plans to return, and they were joined by others who had heard of fabulous discoveries in McNulty Gulch. Early in 1861 they embarked on frosty trails to begin the hard journey. Once the mining season began in April, the miners preempted land, bought and sold claims, and washed out the gold wherever they could. Although many argonauts reworked the ground placered in 1860, this year the excitement and euphoria gave way to a more thoughtful, more systematic development. While the day of spectacular cleanups had passed, with steady work a company of miners could still earn about five dollars a day, the average return in the high country. Yet many got less, and some got nothing. Edward Seymour, an Ohio farm boy who came out to California Gulch that spring, wrote in his diary that his uncle had returned from McNulty empty-handed. [21]

While most men hoped to find their El Dorado in the placers, others bent their efforts to opening the silver lodes. Veins ranging from two to five feet across cropped out sharply on the surface, and it became obvious that they ran in a northeast to southwest direction through the Ten Mile Range. Before summer passed, the miners had located (or relocated) the Balahoo, Sublunar, Detroit, Newark, Merrimac, Hard Cash, and others christened with equally colorful names, and at least one group began driving a crosscut tunnel from Clinton Gulch into Fletcher Mountain hoping to strike rich ore at depth.

If the discoverers had not done so the previous year, then in 1861 they shipped ore samples east to be assayed. Several lots went to Boston, Massachusetts, where they were examined by A. A. Hayes, the state assayer. He described the ore as a silver-bearing galena—that is to say, a silver-bearing lead mineral. He also determined that some samples held iron pyrites laced with gold. After completing his assays, Hayes wrote that the ore ranged from $30 to $27,000 per ton, although he estimated the average value at $100 per ton. [22]

Reports such as this might have prompted a silver rush to Ten Mile, but nothing happened. Hard-rock mining required technology, capital, labor, transportation, and a feasible method of recovering silver and lead from complex ore. At this early stage in Colorado's development, most of this essential infrastructure was simply not in place. If mined, the ores might in theory have been shipped to Europe for smelting and refining, but in 1861, given the primitive western transportation system, it was impossible to send a ton of ore worth $100 more than halfway across the continent, let alone the vast ocean beyond, and still earn a profit. Moreover, the angry fires of civil war had just begun to consume the men and money who might have supported development. The silver mines would have to wait.

How many of the boomers of 1860 returned in 1861 is, of course, conjectural. Sarah Grannis went back to California Gulch, where she took up a claim in the Sacramento District. So, too, did James Sulivan. McNulty's associate, John Gibbs, made his headquarters in California Gulch, where he was elected recorder of the California District and his firm, John Gibbs & Company, did a considerable amount of placer mining, no doubt aided by Gibbs's crucial position in local affairs. Scott J. Anthony also returned to the central Rockies, but later that year he obtained a commission in the Union Army. [23]

While it seems likely that these people went back to Ten Mile at least briefly to look after their claims, no one can be sure. What is certain is that in 1861 the miners in Ten Mile enjoyed a better system of transportation. What had been nothing more than trampled-down trails the year before evolved into rough wagon roads, particularly the route over Arkansas Pass. With these, the people toiling away in the valley received more regular and more abundant supplies. [24]

But when the brilliant hues of aspen leaves signalled the arrival of fall, most miners in Ten Mile began loading their gear to retreat from the mountains, this time for good. There seemed to be no future in silver, the placers seemed to be exhausted, and the easy money was gone—if any had ever been easy money. Although some miners would return in the next few years, they would find ever less gold because the ground had been worked over four or five times. Given the technology of the day and the small size of the 100-foot claims, the placers could no longer be worked at a profit.

As the boom petered out, the unchinked log cabins, lean-tos, and other dwellings slowly deteriorated, and nature began to reclaim the ground. And there was much to reclaim. The miners had not been careful. They left behind all the paraphernalia they no longer wanted. Broken sluices, rusty nails, rough furnishings, squashed cans, old clothes, broken gear, and piles of junk littered the gulch from one end to the other.

It was just as mining in McNulty collapsed, however, that the miners found themselves organized into a territory. Ever since the faint beginnings of the gold rush in 1858, the people who lived in the region had demanded some sort of official organization, but their wishes had been caught up in the growing sectional antagonism. To most Americans living east of the Mississippi River, a relative handful of gold miners in the Rocky Mountains mattered little. With inaction in Washington, the fifty-niners had taken matters into their own hands by creating the extralegal Jefferson Territory, but it received little recognition in the Rockies and none in Washington. Not until April 1861, in the midst of the secession crisis, did Congress create the Territory of Colorado. A few months later the first governor, William Gilpin, and the first legislature drew up the first counties. Gilpin County took in Central City, Black Hawk, and all the camps on North Clear Creek. Clear Creek County gathered up all the towns on South Clear Creek. Lake County incorporated all the diggings in California Gulch. And Summit County collected all the camps drained by the Blue River and its territories, including Ten Mile, and virtually all the land to the Utah border. Breckenridge emerged as the county seat.

From 1861 onward, the heart of Colorado's mining industry lay in Gilpin and Clear Creek counties. The placer mines gave out, just as they did in California and McNulty gulches, but the rising production of lode mines more than made up the difference, and the territory's shipments of gold rose until 1863, fueled by the digging of easily mined and easily processed ore. [25]

Then the world of Colorado turned upside down. A hot, dry summer in 1863, a long hard winter, an Indian War in 1864, the collapse of a frenzied stock speculation, and a sudden technological impasse created by the production of sulfide ores that resisted stamp milling, all combined to crush out the life of the industry. Shipments of gold peaked at $4.5 million in 1863, then plunged. By 1867 mines were boarded, houses shuttered, doors locked, and much of the population trying to get away. A writer for *Harper's Magazine* termed the country "a land of disappointment." It was in that season of despair, however, that Nathaniel P. Hill, an eastern chemist of stocky frame, handlebar moustache, and combative personality, introduced a European smelting process that could recover gold from these "rebellious" ores, but despite the success of his Boston and Colorado Smelting Company, which opened for business in 1868, not until the mid-1870s would the mines of Colorado ship as much metal as they had in 1863. [26]

As the depression ran its course, the mining camps in Summit County fell into the backwash of life in Colorado, but even so, some miners remained interested. In 1864 a group of prospectors from Empire climbed over the continental divide to the headwaters of the Snake River, and prospected on the slopes of Glacier Mountain. Here they found the grey-black outcropping of a silver-bearing galena, a discovery often, though incorrectly, reported as the first location of silver in Colorado. Unlike the earlier finds in Ten Mile, this one prompted a silver rush. Along South Clear Creek, the boom revived dying camps like Georgetown, where miners relocated many abandoned gold mines now known to hold silver. And in Summit County prospectors found other promising silver properties, the most important of which was the Comstock lode, cleverly named after the fabled mineral deposit in Nevada. These finds gave root to new silver camps like Saints John and Montezuma. [27]

The opening of the Comstock lode rekindled interest in Ten Mile. In March 1865 a group of prospectors discovered gold near Chalk Mountain on the southern perimeter of the valley. Although the news did nothing to revitalize the frenzy of 1860, several men drew up the laws of a Chalk Mountain Mining District to form the basis of their claim to what they christened the Jackson lode. This time not all the organizers were new to Colorado, nor even to this section of the territory. Bennett Seymour for one had mined in California Gulch since 1861, and Wolfe Londoner for another had already launched his colorful career in the same precincts. Despite their experience, however, flush times did not return to Ten Mile, and before long the Chalk Mountain District drifted into oblivion, another hope for wealth gone awry. [28]

Although Seymour and Londoner apparently made little profit in gold, others hoped to open the silver lodes in tandem with the Snake River excitement. The most important of these people was Joel Parker Whitney. Born in Massachusetts, Whitney sprang from an old New England family of good means and Puritan ethics, a background that belied his own passions for hunting, fishing, traveling, and living the life of a bon vivant. But Whitney was also an energetic businessman. In the 1850s, having joined his father and brothers in the mercantile business, he had plied the long trade route from Boston to Cape Horn to San Francisco, and when not sailing on Neptune's world, he had helped his family establish a sheep ranch in California. Although he did not join the rush to Pike's Peak, it seems that the inclination burned inside him, a wish interrupted by several tours of duty with the Union Army during the Civil War. [29]

Once the conflict ended in 1865, Whitney decided to go to Colorado, ostensibly for a vacation, but more likely for a busman's holiday. That was his style, mix business with pleasure. Thirty years old now, he was in the prime of life. A bachelor, perhaps something of a dandy, he certainly looked the role with his tapering handlebar moustache, alert eyes, and ruffled hair swept back from a balding forehead. Once he arrived in Central City, he wasted no time in acquiring ore samples and putting together a hunting party. Then he was off. He crossed the continental divide, descended Snake River, and followed the path to Ten Mile; then he crossed Arkansas Pass and headed south to California Gulch. All along, he found the game plentiful, for like the land, the animal life had regenerated after the miners had gone. Deer, bear, and elk fell to Whitney's guns. It was a splendid foray!

Why Whitney chose this particular itinerary for his hunting trip is something of a mystery. Perhaps it was happenstance, but in the light of subsequent events, it seems more likely that he wanted to look at gold and silver mines as well as hunt. What is certain is that Whitney saw the silver lodes of Ten Mile and acquired ore samples en route. [30]

Once he returned to Central City, Whitney took his samples to different assayers for analysis, then went home to Boston to have the tests repeated. While he waited for the results, he explored the venture capital market to see who might be willing to invest in the mines—not an easy task, for hundreds of people had lost thousands of dollars in the Colorado stock speculation that went bust the year before. Yet Whitney was well-connected, persuasive, and persistent, and it seems that he obtained some commitments. Then he returned to Colorado to buy options or take control of various properties in Central City and Ten Mile. [31]

On his return to Boston, Whitney published a slender pamphlet, *Silver Mining Regions of Colorado*. He conceded that it was "hastily written and compiled . . . for the purpose of attracting the Capitalists to the inviting silver fields of the Cordillera Range," but even so, he never let the silver deposits of Ten Mile slip very far from his reader's attention. "In prominence and value," he claimed, the mines were "beyond any known in the world." Their development would "constitute an epoch in the history of silver mining." Experts—all unnamed—familiar with the richest districts in Mexico, Nevada, and elsewhere, had agreed that "those particularly of the Ten Mile District [were] fully equal to any they [had] ever seen; in fact superior in their surface indications. . . ." Although miners had done relatively little development, they had sunk shafts deep enough to reveal the "solid and massive proportions" and prove that the deposits were "practically inexhaustible."

Whitney then marshaled his evidence. He presented assays done by Hayes, who stated that the ores ranged from $106 to $141 per ton in coin value (a dollar in coin being worth far more than a dollar in paper). And Hayes added that galena was "one of the most economical silver ores" because smelters could recover the silver and other metals "at a comparatively small cost," particularly when the mineral was mixed with pyritous gold ores. But neither Whitney nor Hayes bothered to mention that Colorado had no successful smelting plants. Whitney also published a letter from A. A. Hodges of Nevada City, Colorado, who stated that recent assays had revealed "some of the richest silver mines extant . . . especially those of the Ten Mile District." They would "equal if not surpass any silver mines heretofore known." Some assays ranged as high as $7,000 per ton. What was more, said Hodges, "the climate in the Ten Mile Valley was milder and storms less frequent than any portion of the mountains east." Whitney also printed a letter from a Judge Cowles of "Empire City," who said that in 1864 he had ascended Ten Mile Creek where he had seen "the perfection of silver lodes." Unquestionably, they formed part of "the richest silver mining district in the United States, if not in the world."[32]

With his promotional tract in press, Whitney put together two firms that would acquire the mines in Colorado. One was the Bullion Consolidated Mining Company, organized in Boston on December 6, 1865; the other was the Incas Consolidated Mining Company, organized a few months later on March 3, 1866. Both enterprises were remarkably similar. Each had mining property near Central City and in Ten Mile, a nominal capitalization of $300,000, and a similar, though not identical, board of directors. George W. Messinger, president of the Globe National Bank of Boston, was president of both companies; Whitney, the corporate treasurer; and W. A. Whiting of Central City, the agent. Among the directors of the Bullion Company was Oakes Ames, a wealthy Massachusetts manufacturer and influential figure in the Union Pacific Railroad, then building across the plains.[33]

When Whitney returned to Colorado in 1866, he began the task of turning what were little more than paper companies into bona fide ore producers, and what a herculean task this was! The depression that began in 1863 had still not run its course, and if problems at Central City were bad, they were far worse in distant Ten Mile. Quite simply, Whitney and everyone else were stymied by the lack of infrastructure. The essential transportation, communication, and ore reduction facilities were simply not in place. What was more, capital and labor were hard to come by, which helps explain why Whitney ran advertisements for the Bullion and Incas companies in the *Daily Miner's Register* of Black Hawk for more than a year. [34]

In the face of mounting adversity, Whitney seized a chance to promote his mines as Colorado's commissioner at the Paris Universal Exposition of 1867. He set up the territorial display and brought home first prize, but he also took advantage of the opportunity to publish a second promotional pamphlet that described Ten Mile and other ores in English, French, and German. Even so, it did the Bullion and Incas mining companies little good. After that, they faded from the record, although they were not dissolved until the 1890s. [35]

As Whitney's efforts dwindled to nothing, hard-rock mining in Ten Mile languished, just as it did throughout Summit County. In 1868 a writer in Breckenridge talked of "the great richness" of the valleys and the first efforts to build mills and smelters, but he lamented that much of the work was in "great trouble" because of "the scarcity of hands." A year later another man pointed out that the greatest hindrance to developing mines and reducing ore was the "enormous cost of transportation." He hoped that the wagon road then under construction on Loveland Pass would lower shipping costs. Then in 1870, Rossiter W. Raymond, the United States commissioner of mining statistics, noted that Saints John, Montezuma, and Breckenridge all had mines under development, many of them "exceedingly rich." And in Ten Mile were the Bullion and Incas companies, which had opened some promising veins near the head of Clinton Gulch and driven an adit some 800 feet into the Ten Mile Range. Evidently, Whitney had continued the work begun in the early 1860s. [36]

By the end of the decade, hardly anyone lived in Summit County. The Census of 1870 found only 258 people, with men outnumbering women 217 to 41, and these hardy souls apparently had little connection with the more populous regions of Colorado. The seasonal cycle of immigration and emigration still continued. In February 1870 a person waiting out the winter in Breckenridge complained to the *Colorado Tribune* that he rarely saw the county represented in the paper because of the "absconding" of the summer population, an exodus that left behind only a few "hale and hospitable" neighbors with whom to spend "the long dreary winter months." Although the heavy snows had cut the mining season short as usual, the people who remained spent their time "about equally between indolence and reading" the letters and other items that the mailman brought but once a week. He was the only link to the "outside world." So isolated were the small camps in Summit County that they did not even receive "ministerial exhortations" or judicial counsel. Even the county functionaries had left for the winter. [37]

By this time mining in Ten Mile had reached its nadir. The feverish days of the McNulty Rush had long since passed. So too had the silver excitement sparked by Whitney's promotions. Both had left little more than nostalgic memories. For the handful of miners who still hoped to make a living in Ten Mile, the only avenue open was placering the old ground that had been worked before. And with that, a third era of extraction began.

The new placer mining, however, was vastly different. In the early 1860s mining district rules had provided for small claims so that everyone would have a chance to make a fortune through individual effort. The new miners, however, had other ideas. Simply put, they hoped to take advantage of the economies of scale. This meant eliminating the small claims, acquiring large tracts of land, and developing water supplies.

The pioneering efforts to consolidate placer ground took place in South Park during the mid-1860s, sometimes with techniques that stretched the law. In some cases, one or more miners would simply buy out other claimants, a practice that was perfectly legitimate. In other cases, however, two or more persons would take out a certificate of incorporation under the general territorial law and designate their claim on the certificate. Still another method was to hire individuals to relocate land under the old 100-foot rules of mining districts and then buy out these dummy locators for a prearranged price. [38]

In addition to large tracts of land, the new system required vast amounts of water. Miners constructed reservoirs and built systems of ditches and flumes. Then they turned to one of two techniques for mining. In the less sophisticated (and cheaper) method known as "booming," they discharged a huge volume of water through the gates of a reservoir, or simply blew up the dam, releasing a man-made tidal wave that rumbled down the gulch and dug out huge amounts of gravel. Booming, however, was very inefficient. It consumed large quantities of water and kept vast amounts of gravel in motion as mud, though it often freed enough gold to make a profit. More sophisticated, precise, and expensive was hydraulic mining. Invented in California in the early 1850s, it used a system of iron pipes laid from a reservoir to a placer site. Once the valves were opened, water charged down through the pipes with enough force to cut away a hillside, washing the pay dirt into a system of giant sluice boxes faster and more efficiently than in booming. [39]

These techniques came to Ten Mile in the late 1860s and early 1870s. The first practitioner was probably Sylvester Ferguson, who mined near Gilpin Gulch, but he was soon followed by others. In August 1872 a group of thirty miners arrived in nearby Clinton Gulch. They preempted the land for three miles from the mouth of the gulch east toward the mountains and for some three hundred feet on either side of a line drawn down through the center. They also made certain to lay claim to the water rights. While there is little known about the group's activities, it seems likely that most of the thirty individuals who signed the claim were dummy locators who later sold out to the principals who included Charles F. Adams, the Ute Indian agent, and William P. Pollock, an early miner turned county functionary. [40]

Despite these efforts the systematic reworking of the Ten Mile placers went slowly. Many prospectors roamed through the hills and gulches, and then moved on; by 1875 the valley was all but abandoned except for a handful of miners like Ferguson who relied on booming to make what money they could. These men included Jonathan H. Follett, the three Recen brothers, Colonel James McNasser, Benjamin F. Brandon, his brother Frank Brandon, and perhaps twenty-five or thirty others. But every one of them found that the laws of the McNulty District, particularly the strictures demanding small claims, hindered the development of large-scale operations. A new order was essential.

On July 24, 1875, Follett and others gathered to change the laws of what they called the "Old District." That day, they created the Consolidated Ten Mile Mining District out of the hodgepodge of older districts and defined the boundaries to encompass all the land drained by Ten Mile Creek; in other words, the entire valley north of Fremont Pass, the name that was fast replacing Arkansas Pass. They also declared the mining laws of the old McNulty District null and void; miners would henceforth take up placer claims under the laws of the United States and the Territory of Colorado. They also stated that all claims held under the laws of the Old District would be forfeited unless the owners claimed them by August 1, which was scarcely one week away, but all claims held under the old laws and represented on that day would be regarded as legal—and representation meant the payment of $100, no small sum in that era. Finally, they specified that the laws of the consolidated district had to be recorded at the office of the county recorder within ten days. [41]

In creating the new district, the miners of 1875 tried to extinguish the old claims held under district law, and bring all claims within the new federal mining law. Although of questionable constitutionality, their action had the effect of dispossessing anyone who had abandoned their

DeRobert Emmett. Something of a soldier of fortune before he came to Ten Mile, Emmett used his success in "booming" to become one of the valley's first important mine-owners. From O. L. Baskin & Company, *History of the Arkansas Valley.*

property, for stating that all claims had to be recorded in Breckenridge within ten days effectively meant that none of the old titleholders could pay the representation fee unless they had attended the organizational meeting or else lived close by. Thus Follett and his cohorts could acquire the land they needed. What was more, new claims were controlled by the new federal mining law which permitted larger placer claims, a change which naturally benefitted large-scale placer mining.

Among the first to take advantage of these changes were DeRobert Emmett and his partner, Edward Lowe. Emmett had been something of a soldier of fortune before he arrived in the Rocky Mountains. Born in England, apparently the son of well-to-do parents (he went to school until he was twenty-one), Emmett had toured North Africa, served in the Confederate Army, and worked in a St. Louis dry goods store before setting his sights on Colorado. In 1868, when thirty years old, he began toiling in the mines near Central City, but before long he set off on a prospecting trip to the San Juan Mountains, a journey that took him through Ten Mile. Here in 1869, he found placer gold in Clinton Gulch. But even this failed to detain him—not until the early 1870s did he return, presumably because the Clinton Gulch placer was the richest he had come across in his travels.

By this time Emmett had met up with Edward Lowe, an American from Illinois. Lowe had left school at thirteen, worked on a river steamer, served in the Illinois infantry during the Civil War, and then farmed for two years, before the lure of gold and silver carried him west. Not until 1871, however, did he come to Colorado, where he did some lead mining in Hall's Gulch before fate carried him over the mountains to Ten Mile.

As the summers drifted by, Emmett and Lowe searched for placer gold in the hills above Ten Mile Creek, but if they engaged in mining, it was on only a limited scale. Eventually, they decided to acquire ground in the lower reaches of Clinton and Mayflower gulches, although they did nothing until the formation of the Consolidated District. The new federal mining law permitted an individual to take up twenty acres of placer ground—which was not enough for the large-scale operations that Emmett and Lowe had in mind—but the statute did allow groups of as many as eight people to locate what were known as "association placers" encompassing up to 160 acres. Needing a larger area, Emmett and Lowe adopted the questionable practice of using "dummy" locators to secure more land. On September 18, 1875, they formalized their partnership, and with six other men—including the ubiquitous Pollock—acting as dummy locators, they acquired the lands for a Clinton Placer and an Emmett & Lowe Placer, 300 acres in all. Then on the day the claims were recorded, Pollock and the others deeded their interest to Emmett and Lowe. [42]

Less than two weeks later, Emmett and Lowe were joined by a group headed by Jonathan H. Follett, the first chairman of the Consolidated District. Using dummy locators, Follett and his partners, Leonard H. Ballou and Henry O'R. Tucker, preempted a tract of land near the confluence of Clinton Gulch and Ten Mile Creek that was either across or downstream from Emmett and Lowe. They called their placer Troy Bar, apparently because Tucker hailed from Troy, New York. [43]

Three other figures in these consolidations were Frank Brandon, Benjamin F. Brandon, and their partner, Colonel James McNasser. Very little is known about the Brandon brothers, but McNasser had made his mark in Colorado through farming, cattle raising, and operating hotels—some said his American House in Denver was first-class. He had also speculated in real estate and mining property, but his credit was shaky, and while some people said he was "an active popular fellow," others thought he was "a pretty hard man." Still, he was a venture capitalist, at least on a small scale. In this three-cornered partnership, McNasser ap-

JAMES MCNASSER. An entrepreneur of diverse interests, McNasser acquired shares of various mining properties in Ten Mile, including Bradshaw's Placer, the future site of Carbonateville. Courtesy Colorado Historical Society.

parently provided the money while the Brandons directed the mining. Together, they planned to rework the old placer ground in McNulty Gulch under a lease from Sylvester Ferguson or his heirs, since Ferguson died about this time. [44]

Also coming to the fore in 1875 were three emigrants from Sweden—Henry, Andrew, and Daniel Recen. Henry had left the shores of Europe in the late 1860s, took ship for North America, and made his way to Colorado. Finding the country to his liking, he returned to Sweden, where he married, encouraged his brothers to emigrate, and then returned to Colorado for good. Recen made his first home at Central City, where he anglicized his name into Recen, which was pronounced "Raseen." Later, he moved to Summit County, where he hewed aspen to build the first cabin in what became the town of Frisco, located a short distance from the entrance to Ten Mile Canyon. No doubt Recen ventured into the valley during the 1870s, perhaps in company with his brothers, who arrived from Sweden about this time.

While they probably knew little of mining before they came to America, the Recen brothers became intrigued with the possibilities of large-scale placering. When the new miners turned their attention to Ten Mile, the Recens were among the first on the scene and helped organize the Consolidated District. Unlike Emmett and Lowe, Follett and his partners, and the Brandon-McNasser group, the Recens chose to mine on the west side of the valley beneath the slopes of what later became known as Jacque Mountain. Ultimately, they assembled a group of dummy locators and on October 13, 1875, they located the Herculean Bar Placer. [45]

By the time these men had acquired their placering ground, however, the season was all but over, and they had to retreat from the valley to wait until the warm spring sun melted the ice and snow. Then, in 1876, they began placering in earnest. They built cabins, reservoirs, and flumes, dug the ditches they needed, and made what money they could through booming. Follett and his partners mined gravels that held only two to five cents in gold per pan. While there are no figures for cleanups in 1876, they took out $2,500 in gold in 1877, and their successors took another $1,000 in each of the next two years. McNasser and the Brandon brothers did better. They recovered $7,500 in 1877 and another $5,000 in 1878. What amount of gold went to Emmett and Lowe and the Recen brothers is a matter of conjecture, but the suspicion is strong that Emmett and Lowe did reasonably well and the Recens did not—the brothers abandoned their claim at the end of 1877. In any case, the cleanups in Ten Mile failed to match the returns from South Park or Blue River. Gone indeed were the days of "Aladdin-like fortunes" that Frank Fossett described in the early boom. [46]

Aside from placering, these men took time to prospect for lodes. Emmett and Lowe were quite active; so were the Recen brothers and two of their dummy colocators, Peter Norling and William A. Bartlett. What they found, for the most part, were the gray-black outcroppings of silver-bearing lead ores—cerussite and argentiferous galena, the same carbonates and sulfides discovered as early as 1860.

A few men took time to locate lode claims. John Moore, Sylvester Ferguson, and James McNasser reclaimed the old Gilpin lode at the head of Mayflower Gulch as early as 1875. Follett and Charles Bledsoe located the Winter Green above Searle Gulch on the west side of the valley the next year. And there were others. A few miners tried to open these deposits, and some formed enterprises like the Bartlett Mountain Mining Company. But as ever, hard-rock mining went nowhere. The essential infrastructure was still lacking, and no one working in Ten Mile had money enough in his own right to make the capital investment required. What made this work important was that it spread the knowledge that silver-lead ores abounded in the mountains above Ten Mile Creek, and it allowed the placer miners to acquire large tracts of land. But while these people may have hoped and dreamed, they had no way of knowing that their knowledge and their land would prove very advantageous in just a few more months.

As 1877 drifted down to its close, it brought to an end nearly two decades of sporadic mining in Ten Mile. And what was the result? While statistics on production are suspect, particularly for the early years, the best records suggest that Summit County yielded about $5,150,000 in gold from 1859 through 1867. Perhaps Ten Mile accounted for one-fourth to one-third of this, or about $1,500,000. For comparison, the gold that came from Lake County—mostly California Gulch—amounted to an estimated $5,272,000. Ten Mile's silver production was just about nil. And that leaves only the era of sporadic placering from 1868 through 1877. Again there are few records for Ten Mile, but the scant data extant suggest that output amounted to $150,000 at most, or scarcely ten percent of Summit County's production of $1,560,000 in placer gold during the decade. Except for the gold rush, the valley did not have a great showing. [47]

So as winter settled over Ten Mile in 1877, the old cycle repeated. The miners departed for milder climates and warmer hearths, the cold weather turned the streams into ice, and the early snows cast a white blanket over the flumes, dams, and ponds of the placer mines. The frigid winds howled off the high, barren peaks, and the swirling ground blizzards blinded anyone who may have chanced to pass through the lowlands. An occasional cabin nestled here or there in the evergreens while large bulky implements poked their white tops through the snow, suggesting that a handful of people labored here in other seasons. But there were no towns, no ranches, no farms, no railroads, no telegraph lines, nor anything else to pretend that this was a settled-up country. Yet as the snows drifted through the woods, filled up the gulches, and settled on the evergreens, it would be the last winter that such peace prevailed in the valley for decades to come.

CHAPTER 2

Fever Heat

As Ten Mile went through its cycle of boom, bust, and fitful recovery, so too did the better known camps in California Gulch. Oro City and other small hamlets had seen their best days in the early 1860s. Some say that as many as ten thousand energetic miners rushed into the narrow, twisting ravine in hope of finding a placer claim that might have enough gold to make them rich for life in return for the hardships they had to endure.

But there were problems. The stream that tumbled down through California Gulch had too little water to supply the countless claims. By the time the precious liquid flowed to the lower mines, it had turned into a substance the miners called "liquid mud." And there were large iron-stained rocks that had to be picked out of the sluices by hand—hard, time-consuming work. And if the lack of water and the large rocks were not enough, there was even a third barrier to instantaneous wealth—heavy black sand that fouled the pans, rockers, and sluice boxes. In polite company the miners called it "black cement," at other times "the damned blue stuff," which was strong language in Victorian America. [1]

And so the mining camps in California Gulch dwindled down to nothing, like their counterparts in Ten Mile. Many a man who had bent body and soul to reach the Arkansas Valley spent but one season in placering, others more determined spent two, but not many endured the privations for a third season. Even Horace and Augusta Tabor, who had done far better than most, departed for more promising mining towns in

South Park. By the mid-1860s, Oro City and the other hamlets had been all but abandoned. [2]

Change came slowly. Not until 1868, a full eight years after Abe Lee had panned his first "colors," did someone start mining lode gold. The opening of this claim, the Printer Boy, gave the district much of what little prosperity it enjoyed in the early 1870s, and also stimulated the search for other lodes. Prospectors prowled the slopes of California Gulch, as well as the rocky ravines and timbered hills nearby. What they found, however, were not minerals bearing gold as in the Printer Boy, but silver-lead ores, the source of the "damned blue stuff" that had fouled so many sluice boxes for so many years. The news of these discoveries increased interest in the Arkansas Valley—it even induced the Tabors to return to Oro City—but neither the gold nor the silver prompted another wild rush like the frenzy of 1860. [3]

What frustrated development more than anything else was the lack of a place to sell ore. California Gulch was extremely isolated. The wagon roads to the upper valley were rude, to be charitable, and the nearest railheads were many miles away across the high, rugged mountains. As for reduction works, except for a few marginal smelting plants far from Oro City, Colorado had no smelters that could have reduced the ore to silver-lead bullion, even if the miners had enjoyed better transportation. As early as 1873, Tabor and others tried to pool their limited capital to build a local smelter, but their efforts came to nothing. So, even though the people who lived in the upper valley knew about silver-lead ore, they had little incentive to mine, given the inadequate transportation and reduction systems. [4]

Meanwhile, in April 1874, Alvinus B. Wood, a veteran miner from South Park, began working the Starr Placer in California Gulch. Intrigued by the minerals that had frustrated placering for so long, he took samples over the range to Alma to be assayed by the Boston and Colorado Smelting Company. The result? The ores were rich in silver! Wood quickly formed a partnership with William H. Stevens, a prosperous miner in South Park. The next year, as they worked the Starr Placer, they took time to prospect for silver, and before winter set in, they located three promising claims on what would later be named Iron Hill. [5]

After a short time spent in test mining, Wood and Stevens knew they had a group of valuable claims, but only if they could find a place to sell ore. This of course was an old problem. Just then, however, the St. Louis Smelting and Refining Company, which had a large plant in Missouri, was busy establishing an ore sampling agency at Alma. The person in charge was August R. Meyer, a young, dapper, garrulous American who had studied mining and metallurgy in Europe. In 1876, Wood and Stevens lured Meyer over the mountains to look at the claims. Meyer immediately saw the potential for profit in shipping the ore to St. Louis, and he managed to get some out before winter. These shipments returned a profit to everyone involved. The news sparked the interest of many who knew of the silver-lead ore in the hills above California Gulch. And as the first snows closed down on this isolated, sparsely populated country, Colorado had quietly moved to the eve of a new mining boom that would dwarf everything that had gone before. [6]

Early in 1877 the St. Louis Company shifted Meyer's base of operations over the mountains from Alma to Oro City, and once the trails cleared, Meyer began shipping ever larger quantities of rich ore to St. Louis. And never a man accustomed to brevity if length would serve, Meyer dispatched enthusiastic epistles that brooked no doubts about the burgeoning development of the mines, the frustrating inability of Colorado's works to handle the output, and the continued demand for a local smelter to buy ore.

With ever more encouraging reports streaming into St. Louis, Edwin Harrison, president of the company, and his colleagues decided to build a branch smelter in the mountains. In June, Harrison arrived in Denver, put Meyer in charge, and then went to California Gulch to decide on a smelter site. He and Meyer found the gulch too narrow for what they had in mind; instead, they selected a place on more open, but hilly, terrain about two and a half miles away. Meyer acquired a large tract of land, and over the brisk summer months, dirt flew as he directed construction. When completed, the plant looked something like a large barn with a few slender pipes stuck through the roof—like most smelters of the day. When Meyer opened for business in October, the Harrison Reduction Works at last offered the miners a local plant that could reduce their ore to bullion. [7]

The boom gathered its strength all through 1877, as Meyer pushed construction of the smelter, but the old towns in the upper valley received little growth. The new people focused their attention on the Harrison Works, where a small village sprung to life, with perhaps two hundred souls, rough log cabins, the inevitable dusty streets, and a few stores with the essential false fronts. It was nothing pretentious. In March 1877 an itinerant correspondent for the *Engineering and Mining Journal* noted that the country was "laying the groundwork for more extensive operations in the future," which was true enough. A year later, however, another legman for the journal confessed that the hardest part of his task would be to "keep within the bounds of reason" and not say so much as to "border on the realms of puff." For during the winter of 1877 and 1878, Meyer, Wood, Tabor, and others had organized the City of Leadville out of the humble abodes that surrounded the Harrison Works, the breathtaking news of silver had burst over the continent, and the rush was on. [8]

The Leadville frenzy was phenomenal even in terms of the hyperbole of mining booms. Here was a town, said one newsman, with "its closely built streets, its bustle of trade, its throng of teams that fill and block the way, and its surging mass of humanity that move in ceaseless currents." Here was a town where "everyone was on the jump," where "the rasp of the saw and the tattoo of the hammer [could be] heard from daylight to dark seven days in the week." Here was a town "overrun with multitudes of half famished, diseased, and nearly desperate people," where teams, horses, vehicles of all sorts clogged the streets, where people had to push and elbow their way through the crowds on the sidewalks. By 1880, Leadville had become a mountain metropolis of fifteen thousand people. They lived along twenty-eight miles of streets gladdened by the flicker of gaslights, and they enjoyed the services of a waterworks, several banks, three hospitals, thirteen schools, 114 saloons, no one knows how many bordellos, and fifteen smelters reducing ore into bullion. And with all this came the spectacular rise in the production of silver and lead: worth a scant $21,000 in 1875 and another $27,000 in 1876, then surging to $550,000 in 1876, $2 million in 1878, $9.4 million in 1879, and an astounding $11.5 million in 1880. [9]

From these underground riches came instant wealth—to a few. The first such overnight fortune went to John, Charles, and Patrick Gallagher, who reportedly divided $225,000 after selling out to the St. Louis Company. And there was Horace Tabor, the merchant whose charismatic personality, hard years in rough country, and sudden fortune embodied the hopes of so many. It was Tabor who grubstaked two prospectors, August Rische and George Hook, to about seventeen dollars worth of supplies and equipment in return for one-third of whatever they found—and what they found was an exceptionally rich ore body christened the Little Pittsburg. And if one bonanza were not enough for Tabor, then in the same year a nefarious sort bamboozled him into buying a salted claim named the Chrysolite. After some exploration, however, Tabor's miners discovered another rich ore body. By 1879, Tabor was the epitome of the bonanza king. [10]

It was just this crescendo of silver riches that quickened the heart of George B. Robinson, a retiring, perhaps even introspective, man snowbound in a railroad car on the cold Nebraska prairie. He had no experience in mining, but then neither did most people heading to Leadville.

Robinson had been born in Gun Plain, in Allegan County, Michigan, on January 28, 1848, the son of Mary Voke Robinson, an English immigrant, and John Robinson, a wood turner from Massachusetts. Although his parents met while living near Rochester, New York, once married, they moved west to take up farmlands in Michigan. George B. Robinson was the third and youngest of their surviving children. Although he began his life at Gun Plain, the family soon moved a few miles away to Kalamazoo, where George spent his early years. His youth was marred by the death of his father in 1854, though what effect this had on his development remains unknown. Two years later, when George was eight, Mrs. Robinson married John Forbes, a native of Scotland, who had also taken up farmland in Allegan County. The Forbes household must have enjoyed some measure of prosperity, for the surviving accounts of Robinson's life make no mention of any rise from poverty. He attended public school in Kalamazoo; then in the 1860s he went to Detroit, where he studied for two years at Bryant and Stratton's Business College. When he left there in 1865, he had an exceptional education, given the standards of nineteenth-century America.

Robinson now made his way in the business world. He took his first job as an assistant to the register of deeds in Kalamazoo, remaining there for two years until 1867, when he left to become a bookkeeper for Kendall, Mills & Company, which had a lumber business in Kendall, Michigan. Robinson may have been a minor partner in the enterprise, but if so, he did not remain long in Kendall. In June 1868 he returned to Kalamazoo to become a bookkeeper in the Michigan National Bank, where he worked for three years. Then he moved to Allegan to become a founder, director, and cashier of the First National Bank. It was on this job, wrote one admiring biographer, that "his careful business training and acknowledged ability and integrity brought him well merited success." Robinson worked at the bank for six years, but early in 1877, he abruptly quit, took ship for Europe, and toured the continent for the rest of the year.

After his sojourn abroad, Robinson returned to Michigan, but by this time he had decided to strike out anew in California. He purchased a train ticket for San Francisco, made his good-byes to family and friends, and in February 1878 he left for the coast. His itinerary took him through Nebraska, and here he ran into trouble. West of Omaha, the train encountered a prairie blizzard, and before long Robinson and his fellow passengers were snowbound. There was little he could do except wander through the cars, talk to other people, and wait for the storm to abate and the railroad to clear the tracks. As he whiled away the time, he heard excited talk of Denver and the new mining boom at Leadville. Intrigued, he decided to change plans. When he finally reached Denver, he heard even more excited reports about the new boomtown. Wasting little time, Robinson set out by stagecoach, but once he arrived in South Park, a ground blizzard swirled across the road, the driver got lost, and Robinson and his companions had to camp out for several nights in freezing conditions before they could cross the range into Leadville.

Businessman that he was, Robinson quickly perceived the exciting commercial opportunities. He purchased a lot at the corner of Pine and Chestnut streets and opened a general store. As thousands of people rushed into the carbonate camp, Robinson's enterprise boomed. Before long he had developed one of the most successful mercantile houses in Leadville, knew all the right people, and moved in the best circles. With some of his early profits he erected a two-story building known as the Robinson Block. Once it was completed, he ran his business from the first floor, rented office space to others, and lived in comfortable quarters upstairs. Within a year, he was said to have the largest single assortment of groceries in town, more freight teams on the road than any other merchant, and a building thought to be grossing more than $7,000 per month.

When he arrived in Leadville, George B. Robinson was barely thirty years old. He had developed into a man of medium stature with a moustache and full beard, which combined with his already balding forehead to make him look far older than he actually was. One future biographer related that he was "a finely-cultured gentleman," while another reported that he was shy and retiring, courteous and polite, characteristics that belied the popular stereotype of the raucous, brawling men who filled the bustling town. But if Robinson was shy, quiet, and retiring, this outward appearance only served to conceal a determined, perceptive, aggressive entrepreneur, a man who wanted to be far more than a successful merchant. Only a short walk from his store, Robinson could see the new headframes that pierced the sky above the mines on Fryer and Carbonate hills, he could hear the dulled crack of explosions underground, and he could see the wagon teams hauling rich ore down the dusty roads to Leadville's booming smelters. Like many others, Robinson the merchant wanted to be Robinson the bonanza king. [11]

Robinson had absolutely no background in mining, but this was no deterrent. The problem was to find a good mine. And for that there was a practical solution ready at hand. This was grubstaking. Generally, prospectors would agree to share any claims found with a person who would furnish the wherewithal required. A "stake" amounted to little more than goods, supplies, and hand tools, and merchants like Robinson found grubstaking an easy way to participate in the search for new mines since they had direct contact with prospectors and could provide supplies at cost. The most celebrated example was Horace Tabor, who had spent nearly twenty years keeping store and grubstaking prospectors before he struck the big bonanza. [12]

In the spring of 1878, as Robinson got his mercantile business underway, he began grubstaking prospectors himself. He may have entered into many such agreements, as Tabor had over the years, but no matter how many contracts he made, two had consequences that outweighed all the others.

It was in April that two veteran prospectors walked into Robinson's life. They were John Y. Sheddon and William W. West, who had formed a partnership months before Robinson even arrived in Colorado. They had found a number of promising claims on Carbonate Hill, now the site of many bustling mines, and they were looking for a new grubstake. By this time Robinson had opened his store at Pine and Chestnut streets. Sheddon and West stopped in to talk, and before long the two parties had worked out an agreement that would last three months, from mid-May to mid-August. As his part of the deal, Robinson would provide mining tools, food, a horse, and other equipment worth about $200; in return, he would receive one-half of whatever was found. Sheddon and West would each get one-fourth.

For the rest of May and on into June, Sheddon and West prospected in the Mosquito Range east of Leadville, but they found nothing that held any promise. Then, after a month's work, the prospectors disagreed over some trivial matter, and West decided to withdraw from the partnership. When Sheddon asked who he should get for a replacement, West recommended a Charles Jones, who, said West, had been "a very successful prospector," although he was now "hard up and dead broke." Sheddon thought well of the suggestion, and West agreed to approach Jones to see if he was interested. [13]

For West to say that Jones was "hard up and dead broke" was to put the unfortunate Jones in the best of all possible lights. Not quite fifty years old, Jones was a man with blue eyes, a Roman nose, and a strong, upright build, but his reputation was unsavory, and he had become an incurable alcoholic. People who wanted to find him looked in the saloons.

Jones had been born Charles Julian in Quebec about 1830, but when he was two years old, his family took up a farm in Vermont and Charles

Julian became Charles Jones. He never learned to read or write, and as he grew, he apparently supported himself as an itinerant laborer on local farms. Then came the Pike's Peak gold rush, and in 1859 or 1860—the record is unclear—Jones headed west. He spent most of the next five or six years near Central City and Black Hawk, but in 1866, he suddenly reappeared in Vermont, not wealthy, although he had money. He married the daughter of a local farmer, but before long, he returned to Colorado, leaving his wife who later sued for divorce on the grounds of desertion. Jones now remained in Colorado, spending his sobriety in prospecting and mining near Central City, and drinking away his earnings at various bars. Everyone who knew him agreed that he was a fine prospector when sober, which was not often enough, and they remembered that he often bragged that he had once been rich and would be so again.

Not surprisingly, the Leadville rush put a premium on the one skill that Jones had in life. He quickly found himself in demand as a prospector, first by a group in Denver. They found him in the saloons on Blake Street. He had a black eye from a fight, and he had gone for some time without food, been thrown out of his room, and had only barely managed to avoid going to jail. Jones was glad to get work, and off he went to Leadville on a grubstake. He prospected for a time, but as before, the bottle caught him up, and he drank away whatever he had, got thrown out of one boardinghouse, ran up debts in another, and was about to be evicted when West found him at the Denver House.

Jones asked for a meal, West obliged, and while Jones ate, they talked. Though West may have suspected, only now did he learn for certain that Jones had nothing but the clothes on his back—no money, no tools, no provisions, no horses—nothing a man would need to go prospecting. Nonetheless, West still held him in high regard as a prospector. He asked Jones if he wanted to become a partner of Sheddon and Robinson, and Jones said he was interested—he had little choice. A short time later, Sheddon and Robinson agreed to the change. Exactly what Robinson knew about Jones is a matter of conjecture, but it appears that he knew very little. One thing Robinson almost certainly did not know was that two months before, Jones had sold one-half of whatever he discovered that year to John W. Burkhardt. [14]

By this time Robinson had struck up a friendship with Captain John W. Jacque, a Civil War veteran from Pennsylvania, but now a seasoned mining man who had joined the rush to Leadville. They met shortly after Robinson arrived in camp, and Robinson became a frequent visitor to Jacque's home. That spring either Robinson or Jacque became intrigued with the possibility of finding carbonate ore in Ten Mile, and in May they decided to go there. It was barely spring when they arrived. Snow still covered the mountainsides, drifts piled high, and Ten Mile Creek was beginning to rise with the tumbling spring runoff. Despite the snow and cold, Robinson and Jacque decided to prospect on the lower slopes of Sheep Mountain, which rose on the west side of the valley about a mile away from McNulty Gulch. They located a number of claims, although they did not find any ore. Still, they were encouraged, and Jacque decided to spend the rest of the year in the valley, work that allowed him to give his name to Jacque Mountain.

It was shortly after Robinson returned to Leadville that Sheddon and West disagreed over some matter. Jones agreed to take the place of West, and Robinson gave his assent to the substitution. The only item to be resolved was where to continue prospecting. Because Robinson was providing supplies, he had the greatest say, and having just returned from his promising trip with Jacque, he had little trouble in persuading Sheddon and Jones to set their sights on Ten Mile. Once they agreed, Robinson paid off Jones's bills in Leadville, gave the prospectors new provisions, and helped them move over Fremont Pass into the valley. [15]

No doubt because of his visit with Jacque, Robinson had Sheddon and Jones set up their new camp at the foot of Sheep Mountain. The prospectors then began to look for outcrops of silver-lead ore. Almost immediately, they found a rusty-looking, manganese-stained limestone ledge, and here they began to dig. On June 30, at a depth of thirty feet, they discovered a streak of pyrite, galena, and carbonate mineral extremely rich in silver. They named this claim the Ten Mile. Once Robinson heard, he was elated, and the search grew more intense.

Rather than focus their efforts on this discovery, Sheddon and Jones decided to look nearby. About two weeks later, on July 16, they located an even more promising claim that they named the 78. Jones realized that he could now command enough money to keep himself in liquor almost indefinitely, and he offered to sell out to Robinson. But Robinson demurred, and the partners apparently decided to extend their agreement several more months. Robinson brought in more supplies from Leadville, as he had done from time to time since June, and Sheddon and Jones resumed the search for claims. Again they had success. On September 3 they located the Big Giant and on September 14 the Undine. Before long, Robinson filed the proper location certificates at the Summit County Courthouse in Breckenridge. [16]

Robinson wasted no time in beginning development. He brought in miners to open the claims, and in late September, he shipped the first ore to Leadville. On September 25, he sold two small lots to an ore-

buying agency. The larger consignment assayed fifty percent lead and
250 ounces of silver per ton, and the smaller, thirty percent lead and 180
ounces of silver per ton. Rich ore by anyone's standards! Two weeks
later Robinson sold a second lot and in late October a third. Although
these shipments amounted to little more than six tons in all, they suggested that Sheddon and Jones had found a very rich ore body, but two
very large questions remained unanswered. Did the rich ore exist at
depth, and if so, how extensive was it?

Even though the answers were still unknown, the news began to
spread that rich carbonates existed outside Leadville, and the men in
Ten Mile heard it first. The word revitalized the interest of DeRobert
Emmett, James McNasser, and the Recen brothers, who knew the valley
well. Newton B. Lord and Leonard H. Ballou, then working in the placer
mines, immediately assembled a huge exploring party to begin searching
the hills and gulches. And Benjamin F. Follett, who had placered in Ten
Mile for years, decided to stop mining to trace Mayflower Gulch to its
head, where he discovered a deposit of carbonate ore. [17]

By mid-fall a rush to the valley seemed imminent. The news of
Robinson's shipments was spreading through Leadville, Sheddon and
Jones made no pretense to secrecy, and many men were beginning to
think that Ten Mile might be another Leadville. If so, they had to get
there before everyone else despite the impending winter.

All this worried the older Ten Milers, who wanted to share in any
new boom but also wanted to protect their interests. Much was at stake.
On the evening of October 3, 1878, thirty miners, a majority of the district's people, gathered at Benjamin F. Brandon's cabin in McNulty Gulch
to revise the local mining regulations. This group included Brandon, of
course, as well as Ballou, the Follett brothers, Andrew Recen, and
William R. Bartlett, all men who had worked the placer mines over the
past few years. There too were Jacob Hecht and John Still, who may have
been relative newcomers to Ten Mile.

In the flickering light of this chilly eve, the miners adopted several
resolutions to "avoid litigation and destruction of the best interests of the
district." They declared their adherence to state and national mining
laws—but only as further defined by the "regulations" adopted at the
meeting. The new district rules specified the size of the shafts, adits,
drifts, or tunnels that had to be blasted or dug on a claim in order for the
owner to maintain his rights from that night until July 1879. (This was a
reaffirmation of the old laws of possession and use.) The men at Brandon's cabin also expected a new mining camp to rise near the confluence
of McNulty Gulch and Ten Mile Creek, and they resolved that it would be

THE RECEN BROTHERS. Andrew Recen, Henry A. Recen, and Daniel A. Recen. They shrewdly converted their unsuccessful Herculean Bar Placer into a townsite, which ironically became known as Kokomo. Courtesy Henry A. Recen, Jr.

known as Carbonateville, although they did not expect any work to be done before June 1879. Beyond that, they resolved to resist claim jumping, "maintain good order and decent and proper individual conduct," and stand by one another in enforcing the district, state, and national laws "in consequence of the failure of the United States government and of the state of Colorado to supply the wants" of the district. [18]

That fall the weather remained stable and moderate far longer than usual, and the expectant men in Ten Mile took full advantage. One group working on Chalk Mountain located a claim they named the Grand Union and managed to get a shipment of ore to Leadville before the end of the year. More important were the strenuous efforts of men who had set their sights on Elk Mountain, which lay a short distance north of Sheep. It was there in the October chill that DeRobert Emmett, Edward Lowe, and Peter Norling (one of the dummy locators who had worked for the Recens) staked their claim to what they named the White Quail, which ultimately proved to be the most important mine on the mountain. A few weeks later, in November, Charles E. Ellis and Val Jones located the Aftermath claim a short distance away.

But it was Sheep Mountain that attracted the most attention. Sheddon and Jones had not been alone that summer, and more men joined the search for mineral that fall. D. F. Snooks and James Daley began working a claim they called the Smuggler, which was hard by the Undine line. Emmett and Lowe took up the Sunset, Pleasant View, and Carbonate Vault, which they quickly sold to George B. Robinson, who also purchased the Smuggler from Snooks and Daley. Jacob Hecht and John Still struggled all the way to the top of the mountain, where they discovered some rich carbonate ore a mere eight feet from the summit. They named their claim the Wheel of Fortune and sunk a discovery shaft that went through a massive ore body for seventeen feet. When they managed to get the first ore to Leadville that winter, the mineral ranged from 80 to 125 ounces of silver per ton, and rumors insisted that Hecht and Still had sold out for as much as $250,000. That was heady news—a quarter of a million dollars for an unproved claim on the top of a windy mountain! And near "the Wheel," as it came to be known, other prospectors located the Little Ruby, Idalia, Chelsea Beach, Silver Tip, and Tip Top; the first shafts sunk on these claims struck ore at depths of less than fifty feet. [19]

The first shipments from the Robinson, Grand Union, and Wheel of Fortune proved beyond all doubt what had been rumored to many and known to a few—that the Ten Mile Valley had rich carbonate minerals— and the spectacular growth of the Leadville smelters at last offered miners in Ten Mile a place to sell ore. By January 1879, the rush was on.

All winter long, prospectors, merchants, and speculators poured into the valley. Nothing could reduce "the fever heat of excitement," wrote Frank Fossett. The boomers struggled through deep snow, bowed their heads against the frosty winds, trudged over the bare passes, and braved routes that Fossett described as "terrible to think of." And they endured the hardships little knowing that the two best claim groups, the Robinson and the White Quail, had already been taken, let alone a number of rich secondary properties such as the Aftermath and the Wheel of Fortune.

Once in the valley, the boomers had to contend with the bitter cold, swirling winds, deep snow, and the absolute lack of shelter. The only habitable dwelling was the single cabin in McNulty Gulch owned by the Brandon brothers. Yet nothing could deter the men bent upon sudden fortunes. For travel they strapped on skis and snowshoes. For shelter they pitched tents over the snow. And despite subzero temperatures, six-foot snowdrifts, and the high chance of frostbite, they looked for signs of ore. "The lack of indications," wrote Fossett, was overcome "by a superabundance of faith." And by luck and guile. Honest prospectors and brazen speculators laid out claims over the snow and sunk discovery shafts through the white mantle; once in a while, this haphazard style of prospecting proved successful, and when it did, the news of a strike did nothing but spur the rush still more. By early February the *Engineering and Mining Journal* reported twenty to thirty men arriving each day, and John G. Vandemoer, the correspondent of a New York newspaper, observed from his chilly post in Leadville that prospectors coming to town continued right on through to Ten Mile. He estimated that one thousand men were already at work. [20]

But not everyone came to mine. A few came to lay out towns, sell lots, and take advantage of the boom indirectly. One of these men was Colonel John W. Jenkins, a former territorial officer, but now a townsite promotor, a man "identified with Colorado and the development of her best interests," according to one promotional tract. Jenkins got to Ten Mile early in the rush, in December 1878, possibly at the invitation of the other "colonel," James McNasser. He wasted little time in searching the valley for a potential location, and although snow hampered his efforts, he finally decided that the best site was Carbonateville, the mining camp designated at the district meeting two months before. The land that he wanted was known as Bradshaw's Placer, which was owned by McNasser and the Brandon brothers, but this did not deter Jenkins. He either preempted the land, bought out McNasser and the Brandons, or worked out an arrangement that united his interests with theirs. Jenkins now emerged as the principal figure in Carbonateville's development, and in early 1879, as the boomers arrived in force, there was the colonel with town lots to sell. [21]

Jenkins had selected what appeared to be an ideal site. Carbonateville lay on a level plateau near the confluence of McNulty Gulch and Ten Mile Creek. And since McNulty was the first gulch down from Fremont Pass, this put Carbonateville on the direct line to Leadville—the first stagecoach service between the two began just a few weeks later in February 1879. Above town, a good-sized lake offered a natural water supply untouched by placering and well-suited for trout fishing. And the setting was magnificent! Carbonateville sat high in Ten Mile at an altitude of 11,200 feet, which made it higher than Leadville. Chalk Mountain, Fletcher Peak, and Bartlett Mountain formed a spectacular backdrop to the south and east, while across the valley loomed Sheep Mountain with the Robinson mine suggesting thoughts of wealth to enhance the majesty of the setting. Farther away rose the famous Mountain of the Holy Cross. Augustus A. Hayes, Jr., an Englishman who traveled through Carbonateville, described the view of this peak as "stupendous." [22]

As hundreds of miners poured across Fremont Pass, Carbonateville boomed just as Colonel Jenkins had hoped. In February, Vandemoer wrote his newspaper that "Carbonate City" was the leading settlement in the district. It had twenty-five new homes, rough-hewn cabins hurriedly built for shelter, protection, and business. Another 250 were under construction, and town lots sold anywhere from $25 to $250. [23]

Jenkins had gotten Carbonateville off to a fine start, but he was not to have Ten Mile all to himself. Another promoter with the valley in mind was Amos C. Smith, who had arrived in the Pike's Peak gold rush. By the late 1870s, Smith was no longer young, but he was still an entrepreneur looking for profit, and the news from Ten Mile looked very good from his home in Denver. As winter set in, Smith and others put together the Ten Mile Land & Mining Company. Their corporate charter emphasized mining, but Smith and his associates were nothing if not adaptable, and they may have used mining as a smoke screen to hide their real objective, which was town development.

As the heavy snows drifted through the mountains, Smith and his associates set out from Denver. They probably traveled by stagecoach, but once in the upper Arkansas Valley, they may have shifted their mode of transportation to Norwegian snowshoes—not the broad, basketlike attachments that one tied to shoes, but rather long, cross-country skis often used for fast travel across difficult terrain. However they went, Smith and his friends battled the winds, cold, and snow from Leadville to the summit of Fremont Pass, from where they slid down into the valley, stopping at Carbonateville, as most travelers did. [24]

Once they arrived, Smith and his men could see they had no chance to locate a townsite in McNulty Gulch; instead, they set their sights across the valley to a point north of Robinson's Camp. After hauling their gear through the lowlands, they pitched their tents on a wooded hillside along the flank of East Sheep and Elk mountains, a stone's throw above the Herculean Bar Placer, owned by the Recens. Smith may have selected the high ground to avoid any conflict. Although he later said that he and his companions were only hoping to find a base for their mining operations, they developed a townsite large enough to serve as a supply center for many mines, and on February 8, 1879, they established a camp they called Kokomo, probably after Smith's hometown back in Indiana. [25]

As the snows piled up, Smith and his associates hired a surveyor to prepare a plat and held a public meeting at which Smith was elected recorder. This was important, for it gave him the legal power he needed under a law designed to give people title to land on which towns had sprung up—the "act to relieve the inhabitants of the public domain." Smith then went into business in a tent that combined offices with living quarters. "From that time out," wrote a contemporary, Smith's headquarters were "fairly besieged by eager applicants for town property." Men trudging in from Leadville, Breckenridge, Georgetown, Montezuma, and who knew where, beat a snowy path to his canvas. So great was the rush that before long he had sold off nearly all the eligible lots, and some buyers had begun to resell them to newer arrivals. And prices rose fast in what was no more than a conglomeration of tents that rippled and quaked in the wintry gusts blowing through Ten Mile.

Like their compatriots at Carbonateville and Robinson's Camp, the Kokomo pioneers had to contend with the deep snow and piercing cold as they struggled to survive in the heart of a mountain winter. For many, remembered one observer, there was nothing except "coarse fare and blanket laid upon the snowdrift, with no covering save the starry heavens." But few could survive that way for long. In frigid weather, the boomers felled trees to build primitive log cabins that were unchinked and ungabled and had earthen roofs piled high over pine boughs. Rude structures like that served "the toil hardened miner and the child of luxury" equally well. When the snow melted in the spring, the pioneers would see tree stumps six feet tall dotting the townsite to remind them of their struggle with the cold and snow. [26]

Kokomo grew rapidly after its founding in February, but from the outset it had a rival below on the Herculean Bar Placer. Although the Recen brothers had worked the ground since 1876, the returns had been so small that they had not bothered to file the required affidavits for labor in either 1877 or 1878. By the onset of the rush they had virtually abandoned the ground. But the boom changed everything. As people stormed into the valley, the Recens realized their claim might be worth more than they had ever expected. On February 21, 1879, less than two weeks after Smith had founded Kokomo, they formally relocated the placer. In retrospect, it seems likely that they knew the land held little gold, but like Jenkins and Smith, they had perceived the opportunity for townsite promotion and moved quickly to firm up their rights. But even then the Recens acted slowly. Although they shivered through the winter like everyone else, they did not plat their site, lay out streets, and begin selling lots until spring. As a result, the town of Recen got off to a slow start. [27]

And during the winter, a fourth rough community got its start. This was Robinson's Camp, which was also known as Ten Mile City, Summit, and Summit City. It grew more haphazardly than Carbonateville, Kokomo, or Recen, but it was just as important because the tents, log cabins, and other rude structures were clustered around the portals of the Robinson mine, the most important in Ten Mile. Although it had no organized plat, Robinson's Camp was more of a proto-industrial mining town with steady workers than were Carbonateville, Kokomo, and Recen with their high percentages of prospectors, merchants, and speculators. George B. Robinson was the first to begin hard-rock mining on any scale, and he had to have miners. [28]

As February 1879 drew to a close, the *Engineering and Mining Journal* reported that "the excitement regarding the new mining district of Ten Mile" continued unabated. Although snow now blanketed the valley and real shelter was virtually nonexistent, prospectors, miners, and merchants—people of all sorts—were still heading there by foot, horseback, and stagecoach. Most came from Leadville or via Leadville and stopped in Carbonateville, the first "town" they came to as they descended from the windy shoulders of Fremont Pass. Sitting in the hollow of McNulty Gulch, Carbonateville offered more natural protection from the wind, snow, and cold than did the embryonic towns across the valley, but even so, the protection was not very much. The *E&MJ* echoed Vandemoer's claim that some 250 "homes" were under construction, but the fact was that Carbonateville had few cabins to house the boomers.

Like Vandemoer, the *E&MJ* gave a conservative estimate of one thousand people, but noted that others had mentioned significantly higher numbers. [29]

All through March, the rush grew. Despite a cold blanket of snow running deeper than ever, the number of pioneers continued to climb, and in Carbonateville, the center of the rush, even more "houses" were reported under construction, although they were little more than crude, rough-hewn log cabins chinked with almost anything to prevent the snow and winds from knifing into the inside. New reports confidently predicted that some 200 dwellings would be constructed by the first of April, but even in March, Carbonateville had a bank, an assay office, a hotel, a grocery, two feed stables, two dance halls, and five saloons. And, thought the *E&MJ*, the camp would "probably show up pretty well from a mineral point of view by May 1." [30]

That was the key. Although Carbonateville, Kokomo, and Robinson's Camp were the points of destination, the lean and hungry men who had thrown caution away to endure so cold a winter in the open had done so only because they hoped to find mines. They may have huddled around campfires, shivered in blankets, and crouched in tents, but they all had ore on their minds. Without the location of promising claims, everyone knew that these boomtowns would melt away in a single season like the snow that covered the valley floor.

While some men speculated in town lots and others staked out claims over the snow, a few kept mining as best they could. Robinson, for one, kept a small crew working all winter on Sheep Mountain, and managed to ship a few sleighs of ore over Fremont Pass. Higher up, in fact well above timberline near the summit, Hecht, Still, and others braved extraordinarily severe conditions to open the Wheel of Fortune. By February they had reportedly sunk a shaft some forty feet and blocked out ores assaying as much as 152 ounces of silver per ton. Their efforts were heroic. By March they had twenty men working around the clock. From the main "shaft"—little more than an open quarry—they drove four drifts that encountered what was called "a horse" of limestone here and there along the vein. Despite the treacherous weather and the problem of hauling ore down the mountainside, they sent several small shipments to Leadville, but on the mine dump lay another 300 tons worth anywhere from $100 to $500 each. Even here in the dead of winter, Hecht and Still were looking ahead, for they were driving a tunnel that would drain the entire property come spring. [31]

As the weeks passed, it seemed ever more possible that Ten Mile would soon rival Leadville. The news from the Wheel of Fortune continued to be promising, the reports from the Robinson claimed that the mine had a vein of mineral seven feet across averaging 150 ounces of silver per ton, and if the Smuggler, Grand Union, and Giant were not quite so rich, then their ore still averaged 100 ounces of silver per ton, and that was very high grade. Still more reports claimed that mining done on at least fifty other claims had revealed veins ranging from three to thirty-four feet wide and averaging a spectacular 280 ounces of silver per ton! And as the weather improved, more mineowners were getting small shipments to the smelters at Leadville. But even then, the *Engineering and Mining Journal* cautioned that so little important work had been done that it was impossible to tell what the prospects really were. [32]

Despite this caveat, the news from Ten Mile continued its spectacular run, and the *E&MJ* did little to lessen the impact. In May it published the account of a reporter from the Denver *Tribune*. He found that the Wheel of Fortune, Undine, and Smuggler, "mines which in themselves would warrant the location of three smelters," proved worthy of their repute. What was more, the owners had "but scratched the ground," having taken out only the ore necessary to drive drifts that increased in thickness and extent as they were developed. Even after deducting transportation and smelting costs, the margin of profit was some 200 to 300 ounces of silver per ton. The Ruby, Chelsea Beach, Star of the West, Big Giant, and Silver Tip were shipping small quantities of ore to Leadville, and of this group the most spectacular production came from Robinson's Big Giant, whose first output was said to average from 500 to 2,000 ounces of silver per ton! While the Big Giant seemed destined to become "one of the richest mines on record," others nearby seemed to "bid fair to outstrip their elder sisters." [33]

Sheep Mountain could not hold everyone, however. Directly to the north, some men did what prospecting and mining they could on Elk Mountain. The White Quail and the Aftermath continued to sustain the promise shown the previous fall, and joining them came the newly discovered Climax, a short distance away. The first shafts sunk on these claims penetrated ore bodies six to ten feet thick. While some reports alleged that these properties were as rich as any on Sheep Mountain, the actual assays suggested that Elk Mountain's deposits were not quite so valuable. But that mattered little. The ballyhoo continued. One boomer called the White Quail "one of the largest bodies of mineral yet uncovered in this district" (which was true enough), but he also enthused over "dozens of equal promise" (which would not prove out), and he claimed that the supply of smelting ore seemed "almost inexhaustible" (which was nonsense).

North of Elk Mountain came good news from Jacque, Red, and Copper mountains. The first shipments from the Addey and the Rising Sun assayed more than 300 ounces of silver per ton, and those from the Reconstruction showed equal promise. What was more, these discoveries suggested that the mineral belt along the west side of the valley ran all the way from Sheep Mountain north. How far, no one knew. [34]

By spring Carbonateville had become the leading camp in Ten Mile. It had some 200 log cabins along its muddy streets and another twenty in various stages of construction. And according to one account, it now boasted a theatre and an opera house! Quite an accomplishment for a town scarcely six months old. Such rapid growth reflected not only the energies of Colonel Jenkins, but also the ideal location, for Carbonateville commanded the most direct route from Leadville to the mines.

As summer approached, however, some ominous thoughts were expressed about the future of Carbonateville. In May a correspondent for the *Engineering and Mining Journal* relayed his impression that Kokomo would become "*the* town of the Ten-Mile District." And indeed, the tide of settlement appeared to be swinging that way—Kokomo was so much nearer the mines on Sheep, Elk, and Jacque mountains. "In Kokomo," said this scribe, hotels, business houses, and dwellings were "springing up as if by magic." So many "capitalists" were investing in houses and lots that speculation was rampant, and some people were already claiming that they had been duped in buying land. It was also said that machinery for the town's first smelter had been shipped from Pittsburgh.

But Kokomo was more than "the mean exponent of mineral wealth" that surrounded it, wrote the *E&MJ*'s correspondent in June. One story told of a group of miners who were digging a grave in town only to strike a deposit of high-grade ore; since the departed could do them no good, they left the frozen corpse in a snowbank and rushed over to Breckenridge to record the claim. While this tale was probably apocryphal— nearly every mining camp had a similar story—there was wealth to be found in the heart of town. One group digging a hotel foundation struck a deposit of sand carbonates running $45 per ton in silver and $425 per ton in gold. Another crew grading a lot for Captain S. D. Ware, a veteran Colorado miner, found a vein that showed mineral from the grass roots. The first assays from this property, named the Jennie W., revealed ore worth several hundred dollars per ton. Ware tried to open the deposit, but the spring runoff from Elk Mountain flooded the workings, other men claimed part of the ground, and not until summer could Ware and his rivals submit the dispute to arbitration and agree to a compromise.

After such authenticated finds, however, there were fewer complaints about speculators. Such discoveries "put a new face on affairs," said the *E&MJ*, and sent the whole camp into "a flutter of excitement." No wonder property skyrocketed in value, prompting Frank Fossett to write that "the prices of town lots compared in altitude with the places in which they were located."[35]

But as the rush continued, no one could deny that Kokomo was beginning to outstrip Carbonateville. The *E&MJ*'s correspondent, who had left on May 15, returned on June 8 to find himself "astonished at the growth of the place." Kokomo was becoming "quite a city." The whine and buzz of the sawmills could be heard day and night. Houses and businesses had mushroomed, and the machinery for Kokomo's first smelter was en route. [36]

During the spring the boomers took time to firm up their rights. About April 1, Colonel Jenkins spearheaded a group that drew up a petition to incorporate Carbonateville. They obtained the requisite number of signatures, presented the document to the county clerk in Breckenridge, and two months later in June, Judge Adam L. Shock of the Summit County Court ordered an election. He appointed five election commissioners, including some of the leading men in Carbonateville. The vote was scheduled for July 19 at the Store Saloon on Chestnut Street, the main thoroughfare in town, but on the day of the poll, two commissioners failed to show up. Undaunted, the remaining three summarily appointed two bystanders to the commission, one of them the proprietor of the saloon. By this rough and ready tactic, later approved by Judge Shock, the election went forward on schedule; and the vote for incorporation was overwhelming. [37]

Kokomo was incorporated the same way. Amos Smith and his people got up a petition, obtained a large number of signatures, and held a vote that went 312 in favor and 2 opposed. On May 17, 1879, Judge Shock entered an order declaring Kokomo incorporated, the first town in Ten Mile, besting Carbonateville by almost a month. The voters also chose Smith the first mayor, a choice that may have been more than political or honorary because the townsite was on public land, and it was essential to obtain a formal patent under the Act of March 3, 1867, which was designed "to relieve the inhabitants of the public domain." It was this law that empowered Smith first as recorder and now as mayor to hold title to lots in trust for the inhabitants. But the federal machinery turned slowly. Not until October 19, 1881, nearly two years later, did the government issue the patent. By then Smith's town of Kokomo no longer existed! [38]

In the meantime, less than two weeks after Judge Shock declared Kokomo incorporated, the Recen brothers filed their plat for the town of

Recen, which encompassed the Herculean Bar Placer. The brothers, however, encountered a number of legal problems, which they handed to Judge Marshall Silverthorne of Breckenridge to resolve. This took time. Although the Recens filed their plat in May 1879, not until March 1880 could they get up the appropriate papers and petition the court for incorporation. But trouble still loomed. Only now did they find that a small strip of land on the south end of town overlapped some ground claimed by Kokomo. To settle the impasse, the Recens turned to George B. Colby, an up-and-coming attorney in Ten Mile. He did his job well, and on April 20, 1880, nearly a year after they had filed their plat, the Recens finally completed the incorporation of their community. [39]

By the summer of 1879, Carbonateville, Kokomo, and Recen, along with Robinson's Camp, had emerged as Ten Mile's principal towns, but three satellite communities developed as well. One was Beuffers, a small village located by an attractive lake near the summit of Fremont Pass. It became a high-altitude agricultural settlement that supplied miners in Ten Mile with milk and eggs. The second was Chalk Ranch, situated below Fremont Pass in the upper Arkansas Valley. Chalk Ranch was technically outside Ten Mile, but because of its proximity, it was a Ten Mile town. The third and most important was Wheeler, or Wheeler's Ranch, located at the north entrance to the valley.

This town drew its name from its founder, Judge John S. Wheeler. Originally from Massachusetts, he had arrived in the gold rush and mined near Black Hawk and Fairplay, but without any degree of success, much like James McNulty and Horace Tabor. Unlike them, however, Wheeler abandoned the mining industry entirely in favor of agriculture. He homesteaded a plot of land near the future city of Greeley, became active in Democratic politics, and was elected a county judge. He also represented Weld County at the state constitutional convention, and ran unsuccessfully for the post of secretary of state. Yet, like other fifty-niners, Wheeler never gave up the hope of becoming a bonanza king. When the news of the Leadville boom swirled across the plains like a prairie fire, he hurried to the Arkansas Valley; but once again he had little luck, and he was about to move on when the work of Robinson, Sheddon, and Jones touched off the Ten Mile rush.

Early in 1879, Wheeler trudged across Fremont Pass into the valley, not so much to mine as to take advantage of the demand for wood—he set up a sawmill in Carbonateville. Although he worked there for a time, he recognized the potential of townsite promotion, and before long, he went north to the confluence of Ten Mile and West Ten Mile creeks,

JUDGE JOHN S. WHEELER, 1875. Like John W. Jenkins and Amos Smith, Wheeler took advantage of the carbonate boom through townsite promotion, not mining. Courtesy Colorado Historical Society.

where he located what he called the Junction Placer. Wheeler did so little mining, however, that it seems certain he wanted to take up land under the mining law but use the ground to develop a townsite, particularly as the location was so strategic, sitting as it did at the entrance to the valley. That summer, as he profited from his share of the sawmill, he built a home for his wife, Amelia, and their three children, and that done, established a second sawmill, a hotel, a billiard hall, and a general store. Later he obtained a post office. From summer on, Wheeler's Ranch became a popular stopping point on the road to the upper valley. [40]

As the warm summer rays melted the snows that covered the land, any old-timer could notice the changes that winter had wrought. Where a few months before, only a handful of people made the valley their home, now more than a thousand plied one trade or another. Where nothing had been but a few scattered cabins, now several log towns offered shelter and housing. Even the tents that remained reflected vitality. At the southern end of the district stood the beginnings of Chalk Ranch and Beuffers, while away to the north lay the foundations of Wheeler. On the east side of the valley sat Carbonateville; a mile or so west clustered Robinson's Camp; while Kokomo and Recen snuggled together beneath the slopes of Elk and Jacque mountains, Kokomo on the hillside above and Recen on the level below. Although they were legally separate, Ten Mile Avenue joined them together via the dogleg it made as it angled from one plat to the other.

CHAPTER 3

Nothing but Muscle

DESPITE the hardships endured by the boomers who stormed into Ten Mile, hardly any mining got done in that first harsh winter. The winds were too high, the snows too deep, and the temperatures too low to permit much systematic work. Most people concentrated on survival. Moreover, the transportation and communication system between Ten Mile and Leadville was no better than abysmal. George B. Robinson had shipped only a few tons of rich ore before the snows virtually precluded further mining, and all winter long, only an occasional ore sleigh managed to struggle over the summit of Fremont Pass.

None of this, of course, was very new. Writing from the close vantage point of 1880, the journalist Frank Fossett noted that "the Snowy Range" had long acted as a great barrier to growth. The heavy snows blockaded the region throughout the winter and at other times the high, rocky peaks "caused freighting and traveling to be slow and very expensive." Would it be any different when the veterans of the Ten Mile rush tried to develop their mines in the spring of 1879?[1]

Clearly, the boom at Leadville had done much for mining in Ten Mile. The wagon roads from Breckenridge and Georgetown had been upgraded, and as the snow melted in 1879, they appeared to be in relatively good shape except for several spots on Loveland Pass and a few soggy places along Ten Mile Creek. The approach of summer, however, put so many horsemen, wagons, and teams on the trail that the passage deteriorated because of the pounding. Three or four work gangs tried to maintain, even improve, the route, but so great was the traffic they had little success. The road over Fremont Pass proved even worse. The heavy spring runoff and even heavier traffic turned the trail into a quagmire. Heavy ore wagons floundered in axle-deep mud, flimsy vehicles simply broke down, and the innumerable carcasses of draft animals littered the route. The cost of shipping to and from Ten Mile ranged up to $100 per ton. [2]

Yet change seemed to be in the offing. In April, Western Union announced plans to double its heavily burdened telegraph line from Denver to Leadville and extend service to Ten Mile. Also that spring, the Colorado Central Railroad sent its chief engineer, Edward L. Berthoud, to survey a route over Loveland Pass to Ten Mile and Leadville. He planned a line that would take iron rails past the beaver ponds in the lower valley and on through Carbonateville, which he hastily sketched in his level book. The results of these plans were mixed, however. The telegraph arrived before the year was out, just as Ten Milers had hoped, but the Colorado Central put down nary a rail on Loveland Pass. Not this year. Not ever. Miners in Ten Mile remained dependent on undependable wagon roads. [3]

By summer the lack of a place to sell ore had become a stumbling block to development. "Everyone here is satisfied with the country," wrote a correspondent for the *Engineering and Mining Journal* in June, "but at the same time everybody feels poor: for the smelters not being in operation here causes miners and others to feel so, there not being any market for their mineral." No market for any mineral, and Leadville, the largest silver-lead smelting center in the West, scarcely twenty miles away! The equipment for Ten Mile's first smelter was on the muddy roads from Webster, but it would be weeks, even months, before the plant could get into operation. That would "give new life to everything," said the *E&MJ*'s legman. In the meantime, rich ore piled up on mine dumps. [4]

Even though the improved though inadequate infrastructure continued to hinder development, it was enough to allow many miners to begin working the rich surface ores. And throughout the spring, summer, and fall, the crack of blasting powder echoed across the valley, miners trudged up and down the narrow mountain trails, and heavy ore wagons creaked along the roads. The mining industry had come to stay.

On Chalk Mountain work resumed on the Grand Union, or Lennon, mine discovered in August 1878, but closed for much of the winter. As the snows cleared in 1879, the owners built housing for miners and pushed development with a twelve-man crew. They sunk an eighty-foot shaft and blasted out various crosscuts giving the Grand Union about 250 feet of workings. The ore, however, ranged only from thirty-five to fifty ounces per ton in silver-bearing galena and "black sulphurets"— much less than ore from the Robinson and White Quail. The only solace to the owners was the occasional indication that the mineral was growing richer with depth, a trend that boded well for the future, if it continued. But not until fall did the mine ship any ore, and then in November, it passed into the hands of the Inter-Ocean Mining Company, reflecting an important trend in the Ten Mile industry. [5]

Across Robinson Flats, miners swarmed over the slopes of Sheep Mountain. Jacob Hecht and John Still enlarged their open cut in the Wheel of Fortune, and the few shipments they made to Leadville apparently brought decent returns. Despite persistant rumors, however, they found it difficult to sell the mine, at least for the huge sum they wanted. Elsewhere on the mountain, the Chelsea Beach, Tip Top, and Silver Tip continued to attract attention, while new properties like the Crown Point, Grey Eagle, and Champion held so much promise that capital flowed in to support their development.

However important those mines were, the real focus of interest was the property owned by Robinson and his mentor, John W. Jacque. Early in 1879, Robinson consolidated his holdings. He bought the Sunset, Pleasant View, and Carbonate Vault from DeRobert Emmett and took up the Hoosier, G.B.R., and Little Giant. Jacque acquired the Badger, Justice, and Silver Queen, and for a time the two men worked the Smuggler. As 1879 unfolded, the Robinson mine became the largest in the district, a sight that must have quickened the hopes of many who had not been so successful. [6]

It soon became apparent that aside from Sheep Mountain, the most valuable mines in the valley were a short distance north on the slopes of Elk Mountain. The melting snows gave prospectors a chance to search for new deposits, and these men showed as much energy here as they did on Sheep Mountain. Miners also opened the Aftermath and the Climax, which had been known for a time, along with the Milo and Greenville, which were apparently discovered that spring.

From the beginning, however, it was apparent that the most important mine on Elk Mountain was the White Quail, owned by DeRobert Emmett, Edward Lowe, and Peter Norling. During the winter they, like Hecht and Still, quarried ore from an open cut, but come spring, they began a more systematic approach. With capital no doubt drawn from placer mining and from Emmett's sales to Robinson, they blasted a discovery shaft which revealed a vein of carbonates and galena averaging 40 to 60 percent lead and fifty to one hundred ounces of silver per ton—rich ore by anyone's standards! From the bottom of the shaft, they drove an eighty-foot incline through a continuous body of mineral.

This find was spectacular, but it suggested that proper development required that an adit be driven into the mountainside from below. This would drain the workings and allow ore and waste rock to be trammed downhill to the surface, which would be far less costly than lifting everything up the main shaft. Although one observer claimed they had "nothing but muscle for capital"—which seems doubtful—Emmett, Lowe, and Norling selected a point about 380 feet down the mountainside, then drove through 128 feet of rock, ultimately cutting a six-foot vein of ore about 226 feet below the outcrop above. Before the end of the year they hauled 460 tons of ore to the new Kokomo smelter, the largest shipment it received from any mine that year. The furnaces then reduced the ore into 200 tons of silver-lead bullion worth more than $40,000. By December, however, operations at the White Quail had slowed to a virtual halt, with only six men at work mining a miniscule six tons of ore daily. Winter in Ten Mile was still a problem. [7]

Meanwhile, other men bent their backs in prospecting and mining the slopes of Jacque Mountain, which stood farther north. The most important were the Recen brothers. The summer before, they had located several claims, but their most important discovery came on September 9, when Daniel Recen was prospecting near timberline above the Herculean Bar Placer. As he worked his way through the thick ground cover, he noticed fragments of iron-stained quartz, or what prospectors called "float," which was mixed in with flat pieces of pinkish brown sandstone and fragments of gray porphyry. Near the last few trees, he dug a small discovery pit and located a claim he named the Queen of the West. But he could do little work before the cold and snow drove him off the mountain.

While 1879 might have been a propitious year for Recen to develop the Queen of the West, he had little time because he and his brothers were launching their town on the flat below Kokomo. All he could do was build a long switchback up from the valley, a road that looked like a huge sword slash on the mountainside. The only mining Recen did, it seems, was enough to maintain title and suggest the Queen of the West's great potential. That, of course, would attract buyers.

Toward the end of summer Recen made his first effort to sell. On September 1 he entered into a title bond that obliged him to sell the property to the old Summit County pioneer William P. Pollock, now living in Kokomo, and Henry Bowman, the Kokomo druggist, who speculated

TEN MILE AVENUE IN KOKOMO, 1879. Looking north past the Boss Bakery, the street is a jumble of wagons and debris. Note the tree stump and log buildings at right, remnants of the midwinter rush. Courtesy Denver Public Library Western History Collections.

in mines. The price was $8,000 if Pollock and Bowman could pay in three weeks. On the same day, however, Pollock and Bowman turned around and bonded the property to A. D. Rosenthal for $15,000. Neither Pollock nor Bowman nor Rosenthal completed the purchase, however, and Daniel Recen remained in possession. He continued his efforts to sell, and on November 8, deeded a quarter interest for $2,000 to William Graff, who had built the Kokomo smelter. [8]

In the meantime, a few men did some prospecting and mining on the east side of the valley. Both Emmett and Lowe, as well as James McNasser, kept small crews at work in placering, but they took out less gold this year than before the rush, perhaps because it was hard to get workers. Emmett and Lowe also tried to find new deposits, particularly near the head of Clinton Gulch above their placer ground. There they located the Lucky and Black Warrior and shipped a few tons of gold-bearing ore from the Golden Eagle and Golden Belle. Some other prospecting and mining went on here and there, but nothing that compared to the feverish activity across the valley. [9]

Mining itself was arduous business. It was almost entirely hand work, mostly double jacking, in the parlance of the day. One miner would hold a long drill steel while his partner drove it into the rock face with the repeated blows of a sledgehammer. After so many blows they traded places. Muscle was the driving force, but the work also required accuracy and faith, for an inaccurate blow or a weak hold often led to broken bones. Besides double jacking, there was some single jacking—one miner holding the drill steel in one hand and hammering with the other—and there was some triple jacking—one man holding and two men driving. But in all cases it was hard work that put a premium on youth, size, strength, and endurance. It was no coincidence that the first census taker found that the populace consisted mostly of men in their twenties and thirties, and that most of them listed their occupation as "miner." [10]

Once the miners had drilled small holes in the rock face, it was time to blast. They filled the drill holes with small cartridges of black powder, then fired the charges with a Bickford fuse, being careful (if they were smart) to count each blast so they would know if any charges had failed to go off. An unexploded charge was a fearful thing; not knowing could bring sudden death or dismemberment. After blasting, the muckers and trammers shovelled the broken rock into cars, then pushed it to a shaft or a portal, in some cases by hand, in other cases with the help of a jackass or mule.

In these days before machine drilling and extensive mechanization, a miner's work was hard, and he performed it under very difficult conditions. The air was often foul, and the timbering frequently poor. What illumination there was came from candles or oil lamps. Sometimes workings were less than the height of an average man, so that it was impossible to stand at many points underground. Cave-ins and explosions were not unknown in Ten Mile, nor were falling rocks or plunges down mine shafts. But if the work was hard and dangerous, the early miner in Ten Mile was not exposed to the horrors of silicosis and the danger of electrocution that would accompany the changeover to large-scale, mechanized mining in the late nineteenth and early twentieth centuries.

Most miners got ready for work in the first light of dawn, if not before. They dressed in heavy shirts, baggy pants, and put on their battered felt hats, for the lighted hard hat was unknown in that day, and mining companies did not provide clothing. A few miners lived in shacks or boardinghouses at the mines, but most men lived in Robinson, Kokomo, or Recen and walked to work, which helps explain the success of these towns, which were right below the mines on Sheep, Elk, and Jacque mountains, and the decline of Carbonateville, which was across the valley too far for a miner to walk. Up from Robinson, Kokomo, and Recen ran switchbacking trails to the Wheel of Fortune, Queen of the West, White Quail, and other mines, and in the morning and again in the evening it seemed as if there was a procession of men. The glimmer from the lights of miners walking these trails in the dark of the morning or in the fading glow of evening were a fond memory to those who lived in these towns.

While prospecting and mining continued apace, the miners in Ten Mile slowly witnessed the rise of the smelting industry. One group of entrepreneurs, headed by a Colonel Robinson, no relation to George B. Robinson, built a small plant in Carbonateville, but this venture never smelted a ton of ore, in fact, never even opened for business, which was the fate of many such firms. Another who hoped to enter the industry was William Graff of Pittsburgh, Pennsylvania. While his background is obscure, he was apparently the head or chief field representative of a group of investors looking at mines near Gothic and Irwin, as well as Leadville and Ten Mile. One contemporary described Graff and his colleagues as men who "looked before leaping," and not until his third trip to Colorado did they decide to build a smelter in Kokomo. They may have decided to buy mines as well—or at least Graff did, for within the year he had purchased a share of the Caledonia, the Wild Cat, and the Queen of the West. [11]

By June 1879, Graff had his plans in motion. He had acquired a plant site in the valley east of Kokomo. On the road from Webster were the machinery and equipment, and on the way from Leadville was Louis Homan, a balding, moustachioed metallurgist who looked far older than his thirty years. He would become superintendent.

After persuading the sawmills to donate some of the lumber needed, Graff let a contract to Cook & Gordon to put up the plant. The main building emerged as a long, rectangular structure with vertical plank siding, large doors in the sides, and a narrow clerestory perched along the roof apex to provide light for the interior space. Inside, Graff and Homan installed a single blast furnace with an ore capacity of fifty tons daily, which was about the average size of such units in the isolated mining camps of the West. Like their counterparts in Leadville, they dispensed with roasters that would have been used to give sulfide ore a preliminary treatment before smelting. They intended to rely on a large production of silver-lead carbonates that could be reduced directly from ore to bullion. This was easy to do from a technical perspective and far more profitable from an economic point of view. [12]

By late fall Graff and Homan got ready to begin operations. While Homan attended to metallurgy, Graff bought ore throughout the district, the largest quantities coming from Sheep and Elk mountains. The Robinson mine sold Graff its third-class mineral, which could not bear the cost of transportation to Leadville; these ores averaged about ninety ounces of silver per ton, although a few small lots held as much as 1,100 ounces per ton, continuing testimony to the great wealth of the Robinson property. The largest shipments, however, came from the White Quail, which was located high above the smelter itself. The silver in these ores ranged from 74 to 150 ounces per ton, and they held as much as 50 percent lead—very good smelting ores. Once Homan reduced these minerals to bullion, Graff shipped it to refineries in Omaha, St. Louis, Chicago, and points east for separation into silver and lead. [13]

Operations, however, did not go well. Before long, Graff found himself "somewhat embarrassed" for want of coke. This may have reflected bad management or inadequate capital or both, but it also reflected the substandard transportation system. The winter had proved so hard that even some of the best-situated plants in Leadville had had to close for a time. To keep going, Graff and Homan switched from coke to charcoal, but charcoal proved equally hard to come by. Even worse, the ores purchased had more sulfur than expected and proved far more difficult to reduce into bullion. One commentator ascribed the large percentage of "sulphurets" to the fact that Ten Mile had large amounts of water below ground, the mines were very wet, and the water had prevented a thorough natural oxidation such as had occurred in the "carbonate fields" of Leadville. [14]

As 1879 drifted down to its end, it could not be denied that despite the rush, the spectacular urban growth, and the sudden arrival of nearly 2,000 people, the output of the mines had not been large. The year had seen much prospecting, considerable development at the White Quail and Robinson, and an enormous amount of promotional brouhaha, but the cold, hard statistics showed that the production of Summit County had come to only about $309,000 in silver, gold, and lead, although $172,000, or 56 percent, had come from Ten Mile. Graff's smelter had accounted for $67,000, or nearly half the amount shipped from the valley. This was very small, even miniscule, in terms of the statewide output of $18,600,000—Ten Mile's share amounted to less than one percent of the total. Leadville, in contrast, accounted for nearly 61 percent of Colorado's production. [15]

So as the snow settled over Ten Mile, work at the mines slowed and people drifted away. Freight wagons gave way to ore sleighs, which meant that the transportation problem only grew worse, for without railroads to break through the snow and ice, ore shipments grew more expensive, supplies became more difficult to obtain, and with that, the cost of both mining and living rose sharply. Many mines closed down completely; others like the Robinson and the White Quail reduced their work force and cut production. Demand plummeted in Kokomo, Recen, and Carbonateville, businesses closed, and many proprietors decamped for the winter. In many ways the exodus resembled the annual departure of placer miners in bygone days. If the boom did not exactly come to an end, it certainly went into hibernation for the winter.

This winter, however, proved far more difficult than the one that saw the rush. The heavy blizzards, cold winds, and drifting snows cut the roads and trails, sometimes for days at a time. Supplies dwindled, and mining ground to a virtual halt. More people boarded their property and decamped for Leadville, Denver, or almost anywhere else that might prove less arduous. The stagecoaches gave way to sleighs, which ran as regularly as anyone could have expected, the passengers bundled together inside the unheated vehicles and the drivers swathed in clothing outside.

But even as the frigid weather embraced the valley, some mining still went on. The Forest, Tiger, and Robinson on Sheep Mountain, the White Quail on Elk, the Mayflower on Jacque Mountain, the Reconstruction on Copper Mountain, and the Kokomo Giant on Gold Hill kept small crews at work. An occasional jack train gingerly wound its way down the slippery mountain roads to town, Graff and Homan ran their smelter from time to time as their supplies of ore and fuel permitted, and an occasional ore sleigh struggled over the snowy roads to Leadville. [16]

Despite the sluggish pace of work, Ten Mile continued to attract attention in mining circles. In February, for example, Colorado's well-known assayer E. E. Burlingame reported that ore from the Toledo mine held 1,050 ounces of silver per ton and mineral discarded on the mine dump as much as 295 ounces per ton. What made this strike more important than others was the news that the Toledo was located "on the same line as the Robinson mines," a fact that inevitably put the Toledo "among the most promising in Ten Mile," according to the Leadville *Weekly Herald*. The Delmonico Restaurant in Kokomo set up an exhibit of ore from the Grand View mine on Gold Hill, and rumors suggested that Ten Mile would get another smelter, come spring, this one to be built by Messrs. Thomas and Greer of New York. [17]

As spring approached, life in Ten Mile perked up again. The population of Kokomo, which had dropped to perhaps 200 people, rose steadily as miners, shopkeepers, and professional men hurried back to town. The renaissance also came to Robinson and Recen, and even to Carbonateville, whose future seemed ever more dubious. Hopeful reports appeared that a group of Bostonians intended to open Colonel Robinson's defunct smelter. Other stories claimed that Homan and Graff had signed new contracts for the Kokomo works, and even better, the mysterious Mr. Greer was about to begin construction of the valley's third smelter. The newspapers, never ones to downplay anything that resembled a mining rush, confidently predicted that a revival had come. [18]

Despite the muster of confidence, the spectre of bad transportation held the valley in what seemed like an unbreakable vise. If the deep snows had thwarted freighting for much of the winter, then in the spring the warm winds and bright sunshine melted the snowpack into cascades of water. The heavy runoff turned streams into torrents, washed out whole sections of road, and converted flat terrain into quagmires of mud. In May, J. C. Morehouse, justice of the peace in Carbonateville, reported that the roads were in "frightful condition, impossible for teams." Stagecoaches from Leadville could get no farther than Chalk Ranch, from where the passengers had to ride shanks' mare to Carbonateville and Kokomo. Mail had to be transferred to hand-pulled sleds. Mines like the Robinson, which had shipped ore by sleigh all winter long, now simply gave up. The Leadville *Weekly Herald* predicted that not until June would the roads be dry enough for regular freighting, but when June arrived, the roads remained in horrible condition. [19]

Even so, Ten Mile was receiving more attention than any other district revolving in the orbit of Leadville. Although reports of new strikes like the Toledo helped rekindle the boom, the deep snow refused to permit much prospecting, and most new discoveries came in properties developed the year before. Many took place in the depths of Sheep Mountain, which received more than its share of attention because of the Robinson group. The Tiger mine, owned by Simon Foss, a Leadville venturer, and Fernando H. Sutherland, a Ten Mile physician, created a sensation. So too did the Snow Bank. But interest extended all the way to Copper Mountain, where new strikes created such a stir that the *Weekly Herald* predicted the peak was destined to become another Sheep Mountain. [20]

It was exuberant news like this, whatever its flimsy basis, that lured venture capitalists, men like August R. Meyer, the man who had built the

KOKOMO'S BUSINESSMEN, 1881. Local merchants and perhaps a few miners posed for the photographer on one of the town's boardwalks. Courtesy Denver Public Library Western History Collections.

Harrison Works, which had done so much to touch off the Leadville rush. Whatever the problems with travel, Meyer brought a party of potential investors to Ten Mile in May. Newspaper reporters, who followed the trip, claimed that Meyer's group "took hold of an important combination of mines." While Meyer and his associates did not follow through—they had many opportunities in Leadville—the visit portended the sale of many mines in Ten Mile to outside investors, a theme that characterized the district's future development.

Many properties changed hands that spring, as the speculative fever returned, though many mines went for comparatively small sums of money. A third of the Clipper sold for as little as $300; a fifth of the Bunker Hill went for $1,000; one-half the Blazing Star changed hands for $2,500. Even properties on the famous Sheep Mountain could sell for small sums—witness the quarter interest in the Bull Dog that brought only $500. [21]

As 1880 unfolded, the chief focus remained Sheep Mountain, largely

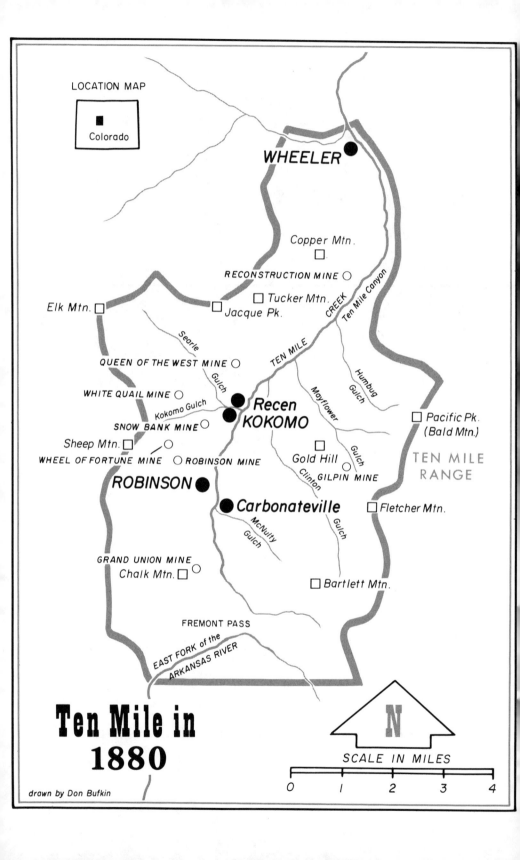

LOCATION MAP

Colorado

WHEELER

Copper Mtn. □

RECONSTRUCTION MINE ○

Elk Mtn. □ □ Tucker Mtn.
Jacque Pk.

Searle

QUEEN OF THE WEST MINE ○

Gulch

TEN MILE

CREEK

Ten Mile Canyon

WHITE QUAIL MINE ○

Kokomo Gulch

● Recen
KOKOMO

Mayflower

Humbug
Gulch

SNOW BANK MINE ○

Sheep Mtn. □ ○

WHEEL OF FORTUNE MINE ○ ROBINSON MINE

Gold Hill □

Gulch

Pacific Pk. □
(Bald Mtn.)

TEN MILE
RANGE

ROBINSON ●

Clinton

GILPIN MINE

● Carbonateville

Fletcher Mtn. □

McNulty
Gulch

Gulch

GRAND UNION MINE

Chalk Mtn. □ ○

□ Bartlett Mtn.

FREMONT PASS

EAST FORK of the
ARKANSAS RIVER

Ten Mile in
1880

N

SCALE IN MILES

0   1   2   3   4

drawn by Don Bufkin

because of the now-famous Robinson mine. But Sheep Mountain had more sensations than this. There was also the Snow Bank, the site of that breathtaking strike in the heart of winter. Located only a short distance away from the Robinson, it had been the scene of some episodic development. In May, however, a second rich strike there created headlines. To exploit the deposit more fully, the owners built up the work force to forty men, giving them one of the largest crews in the district. By the end of the month, these men had blasted and stoped more than 200 tons of silver-lead ore, which was sold to the Greer smelter that went into blast at this time. As June came, shipments from the Snow Bank created what one newspaper called "a furore of excitement." Prospects seemed so rosy that the owners decided to sell out to a new firm, the appropriately named Snow Bank Mining Company, controlled by Messrs. "Stettaur, Neely, Fenlon, and others," but managed by that astute Ten Miler DeRobert Emmett, who now directed his interests from Leadville.

Emmett wasted no time. He built a frame boardinghouse, bought new machinery, erected a new shaft house complete with a blacksmith's shop and a carpenter's bench, and installed a new engine and hoister over the workings. He blasted the shaft down to a depth of 100 feet, passing through ten feet of ore consisting of "sulphurets" mixed with galena. He built several stations in the shaft in order to begin drifting into the ore body, but just as his men were ready to begin this work, the spring runoff flooded the workings, and since Emmett had no pumping machinery, he had to cease work and lay off miners. Some weeks would elapse before the Snow Bank went back into production. [22]

A short distance away were three other mines that loomed larger in 1880. One was the Nettie B., owned by a Colonel Ketchum; the other two were the Forest and the Tiger, owned by Simon Foss and Fernando H. Sutherland. Both parties had opened their claims in 1879, but before long, they disputed the title to a piece of overlapping ground, and although they shipped a combined total of about 275 tons to Leadville, the contentious issue of land put an end to further work. But over the winter both parties sensed wealth below ground. Rather than sending armed parties to seize the contested land or fighting an expensive legal battle that might take years to resolve, Ketchum, Foss, and Sutherland decided to negotiate, and in the spring of 1880, they merged their interests into one firm, which became known as the Forest Consolidation.

Once the merger had taken effect, Ketchum, Foss and Sutherland hired Thomas Gowenlock, a mining engineer, to manage the property. He decided to work the mine through an incline that ran down from the

Nettie B. through the Tiger and from which he could drive levels into streaks of high-grade ore. As his miners blasted away, Gowenlock found that his mineral averaged about sixty ounces of silver per ton, although small pockets held much more. By June, Gowenlock had turned the Forest into a steady producer, but more than that, he had developed plans for a shaft house, ordered more machinery from Denver, and let contracts for building a boardinghouse for his miners. Clearly, Gowenlock and the owners recognized that if they were going to continue production, they would have to improve what one observer thought were "very primitive" surface facilities.

The Forest Consolidation was by no means the only property that Gowenlock managed on Sheep Mountain. High up near the windy summit loomed the Wheel of Fortune. So far as anyone knew, Jacob Hecht and John Still had long since abandoned Ten Mile, but their legend lived on, particularly the unconfirmed report that they had finally sold out for $250,000, and that the buyers had resold the mine for $1,250,000. By 1880 the Wheel had come into the hands of Foss, Tim Foley, and Horace Tabor, who were partners here as they were in Leadville. When Gowenlock took charge, he found the main shaft down to a depth of sixty-two feet, and from that the mine had 240 feet of drifts and a 138-foot drainage tunnel. He thought the best way to continue development was to sink a new shaft, a decision that prompted some questioning comments from outsiders. Even so, Gowenlock and his bosses were undeterred, although the mineral shifted to what Frank Fossett described as "galena and sulphurites carrying silver." Gowenlock had the ore shipped to Leadville, but few smelters had any capacity to reduce sulfides. Before the summer was out, the Wheel had ceased to be a steady producer.

Off to the north, the spring of 1880 also witnessed a renaissance on the slopes of Elk Mountain. The Badger and Milo seemed likely to become steady producers. And they did yield some high-grade ore and higher hopes, but neither mine could work steadily, no matter how great the promise. Water rushed in and flooded the workings, and the sudden appearance of sulfides, for which there was so little market, crimped operations. On Elk Ridge other miners blasted away on the Raven, the Eagle, and the Colonel Sellers (another property partly owned by the ubiquitous Emmett). They shipped some ore, but again, operations were intermittent and might have been even less save for a stroke of good fortune that came when the Raven adit, driven into the mountain 350 feet below the White Quail, served the unintended purpose of draining many of the mines above.

Another property sparking much interest this year was the Aftermath, which had been closed for much of the winter. New mining crews blasted away below ground as the owners ran a drift off the main incline and used a horse whim to haul the ore to the surface. Such rough development yielded 1,500 tons of pay rock, making the Aftermath one of the larger producers in Ten Mile; but not all the ore lifted could be shipped, because of the freighting and smelting costs. What could not be sold was stockpiled near the mine portal to await a more profitable day. Inadequate capital also seemed to trouble exploration. Not until the end of the year did the owners install more modern equipment and improve the surface facilities.

These properties aside, the mine that drew the greatest interest this spring was the White Quail. Although Emmett, Lowe, and Norling had curtailed operations during the winter, they resumed mining in earnest once the snows cleared. In May they made one large strike after another and blocked out a huge mass of galena averaging 180 to 240 ounces of silver per ton and said to be "very heavy" in lead—truly an outstanding ore. Unlike their counterparts on Elk Mountain, Emmett, Lowe, and Norling managed to ship twenty or thirty tons daily all summer long.

Despite the mine's promise, Emmett, Lowe, and Norling wanted to sell out. Why is a mystery, but they may have desired a quick payoff, or they may have lacked the capital to develop the mine properly. Emmett seems to have been the only one of the three with any money, and he was now heavily involved at Leadville. Early in 1880, the three dickered with a group of eastern investors who were interested in buying the mine and the Kokomo smelter to form an integrated mining and smelting company that might lower costs and increase profits. These negotiations ultimately miscarried, but the idea of merging the mine and the smelter did not. As the year passed, Emmett, Lowe, and Norling granted additional options, but always the plans fell through, one after another, until a group of investors in Philadelphia, headed by General B. K. Jamison, agreed to buy the mine and the Kokomo smelter and transfer them to the newly organized White Quail Mining and Smelting Company. But no sooner had the Philadelphians taken control than the onset of winter forced the mine to reduce operations until the season passed by. [23]

Meanwhile, across the valley in Mayflower Gulch, the carbonate boom revived interest in the old Gilpin lode. John Moore had found mineral at grass roots as early as 1866, but he soon dropped his claim. After that, the property appears to have been staked and abandoned repeatedly for the best part of a decade, as no one had any success in mining or shipping ore, and no one, it seems, bothered to file an official certificate of location, at least not until August 15, 1875, when Moore, James

McNasser, and Sylvester Ferguson finally got around to it. What work they did on the property remains conjectural, but it could not have been much until the beginnings of the Leadville rush. Ferguson died about 1877, and his heirs sold his share to McNasser for $10,000. Then in May 1879, after at least one effort to sell out, Moore sold his interest to McNasser.

Rather than do any real mining, McNasser continued his efforts to sell. He had little luck in 1879, but undaunted, he continued his efforts as the carbonate revival of 1880 boomed the prices of mining property, and in April he sold the Gilpin to George Daly for a reported $65,000. A mining engineer of long standing, Daly had come to Leadville to manage the Little Chief and Chrysolite mines, shortly after they were incorporated by a group headed by George D. Roberts, an old California speculator who was making quite a name for himself in the mining circles of Ten Mile, Leadville, and New York. Whatever good things might be said about Daly the mining engineer or Daly the mine manager, he was a man of dubious integrity except for his loyalty to the unscrupulous clique for which he worked. Ten Mile would see.

Soon after he purchased the Gilpin, Daly had the property incorporated as the Gilpin Consolidated Mining Company, perhaps in hope of selling shares to a naïve but enraptured public. He initiated development, blasted an incline, and sunk several shafts, and before the end of the year, he sold several loads of ore. During this time Daly had become associated with the new Robinson Consolidated Mining Company, and he sold some ore to the new smelter in Robinson. Whatever Daly intended before the shocking events of that fall threw his plans into disarray, it was clear that the changed economic conditions created by the carbonate boom had made this property attractive for the first time since its discovery some fifteen years before.

While the Snow Bank and the Wheel of Fortune, the White Quail and the Gilpin, to say nothing of the spectacular Robinson, were the mines that garnered the most publicity, what happened to them was in some degree typical of what happened throughout Ten Mile. Many enterprises mined some ore, and if others produced nothing, then at least prospecting and exploring continued in hope that another Robinson or White Quail might yet be found. But as mining continued throughout 1880, it became obvious that the carbonate ores near the surface were giving way to sulfides below far sooner than expected (if it was anticipated at all), and the trend was far more pronounced than it was in Leadville.

Overall, the year 1880 witnessed much larger and more systematic development, which reflected the arrival of professional mining engineers and mine managers like Daly and Gowenlock. If most enterprises had sunk only twenty- or thirty-foot shafts in 1879, this year they blasted down to an average of perhaps 100 feet, although larger ones like the White Quail went down to about 200. The year also saw a far greater need for buildings above ground and far greater use of machinery both above and below. For the first time water became troublesome, and more than one enterprise had reason to rue the old saw that when the water ran in, the profits ran out. The Badger and Milo were by no means the only mines to be drowned. Mining crews grew larger in 1880, but even at bigger operations like the Snow Bank and White Quail, the size of the work force was relatively small. Except for the Robinson—which was generally an exception—no more than fifteen or twenty men toiled away on a typical property, and only a few like the Forest Consolidation could offer a miner room and board.

As 1880 passed, outside capital became more interested in Ten Mile, and the year saw much speculation and sharp increases in the price of mining properties. For some, returns could be fantastic: witness McNasser's huge profit in the sale of the Gilpin to Daly. But perhaps more typical were the efforts of men like August R. Meyer, who brought in those investors in May. Although they failed to buy, others certainly did; and with that, the mining corporation became the mainstay of large-scale work in the district. The White Quail and Snow Bank were but two examples, and they paled before the sensational incorporation of the Robinson group. Leadville, of course, played a key role, but the mines of Ten Mile also rippled the financial waters of New York, Chicago, and Philadelphia.

Meanwhile, what of the smelters? As the year began, the valley had two plants, Colonel Robinson's defunct unit at Carbonateville along with Homan and Graff's struggling works at Kokomo. Colonel Robinson never opened his smelter, however, and that left a monopoly to Homan and Graff. They bought ore throughout the district, but the largest shipments came from Elk Mountain, notably from the Aftermath and White Quail, and from Sheep Mountain, notably from the Snow Bank and Robinson.

Operations at the smelter continued sporadic, however. Homan and Graff could never acquire enough fuel, not even during the summer, perhaps because they had too little working capital, given the relatively large sum they had to tie up in ore and bullion. The rich carbonates were also giving way to poorer sulfides, and Homan and Graff had not installed roasters to treat such minerals before smelting. All summer long, the plant limped along. Then, in November, the water jacket used for cooling the blast furnace burst, forcing Homan and Graff to shut down completely. Their predicament might have been worse than it was, but just at this time Jamison's group bought the smelter for the White Quail Mining and Smelting Company. While Homan continued as superintendent, since he was apparently a minor stockholder in the new venture, Graff severed his connections to concentrate on the Queen of the West and other mines. [24]

Whatever their problems with fuel, capital, and sulfides, another reason why Homan and Graff could never run their plant steadily was that they had to compete with a new smelter across town. This was launched by the firm of the Greer brothers, particularly Thomas A. Greer, who had come out from New York in January. For Greer entering the smelting industry was a remarkable change in career. Forty-three years old, he hailed from Albany, New York, where he had worked in the tobacco business and served a term in the state legislature.

Greer acquired a plant site near the base of Elk Mountain, which meant that his smelter would be sandwiched between Kokomo and the steep slopes. It was not a good location, but perhaps Greer thought that being nearer the mines than Homan and Graff would make his works more competitive. Once spring appeared, construction began, and by June, Greer was ready to begin. He bought ore from mines on Elk Mountain and acquired other mineral from the Texas Star on Jacque Mountain, a mine that he and his brother had bought. Greer smelted these ores into silver-lead bullion, but after a brief time he had to shut down, not so much for lack of ore but because of the lack of fuel, the ongoing problem of transport, and a failure to obtain the right mixture of mineral for optimum reduction—the same problems that plagued Homan and Graff. Greer could do little work for much of the summer and fall, and as winter closed in, his investment hovered on the brink of disaster, and there was no White Quail company on the horizon to rescue his fortunes. [25]

As if the Kokomo and Greer smelters were not enough, Ten Mile witnessed the construction of still another plant this year, the one launched by George B. Robinson. The failure of the railroads to reach Ten Mile and the relatively high costs of shipping ore to Leadville frustrated the young merchant. While his rich mineral could stand the freight—so long as the wind, snow, and mud permitted—second-class ore had to be piled up on the mine dump, worthless for all practical purposes. Despite the rumors that Colonel Robinson would sell his plant to investors in Boston, it was George B. Robinson who bought the Carbonateville smelter. Once in control, he moved the machinery across the

THE ROBINSON SMELTING WORKS. Hoping to lower reduction costs, George B. Robinson had the smelter moved from Carbonateville to the Robinson mine, where it was rebuilt by Albert Arents, one of the foremost metallurgists of the day. From O. L. Baskin & Company, *History of the Arkansas Valley.*

valley, put up a new plant, and had the sagacity to hire Albert Arents, one of the most respected metallurgists in the business, to direct operations.

Despite the enviable reputation of the German-born, German-educated Arents, not until October could he rebuild the smelter and set the furnace in blast. And when he was finally ready, he had to enter the Ten Mile ore market to buy certain classes of mineral, because the ore from the Robinson mine did not have enough lead, the metal essential to collect and hold the far more valuable silver. Just at this time, however, the White Quail furnace burst its water jacket, which shut down the smelter indefinitely. Moving quickly to take advantage, Arents bought lead-bearing ore from the White Quail, Aftermath, and Snow Bank, mixed it with Robinson's mineral, and finally got the smelter into blast by the end of the year. [26]

While the inclement weather shut down most mines in the district, frustrated prospectors, and brought life in the valley to something of a standstill, a revitalization rushed through Ten Mile with the warm breezes of spring. Yet, aside from the Robinson, whose sensational output captured the breathless attention of the press (by corporate design), the mines in the Ten Mile worked with far less fanfare in 1881 than in the two years just past. There was now less delirium about the fantastic wealth to come, and more prosaic, systematic efforts to mine and ship what ore was at hand. While many mines continued to operate sporadically, the blasting and clanking continued all summer long from Chalk Mountain to Copper Mountain, and here and there in the Ten Mile Range. On Sheep Mountain the Wheel of Fortune, Grey Eagle, Crown Point, Tiger, Snow Bank, and others shipped anywhere from fifteen to sixty tons daily, to say nothing of the Robinson, which probably yielded more ore than the rest of Ten Mile combined. On Elk Mountain the White Quail, Aftermath, Badger, and Milo sent out as much as 100 tons per day, though in general they shipped something less. But far fewer ores came from Jacque Mountain, although the Queen of the West, Mayflower, and others sold small amounts to the smelters. Unhappily, there was no production from the Graff, the Reconstruction, and other mines on Copper Mountain.

The production of some mines was huge. Apart from the Robinson, a story in itself, the White Quail shipped 9,000 tons; the Badger, 4,800; the Milo, 3,500; and the Wheel of Fortune, 2,500. Some mines did not release figures, but the Aftermath probably rivaled or surpassed all but the White Quail. In contrast, the leading producer in the Ten Mile Range was the Gilpin, which shipped no more than ten tons according to published accounts.

Although they were not among the large shippers, Daniel Recen and William Graff finally got the Queen of the West into production in 1881. They spent much of the summer building a log shaft house, sinking their shaft nearly fifty feet into Jacque Mountain, and driving a drift along a four-foot vein that was rich in silver, though not rich enough to defray the costs of mining, lifting, and hauling, let alone smelting. This must explain why the mine worked so sporadically, and why it received so little publicity in the early days of the boom. Recen and Graff stockpiled what ore they lifted right by the shaft house. Not until that fateful October 13, 1881, did they ship their first ore to Leadville—thirty-seven tons averaging forty-five ounces of silver each. While the profit was small, this shipment was the harbinger of more profitable days to come. [27]

Mining of course was no less dangerous this year than before. In May, Gideon LaChapelle was crushed to death in the Greenville mine, a unit of the Milo Consolidation. A short time later a miner named Hogan lost his leg at the Robinson. What LaChapelle's family did is unknown, but Hogan sued for $50,000 in damages and eventually received an award of $4,900, a large sum in that day yet still "rather slight compensation for the loss sustained," opined a Breckenridge newspaper. Hogan decided to stay on in Ten Mile. Despite his limited mobility, he found a job with the *Summit County Times*. [28]

The smelters also went back into blast. The Summit works that Robinson had brought over from Carbonateville resumed operations processing ore from the Robinson and other mines, and it ran longer this year than any of its rivals in Ten Mile. Arents had done his job well. The Greer smelter, however, made a very tardy reappearance. In April, the *Mining Record* of New York announced that there was only the "meagre prospect" that the plant could resume work, because the owners had been "so dilatory." Not until August did the Greers get under way with ore from the Aftermath and the Wheel of Fortune.

In contrast was the White Quail smelter. Early in the year the company announced plans to make the plant "the most complete in this section of the state," so that mines like the White Quail and Milo could ship steadily, but the firm apparently made few improvements. By the end of the year the smelter had run some 140 days, producing 950 tons of bullion worth about $475,000, in sharp contrast to the Greer works, which had run only seventy-six days, producing about 240 tons of bullion. And while the Robinson company released no figures on the output of its plant, the smelter had run for 180 days. [29]

As 1881 drifted on to its close, it marked the end of three years of increasing production. Output had soared from virtually nothing in 1878 to $309,000 in 1879, $439,000 in 1880, and a spectacular $2,600,000 in 1881, much of it due to the Robinson mine. From this trend alone, the future looked good, but the fact was that the carbonate boom had played out, the easily worked ores were gone, and tragedy had numbed the valley for the second time in scarcely a year. In many respects the future was uncertain. Yet whatever doubts Ten Milers harbored, those who stayed on looked forward with optimism. And no wonder. Mining had brought profound change to life in the valley. A wilderness three years before, Ten Mile was now settled-up country.

CHAPTER 4

Surrounded by Paying Mines

IN the summer of 1878, Ten Mile was a virtual wilderness. From the summit of Fremont Pass to the lowlands at Wheeler's Flats, there was almost nothing to mark nearly twenty years of sporadic mining. An occasional cabin, some rusting equipment, and a few ruins suggested that people had toiled here in the not-too-distant past, but there were no roads, no villages, nor even any large ruins that might have suggested a larger, more permanent presence. Ten Mile was covered with forests, graced by streams, and surrounded by mountains capped by snow. Altogether a peaceful, if rugged, place. This was the Ten Mile that Robinson, Sheddon, and Jones saw from the slopes of Sheep Mountain in the course of that fateful summer—the last summer that Ten Mile would ever look quite this way.

As early as July 1878, as the rush to Leadville rose to ever new heights, a group of businessmen at Georgetown recognized the commercial potential of a fast, safe, and efficient stagecoach line from their town to Leadville via Ten Mile Canyon. There was some talk of opening that summer, but nothing happened. Not until February 1879 did the Georgetown *Courier* report "a movement . . . on foot to establish a regular coach line between this place and Leadville, or rather a line of sleighs and light wagons," which would be quicker and more comfortable during the winter. The leading figure in the venture was Silas W. Nott, a New Yorker who ran a livery stable in Georgetown. Nott and his associates planned to open a route over Argentine Pass, down the Snake River to Ten Mile

Canyon, and then through there to Fremont Pass and Leadville, about forty miles in all. Later that month, however, Nott announced a change— the stages would cross Loveland Pass, because it was 1,500 feet lower than Argentine and would be easier to keep open when the snow flew.

During the winter Nott began work on what was soon known as the High Line. The *Courier* predicted that the cost would be three times greater than if Nott had waited for summer, but so great was the rush to Leadville, and now a surge to Ten Mile, that Nott saw no point in waiting. Delay might let others preempt the trade. Despite the heavy snows and harsh winds, Nott pushed his construction crews. He also tried to persuade the Union Pacific and Colorado Central railroads to send their passengers forward on his coaches. Nott drove the High Line to completion about June 1, and later that month began his triweekly service between Georgetown and Kokomo, a town that had scarcely existed when he began construction. His stages left Georgetown on Monday, Wednesday, and Friday, and returned from Kokomo on Tuesday, Thursday, and Saturday. The last leg between Leadville and Kokomo was handled by Ed Cook and Pearly Wasson, who had established a line over Fremont Pass.

During the summer Nott expanded his business. He obtained a government contract to carry mail from Georgetown to Kokomo, and either bought out or merged his interests with Cook and Wasson. By midsummer Nott ran his coaches all the way to Leadville, and Cook and Wasson now drove for him. The stagecoaches left Georgetown at 5:00 A.M., in other words before dawn, and reached Leadville at 7:00 P.M. if they were on time. The fare from Georgetown to Kokomo was $7; and from Georgetown to Leadville, $10. Nott advertised that on his line there was "no walking—no dust—no danger," which overdid the truth, but few could deny that he had developed a prosperous business, so prosperous, in fact, that in the fall of 1879 he bought three Concord coaches.

Despite the line's utility, it could not be denied that this was still a hard passage. A. A. Hayes, Jr., who rode atop a coach from Leadville to Breckenridge in the summer of 1879, remembered that he suffered from the early morning cold and that despite the driver's warnings of a "bad road ahead," they had to dodge tree branches until the team stopped at Chalk Ranch to let everyone have breakfast. From here the coach lumbered on through Ten Mile. Hayes related that the road was "confidently stated to be an improvement over the old one, but neither is very kind." Abandoned wagons and dead horses littered the route. One dead bronco stuck in Hayes' mind because it appeared that someone had "attempted to relieve his suffering, for some grim soul had put a whiskey bottle between his stiffened jaws."

The section from Kokomo to Georgetown was no better. The route was narrow and the surface rough. Hayes complained that despite its recent construction, the road was only "wide enough to let the wheels pass between the stumps and rocks, and no more. The strain on the driver was tremendous. To travel at night would be impossible."

Other travelers echoed these views. Professor R. Weiser, a mining engineer, thought it "a duty" to say that the High Line was "one of the great internal improvements of Colorado . . . a fine specimen of engineering skill." But Weiser also saw the need for many new bridges, as the ground was low and marshy, making travel nearly impossible in the late winter and early spring; and he thought there would have to be many other improvements before the road could be traveled "with safety and comfort."[1]

Nott's stagecoach line was the only improvement in transportation that really benefited Ten Mile in 1879, but along with the limited wagon and freight service, however expensive, it was just enough to help the professional and commercial people. They were less hampered than miners by the shortcomings of the transportation system.

As more and more people arrived in Ten Mile, they created a thriving business for loggers. Most mining enterprises had ample amounts of timber, and they hired many an axeman to cut down trees that were used on the spot where they had grown. But in places where prospectors found no trace of mineral, the independent loggers set to work to satisfy an almost insatiable demand. "The echo of the woodsman's axe could be heard at any time of the day in the previously uninhabited but stately forests of pine," wrote Frank Fossett a year later. [2]

Not only did the loggers work for miners and cabin builders, they also sold to the sawmills. Among the first to see the potential of this business was Judge John S. Wheeler, the old fifty-niner. He formed a partnership, eventually known as the Ten Mile Saw Mill Company, which put up a plant in Carbonateville and advertised that the owners were "manufacturers and dealers in all kinds of lumber." Hard on the heels of Judge Wheeler came James McNasser, who set up a sawmill in McNulty Gulch, as did the firm of Holland & Eckley. Besides lumber, these companies sold shingles for roofing and siding. No doubt all three expected that Carbonateville would dominate the Ten Mile trade, but as summer passed, the real growth shifted across the valley to Kokomo. By the end of the year, this community could claim four sawmills, five shingle mills, and even a planing mill established by Donald Doncaster. This shift highlighted Kokomo's emergence as the leading town in Ten Mile.

The loggers and sawmillers were only the first two links in the build-

THE APEX OF DEVELOPMENT IN KOKOMO-RECEN. Here in the summer of
1881 a group of Rio Grande boxcars waits on a siding in Recen while the
White Quail smelter belches smoke in the valley east of Kokomo. Chalk
Mountain looms away to the north. In just a few more weeks nearly all the
buildings on the hillside would be lost by fire. Courtesy Colorado Historical
Society.

ing chain. After them came the contractors and carpenters. Carbonateville had at least three contractors who established offices on Chestnut
Street in the heart of the business district. Over in Kokomo it was much
the same. By the end of the year the town had at least twenty-four
people who proclaimed themselves carpenters. This group included the
aspiring firm of S. Reese & Company, a multipurpose outfit whose members advertised themselves as "Architects, Contractors, and Builders,"
and whose broadsides proclaimed that "estimates given, and contracts
taken at low rates," were company policy.

Retailers also took advantage of the rush. In Carbonateville there
was James Coffey, who sold meat, suggesting that it was no longer es-

sential for miners to hunt as they had for two decades. There was also Burnham & Company, which specialized in drugs and medicines, paints and oils. But more typical of Carbonateville, perhaps because of its small size, were the general stores, such as that of Enfield and Ralph, who claimed they had "General Merchandise, Miners' Supplies, Storage and Commission, and Livery and Feed Stable." Enfield and Ralph had at least three other competitors, but they were probably the most successful, in light of Ralph's future career in Ten Mile.

Retailing was different in Kokomo, where there were more firms and greater specialization. Few enterprises took the approach of Enfield and Ralph, who seemed to be all things to all people. Kokomo had two shoemakers, one firm that sold only "sashes and doors," two enterprises that concentrated on sign and house painting, four outfits that dealt solely in hay and feed, two confectioners, five emporiums selling "Gents Furnishing Goods," and several shops that did nothing but baking. If Carbonateville had one enterprise specializing in drugs and medicines, paints and oils, then Kokomo had four, including the firm of Gustave H. Lippelt, Jr., and Henry Bowman. In grandiose fashion, they advertised themselves as "Druggists & Apothecaries" headquartered on Ten Mile Avenue, where they were "dealers in drugs, medicines, chemicals and perfumeries" as well as "assay and dental goods," to say nothing of their "paints, oil, varnishes, window glass, etc." Their prescriptions were "carefully compounded at all hours." Even the general stores in Kokomo seemed to be more specialized than in Carbonateville. Firms like A. Eckstein's Boston Square Dealing Clothing House sold more than clothes, but not everything that people would need; while Jacob Bergerman had drygoods and clothing as well as groceries and provisions.

The hotel keepers arrived early, too. The prospectors, miners, and merchants needed places to live, and the valley attracted all sorts of people who needed a bed for a night or two. Most innkeepers formed partnerships to pool their capital, spread the risk, and ease construction and operation. Hotel building, of course, increased the demand on loggers and sawmillers, and the structures erected were generally larger than ordinary cabins or houses. Even so, most hotels were probably little more than large cabins constructed of logs and boards and covered with high false fronts to create an air of respectability and permanence. The rooms were small, the washing facilities shared, and the plumbing outdoors. Several men often slept in the same bed together, others rolled up in blankets spread on the floor, and the minuscule number of private rooms were little more than cubicles offering a scant degree of privacy. Most hotels served meals, generally family style at a common table.

By the end of 1879, Carbonateville had at least five hotels, all except one going by the name of house—the American House, the Carbonateville House, and so forth. L. R. Harrison advertised his establishment on Chestnut Street as "centrally located" with "terms reasonable" . . . meals served at all hours [and] good stabling connected with house." If the Harrison was typical, perhaps the most ambitious was the Delmonico of the Pacific, a name borrowed from a hotel on Denver's fashionable Larimer Street, which had taken the title from the posh Delmonico's in New York City. M. W. Brandenburg, the proprietor in Carbonateville, claimed that he had "the only first-class hotel in the Ten Mile Valley . . . magnificent . . . 36 by 60 feet, and two stories high, and capable of accommodating One Hundred Guests." If that was true, Mr. Brandenburg must have packed in his patrons like sardines in a tin can. [3]

If Carbonateville had five hotels, then Kokomo had at least twelve. Most firms were partnerships. Goss and Skinner opened the Camp Comfort Hotel; Billingsley and Carleton, their own Delmonico, Hinman and Mix, the Home Lodging House; Cornwild and Taylor, the Palace Lodging House; and Mrs. J. F. Cooper, the Pacific Hotel. Since these people generally claimed they operated hotels, rather than boarding-houses, their buildings were probably larger and better equipped than those in Carbonateville. But the innkeepers of Kokomo were no different when it came to advertising. Woods and Gallegher claimed that theirs was "the only first class hotel in the city. Table bountifully supplied. Terms moderate." These inns, however, were something less than advertised. Charles S. Thomas, a judge who rode circuit, remembered years later that "nearly all the outlying hotels were more popular with bedbugs and body lice than they were with travelers," and the food made lodgers "forget all their other troubles." [4]

Whatever the hotel conditions, Ten Mile did not lack for "liquid refreshment." The saloon keepers made sure of that. Theirs was always a good business in isolated mining camps dominated by single men who worked long, hard hours below ground. At least ten firms entered the trade at Carbonateville. Most were partnerships like that of O'Rourke and Cassidy, who opened "The Miners," or Morris and Company, who ran "The Store Saloon." Kokomo had at least twice as many saloons, but the barkeeps generally listed themselves under the more dignified sobriquet "Wines and Liquors," and most doubled as purveyors of "Cigars and Tobacco." Some served meals. Perhaps typical was Sanders Place, located on Ten Mile Avenue like most of its counterparts; here the proprietor, Cyrus F. Sanders, sold what he claimed were "the choicest wines, liquors, and cigars in the Ten Mile district." What was more, he had a "club room attached."

Kokomo also offered more entertainment connected to its drinking establishments. "Prof. Graff," who managed the smelter, established himself as the "musical director and leader of the Kokomo Brass Band." The town also boasted of "concert saloon and dance halls," in fact, four of them. Charles Bell had his Jardin Mabille; G. Wisner, his Red Light Dance Hall; N. Huddle, his Light Fantastique; and M. A. Curcis, his Variety Theatre Comique. A year later Robinson topped both Carbonateville and Kokomo by claiming some twenty-four saloons where a parched miner could quench his thirst. No doubt a few of these bars offered what Victorian America called "soiled doves," who offered lonely miners a few moments of pleasure for pay.

If the saloon keepers carved out an important niche in Ten Mile, so too did the bankers, although their number was disproportionately small. Quite naturally, the first bank opened its doors in Carbonateville. It was here that Anthony Blum and A. H. Reynolds, president and cashier, respectively, launched the Merchants' and Miners' Bank. They advertised that their firm was incorporated under the laws of Colorado and that their "capital paid in" amounted to $50,000. For business they loaned money on "approved personal security," bought and sold domestic and foreign exchange as well as gold dust, and received accounts "on favorable terms." They also made it clear that their safe was "guarded by a Yale Time Lock" to discourage bandits in a town with only the most rudimentary form of public security.

Blum and Reynolds appeared to prosper, but Blum apparently engaged in several dubious business ventures which led to internal problems. In September 1879, he wrote a number of questionable bank drafts, then decamped with several thousand dollars belonging to individuals like James Coffey, the proprietor of the meat market, and Patsy Gillin, a local miner; and firms like the Summit County Bank of Kokomo. A warrant was issued for Blum's arrest, but just then the new telegraph wire went down, and Blum made good his escape via Chalk Ranch to Leadville. From there he was traced to Denver and finally to points east, where he disappeared. Though Blum was denounced as "a rascal," Coffey, Gillin, and others were out a considerable amount of money. In October the bank failed. [5]

While Blum and Reynolds founded their bank during the rush in February 1879, Kokomo had to wait another three months for its first financial institution, the Summit County Bank. The chief organizer was A. L. Ordean, a Pennsylvanian. Though only twenty-two years old, Ordean had four years experience in banking through previous jobs in Ohio and Kansas and, most recently, at the Miners Exchange Bank of Leadville. When he opened his doors, he served as cashier, and his firm appeared to prosper, unlike the Merchants' and Miners' Bank. [6]

Along with the merchants and bankers came the newspaper publishers. At the outset there were several papers projected for the district. One was the *Ten Mile Clarion*, which was to be published in Ten Mile City, the hodgepodge of tents, shacks, and cabins clustered near the portals of the Robinson mine. Another was the ponderously named *Carbonateville Daily Ten Mile News*, a promotion of the ubiquitous Colonel Jenkins. But neither paper ever went to press.

Not until the second half of 1879 did the Ten Mile publishing industry get under way with the arrival in Kokomo of Cassius M. Coe. Like so many others who came to the valley this year, he was young—only twenty-four years old. He was also a college graduate from the University of Iowa—an unusual background for a journalist in nineteenth-century America; and he had experience with several dailies in Denver.

In mid-1879, Coe formed a partnership with Ben Macready, a man whose background is more obscure. They rented an office on Ten Mile Avenue, and on September 27 they sent the *Summit County Times* to press for the first time. This was not only the first newspaper published in Ten Mile but also the first ever published in Summit County. On the masthead Coe and Macready boasted that their paper was published "at a higher altitude than any other newspaper in the world," a claim that soon drew the derision of rivals who entered the business in an age when newspapers seemed almost unconscious of libel. But the *Times* provided an important service by offering news, publishing legal notices, and selling advertising space to local firms, others in Leadville, and some as far away as Denver. [7]

If small businessmen hoped to profit from the boom, so too did professional people like doctors and lawyers. At least two physicians hung out their shingle in Carbonateville in 1879 and another two in Kokomo. Others came and went over the next few years. Among them was George O'Connor, a Canadian via Jackson, Michigan, who had immigrated to Colorado because of failing health. He set up practice in Kokomo and eventually became county physician. Another doctor was J. J. Hendricks, a graduate of the Keokuk Medical College of Iowa. He had a drugstore and medical practice in Leadville, but was more interested in mines. When the rush to Ten Mile began, he was among the first to start for

Fremont Pass, but he had little success in finding mineral wealth. The next year he opened another drugstore and medical practice in Kokomo.

Despite the arrival of such physicians, no one in Ten Mile ever established a hospital. The camps were too small. The nearest facilities were in Leadville, where the Sisters of Charity erected St. Vincent's Hospital in 1878, and an association of Civil War veterans built a second hospital in 1879. Lake County put up a third hospital several years later. Anyone who had the misfortune to be sick, injured, or shot in Ten Mile was first treated at home, in a public building, or in one of the local hotels. Only later could a convalescent be taken to Leadville.

The Ten Mile bar also flourished during the boom. Despite the valley's isolation, mining was an essentially urban activity and, as such, required an essentially urban approach to the practice of law. The miners' courts and the other ad hoc arrangements of the Pike's Peak rush no longer sufficed; by now there were federal and state laws that dealt more directly with the disposition of water rights and public lands. Although the new statutes still permitted individuals to locate claims and acquire water rights on public lands with a minimum of government supervision, conflicts were inevitable in the rush for riches. They provided plenty of work for lawyers, particularly in Ten Mile where the carbonate deposits did not fit the classic notion of a vein as hypothesized by the men who drafted the federal mining law.

The legal work varied. Some of it was mundane, some of it sophisticated. The documentation and transfer of mining property provided a steady, if prosaic, business for attorneys. Individuals forming partnerships and corporations needed legal advice. Others sought charters for toll roads. Railroad men struggled to secure rights-of-way. And there were suits and countersuits as the people of Ten Mile proved just as litigious as any other group in America. The boom conditions also resulted in considerable lawlessness, some of it violent. The consequence was the creation and operation of a system of law enforcement and criminal justice that provided additional work for the legal profession.

Like the physicians the attorneys who came to Ten Mile had diverse backgrounds. The first lawyer to hang out his shingle in Carbonateville was John W. Jenkins, who continued to practice in Ten Mile until the time of his death. The first lawyer in Kokomo was James A. Clark. A Georgian by birth, Clark had studied law at the University of Virginia and then practiced in Balitmore, Maryland, before coming to Georgetown in 1877. No sooner had he set up office in Kokomo than he was joined by the firm of Lorin A. Staley and Ben Safley. Both men were in their mid-twenties and had studied at midwestern universities before moving to Denver, where they had read law and entered private practice. Their clientele was not so well established, however, that they could not move on immediately. Like Clark, Staley and Safley joined the mid-winter rush to Kokomo, and before long, Staley moved into public life as the first city attorney. [8]

By midsummer Kokomo looked like most mining camps, and a stroll down Ten Mile Avenue told much about life there. The street was narrow, though not unduly so. Most buildings were one or two stories high with gabled roofs, most of them covered by high false fronts to lend an air of permanence and respectability. That was the style of the day. Most structures had a single, narrow door flanked by tall narrow windows. Around to the side, however, these structures revealed more about themselves. Some had clapboards covering wooden frames, but others showed nothing more than logs, or logs covered with vertical planking. A few sat very obviously on stilts, which were necessary because Kokomo lay on a hillside. In front of just about all these buildings were long, wide boardwalks that stood high off the street, to which most had long, wide flights of stairs. Some businesses put a porch over their walkway, and just above eye level on each protruded a huge white sign with dark letters that proclaimed this business or that. Ten Mile Avenue, however, was no picture of order. The street was unpaved, crisscrossed by ruts and ditches, and littered with refuse.

Along the boardwalks strolled the people who lived in Ten Mile. Businessmen wore dark suits, white shirts, and tall hats; miners their baggy overalls, colored shirts, and slouchy hats. Women, what few there were, wore long dresses that flared out to the ground. Even a few children played here and there. And everyone posed when a photographer set up his equipment.

Although most business people lived over their stores, shops, and offices on Ten Mile Avenue, the side streets did have houses and log cabins. For the most part these homes were affairs of hasty construction, particularly the log cabins assembled the previous winter. By late 1879 there were some more substantial dwellings, though they were built partly or wholly on stilts, with the bottoms covered, to guard against snowfall. Outside a few enterprising people built platforms to hang out the laundry over deep snow. A few homeowners put down boardwalks across the fronts of their houses, and some fenced off small plots for grass, flowers, and even a small vegetable garden. Inside, the rooms were few, and offered little privacy, at least by twentieth century standards. Heat came mostly from fireplaces or woodburning stoves, and most walls were covered with newspapers for decoration and insulation. Those who prospered could buy wallpaper later. Obviously, life in Kokomo offered few comforts, and the other hamlets in Ten Mile offered much less.

It was just because of these primitive accommodations, and because the mines were closing, that as winter approached, most people in Ten Mile pulled up stakes and left. Businesses and homeowners boarded their doors; the population plunged, just as in seasons past. There was little work, supply was difficult, and the cold and starvation posed threats to survival. By January 1880 life in Ten Mile had come to a standstill.

Throughout the winter it seemed that aside from the telegraph line the valley's only steady link to the outside world was provided by Silas W. Nott, a man determined to keep his express line open, no matter what the weather conditions. His advertisements featuring the Concord coach stated emphatically, "This Line Will Run All Winter." But the season presented special problems on the High Line where the temperatures were cold, the drifts deep, and the winds high. Before long Nott had to abandon his Concord coaches for light wagons and sleighs, and put his lightest horses in the lead to lessen the danger of starting snow slides. To keep warm, his drivers dressed in long overcoats and caps and covered their feet with burlap, which was warmer than overshoes and less liable to slip on snow or ice. Nott unshod his horses for the same reason. As the weather deteriorated, he switched his route from Loveland Pass to the much higher Argentine Pass, where the winds blew the snow off the road. But the howling winds and the exposed terrain presented special problems. To get over the top, the drivers had to rest the horses a short distance below the summit, then dash over the top to shelter below. This also meant that baggage sometimes had to be abandoned—it was piled under a tarpaulin to await more favorable weather. At lower elevations Nott hired several men to keep the trails open with shovels and small, homemade plows, and to help get his horses back on the road when they slipped off. In some cases the horses became so snowbound that Nott's crews had to use a wagon tongue as a derrick to lift the animals back on the trail with a block and tackle.

Travel under such conditions was hazardous. In January 1880 the *Summit County Times* wrote that "trusting one's life in the sleighs and wagons that are now crossing the range is almost as dangerous as walking out after dark in the streets of this city used to be." The peril came not from the carelessness of the drivers nor from the insecurity of the vehicles, but from the conditions of the road. It was full of ice and snow.

The most dangerous part of the journey was over Argentine Pass, a hard route under any circumstances and a perilous one during a snowstorm. One traveler related that it snowed all day as he rode a sleigh from Kokomo toward Georgetown, but the full force of the snow and sleet did not strike until the driver crested the 12,000-foot summit of the pass. Then the fury of the storm "burst with full force upon the benighted passengers." As the descent over the switchbacks began, a formidable snowslide crashed down a steep slope and blocked the road. The travelers had little choice. Everyone, even a sick passenger, had to get out and help clear the trail, with the aid of some horsemen and freighters who happened along. After an hour's work, they had just about opened the road when an even larger snowslide thundered down the slope, caught some of the horses, and buried the trail six to ten feet deep. This time the driver turned the horses loose to escape from the drifts by themselves while the men once again set to work clearing the road. Only after "much wearisome labor" did the travelers break through, round up the horses, and make "their safe exit from the ordeal of trial."

Despite such difficulties, Nott apparently increased his business during the winter and proceeded to expand with the approach of spring. He added branch lines to Decatur, Chihuahua, and Breckenridge, bought more horses, hired more drivers, and built up his snow-shoveling and road-repair crews. He also changed his departure times to make better connections with the railroad to Georgetown. With such steady service, it could not be denied that Nott was promoting the region's development, and the *Times* went so far as to say that Nott was "doing more for Summit County than almost any man in it."[9]

As spring approached, life in Ten Mile perked up again. The population of Kokomo, which had dropped to an estimated 200 people, rose steadily as miners, shopkeepers, and professional men hurried back to town. The renaissance also came to Robinson and Recen, and even to Carbonateville, whose future seemed ever more dubious.

Whatever doubts there had been about Kokomo's place in the district, by June 1880, Amos Smith's camp had established itself as Ten Mile's metropolis. Miners and merchants, along with a handful of families, flocked to town with the arrival of summer, the reports of new discoveries, and the start-up on mines closed for the winter. By now there were no vacant buildings in camp, and contractors hammered away on new structures as trade and commerce flourished again. So too did inflation. Rents doubled in less than two months because housing was short again. Publicity about Kokomo continued optimistic. The business houses compared "very favorably with those in the larger towns," wrote the Leadville *Herald* in June, and the hotels and homes were "fully up to what is generally found in mining camps."

The men and women who cast their fate in Kokomo this year did what they could to fix up the old buildings, not all of which had fared well, abandoned to the fury of the winter just past. Businessmen added new storefronts, hammered down planks on new boardwalks, put on new porches, applied liberal coatings of paint—particularly white—and propped up old sagging roofs. A benefactor of the Catholic Church donated lots to a society that hoped to construct a church, school, and eventually a cathedral. The city council appropriated money so that Kokomo and Ten Mile avenues could be graded, cleared of rubbish piles, and filled with sand and broken rocks. The city also asked contractors to submit bids to build waterworks south of town near the foot of Sheep Mountain. By early summer, a Kokomo that had been nearly deserted a few months before now seemed destined to dominate the valley for years to come. With Sheep, Elk, Jacque, and Tucker mountains flanking the city on the west, and Gold and Mayflower hills across the valley to the east, the bustling town was "absolutely surrounded by paying mines," noted the enthusiastic editors of the *Herald*. [10]

The year 1880 was also the time of the decennial census, and in June a government agent toured the valley to record the populace. He discovered that not everyone lived in towns. He found 40 people on Gold Hill, 67 in Clinton Gulch, 50 on Jacque Mountain, and 173 on Sheep Mountain. In the towns he counted 129 at Robinson's Camp, 161 in Carbonateville, and 818 in Kokomo, more than in all the others combined. There was no record for Recen; it was apparently counted as part of Kokomo, no doubt to the frustration of the Recen brothers, whose town could never escape the long shadow cast by its neighbor on the hillside above.

While the census probably understated the population of Ten Mile, it still outlined the makeup. The largest group consisted of single white men in their twenties, followed by single white men in their thirties. Nearly all listed their occupation as "miner." Ten Mile had only a handful of blacks. It also had very few women. Of the 818 individuals who made their homes in Kokomo, there were only 51 women, of whom 36 were married. They had a grand total of 65 children. The 15 single women listed their occupations as "boarder" or "housekeeper," which may have disguised their real "profession" as prostitutes. [11]

Despite Ten Mile's revival this spring, some of the older commercial houses did not reopen, but other firms took their place, and still other enterprises simply changed hands. In January 1880, for example, Will C. Stainsby, a twenty-five-year-old veteran of banking in New York, bought the drug business of Lippelt and Bowman. Later in the year, he formed a partnership with J. F. Fort and George B. Colby, the young attorney who had helped the Recens incorporate their town. Frank Ralph of Carbonateville and Jacob Bergerman of Kokomo dissolved their respective partnerships and moved to Robinson, where they opened a mercantile house known as Ralph and Bergerman. And like Ralph, many of Carbonateville's businessmen relocated in Robinson, a town that grew in some degree at the expense of Carbonateville.

There were also changes in the banking industry. Early in 1880, A. L. Ordean, who had opened the Summit County Bank in Kokomo, took a new position as assistant cashier of the First National Bank of Leadville. But Ordean stayed there only a short time. In the fall he came back to Kokomo to form a partnership with Herman D. Myers, who had come to Kokomo from Canton, Ohio, in 1879 and probably had run the bank after Ordean moved to Leadville. But with Ordean back, the two men formed an enterprise that went under the style of Ordean, Myers & Company, and they prepared to open a second bank in Robinson.

The year 1880 also saw many changes in the professional ranks, particularly among the lawyers. Jenkins, Staley, and Safley all remained in practice, but they were joined by new men. One was Alfred Kerns, who came from Pennsylvania to hang out his shingle in Kokomo. Two others were Walter M. Bickford and Will A. Harris, who formed a partnership in Robinson. But most important was the new firm of Leonard R. Hill and Benjamin H. Butcher. They had been classmates in law school in Washington, D.C., then set up a firm in Parkersburg, West Virginia. Hill had departed Parkersburg in a few months to establish a practice in Salina, Kansas, where he had married and worked for a year before joining the rush to Kokomo in 1879. Butcher, meanwhile, at the age of twenty-two, had been elected to the West Virginia legislature, besting a former governor in a hard fought campaign. Despite their seemingly divergent careers, Hill and Butcher had never lost contact, and in May 1880, Butcher abandoned his law practice and his seat in the legislature to rejoin his former partner in Kokomo. [12]

But aside from these changes in business and professional life, the truly big news of 1880 was the railroad. For this year, at last, it seemed as if the Denver and Rio Grande Railway would break the old bottleneck that choked the flow of ores and supplies and strangled development throughout Ten Mile.

The Rio Grande had been the creation of a group of businessmen and financiers headed by William Jackson Palmer, a handsome man of dapper dress and kindly looks accentuated by a pale moustache. He and his associates saw the carbonate boom at Leadville as a spectacular opportunity, but so did another line—the Atchison, Topeka & Santa Fe Railroad. As it became ever more obvious that Leadville offered fantastic potential for profit, both railroads decided to build there, the Rio Grande directly, the Santa Fe through a subsidiary known as the Pueblo and Arkansas Valley Railroad. Two competing lines might have served Leadville well, but this was impossible, for near Canon City, at a place known as the Royal Gorge, the narrow, high-walled canyon of the Arkansas pressed in so tightly that it would allow only one track to be put through. Neither road was willing to concede this crucial passage to the other, and in April 1878 both lines built forts to prevent the other from building. This was the apparently bloodless Royal Gorge War.

After suits and countersuits that wasted time and cost money, the railroads decided to end the dispute through negotiation. On March 27, 1880, they signed the so-called Treaty of Boston. It gave the Santa Fe the right to build south over Raton Pass to Santa Fe and Albuquerque, while the Rio Grande acquired the Pueblo and Arkansas Valley line. Because the Santa Fe had already graded much of the roadbed to Leadville, it took the Rio Grande little time to finish the railway. On July 20, Palmer ran his first train to Leadville with former president Ulysses S. Grant on board for the celebration.

Palmer and his men did not stop in Leadville. So energetic was the road in tapping new sources of revenue that a popular joke claimed that if someone had nothing more than a wagonload of pumpkins for sale, Palmer would put a branch line over the mountains to get the trade. Palmer and his lieutenants wanted all the business they could get from the bustling mining camps spawned partly by the Leadville boom, camps like those in the valley carved by the waters of Ten Mile Creek. [13]

Even before Palmer ran his first trains to Leadville, he set his crews to work grading a line up the east fork of the Arkansas River toward "the Ten Mile Pass," but no sooner had he begun building than he learned of a rival company. This was the Leadville, Ten Mile & Breckenridge Railroad Company, controlled by a group headed by Charles Mater, a Leadville merchant, and George B. Robinson. They had organized a construction company, acquired a right-of-way on the Ten Mile side of Fremont Pass, and set to work grading. By late July, about the time the Rio Grande steamed into Leadville, Robinson had put thirty-eight men and twelve teams to work, and was building a construction camp a scant ten miles from Leadville. [14]

The motives that lay behind the efforts of Robinson and his associates have drifted away with the passage of time. Did they actually intend to build a railroad from Leadville to Kokomo, and from Kokomo around the mountains to Breckenridge? Or did they hope to scare the Rio

Grande into rushing its track over Fremont Pass, thinking it might lose this important trade forever if it waited for even one season? Or did Robinson and his colleagues simply hope to make a fast buck by organizing a railroad to control the best right-of-way and then force the Rio Grande to buy them out at a very good price?

To protect their interests, Palmer had his associate, Robert F. Weitbrec, open negotiations with Robinson. Through late July and early August telegrams and correspondence flowed from Leadville to Denver to New York and back. Ultimately, Weitbrec telegraphed in code that he thought "a little concession will squelch the local line" and he was "looking after it." Soon Weitbrec and Robinson reached a tentative agreement. When Palmer heard the details, he telegraphed Weitbrec, "if definite and complete, accept proposition local 10-mile road avoid any danger of their turning around and trying game with Gunnison."[15]

Finally, on August 2, Weitbrec and Robinson met at the Miners Exchange Bank in Leadville to hammer out the last details. Then, in the contracts signed that day, the Ten Mile railroad and its construction company agreed to transfer their grading, rights-of-way, all their property, and "everything else not enumerated" to the Rio Grande, to do this in the most expedient manner, and to "desist from any further prosecution of railroad work" along the line. In return, the Rio Grande agreed to pay Robinson and his associates $15,000—$5,000 that day as a first installment and $10,000 as soon as the corporate headquarters in New York could formally approve the agreement.[16]

Palmer was now poised for the final push into Ten Mile. On August 10 he telegraphed Weitbrec that they "must economize in building to Kokomo" but "must arrive before winter detention," although there was "no longer any reason for speed regardless of cost." They would stop in Kokomo that winter. As summer drifted on into fall, dirt flew as Weitbrec pushed his crews to lay as much track as possible before the freeze. By mid-fall he was hard at work on the broad loop that swung around the southern flank of Fremont Pass, and on November 15 he put his first rails across the summit. Then began the broad descent to what remained of Carbonateville. The temperature dropped sharply, the earth froze, and snow began falling, but the crews put down ties and rails over the hard, unyielding ground, "affording a striking instance of the energy and contempt of obstacles characteristic of Western railroad builders," according to one admirer. At last, on December 27, 1880, the Rio Grande ran its first train to Robinson and pushed its line into Kokomo a few days later. Here the road stopped for the winter, just as Palmer had said.[17]

The Rio Grande now turned its attention to service. It built a "roundhouse" big enough to accommodate one engine on land it bought in Robinson, and by February 1, 1881, it had established regular service offering two trains each day between Robinson and Leadville. Each trip took one hour and forty-two minutes to cover the 16 1/2 miles between towns; this meant the average speed was 9.7 miles per hour, which was regarded as fast service. These trains were not large, however. Most consisted of a single passenger car pulled by an engine and tender, sometimes with one or two freight cars attached. [18]

Because of the celerity of construction, the line was badly built. The winter prevented the company from doing anything more than cursory repairs, and as a result railroad crews spent much of the next summer repairing and ballasting the roadbed. Still, derailments occurred all too frequently, and there was one serious accident. Nonetheless, it could not be denied that the line was performing an important service. The Rio Grande set a rate of just three dollars per ton on ores shipped to Leadville—a rate one-tenth the lowest charge of the wagon freighters! Although miners were later to complain about high railroad tariffs, cheap transportation had arrived for the first time.

A journey on the train from Leadville to Ten Mile offered a spectacular passage. Ernest Ingersoll related in his book, *The Crest of the Continent*, that as he approached the summit of Fremont Pass, he turned his thoughts from musing about the heroic destiny of the Arkansas River to admiring the grandeur of the mountains. "Almost in the very springs of the river," he wrote, "where an amphitheatre of gray quartzite peaks stand like a stiffened silver-grey curtain between the Atlantic and Pacific, we curl around a perfect shepherd's crook of a curve, and then climb its straight staff to the summit of Fremont's—the highest railway pass in the world." Here, "the pathway is so hidden in great woods, and the grim giants of the Mosquito Range are so inaccessibly high about you, even when you have reached the sterile *oberland* above the trees, that you hardly realize that you are 11,540 feet—considerably over two vertical miles—above the sea." Once his car crested the summit of the pass, he saw Ten Mile Creek flowing away on the other side, and as his train swung around the curves on its descent to Carbonateville and Robinson, he caught a glimpse of the Mount of the Holy Cross glimmering off in the distance. Everyone, it seems, remembered this sight—entranced passengers like Ingersoll, riding along in a warm railroad car, or shivering men like A. A. Hayes, Jr., bundled in blankets atop a lurching stagecoach. [19]

The arrival of the iron horse certainly changed the complexion of winter in Ten Mile. It allowed the mines to keep working, it eliminated the isolation that made life so seasonal, and it diminished the threat of starvation and cold. Even though winter was hardly less rigorous, the railroad meant that life would now be more normal, or at least as normal as it could be in these rude towns.

And the bits and pieces scattered through the narrow columns of the *Summit County Times* on January 1, 1881, told much about life in Ten Mile, now that the railroad had come. One headline took note of the festive New Year:

THE MERRY MOUNTAINEERS.

Their Grand Festivities at Robinson Last Night.
Names of those who Enjoyed the Occasion.

Which referred to an affair at Tuckers' Hall in Robinson, where a social group known as the Merry Mountaineers had given a New Year's Ball attended by people from Kokomo, Leadville, and elsewhere. Dancing had begun at 8:30 and "continued until long after the new year had dawned and the dark shadows of night were dispelled by the long rays of light that came streaming over the peaks beyond Bartlett Mountain." And how did the *Times* know so well? Ah, the revelers included none other than the editor, Ben Macready, along with Mrs. McDonald, Miss Mamie Wanner, Miss Bell Hughes, and of course Jacob Bergerman, Frank Bissell, Walter M. Bickford, and many others such as Miss Pedgriff and Miss Darrow from Leadville. "Many of the ladies present," observed the careful *Times*, "were rendered very charming by the elegant jewelry and bouquets which adorned them." But not to be outdone, "the gentlemen" were also "tastefully adorned" for this party of "rare enjoyment."

Yet the Merry Mountaineers had by no means staged the only bash of the New Year. Not at all. Several women had joined Mrs. Thomas in keeping an open house, where others were invited to call for a "rare good time." This was most commendable, thought the editors, for it promoted good feeling at this time of year. And the *Times* made it a point to recall the "royal old fashioned repast" that Mr. and Mrs. Thomas Gowenlock gave the editors on Christmas Day.

On the last page of the *Times* was evidence of the new permanence. Here was the news that the Society of Hearty Eaters, twenty men strong, had rented the Bon Ton restaurant and "arranged for home refreshments." More important were reports that the "ubiquitous Bob Emmett" had disappeared, Fernando H. Sutherland the physician had gone to Leadville to work on a mining deal, and "several gentlemen" who had left Kokomo for the winter had in fact returned, among them "several victims of the Durango delusion." Even Mr. and Mrs. Benjamin F. Follett—Mr. Follett being the old placer miner—had decided to remain in Ten Mile this winter. Times seemed to be changing indeed. And the Rio Grande Railway had made arrangements to build two intermediate stations between Leadville and Robinson—one at Birdseye and another at Summit. [20]

Yet whatever the good news and glad celebrations, it could not be denied that the New Year had inaugurated a winter far more severe than the one just past. Before long, the cold, the snow, and the drifts had shut down every mine in the district except for White Quail and the Robinson—hard times had returned. Yet the Rio Grande kept open its track to Leadville, maintaining better communications than ever before, while Silas W. Nott sent out the coaches and sleighs that held his share of the network between Georgetown and Kokomo. No doubt it was such change in the infrastructure, but particularly the arrival of the iron horse, that induced the Folletts and others to ride out the winter in Ten Mile instead of decamping in the usual fashion.

Yet for Silas W. Nott this winter was a very close thing. He ran his coaches over the rough route from Georgetown as late as November 1880, but once the snows descended over the mountains, they fell fast and deep. "The snowstorms of the present winter are an unprecedented thing," wrote one newspaper editor. Nott switched to sleighs on the Argentine Pass route, as he had done the year before, but by January 1881 his teams could not get through for days at a time because of high drifts and numbing cold. Chihuahua and Decatur were cut off, so were Kokomo and the other Ten Mile towns; it was impossible to think of getting as far as Leadville. Nott could do little more than maintain his mail contract by sending pouches forward with men who crossed the range on snowshoes or cross-country skis. [21]

Another man undeterred by high winds, deep snow, and shuddering cold was John L. Dyer, a minister in the Methodist Episcopal Church. Sometimes called "the snowshoe itinerant" because of his winter treks to preach the gospel in isolated mining camps, the indefatigable, sixty-year-old Dyer saw his work this year as no different than times past, though perhaps as a concession to age and convenience, he used Nott's line of coaches and sleighs. He remembered years later that Nott's sleighs were "generally full," though it was "not uncommon to be turned over and all thrown out into the snow."

In February 1881, Dyer arrived in Ten Mile, courtesy of a half-fare ticket on one of Nott's sleighs. No sooner had he found lodging than he held "a protracted meeting" in Kokomo, where he hoped to organize a parish. When he returned to the inn that night, "weary" from his arduous day, he found his anticipated rest interrupted by two young couples. "There was a room nearby, with a stove and table and cards," he remembered, and the young people came upstairs and began to play cards. "They were full of noisy fun. Evidently the boys beat, and I supposed the game was what they called smut, as the girls would not stand the application, and ran up the hall, the boys after them, and went back and at it again. I got no sleep till after midnight."

Though Dyer worried how his ministry could succeed "under such usage as this," he made up his mind "to hold on and try," and in the morning, somewhat fresher after his interrupted night's sleep, he resolved to continue. The snow in the valley was six feet deep when he left the hotel, yet he began to visit families and bachelors' cabins, and received several invitations to stay. He finally accepted an offer from Mr. Thomas, "a Welsh Congregationalist." Thomas's small cabin was but six feet high to the eaves, "snow all around," remembered Dyer, and "six feet on top." Someone had carved out steps in the snow to provide passage to the street. For two weeks Dyer slept on a spare mattress in the corner of a room, but he took his meals with bachelors, made rounds, and preached every night to about seventy-five people who braved the ongoing storms. For his efforts, Dyer managed to form a society of sixteen, which, he was proud to relate, built a chapel that spring. [22]

The year 1881 saw the full flowering of the hopes and efforts that had produced the carbonate boom. The production of the mines leaped to a record high, spearheaded by the Robinson, and if prospecting diminished, there was more prosaic work mining what ore was at hand. There was also far less hoopla. People in Ten Mile went steadily about their business of buying and selling, shopping for goods, campaigning for office, launching churches, and enjoying what pleasures of life they could—an outing at Wheeler's, a jaunt to Leadville, a trip to Breckenridge.

And so the year unfolded. The capricious days of summer drifted on to the crystal weather of fall. The brilliant aspens brightened Ten Mile with huge splotches of yellow and orange, and the first light snows added a contrapuntal theme as they dusted the mountain peaks with a mantle of white. Life continued its hum and routine as Ten Milers prepared for another winter, how hard no one knew. Miners strained to produce as much ore as possible, and the Rio Grande crews hurried construction on the Blue River Extension, the formal name of the line from Leadville to Ten Mile, down the valley to Wheeler's Ranch, and on toward Breckenridge, its ultimate destination.

But as the year drifted on toward its close, sudden change caught the valley up short. A headline in the Breckenridge *Daily Journal* told the story:

KOKOMO DESTROYED! THE TOWN WIPED OUT WITH A BESOM OF DESTRUCTION!
THE LATEST PARTICULARS BY TELEGRAPH AND PRIVATE SOURCES!
WANT OF WATER THE CAUSE OF THIS WHOLESALE LOSS!
A LARGE NUMBER OF FAMILIES LEFT SHELTERLESS
A PARTIAL STATEMENT OF INDIVIDUAL LOSSES
THE 13TH OF OCTOBER A DAY TO BE LONG REMEMBERED!

Indeed it was. The fire apparently began in the Summit House, the hotel owned by J. M. Longwell, about seven o'clock that Thursday night. Sketchy evidence suggested that a kerosene lamp had accidently exploded and started a fire that spread so rapidly through the building that Longwell did not even have time to take the money from his cash drawer before he fled for his life. He lost everything.

With the Summit House an orange inferno in the chill night air, the flames leaped across the street and rushed down both sides of Ten Mile Avenue. Buildings burst into flames like so many matches lined up in rows. The Summit County Bank "went down like timber," wrote the *Journal*. Morris' Dry Goods House burned "like a flash." The family got out alive, but nothing was saved. Then on to the Strongs' Western Hotel. Mrs. Strong got to some belongings before the inferno, but a number of horses died in the blaze. As the flames rushed through town, they burned out Haus & Smith's saloon, Shepard's law office, Staat's assay office and fruit store, some vacant buildings, Hardin's grocery, the Kokomo post office, Stainsby's drug store, Boyd & Company's shoe store, and other firms. Some people tore down a building to stop the conflagration, but the flames roared past down the hill toward Recen.

Once the fire touched off the Summit County Bank, it spread in the opposite direction up Ten Mile Avenue. George's Saloon, Wilkins, Hall & Butcher's law office, a fruit stand, Wetsley's livery stable (Wetsley managed to save his horses), a dance house, several vacant buildings, a cigar shop, and finally the *Summit County Times*, including its splendid new power press. All went up in flames.

As fire raced through town, the telegraph operator clicked out the word to Leadville. Without delay, General Agent Williamson and Superintendent Griffen got up a special Rio Grande train filled with firemen and volunteers from the Tabor Hose, the Humphrey Hose, and the Harrison Hook & Ladder Company, but by the time these firefighters hove into Ten Mile, they could do little more than extinguish the small flickerings that still licked away through the ruins. Except for two buildings that stood near the dogleg into Recen, Kokomo lay in ashes. Losses were estimated at $250,000 to $400,000, and while no one had died, all the people who lived over their shops and stores were left homeless. To make matters worse, rumors began to circulate that looters had arrived to prey on the homeless and destitute. "Lynching is too good for such liabilities on the race," thundered the *Journal*, but no one ended up dangling from the taut end of a rope. Instead, the men and women of Kokomo turned to the task of rebuilding their shattered lives. [23]

The burning of Kokomo was hardly unusual. Such jerry-built mining towns had little or no provision for fighting fires. Leadville, Central City, and many others had all been swept by flames at one point, and others, like Creede and Cripple Creek, would suffer the same fate in years to come. But such stoic philosophy (if any there was) mattered little in Ten Mile this October of 1881. The mines were still productive, and this meant that Kokomo would be rebuilt. And in this hour of calamity, loss, frustration, and despair, two firms came forward to help the reconstruction. The first was the Rio Grande Railway. Within a few days the line offered to haul building materials gratis from Leadville to the townsite. While this altruism naturally coincided with the road's best interests, few would deny that it was a boon to the devastated. The Leadville *Democrat* termed the offer "timely and generous," and said that "too much praise" could not be accorded the management.

More important, however, was a proposal from the Recen brothers. They decided to donate lots in their town to any burned-out resident of Kokomo who would erect a building costing at least $300, begin construction within thirty days, and complete the work without unnecessary delay. They took out advertisements announcing that their offer would be good for ten days, although they were careful to reserve the right to select lots for the various applicants and prohibit the transfer of title bonds for a time to prevent speculation.

And so, as the first winter snows drifted over the valley, many of the residents of Kokomo began rebuilding their homes and their lives in Recen. Yet it must have been a cheerless fall and a dreaded winter, seasons filled with great doubts. Not only had Kokomo burned, but by this time it had become clear that none of the towns in Ten Mile would become another Leadville. Aside from the Robinson, the surrounding mines were neither as rich nor as extensive. What production there was to come would be relatively small and more costly. The carbonates had given way to sulfides, the smelters of Ten Mile had no roasters to treat this new ore, and the situation was hardly any better in Leadville. Even worse, the famed Robinson mine, the bellwether of Ten Mile ever since Robinson, Sheddon, and Jones had set their sights on Sheep Mountain, had now fallen under the dark clouds of doubt, its management suspect, its future uncertain.

CHAPTER 5

The Most Brilliant Prospects

AND what of George B. Robinson and the Robinson mine snuggled there at the foot of Sheep Mountain? DeRobert Emmett, Fernando H. Sutherland, and Thomas Gowenlock may have been significant figures in Ten Mile, and the Wheel of Fortune, White Quail, and Aftermath were important mines, but their story paled before the unfolding saga of the young merchant from Michigan and the tumultuous history of the claims he had located with John Y. Sheddon and Charles Jones in that halcyon summer of 1878.

Sheddon and Jones had hauled their gear over the mountains to Ten Mile at Robinson's behest shortly after all the parties had agreed that the troubled Jones could take the place of William West in the grubstake agreement of May. And it was early that summer that Sheddon and Jones located the first important claims on Sheep Mountain—the Ten Mile on June 30 and the 78 on July 16. Jones wanted to sell out immediately, apparently hoping to get enough money to keep himself in booze for months to come, perhaps for the rest of his life. As early as July, he offered to sell his share in both claims to Robinson for $5,000, but the young merchant demurred, no doubt to his later regret. Either he did not have the $5,000, or as seems more likely, he was reluctant to pay so much for two promising but unproved claims. Yet he apparently loaned Sheddon and Jones about $700 or $800, perhaps their share in the initial development costs or an advance to extend the grubstake agreement.

103

GEORGE B. ROBINSON. In this, the
only known likeness, Robinson's dignity and serenity mask the swirl of
events transforming his life from
prosperous merchant to bonanza
king. From O. L. Baskin & Company, *History of the Arkansas Valley.*

Sheddon and Jones kept prospecting, and on September 3 they located
the Big Giant and on September 14 the Undine.

Despite the increasing promise of the claims, Jones resumed his
efforts to sell. He approached William L. Campbell of Arapahoe County,
a man he had known for years, asking for $30,000. Since Jones was
drunk, Campbell was reluctant to buy, although he did take a look. Jones
again offered to sell his share to Robinson for $10,000, but Robinson still
demurred, and one wonders why? He had now shipped his first ore to
Leadville, and the four claims seemed ever more valuable.

But even if Jones had failed to sell, he made a sudden exit from the
unfolding saga of Ten Mile. Somehow, he got hold of enough money to go
on a prolonged drinking spree through the bars of Leadville, and now the
ravages of alcoholism caught him up. On October 15 he began drinking
heavily at the Senate Saloon, and while no one is certain what happened,
that night he died. In the morning a mutual friend took the news to
Sheddon and West, who lived near camp. They hurried down, claimed
the body, and buried Jones in a pauper's grave.

Although Jones was gone, his estate still had to be settled, and
through this happenstance a new figure entered the Robinson story. This

was Franklin T. Caley, a Leadville butcher-turned-speculator in mines and a lower-echelon politician soon to be elected county commissioner. Perhaps through such political connections, the Lake County Court appointed Caley the trustee and administrator of Jones's estate. Caley examined the claims in Ten Mile, liked what he saw, and over the next few months he became an important catalyst in the Ten Mile situation.

Robinson may have been through with Jones the man, but no sooner had the tragic prospector been interred than Robinson learned that Jones had died without a will. This might have made little difference had the claims on Sheep Mountain proved worthless, but by the end of October, a carbonate rush to Ten Mile lay in the offing. And when the boom came, and it became obvious that the four claims were among the richest in the district, claimants to Jones's estate appeared from everywhere. Not for another year and a half—not until the latter part of 1880—did Robinson and the courts resolve the matter. [1]

And then there was Sheddon, a man not so impoverished as Jones, but a prospector who apparently had little money. Sheddon did not try to sell as early as Jones, but as summer turned into fall, he too decided to part with his interest. On September 20 he sold his share of the Big Giant to Robinson for a mere $100. Throughout the autumn he received his portion from the first sales of ore from the 78, but he needed more cash to finance other prospecting ventures or pay off his debts to Robinson. On December 16, with the vanguard of the rush descending on Ten Mile, he borrowed $1,000 from Eddy and James, the Leadville ore buyers then receiving Robinson's shipments, and secured the loan with his interest in the Ten Mile, 78, and Undine. But, three days later, he leased his share in the claims to Caley, a lease that apparently included an option to buy for $10,000. [2]

In the meantime, Robinson seemed ever more intent upon committing his resources to the district. By the end of September he had sold his first ore, and his half interest in the Ten Mile, 78, Big Giant, and Undine looked better and better with each passing day. Yet he still did not buy out Sheddon and Jones (and one wonders why, since they wanted to sell). Nonetheless, he moved quickly to take control of the nearby ground, for he could see other prospectors at work. He bought three claims from DeRobert Emmett—the Sunset, Pleasant View, and Carbonate Vault—probably in partnership with his friend and associate John W. Jacque. But no sooner had Robinson completed the deal with Emmett than he saw two other prospectors working close by the Undine sideline. And that seemed ominous.

The two men in question were D. F. Snooks and James Daley. When they began prospecting is a matter of conjecture, but they were certainly on the site by November. Not much is known about either man; what is important is that on November 15 they laid out a claim they called the Smuggler, which was immediately adjacent to the Undine. Four days later they recorded a location certificate at the Summit County court-house in Breckenridge. Laid out at a right angle to the 78 and the Un-dine, the southwest end line of the Smuggler was parallel to and adjoined the northeast sideline of the Undine. At once, Snooks and Daley sank a discovery shaft that was not only close to the Undine line, but also lined up with the workings of the 78 and the Undine. Even though he had little experience in mining, Robinson perceived that Snooks and Daley were hoping to hit the ore trend disclosed in his claims, or else force him to buy them out. [3]

Robinson reacted quickly, perhaps on the advice of his friend Captain Jacque. Starting near the Undine sideline, a mere eight feet from the Smuggler shaft, Robinson had his men sink a second shaft to a depth of eighteen feet, outdistancing Snooks and Daley, who had gone down only ten to twelve feet. Snooks and Daley now seemed ready to sell, and on November 21, just two days after they recorded their location certificate, Robinson paid them $200 for the entire claim. To this point they had not struck any ore, which seems to be the reason they sold for so little money. Then five days later, on November 26, Robinson sold Jacque a one-half interest in the Smuggler for $100.

Exactly why Robinson bought the Smuggler for a nominal sum and then sold one-half to Jacque eventually became a matter of dispute. Three years later, in 1881, Jacque testified that Snooks and Daley had staked the claim before they discovered any ore on the strength of their belief that the 78 ore body entered the Smuggler some distance below ground. According to Jacque, Robinson knew that this was their expecta-tion; and what was more, he also thought the Smuggler shaft would strike the 78 ore body. Thus he bought the Smuggler to prevent strang-ers from gaining a foothold so close to his valuable claims and to avoid harrassment and litigation. But, said Jacque, since he and Robinson were "upon the closest terms of intimacy and friendship," Robinson induced him to buy one-half the Smuggler and share the cost of developing and mining that part of the 78 that extended into the Smuggler. And, said Jacque, neither he nor Robinson expected to find anything in the claim except the same mineral found in the 78.

But Robinson's successor, the Robinson Consolidated Mining Com-pany, told a different story. According to this account, Robinson and Jac-que had purchased three other claims nearby—the Sunset, Pleasant

View, and Carbonate Vault—and when they saw Snooks and Daley stake out the Smuggler, they perceived that this claim was a threat to their joint interests because the boundaries of the Smuggler conflicted with those of the Sunset, Pleasant View, and Carbonate Vault. To protect themselves, Robinson and Jacque agreed to buy out Snooks and Daley, but because Jacque was short of cash, Robinson paid the $200, took the claim in his name, and only later conveyed the one-half interest to Jacque for $100. At all times, said the company, it was a simple defensive agreement that took place before the continued development of the 78 and Undine made it clear that the 78 ore body ran into the Smuggler ground. [4]

Whatever the truth, after they bought out Snooks and Daley, Robinson and Jacque decided to deepen the Smuggler shaft to see if the 78 ore body entered the Smuggler. Robinson may have provided some or all of the capital, while Jacque directed the miners. Cold and snow hampered the effort, but on January 3, 1879, Robinson and Jacque struck ore at a depth of fifty-five feet. They were elated, but their joy turned to doubt the very next day when Jacque fell ill. His condition deteriorated, and before long, he had to be taken to Leadville, where he lingered for months in the twilight between life and death.

Despite Jacque's illness and the rigorous winter, Robinson continued to develop the Smuggler as best he could, taking pot luck with his miners and joking that the mines of Ten Mile would soon make him rich. At first he abandoned work on the shaft in favor of building an ore house and making other surface improvements that would be essential for exploration once he and Jacque resumed operations; and he charged one-half the cost of labor and material to Jacque's account.

Meanwhile, after obtaining a lease from Sheddon, but working simultaneously as the administrator of the Jones estate, Caley made another trip to Ten Mile. Despite the inclement weather, he carefully examined the Ten Mile, 78, Big Giant, and Undine. For the first time he saw that they were rich in mineral, since Robinson had by now exposed a large ore body in the discovery shaft on the Undine. Caley also observed that the vein of mineral appeared to run from the Undine *up* the limestone footwall toward the 78 and *down* the hill toward the Smuggler. Except for the actual discovery of these deposits, Caley's observation was one of the most crucial in the hurried development of what people were beginning to call the Robinson Mine. [5]

Satisfied with the ore body, Caley decided to exercise his option to buy the quarter share still owned by Sheddon, and on January 17, 1879, he paid Sheddon the $10,000. Yet on the same day he sold half of Sheddon's interest to Robinson. The deed recites that Robinson paid Caley only $500, but it seems likely that Robinson paid a much larger sum and that Caley was either acting as a front man for Robinson or that Caley financed his own purchase by selling an interest to Robinson. As this day came to an end, however, Robinson owned five-eighths of the Ten Mile, 78, Big Giant, and Undine, Caley owned one-eighth, and the Jones heirs, whoever they were, owned a full one-fourth.

With the sale to Caley, Sheddon dropped out of the Ten Mile story. Although he sold before development established the full value of the mine, he still left the Rockies a wealthy man by the standards of the day. He continued his prospecting career in the Southwest, and in August 1882 he discovered a promising silver property near Kingston, New Mexico. Using his old Leadville connections, Sheddon bonded the mine, named the Solitaire, to Horace Tabor and John E. Wurtzebach. Although hopes ran high, the good pockets of high-grade ore near the surface soon petered out, and the mine was not a success. [6]

Meanwhile, Caley returned to Ten Mile to keep watch on his interests. By this time he had decided to act on his observation of the ore trend disclosed in the Undine. Once he arrived at Sheep Mountain, he told Robinson that he thought that the apex, the highest point on the vein, began in the 78 and ran downward into the Smuggler. Because of this, said Caley, Jacque had no right to any share of the ore and should be enjoined from further work. Whatever Robinson's view, said Caley, he intended to claim a full interest in the Smuggler. Robinson replied that he knew the apex of the vein was in the 78, but he had sold one-half the Smuggler to Jacque and did not think it right to deprive him of his interest. [7]

Caley's effort to garner a share of the Smuggler through his part ownership in the other claims may seem unethical, but he had a sound legal basis. The General Mining Law of 1872 provides for two kinds of mining claims: *lodes* and *placers*. Lode claims are appropriate where valuable minerals occur in veins or deposits which are in place within the general country rock. Placer claims are located when valuable minerals are found in stream gravel or other loose deposits. The distinction is significant because the statute permits owners of lodes to mine portions of mineral deposits that extend beyond claim sidelines. Such "extralateral rights," as they were called, were customarily recognized in western mining districts. The idea itself was very old; it had come originally from the mining regions of England, Spain, and Germany and was incorporated into the federal mining laws of 1866 and 1872.

The first miners in Colorado had no trouble in distinguishing between lodes and placers, but this was not so at Leadville and Ten Mile. Here the "carbonate" deposits were often conformable with flat-lying sedimentary rocks. In some instances miners found ore on the surface or covered only by a superficial mass of debris or other moveable material that was distinguishable from the general mass of the mountain, while other deposits were found beneath an overlying mass of rock.

The interpretation of the law made a crucial difference in determining who owned what. If the silver-carbonate ores were "in place," then lode claims would be appropriate, and the owners would be allowed to assert extralateral rights. But if the ores were not "in place," then location would be by placer claim, and the owners could mine only within the boundaries. Early mining at Leadville indicated that many of the richest deposits were nearly flat; thus a legal interpretation that the deposits were lodes, coupled with the finding that one claim held the apex of the lode, would permit a few individuals to control nearly the entire district.

As might have been expected, litigation retarded development at Leadville, and some disputes generated such fury that belligerent miners sometimes tried to seize claims by force. While some headstrong individuals moved so rashly that they induced armed combat below ground, one party or another usually obtained an injunction that closed the mines involved. As early as February 1879, John G. Vandemoer wrote that the contentious subject of sidelines had become a major topic of debate in Leadville. He reported that most individuals favored the use of vertical lines because they would eliminate a source of litigation.

Ultimately, such a practical resolution prevailed. In one lawsuit Judge Moses Hallett ruled that Leadville's blanket deposits were lodes as the term was used in federal mining law; as a practical matter, however, juries refused to find that the lode apexed in a plaintiff's claim, thus precluding the assertion of extralateral rights. So an unwritten law emerged in Leadville. While the deposits were veins or lodes as defined by the courts, they were not such as a matter of fact. One judge, in writing a treatise on mining law, termed the General Mining Law of 1872 "absurd when applied to geological conditions which were not in contemplation by the lawmakers when the laws were enacted." In effect, the miners of Leadville avoided an unjust application of the law without doing any violence to the court's definition of lodes or to the general plan for mining claims adopted by Congress.

But this vexatious issue had not been resolved when Robinson, Sheddon, and Jones located their claims on Sheep Mountain and touched off the Ten Mile rush. The prospectors who arrived chose to stake lode claims, although they were unsure where to place the sidelines and endlines. If the deposits had been the classic type of veins known elsewhere, the claims would have been laid out with the centerline of the claim running along the strike of the vein, with endlines at right angles. Mining could then have proceeded down the vein even if it departed from the sidelines. But most ores in Ten Mile were in blanket-type deposits resembling those at Leadville.

When Robinson and Jacque began to open the 78, Undine, and Smuggler in 1878, they did not know how the veins dipped because the discovery cuts did not reveal the trend, nor did they know that the ore in the depths of Sheep Mountain was in a blanket-type deposit like that at Leadville. Not until late fall, perhaps even early winter, did they begin to perceive that the ore body ran down from the 78 through the Undine into the Smuggler, and even then, they do not appear to have perceived the ultimate implications of the trend. But Caley did. It seems that from the time of his December visit, he recognized the direction of the ore body and what this meant in terms of mining law. Caley bided his time while he negotiated with Sheddon, administered the Jones estate, and watched Robinson and Jacque sink the Smuggler shaft toward the ore body they struck on January 3. Once Caley acquired his share of Sheddon's interest about two weeks later, he immediately ran his own drift from the bottom of the Undine shaft toward the Smuggler shaft a few feet away. It was this work that proved what he suspected—the rich silver-lead ore body ran down from the 78 through the Undine sideline and dipped into the Smuggler ground, and the apex of the system lay in the 78.

By this time Jacque lay abed at his home in Leadville. He was either convalescing or dying, no one was certain, but even so, Caley again urged Robinson to exclude Jacque from the Smuggler on the grounds that Jacque had no right to any ore because the apex of the system lay up the dip in the 78 and Undine. All the mineral belonged to Robinson, Caley, and the Jones estate. Robinson asked Caley what had better be done. Surprisingly, Caley replied that it would not be right to take advantage of a sick man—it would be better to wait until Jacque recovered, which was by no means certain. Nonetheless, Caley later recalled that he and Robinson agreed that when Jacque did recover, Caley should assert what he believed to be his right to a share in the Smuggler and take whatever steps he deemed necessary to secure them. And, said Caley, Robinson agreed to stand by him.

But Robinson, caught in the middle, had apparently not made a final decision. In February, when he completed the ore house over the Smuggler shaft, charging one-half the cost to himself and one-half to Jacque, he resumed work below ground and began hoisting ore for his joint account with Jacque. Caley grew ever more anxious, fearing that he might lose what he believed to be his share of the returns from the Smuggler. Even if Robinson had a moral obligation to Jacque, Caley had none. Finally, in late March, after fighting his illness for nearly three months, Jacque recovered enough to walk, and once on his feet, he made rapid progress toward regaining his health, so fast in fact that Caley made plans to meet him to discuss the Smuggler question. It was at that time that Caley told Jacque that he had a right to a share of the Smuggler because of the law of the apex. [8]

By April, the conflict had developed to a point where litigation seemed imminent, yet Robinson, Jacque, and Caley knew that if anyone filed a suit, the courts would probably issue an injunction halting all work until ownership could be determined. They also knew that in view of the technical nature of lawsuits involving extralateral rights, it would take months to prepare and assess the extensive testimony that would have to be obtained from geologists and mining engineers. A long trial would follow. With the mines closed, perhaps for years, they knew they would make little profit; more than that, they would deprive the new district of its economic underpinning.

Given this scenario, Robinson, Jacque, and Caley tried to reach a compromise. On April 12, 1879 they entered into an agreement "to avoid the trouble and expense of litigation." Instead they desired "to either consolidate said claims to be owned jointly . . . or to arrive at a settlement of the same upon the basis of a cash settlement. . . ." But if they could not agree, a group of five arbitrators would visit the mine, take testimony from each party, and submit propositions for a consolidation or a cash sale. Robinson, Jacque, and Caley each put up a $5,000 bond to secure the performance of the agreement.

The news cheered the miners, merchants, and other boosters of Ten Mile, for it seemed the conflict would be quickly resolved. The negotiations went forward as agreed, and when Robinson, Jacque, and Caley could not reach a compromise, they turned to a team of arbitrators. These people suggested that Jacque be given either $16,000, or his interest in the Smuggler, or a quarter share of the 78, Undine, Smuggler, and other claims that made up the Robinson group. Given this choice, Robinson and Jacque both agreed to the $16,000 payment, but Caley did not come forward with $4,000, his share of the payment to Jacque, and the whole arbitration fell through. [9]

In the meantime, Robinson saw his interests assailed on another front. The first claimant had emerged from the murky past of Charles Jones, now six months dead. On March 20, 1879, Sarah E. Johnstone of Denver filed suit against Robinson and the unknown heirs of Jones, claiming that when Jones and Sheddon discovered the claims on Sheep Mountain, Jones was prospecting on a grubstake that she and her husband had furnished in 1877. If the courts upheld her claim, she would be entitled to a share in the mine. [10]

Unknown to Sarah Johnstone, however, Robinson had found the Jones heirs—the prospector's three sisters who lived in Vermont. How he learned of their whereabouts is conjectural, although the suspicion is strong that he got the information from Caley (which begs the question of how Caley found out). Either Robinson or his representatives contacted Jones's sisters, and toward the end of April, a month after Mrs. Johnstone filed her suit, and just about the time that the Smuggler arbitration fell through, Robinson bought out Jones's sisters for small sums of money—$400 to each. Jones, of course, had wanted far more, and Sheddon in fact had received $10,000 for a less valuable interest. [11]

Thinking that he had extinguished the interest of the Jones estate, Robinson approached Caley, who still owned one-half of Sheddon's share. The two negotiated, and in May, Caley agreed to sell. How much money he received is unknown, but by the end of the month he was gone from the ownership, and Robinson must have thought that he had at last extinguished the interest of his two original partners, leaving him free to deal with Jacque.

Throughout these negotiations, Robinson had by no means abandoned development of the mine. Far from it. Early in 1879, after Jacque took sick, he hired W. E. Musgrove as superintendent, a man experienced in a profession in which Robinson was not. Musgrove began work as the boomers shivered in tents at Carbonateville or out in the open, but he could do little owing to the cold, snow, bad transportation, and, one suspects, the difficulty of finding miners. Inclement weather was one thing, and the lack of shelter another, but most men willing to endure so harsh a life wanted to find a bonanza claim, not toil for wages as hardrock miners. Development went slowly. Although Robinson and Musgrove shipped thirty-six tons of ore in January, the output of the mine fell to five tons both in February and in March, the bitterest months of the Ten Mile year. [12]

Come April, operations picked up, and toward the end of the month, Jacque returned to resume work on the Smuggler. Robinson did not oppose him, and Musgrove and Jacque apparently coordinated operations with Robinson's blessing, although it was just at this time that the arbitration was pending. Before long Jacque had hoisted 100 tons of ore for his joint account with Robinson. This mineral was sold to a Leadville smelter for more than $7,000. Jacque also ran a drift from the Smuggler shaft to the Undine sideline where he stopped, a fact which suggests his view on the question of extralateral rights.

As May slipped by, Robinson and Musgrove continued working the 78, Undine, and other claims, while Jacque continued mining the Smuggler for his joint account with Robinson and in consultation with Musgrove. Operations continued simultaneously for several weeks, but the suggestion is strong that by the end of May, Robinson had come to accept Caley's view of extralateral rights and that the friendship between Robinson and Jacque, once so close, had become severely strained, if not sundered, through the counsels of Caley, the frustrating arbitration, and the quest for the wealth of the Robinson mine. [13]

On June 22, Jacque left Ten Mile to escort his family from Leadville to Denver, and it was now that Robinson decided to make good his interpretation of extralateral rights. With Jacque gone, he seized the Smuggler, set up armed guards, and when Jacque returned two weeks later on July 6, Robinson's foreman denied him permission to enter the mine. The reason? Robinson had given the order. Why? The apex of the Smuggler vein rested higher up in ground controlled by Robinson. [14]

The news swept through Ten Mile, people took sides (mostly Jacque's), and everyone wondered what Jacque would do. He had only two options: he could try to regain possession by force—in Leadville there was ample precedent for just such dangerous action—or he could seek redress in the courts—a long, slow process at best and one with an uncertain outcome, though it was no less uncertain than the option of taking the mine through force of arms. No one knew what Jacque intended. While Ten Milers waited, tension over the prospect of violence began to ebb and flow, and the armed guards at the mine remained nervous and wary as rumors persisted that Jacque was planning to seize the Smuggler.

Yet mining continued. As warmer weather melted the ice and snow, Musgrove put larger crews to work on a steadier basis and made more regular shipments to Leadville. He and Robinson also planned to develop the mine more systematically, and they began to equip the underground workings for larger-scale production, although they did not buy any machinery. By September 1879, Musgrove had extended the main incline some 310 feet, established four levels of production, and begun a tunnel from the surface to intercept the main incline so that ore cars could run downhill to the surface rather than having to be hauled up the main incline.

Throughout these months, Robinson sold his ore to sampling agencies in Leadville, which resold it to local reduction plants. Although he and Musgrove had sent only a few tons across the snowy roads in January and February, they increased shipments to twenty-five tons in April and fifty in May, then leveled off at forty tons in each of June, July, and August. By fall these sales added up to 227 tons worth an average of $206 each. This was exceptionally rich ore, double the average value shipped from the famous mines of Leadville, and the ballyhooed reports did nothing except spread the fame of the Robinson mine, boom the Ten Mile district, and increase the frustrations of John W. Jacque.

No doubt, Robinson's profits were very large. His cost of mining was relatively low, less than $10.00 per ton, perhaps even as low as $3.50, but that had to be balanced against the astronomical costs of shipping and smelting—$42.00 per ton—although these charges were not atypical, given the high price of transportation and Ten Mile's isolation. Even so, the net profit on sales from the mine must have been about $160 per ton, an excellent balance on anyone's books, though some of the return had to be charged against the cost of investment. What was more, Robinson and Musgrove were shipping only the richest mineral. By September there were at least 500 tons—the miners claimed 700 tons—of lower-grade, second-class ore that had been cast away on the mine drump. It was worth $70 per ton.

By fall Robinson and Musgrove perceived that the high costs of shipping and smelting were retarding development. Yet they looked forward to relief, for scarcely a mile away in Carbonateville they could see Colonel A. R. Robinson slowly building his smelter. What sort of background the colonel had in this highly technical business is conjectural, but mineowners gave him their encouragement. And with good reason. When Winfield Scott Keyes, a prominent mining engineer and former smelterman, examined the Robinson property that September, he estimated that ore could be hauled to Carbonateville for one dollar per ton and smelted for another twenty dollars. This would not only eliminate the high cost of shipping the heavy, bulky ore over Fremont Pass but also chop the smelting charges in half! [15]

In November, with the smelter nearly complete, George B. Robinson signed a contract to supply A. R. Robinson with ore for the next six months. Yet the smelter never reduced a single ton of mineral. By now the snow had begun to fly, the drifts built up, and the colonel failed to set his furnace in blast. Nor did he open in the spring. Like many early smeltermen, he may have had little experience in the complex business of ore reduction. The ores from the Robinson mine were also "refractory," as they said in the parlance of the day—that is, they were difficult to reduce because of their high sulfur content. The amount of lead may have been relatively low—too low to collect the silver. And winter was an overwhelming problem. The colonel's failure was not extraordinary, but it did nothing to help George B. Robinson develop his mine.

Meanwhile, as Robinson's miners blasted away in the depths of Sheep Mountain, Sarah Johnstone pressed her suit in the Arapahoe County Court, apparently unaware that Robinson had already purchased Charles Jones's interest. The case continued through the long, hot summer, but in September, when no one appeared to contest her claim, the court entered a default judgment and a decree against the unknown heirs of Jones and ordered one-half the estate—or what amounted to one-eighth of the Robinson mine—conveyed to her.

Robinson was then in New York, but when he heard, he had his attorneys present an affidavit to the court. In this document Robinson claimed that he had received no notice of the proceedings. He also pointed out that he had purchased Jones's estate from the rightful heirs, and that because the court had no jurisdiction over the estate, its decree was null and void. After evaluating the evidence, the court reversed itself and ruled that Jones's sisters were "probably the only heirs" and that Robinson had become the "transferee of these heirs." Then the court substituted Robinson as the defendant and allowed him to file an answer to Sarah Johnstone. This litigation took up much of the fall and as the early winter snows fell in Ten Mile, the case remained unresolved. [16]

As if the Johnstone suit was not enough, there was also the suit of John W. Burkhardt, another obscure individual who had suddenly emerged from the dubious past of Charles Jones. After hearing that Robinson had bought out Jones's sisters, Burkhardt initiated a lawsuit in Summit County, alleging that Robinson's deeds were fraudulent and should be set aside. Burkhardt, who had known Jones for many years, claimed that he had loaned Jones money to pay his bills—money that had not been repaid—and that he and Jones had signed a grubstake agreement by which the unfortunate prospector would convey to Burkhardt one-half of whatever he found for the rest of 1878—and what he had found now amounted to one-eighth of the Robinson mine.

Burkhardt's position was stronger than Sarah Johnstone's. He could prove he had loaned Jones the money to pay his bills, and he could produce a signed grubstake agreement, the last that Jones had signed in his lifetime. What was more, Jones had signed the agreement but days before he went out to Sheep Mountain with Sheddon and Robinson.

If the Johnstone and Burkhardt suits were not enough, Robinson still had to contend with the contumaceous John W. Jacque. Despite his exclusion from the mine, Jacque had no intention of abandoning his claim to one-half the Smuggler. The real question was what would he do? On August 27, 1879, while Robinson was preparing to go to New York, Jacque went to the United States Land Office in Leadville to file an adverse claim against Robinson's application for a patent to the 78. However bizarre it may seem, Jacque based his contention on the grounds that such a patent would deny him his rightful share of mineral because the apex of the 78 lay in the Smuggler! His adverse claim brought little relief, however. The Land Office granted the patent to Robinson. [17]

Far more important than this counterclaim was Jacque's tenacious, relentless effort to obtain redress in the courts, the only legitimate course he had. Over the summer he worked closely with his attorneys, and in September, about the time when Robinson left for New York, Jacque went to Breckenridge, and there in the Second Judicial District, he filed a suit against Robinson and Musgrove claiming that they were denying him his rightful one-half of the ore removed from the Smuggler. [18]

Yet Jacque and his attorneys knew that it would take months for the court to take testimony, try the case, and reach a decision (if it could reach a decision), months that would allow Robinson and Musgrove to mine the Smuggler and pay out the profits. To prevent this, Jacque turned to the First Judicial District Court for an injunction to halt mining. On October 25, Judge William E. Beck granted Jacque a temporary injunction. Both sides filed affidavits, and two months later on December 15, Judge Beck held a hearing in Boulder, the small college town one hundred miles away. After listening to the arguments, Judge Beck ruled that the injunction was unwarranted and dissolved his restraining order. Robinson went back to mining the Smuggler, while Jacque walked away as frustrated as ever. But his case still continued in the Breckenridge court. The issue had only been joined, not settled. [19]

By this time Robinson had met up with an ingenious California promoter who was about to have almost as much influence on his life as Sheddon, Jones, and Jacque. This was George D. Roberts, a prosperous San Franciscan with—to be charitable—a shady past. Everything about Roberts seems to border on the dubious, mysterious, perhaps even the fantastic, except the shipwrecks of mines, reputations, and fortunes that he left in his wake. His origins are obscure, he never gave his age, but long before he arrived in Colorado, he had made quite a reputation on the West Coast. One Californian described him as "a small-sized individual, with a big head, a quick eye, and a pleasant smile," but Roberts was also disposed to bouts of anger and "when riled," said the scribe, "isn't pleasant to tackle." Though not handsome, he had a genial disposition, walked briskly along the streets, and liked to fend off the probes of reporters with a question of his own. In his domestic life, he was said to be "happy as the father of a family—wife, and a sweet, sunshiny girl, the joy of his heart."[20]

Others less charitable might have described Roberts as a shark, and it was his dubious reputation as a promoter that attracted and repelled the business world. No one questioned his skills, energy, or perspicacity; the question was ethics in an age not renowned for high standards in business. Roberts had built quite a record during the 1870s. He had organized many mining ventures in California, New Mexico, and Nevada, most notably on the Comstock lode at Virginia City. And in so doing, he had developed his own unique system. He would investigate a mine in person by moving in with the mine workers and cultivating their friendship to obtain first-hand information about the underground workings—he distrusted mine managers. The California scribe described Roberts well. "When in Virginia," he wrote, "he either luxuriates in the select restaurants or hibernates with the miner—taking pot-luck as it comes, serene, self-confident, and self-possessed," and because of his perception and style, he became "the moving spirit in the Lady Bryan deal . . . and the power that raised Julia from nothing to big figures."

Roberts by no means confined his efforts to mining. He recognized the promotional possibilities of reclaiming swamplands in the San Joaquin and Sacramento valleys in California, and he gained a degree of national notoriety for his role in boosting the great diamond hoax of 1872. This was a brazen scheme to fleece the public by salting barren lands in northwestern Colorado with diamonds from South Africa, then selling shares in a diamond mining company at lofty prices before the ruse could be discovered. Not surprisingly, the New York firm of R. G. Dun & Company, which kept a watchful eye on the finances and ethics of innumerable businessmen, reported in March 1879 that Roberts had the reputation of being "sharp & unreliable in business."[21]

Until the late 1870s, Colorado mineowners had obtained much of their investment capital in New York and Chicago, Philadelphia and Boston. Californians had played only a small, if not negligible, role. They sank their venture capital into the mines of the Golden State and the fabulous Comstock lode, situated close to the California line. By the late 1870s, however, the bonanza days of the Comstock had passed, and many promoters saw their livelihood threatened by tough new regulatory provisions voted into the California constitution, provisions that the chairman of the San Francisco Stock and Exchange Board termed "disastrous." Just when the "California operators" had their eyes open for new fields of promotion, speculation, and investment, the sensational

CHESTNUT STREET, LEADVILLE. Robinson lived over his store one block west of here at the corner of Pine and Chestnut streets. On the west, Mount Massive towers over the city. Courtesy University of Colorado Western History Collections.

reports of the silver-lead boom in the Rocky Mountains whirled across the continent. Although the *Mining and Scientific Press,* based in San Francisco, downplayed the Leadville rush for the best part of 1878, the fever created by a mining district that would prove far richer than Washoe spurred some Californians to leave their warm, salubrious climate for at least one trip to the frigid Rockies. George D. Roberts had not come to Colorado by chance. He had joined the vanguard of investors and bankers, promoters and stockjobbers, who saw new fortunes to be made on the crest of the continent. [22]

Despite the high-country cold and the bone-jarring stagecoaches, Roberts hurried to Leadville, perhaps as early as March 1879. Even though he was now a man of considerable means, and could have lived pretty much where he wanted, he intended to rely on his old system. That meant bunking at the mines, forming friendships with the men who did the blasting, mucking, and tramming, and so obtaining "inside" information as best he could. For a time he took bed at the Iron Silver, the mine that played so large a role in touching off the boom; later he settled in humble quarters at the Little Pittsburg and the Chrysolite, the twin jewels that glittered in Horace Tabor's new empire.

Come spring, Roberts branched out. He criss-crossed the mineral belt from Central City, south and southwest through Breckenridge and Ten Mile, and on down to the San Juan Mountains in southwestern Colorado. On this last trip he traveled with Tabor. It was said later that Roberts considered some eight hundred mining properties—which seems a vast exaggeration—and from these he selected a handful that he thought he could promote in New York, a handful that included the Winnebago-OK near Central City; the Iron Silver, Little Chief, and Chrysolite in Leadville; the Fuller Placer near Breckenridge; and, of course, George B. Robinson's mine in Ten Mile. [23]

By fall Roberts had charted his course, the same one he had navigated through the investment shoals of California and Nevada. He would take an option on a profitable mine—such as the Iron Silver, Chrysolite, or Robinson—organize a corporation with a much higher capitalization than the option price and the known value of the ore reserves, exercise the option, and then list the shares of the company on a securities exchange, in this case the New York Mining Stock Exchange or later the American Mining Stock Exchange, which Roberts helped organize. To instill public confidence, the favorable reports of mining engineers would be ballyhooed before a populace eager to invest in underground treasure, a glittering list of notable men would be asked to join the board of directors (although they would be shielded from the inner workings of the corporation), and then Roberts would import his own operatives from California or Nevada to run the mine. These men would drive for maximum production, pay the largest dividends possible, and fire a constant barrage of good news at newspapers to generate excitement. That pushed up stock prices, giving the insiders a chance to sell out near the top once they had paid the bulk of the dividends into their own pockets and exhausted the easily mined and processed ores, all the while ignoring the demands of systematic development.

It was a clever plan, one eminently practical in the days before securities regulation, and it was through just such schemes that Roberts had earned his dubious reputation. How much Robinson knew of Roberts's designs is a matter of conjecture, but it is hard to believe that he knew nothing at all.

While no one knows how Roberts and Robinson met, it seems likely that they got together in the early summer of 1879. Roberts apparently suggested that a corporation could acquire the promising mine on Sheep Mountain and that shares of the firm could be listed on the New York Mining Stock Exchange. Robinson no doubt seemed amenable to the idea. The judicious sale of stock could provide the capital he needed to develop the mine on a larger scale. Listing shares on an exchange would also offer him flexibility if he wanted to sell some or all of his interest, although as a founder, he would still receive a very large proportion of the dividends so long as he held his shares.

Roberts and Robinson developed their plans through July and August, and in the late summer Roberts hired "General" J. B. Low and Winfield Scott Keyes to examine the mine. Both men enjoyed national reputations as mining engineers, but they were also old friends of Roberts, which suggests that their reports might not have been entirely objective.

The first to arrive at Sheep Mountain was General Low. He examined the mine in August, taking carefully selected ore samples that he had assayed in Leadville. Then he sent his report to Roberts. At the outset he noted in the dry, matter-of-fact style of mining engineers that the Robinson group consisted of forty-eight acres of land, and he listed the various claims that comprised the ground, including "one undivided half of the Smuggler," which, said Low, was valuable solely for timber. Then he described the mineral as "mostly iron pyrites, highly charged with silver, carrying a trace of gold," along with occasional "bunches of oxidized iron and lead, with now and then a streak of galena." The mineral was "exceedingly strong and uncommonly even in richness," and perhaps most important, "the lode outcrops at the mouth of the Main Incline of the Seventy-Eight," which was the apex of the vein.

Then Low presented some heart-quickening calculations. In offering "a decidedly safe estimate," he computed that the average value of the first- and second-class ore was $117 per ton. And how much was there? Well, the main incline had penetrated an ore body that was now 310 feet deep, the parallel and cross drifts indicated that it was at least 72 feet wide, and the average thickness was five feet. This meant that the mine held about 12,180 tons of ore with a gross value of $1,428,000. If the mineral could be reduced at the works then building in Carbonateville, the cost of mining, hauling, and smelting would be roughly $24 per ton. After adding the costs together and subtracting them from the gross value, the net worth of the mineable ore was $1,134,000. Low was astounded! But just to make sure, he returned to the mine, took a second group of samples, and had them assayed at the highly respected Argo smelter near Denver. The second group of figures resembled the first!

From dry facts and lofty figures, Low went on to tantalizing speculations. "It is not just," he wrote, "to estimate the *value* of a mine entirely on what miners term ore in sight, especially when prospecting has been confined to a comparatively small portion of the claim." Although he had "no positive knowledge of other good chimneys of ore," the present development suggested that "in all probabilities" other chimneys would be found. What was more, the present workings were by no means fully explored or exhausted, thus giving "every reason to expect a continuation of the ore in full strength for a much greater distance." Then he moved on to his ultimate conclusion. "Seldom have I seen a mine so desirably located."

Not content with Low's investigation, good as it was, or perhaps thinking that one exciting report required another for the sake of credulity, Roberts dispatched his second expert, Winfield Scott Keyes. Far better known than Low, Keyes was a renowned mining engineer, a graduate of the Bergakademie at Freiberg, Saxony (Europe's most prestigious mining school), a pioneer of successful silver-lead smelting in the West, and a man thoroughly conversant with all phases of the minerals industry. Keyes arrived in Ten Mile in September, a few weeks after Low. He inspected the mine, took ore samples, had the mineral assayed in Leadville, and even obtained sworn affidavits from ore buyers, certifying the shipments made from the mine.

Keyes sent his report to Roberts on October 6. Like Low, he presented the details about size, location, and geology in the same dry, perfunctory fashion, and like Low, he noted that the Smuggler and several other claims were valuable only for timber. Keyes, however, was much more explicit than Low in stating that "the top or apex of the lode is unquestionably with the '78 location, and therefore the right to follow the lode on its dip is part of the grant under the patent." The long, dark shadow of John W. Jacque hovered over the entire assessment, but for all any reader would know, John W. Jacque did not exist.

Keyes went on. To compute the value of the mine, he calculated that the ore reserves amounted to 12,000 tons that would have a net value of about $1,091,000 if smelted locally as opposed to in Leadville. This, in effect, confirmed the two estimates of Low. And Keyes was equally confident about the future. He wrote that he had "never yet sampled a mine where the results were so nearly alike and so high." If the ore body extended only so much as another hundred feet down the incline, the additional profits would run anywhere from $400,000 to $800,000, depending on the thickness of the vein. Finally, he asserted that "such bonanzas are never isolated, and the finding of new ore bodies may be confidently expected."[24]

Buoyed by such splendid reports, Robinson went east that fall. He met Roberts in New York, and there the two men discussed the prospect of forming a mining company that would acquire the mine. The discussions went well, and Robinson agreed to transfer his properties to a firm that would be known as the Robinson Consolidated Mining Company. It also seems likely that, either on this journey or on one of his subsequent trips, Robinson met a Miss Norman, who lived in Connecticut. A romance developed, and sometime in the next year, she and Robinson became engaged to be married.

Once Robinson finished his business in New York, the first signs of change appeared in Ten Mile. At Roberts's direction, Keyes cabled his friend James C. Brown, a mining engineer, to come from California to represent Roberts's interest at the mine, "watch the development," and "look into the mining suit." Brown arrived in November. Roberts also urged Robinson to settle with Jacque, but Robinson was adamant. A couple of months later he told Brown that Jacque was "a very square kind of man," and that he had sold Jacque one-half the Smuggler for a nominal sum in return for a favor: Jacque had persuaded Snooks and Daley to sell. After that, as development revealed rich ore, Jacque had not paid his share of the development costs and refused Robinson's two offers to buy. "Jacque's refusal to accept . . . angered Robinson," remembered Brown, and Robinson had expressed his determination "to let Jacque get what he could legally, and it would be a question of legal technicalities and the longest purse."

As winter approached, Robinson and Musgrove continued to equip the mine for the large-scale production they hoped to begin once the Carbonateville smelter opened for business. Robinson replaced the crude horse whim with a twenty-five horsepower engine that provided power for the new hoisting machinery they installed in the main shaft. Musgrove enlarged the shaft house Robinson had built the previous winter, and constructed a partition within to separate the engine from the shaft itself, a good safety precaution. Below ground in the workings, they built ore platforms at various levels and laid track that ran off through the narrow black drifts to the stopes. Robinson also acquired the Windsor claim lower down the mountain, from which Musgrove began driving an adit to reach the main incline. When completed, this would allow ore cars to run downhill to the surface, which would reduce the cost of mining. Yet in spite of this ongoing development, a slight but perceptable tension hung over the mine and its people. The claims of Johnstone and Burkhardt clouded Robinson's title, Jacque continued to press his case in the courts, and rumors suggested there was some dark plot afoot to seize the mine.

Carbonateville, Kokomo, and Recen took on the look of ghost towns this winter, as mining slowed to a standstill. Yet at Robinson's Camp, where Robinson had put up a boardinghouse to go with a few cabins surrounding the mine portals, Musgrove kept his crews at the rock face, and the dull thud of blasting echoed across the hills. Robinson stopped by between his trips to New York and to court, and operations went fairly well despite unusually heavy snows. In February 1880, Musgrove had four hundred tons of ore hauled on sleds to the summit of Fremont Pass, transferred to wagons, and pulled across the snow-swept roads to Leadville. This nearly doubled what Robinson had shipped in all of 1879, and by now more than one thousand other tons lay on the mine dump awaiting the day when lower freight costs would allow Musgrove to have them shipped and smelted. [25]

During these frosty weeks, however, the mining press fired its first salvos of criticism at Roberts for what became known euphemistically as "California management." By now Roberts had brought to market one of the first of his Leadville promotions, Tabor's Chrysolite Silver Mining Company. In November the New York journal *Bullion* had hailed the firm as "fairly launched with a great property and adequate management" in the person of the ubiquitous Keyes, "the foremost expert on silver lead ores in the country"; and the first dividends from the Chrysolite were breathtaking—$200,000 per month. By January, however, the prestigious *Mining Record* of New York was no longer sure of Roberts. When he began to float the undeniably small Tilden mine in Clear Creek County (a mine ironically named after the reform governor of New York), the editors felt obligated to "cast a light of warning" and then bluntly charged that Roberts and his associates intended "through certain dextrously managed channels to vend their wares at inflated prices which are one day to meet a reaction that must gravely damage, if not swamp, the credit of the whole mining industry."

The Denver *Tribune* was just as blunt a few weeks later. In assailing "California Methods," the editors denounced "the most absurd stock kinards [*sic*] . . . extravagance . . . corruption . . . [and] lying reports from purchased experts." Although the *Tribune* did not mention anyone by name, it charged that a "clique" of insiders hoped "to gull the public with doubtful schemes and fill their pockets with ill-gotten gains."[26]

Despite the onslaught, Roberts and Robinson pushed their plans forward. In early February they conferred in Leadville, and then on the seventeenth Robinson left for New York. Once he arrived, the plans moved swiftly to culmination. On March 5, Roberts and Robinson, along with Anson P. K. Safford, a former governor of the Arizona Territory, organized the Robinson Consolidated Mining Company under the laws of the State of New York. They set the nominal capitalization at $10 million divided into 200,000 shares worth $50 each at face value. Several days later Robinson conveyed the Ten Mile, 78, Big Giant, Undine, and several minor claims, along with an undivided one-half of the Smuggler, to the new corporation in return for the vast majority of the stock, at least 150,000 shares and probably more. The remainder went to Roberts, Safford, and others who joined the firm as directors or officers.

The corporate organization bore the typical Roberts stamp. Roberts himself became president; Robinson, vice president; Stephen V. ("Deacon") White, treasurer; and D. F. Verdenel, secretary. White had been a stockbroker in New York for years. He would soon become president of the New York Mining Stock Exchange and eventually a member of Congress. Verdenel was a promoter from California, no doubt an old crony of Roberts. From the board glittered the names of well-known businessmen—Anson P. K. Safford, John D. Prince, and Jonas H. French. And finally, there was James C. Brown, whom Roberts and Robinson had selected as general manager of the mine.[27]

Even though Roberts had come under attack, the sparkling new Robinson Company still received a warm reception in the press. The

Summit County *Times* hailed the mine as "certainly the best property in the state." The Leadville *Weekly Herald*, which had one of its correspondents go through the workings, enthused about "an almost inexhaustible" ore body that formed "one of the great bonanzas of the world," and the *Herald* stated that the firm itself looked "as safe and profitable an investment as could be made." Perhaps the *Merchants' and Manufacturers' Review* best reflected the heady spirits of the day when the editors wrote that the firm had started "under the most favorable auspices," and that Robinson and his company enjoyed "the most brilliant prospects." And no doubt Sarah Johnstone, John W. Burkhardt, and John W. Jacque shared the same lofty sentiments as they waited impatiently for court to resume. [28]

CHAPTER 6

The Realms of Time

FOR George B. Robinson the spring of 1880 began on the upbeat. His business in Leadville continued to flourish, his mine on Sheep Mountain stood ready to pour forth its riches, a political career seemed within grasp, and his close friend Miss Norman appeared ever more likely to end his days as a bachelor. He was planning to build his own smelter in Ten Mile, launch a new town near the Robinson mine, and even construct his own railroad from Leadville. He moved in the best circles, he knew the right people, he ranked with Colorado's first citizens, and here he was, thirty-two years old, and all this accomplished in scarcely two years. It was the stuff of dreams. Yet in this triumphant crescendo, all but drowned out by the prospect of imminent wealth and certain fame, sounded the faint, discordant notes played by Johnstone, Burkhardt, and Jacque.

The founding of the Robinson Company brought changes in Ten Mile. Continuing his method of operation, George D. Roberts appointed James C. Brown general manager, and while Brown seemed reluctant to serve, he took the post, partly at the behest of his friend Winfield Scott Keyes, whom Roberts appointed consulting engineer. Called "one of the most practical mining men in the country" by the Leadville *Herald*, Brown had managed mines in California and Nevada, where he attended "strictly in person to every move made." Perhaps so, but Brown tended to be autocratic and did not get along well with his miners. His appointment produced tension right at the start, for he and Musgrove did not get along. As a result Musgrove resigned. [1]

126

True to his reputation as a hard driver, Brown pushed all phases of development. On some days he shipped as much as twenty tons of rich ore averaging up to 250 ounces of silver, let alone lead and other metals. Like Musgrove, Brown had the mineral loaded aboard sleds and hauled up the switchbacks to Chalk Ranch, where it was transferred to wagons for the final leg of the trip to Leadville. But he had to store at the mine vast quantities of rock running anywhere from 90 to 150 ounces of silver per ton. Brown also gave the newspapers the weekly development and production figures. This was unusual for mining companies, but not those headed by Roberts. One clever aspect to all his promotions was to feed the newspapers a steady stream of favorable reports. This created excitement, and excitement bolstered stock prices. [2]

By spring, however, Brown's shipments had slowed to a virtual halt. The melting snows turned what roads there were into quagmires of mud that frustrated the movement of wagons and sleds. By May 15 it was nearly impossible for teams to get over Fremont Pass, impossible in fact for virtually every type of vehicle. Stagecoaches like Silas Nott's had to halt at Chalk Ranch to let the frustrated passengers hike down to Carbonateville or Robinson's Camp. In his report for May 23, Brown stated for the record what was obvious to everyone: "The impassible roads have stopped shipments from 'Ten Mile' to Leadville." Even so, he had sold enough ore to allow the company to pay its first dividend of $75,000, or 37½ cents per share, in June.

In the meantime, Sarah Johnstone's suit against Robinson had dragged on over the winter as both sides gathered evidence, and in the spring of 1880 it went to court. There the evidence presented brought to full light the pathetic story of Charles Jones—his origins, youth, wanderings, marriage, divorce, and finally his degeneration into abject poverty and chronic alcoholism. It was a grim litany. But the trial was not about Jones. It was about the Johnstone interest in the Jones estate that Robinson had bought. The evidence showed that Jones had spent the summer of 1877 prospecting in the San Juan Mountains with Sarah's husband, Edward Johnstone. The two men located a few claims near Silverton, but as winter approached, Jones wished to go to Denver, where the climate was milder and the living easier. And so Jones struck a deal. He agreed that if the Johnstones brought him to Denver, provided him room and board in return for chores and handiwork, and gave him a prospecting outfit come spring, he would give Mrs. Johnstone or her children one-half of whatever he found in 1878.

Despite a number of drunken bouts, Jones performed his part of the agreement that winter, and Sarah Johnstone performed hers in the spring. She gave Jones new clothes, found him an outfit, and provided him with the other essentials a prospector would need. Yet she and her husband were worried. They feared that Jones would drink up the grubstake if he went out alone. So they tried to persude him to wait until the snow cleared and Edward could go along too. But with his equipment in hand, Jones was anxious to join the Leadville stampede, and despite the Johnstones' entreaties he left. No sooner had he arrived in Leadville, however, than he squandered the entire grubstake on a drunken spree, just as the Johnstones had feared. After that, he drifted from one thing to another, finally entering into two more grubstake agreements before he turned his sights toward Ten Mile as a substitute for West in the tripartite arrangement with Sheddon and Robinson. In spite of his shortcomings, however, Jones never forgot his promise to Mrs. Johnstone. Shortly before he drank himself to death in October, he remarked on several occasions that he expected to give some part of his interest in the Robinson group to her and her children.

The decision in the case ultimately fell to Judge Moses Hallett, the most noted of Colorado's nineteenth-century jurists. He gave short shrift to the assertions that Jones intended to give the Johnstones a portion of whatever he found. He focused on the original grubstake agreement. Ultimately, he ruled that when one agreement is abandoned and a prospector goes to work for other interests, the party to the first grubstake has no claim to any mines that might be found. Mrs. Johnstone had lost. More important, Judge Hallett's opinion remained the law on the subject for the next century and would be frequently cited in discussions of grubstake law. [3]

While Robinson had triumphed over Mrs. Johnstone, he still had to contend with John W. Burkhardt, who held a far stronger position. Burkhardt could not only prove he had loaned Jones money to pay his bills, he could also produce the last grubstake agreement that Jones was known to have signed in his lifetime. As a result, Robinson had to face litigation on two fronts: an administrative proceeding in the Lake County Court, where Burkhardt hoped to recover the debt money; and a forthcoming trial in the Summit County Court, where Burkhardt hoped to establish the validity of the grubstake agreement and thus obtain a one-eighth interest in the Robinson mine.

In both of these cases, Robinson was not quite so fortunate as he had been in the Johnstone suit. In the Lake County Court the judge accepted Burkhardt's contention that he had a claim to the estate by dint of Jones' debts, and early in 1880 the court ordered the estate sold to satisfy the debts and pay Franklin T. Caley and others for the administrative costs. The court held the sale on April 10, 1880, and the purchaser was none other than the Robinson Consolidated Mining Company, which paid the court $3,000. About this time Burkhardt's other suit came to trial in Summit County, and on May 21 the court upheld the validity of his grubstake agreement with Jones and so awarded Burkhardt a one-sixth interest in the Little Giant and a one-eighth interest in the Ten Mile, 78, Big Giant, and Rambler claims.

But Burkhardt did not hold this interest for long. His attorneys must even then have been negotiating with Robinson's—negotiations backed by the threat of a lengthy appeal and a pro rata assessment in the development costs. On May 25, a scant four days after the court rendered its decision, the Robinson Company paid Burkhardt $8,500 for his interest in all claims but the Rambler. This transfer finally cleared up the title stemming from Jones's share of the Ten Mile, 78, Big Giant, and Undine. After months of litigation, Robinson had at last extinguished the interest of his partners in the original grubstake.

Although Robinson had resolved the lawsuits of Johnstone and Burkhardt, he still had to contend with Jacque, but while both sides dug in for a long battle, Robinson and Brown pressed forward to mine the ore of Sheep Mountain. Despite the axle-deep quags that plagued development, the hard-driving Brown pushed work on two fronts. He had one group of crews extend the main incline farther into the depths, while he had other crews drive the new adit from the Windsor claim toward the Number 4 level. The adit advanced at the rate of about 100 feet per month; it was in 342 feet by April 24, 442 feet by May 29, 522 feet by June 26, and 645 feet by July 28. But Brown was not happy. He claimed the men "loafed too much" because they were on straight wages, and in July he suspended work on the crosscuts and winzes until he could put his crews on a system of contract mining. This way they would be paid only for the amount of work done.

With his labor problems resolved, Brown stepped up shipments to Leadville to increase revenues in anticipation of the September dividend. By this time he had twenty-five ore teams hauling about twenty tons per day over Fremont Pass to the Lake County Sampling Works, shipments so large and so rich compared to other Ten Mile mines that Brown finally appointed one Mr. Fry as the agent to receive and assay the ores before the Sampling Works resold them to the local smelters or shipped them to Denver on the Rio Grande Railway, which by now had run its rails to the carbonate camp. The division was relatively simple because the Leadville smelters took all the carbonates, while the sulfides went to Denver. The Leadville companies did not have the roasters essential in reducing sulfides.

Brown was unstinting in his efforts to spur development. He drove the adit forward at 100 feet per month, and on October 20, some 953 feet into the heart of Sheep Mountain, his crews blasted through to the main incline. Without delay, he had switches and track installed, turning the adit into the main haulageway for the mine. Meanwhile, the simultaneous development of the main incline demonstrated the existence of a spectacular ore body 700 feet long, 100 feet wide, and 6 to 20 feet thick; and prospecting underground suggested that additional ore bodies might lie close by and parallel to this massive structure. Brown himself speculated in October that the probabilities and possibilities were very high that rich ore existed much deeper, perhaps for another 400 feet down the incline.

Encouraged, Robinson and Brown decided to drive a second incline down along the ore body once the adit intercepted the original workings. This "New Incline" would begin only thirty feet to the southeast of the adit connection, and would run parallel to the original incline. In late October, Brown put his crews to work, and by early November, they had blasted their way some thirty-one feet, only a short distance to be sure, but the new incline was entirely in ore. Opposite the workings, Brown excavated ground for a steam hoist and a boiler. He and Robinson strove to mechanize operations wherever possible. [4]

In the meantime, Robinson, Musgrove, and Brown had all wrestled with the problem of sulfide ore. So much of the mineral hauled to the surface had such a high sulphur content that it was not acceptable to the Leadville smelters, no matter how much silver it had. Before Brown joined the company, Robinson and Musgrove had decided to build roasting works at the mine to partially desulphurize the mineral before shipping it to Leadville. And they intended to do this until Robinson could build his own smelter because, by early 1880, it had become obvious that Colonel Robinson's Carbonateville plant was little more than a derelict and the Kokomo works were unreliable.

A few weeks before the Robinson Company acquired the mine, Robinson and Musgrove built some crude roasters nearby. They consisted of little more than rectangular stone walls about twenty feet long, ten feet wide, and two and one-half feet high. For roasting, the enclosure so formed was covered with a floor of fresh pine logs, then piled with finely split dry wood, and finally heaped with about forty-five tons of sulfide ore. Once Musgrove torched the wood, it set the pine logs ablaze, the logs raised the mineral to its own point of combustion, and from that point the sulfur burned off as pungent sulfur dioxide gases. Covered only by crude wooden sheds, the ore burned for about two weeks, then was allowed to cool, and the "desulphurized" product shipped to Leadville. The cost of roasting was about seventy-five cents per ton. It was so cheap because the forests of Ten Mile could still furnish wood for little more than the cost of cutting. [5]

Such crude "furnaces," however, could not be used for long. Although the Boston and Colorado Company, the state's most successful smelting firm, had done heap roasting like this until the late 1870s, the technique was clearly outmoded. Robinson and his associates knew this, too, and during the summer they designed a roaster building for furnaces that would be integrated into the operations of the smelter that Robinson had begun building a short distance away. Construction took time, however, and not until fall was the roaster building ready for operation. [6]

In the meantime, despairing of local entrepreneurs, Robinson announced plans to build his own smelter. Implementing this strategy took time, but by May he had organized the Summit Smelting Company and hired Albert Arents to build and run the plant. This was a sound decision, for Arents was one of the leading metallurgists in the industry. A German-born engineer, educated at Europe's most prestigious mining schools, Arents had been a leading member of the so-called Eureka group, which had done the most to launch the first successful use of blast furnaces in the West. With Winfield Scott Keyes, Arents had been the co-inventor of the siphon tap, an important device for removing bullion from furnaces, and it seems likely that Robinson met Arents through Keyes. [7]

Robinson and Arents selected a plant site near the adit that Brown was driving into Sheep Mountain, and Arents managed to get construction under way by June. Brown predicted that the plant would be ready by August 1, but one delay after another hampered work, much to everyone's frustration. Not until October did Arents acquire the proper fuel and fluxes and the right mix of ores, drawn from the Gilpin, Forest, Snow Bank, White Quail, Aftermath, and Climax, to name only a few mines that sold to the company. Finally, on October 10, Arents set the furnace in blast, and a few weeks later reports claimed the smelter was "running successfully." That was true, but only to a degree. Robinson and Arents found what others had already learned—most ores from Ten

Mile were hard to reduce because of their high sulfur content—and smelting did not go as well as predicted or claimed, although Arents did begin shipping bullion in December. [8]

Dynamo that he was, Robinson extended his interests that spring far beyond mining, roasting, and smelting ore. He also made plans to launch his own town. Up to this time, most miners who toiled on Sheep Mountain lived in Robinson's Camp, the cluster of log cabins, shacks, and frame houses hard by the mine portals. No doubt other men made their homes in Kokomo or in what remained of Carbonateville, and rode shank's mare to the mountain. But in May, with operations going so well, and with Robinson's Camp increasingly congested, Robinson took the initiative to lay out a new townsite. It was hemmed in by mountains on all sides, but open enough to offer a small community ample room.

The town had no buildings, however, until June, when Robinson set construction in motion. That month he began a long, narrow hotel with false front, decorated cornice, and tall, narrow windows. Streeter and Spain put up a livery stable. Other entrepreneurs bent their backs to build several saloons and a billiard hall to slake the thirst of Sheep Mountain's miners. Yet one group, not to be outdone by the purveyors of alcohol, constructed a church that was partly sponsored by Robinson, who purchased a bell for the steeple.

By summer the whack of hammers and the whine of saws resounded across the valley. The town sprang up "as if by magic," wrote an entranced reporter from Leadville, so rapidly in fact that "the pine of its oldest building had not lost its original hue and the leaves from its branches were scarcely withered." By then some 600 people made their homes in shacks or cabins that fringed the commercial area downtown. Georgia Burns Hills, the daughter of a merchant, remembered many years later that "the miners cabins were on the mountainsides; the backs of them against it and the fronts on high stilts with snow piled up under them. The long flights of steps going down from the front door ended on a muddy road or trail."[9]

Whatever hopes Robinson may have held about launching a model community, his town attracted a tough crowd. Many a man who had failed at prospecting became a hard-rock miner or general laborer dependent on wages, and in an isolated environment like Robinson, these toilers in the earth were often lonely and ready to spend their money freely. Although Robinson had few single women, the saloonkeepers wasted little time in providing more along with copious quantities of alcohol. One of the best known, or perhaps most notorious, was the Red Light Dance Hall, which moved from Leadville, girls and all. At least partly because of

the free-flowing liquor and the lack of much semblance of law enforcement, fights and shootings became commonplace in town. One resident
who complained about the "indiscriminate and reckless use of firearms
on slight provocation" claimed that hooligans fired from one to twenty
shots on the streets every night. He also declared that "with the dance
girls, saloons and gambling places we need a marshall and police," and he
hoped that the officials of an incorporated town would "be able to make
an example of some of these scoundrels."[10]

But that was to be in the future. For now the shootings continued. In
early November the Leadville *Daily Herald* reported one scrape involving two men who worked at the Empire lode. One night, they were apparently having a quiet game of billiards in one of Robinson's bistros when
"a desperado . . . somewhat the worse for 'bug juice'" walked in and
started a row. Either the patrons or the barkeep threw him out, but he
swore revenge as he went. In the next few minutes, he hurried to his
cabin, got a pistol, returned to the billiard hall, and opened fire on one of
the billiard players. This man drew his gun and shot back. "Both parties," said the *Herald*, "emptied their revolvers without damage, except
to the building." Yet sudden death loomed large for a frightening instant
during the fusillade, and one little girl had a narrow escape when a bullet
whizzed by her head. Once the shootists had emptied their guns, the
enraged bystanders seized the assailant and hauled him before "Squire
Moorhouse," who levied a fine of $25 for carrying a concealed weapon
and ordered the man to leave the county within twenty-four hours lest he
be arrested and tried for assault with intent to kill.

About the same time as this impromptu duel, the hard life and rough
conditions in Robinson overwhelmed two women who worked in the
dance halls. One was Lillie Lynch, who was described as "distinguishable from the majority of the girls by her modest demeanor and handsome appearance." The other was Lillie's closest friend, known only as
Mabel. Their trade was anything but reputable in Victorian America, although that may have been beside the point, since their dancing probably
served to disguise their real occupation as prostitutes. According to accounts, Lillie had taken a "lover" in Thomas Lynch, but one Sunday in
November, Lynch beat her up, and she sank into despondency. On Monday, Lillie and Mabel walked to Mabel's cabin for the night, and while
getting ready for bed, Lillie told Mabel that she had brought along a poison to kill herself. Mabel replied that she was tired of the dance halls and
did not wish to be left without her only friend; so she decided to put an
end to herself as well. The two made a suicide pact, took Lillie's potion,
and then drifted off to sleep. A while later, someone discovered them

"locked in an embrace," apparently dead. A physician hurried over to see if anything might be done. He made a quick examination, found Lillie dead, but he managed to revive Mabel, who had presumably not taken so large a dose of the poison. [11]

Despite the sordid undercurrent of life in Robinson, the people who moved there pushed forward with plans to incorporate the town. At a poll held on October 18, the voters decided in favor by a margin of 230 to 15, and the next month, on November 26, the town held an election to choose its first municipal officers. A. J. Streeter, who had helped build the livery stable, was elected the first mayor.

The formation of the Robinson Company, the exciting increase in production, the payment of two splendid dividends, and the founding of a boomtown might have seemed accomplishment enough for one individual in the course of a busy year, but not for George B. Robinson. The fame and fortune generated by the great mine on Sheep Mountain—and not the problems created by all those lawsuits—made the young midas an attractive candidate for political office. This year, both the Republicans and the Democrats planned to hold their state conventions in Leadville, which put additional attention on the bonanza kings of the Central Rockies. And George B. Robinson was one of the best known.

Like the majority of mineowners, Robinson belonged to the Republican Party, the dominant force in Colorado politics. Whether he decided to seek office himself, or whether insiders like John W. Jenkins encouraged him to sail on that stormy sea, is a matter of conjecture. By summer, however, Robinson had made up his mind to run for lieutenant governor, a post then held by Horace Tabor. Although the office was largely ceremonial, Robinson knew that it might be used as a springboard to the governor's office or to a seat in the United States Senate.

On August 26, the Republicans gathered at the Grand Central Theatre in Leadville. They gave the morning session over to predictable speeches by party leaders like the veteran politician, gaunt Henry M. Teller, who was then serving his first term in the United States Senate. After Teller came John M. Routt, who was out of office but still honored as Colorado's last territorial and first state governor. But neither Teller nor Routt attracted a full house. The real excitement would not come until afternoon, when the delegates chose their standard bearers for fall. Not until then did the theatre fill to capacity.

Even so, the first order of business was easy and predictable, and that was selecting the gubernatorial candidate. The incumbent, Frederick W. Pitkin, was popular in Republican circles, he wanted a second term, and party leaders had agreed to renominate him. So early in the

afternoon, Lieutenant Governor Tabor stepped to the podium, casti-
gated the Democrats, extolled the virtues of Pitkin, and placed the governor's name in nomination. A well-orchestrated demonstration erupted
in the aisles, a band blared festive music, and the delegates tossed their
hats in the air. When the votes were counted, Pitkin had been unanimously renominated, to no one's surprise.

Now came the nominations for lieutenant governor. And here there
was no unanimity; competition was keen, particularly because the nominee stood a good chance of election. Astute as always, Robinson had his
name placed in nomination by Jenkins, a party stalwart; but once Jenkins
departed the rostrum, four other candidates were nominated. Having
five men in the running worried party officials because no one had a decisive margin, which created the prospect that a bruising struggle could
split the party and cost it the election.

Just at this juncture came a proposal from Judge A. S. Weston, a veteran miner, attorney, and politician, whose career stretched all the way
back to that first rush to McNulty Gulch. He suggested that the delegates consider the first ballot informal. The delegates agreed, and when
this informal poll was taken, Robinson received the most votes, 105,
putting him well ahead of his nearest rival, William D. Todd of Arapahoe
County (which included Denver), who received 76 of the 278 votes cast.
The convention then took its first formal poll, but before anyone could
count the ballots, the Todd forces, perhaps sensing defeat, moved to
make Robinson's nomination unanimous. At this point Robinson was
nominated by acclamation, a more impromptu demonstration swelled the
aisles, applause filled the theatre, and the band played "Turkish Reveille." Once the cheering stopped, Robinson rose from his seat to be
introduced to the convention as the next lieutenant governor. And in
time-honored tradition, he addressed the delegates:

I cannot express my gratification at the support and nomination I have received
at your hands. I do not feel that it is as much of an honor to me as it is to the
district I represent beyond the crest of the snowy range. There is no question
that your action is satisfactory to the Republicans of Summit County, and I hope
equally so to the party throughout the state. And when the day of election
comes, an overwhelming majority for the entire ticket can be looked for from
the Blue River Valley. [12]

The reaction from the newspapers was mixed, as might have been
expected, because most had strong partisan interests. The Leadville
Weekly Herald, with pronounced Republican leanings, claimed that the
convention had done "one of the best things for the party that it was
possible to do." Robinson would make "one of the shrewdest political

workers in the state." But that staunch Democratic organ the *Rocky Mountain News*, taking note of the pro-Denver, anti-Denver split in the state's makeup, growled that "Leadville has not been propitiated by the supercilious ostentation with which Denver has been ignored." And quoting a Republican businessman opposed to Robinson's nomination, the *News* went on to say that "no honorable excuse can be offered for preferring Robinson to Todd." Robinson was not a popular man personally, and it was "an insult for him to come without a single claim shaking his cash in our face, demanding that we bow down and honor him because he is newly rich."[13]

As the fall campaign began in earnest, the partisan attacks grew more virulent. In September, Robinson received an endorsement from the Kokomo *Times*, which claimed "the camp is solid to a man, without distinction of party." But all the *Times* did was provoke "Kentucky," who wrote the Leadville *Daily Democrat* that the individual who had made this claim was "either an ass, or has an utter disregard for the truth." Robinson's name was indeed "soul inspiring, viz: inspires the very soul of an honest man with loathing."

But Kentucky was mild stuff compared to "Barnacle." In a letter to the *Rocky Mountain News*, he denounced the practice of giving even the "unimportant office of lieutenant governor" to bonanza kings "to tickle their fancy" and bestow the title of "governor" for life—a swipe at Tabor as well as Robinson. Then Barnacle attacked Robinson as a man "indifferently supplied with brains," a man who was "no parliamentarian and no orator," a hard employer who cut wages, extended hours, stripped timber from adjoining claims, and who had come within an eyelash of losing the Jacque suit in the Breckenridge court.[14]

The Robinson forces leaped to reply. To refute the charges that Robinson had stolen wood from other claims, they had twelve owners of adjacent properties sign an affidavit, attested by Justice of the Peace Morehouse, that Robinson had always paid for the timber his men had cut. But general manager Brown was far more blunt in reply. He wrote the Leadville *Daily Herald* that Barnacle's accusations were nothing but "libels" and announced his intention to form a Robinson Club. Then Brown wrote the hostile *Rocky Mountain News* that he himself was "a democrat of thirty-eight years' standing" and asked the editors to print his rebuttal to Barnacle. Here Brown termed Barnacle's accusations nothing but a "tissue of falsehoods," and charged that Barnacle must have received his "early moral teachings within the aromatic precincts of a soap factory" because he was "so saturated with 'lye.'" After refuting Barnacle's charges, Brown observed that a barnacle was "a parasitical shellfish," one of the species that clung to the bottom of great ships "through the law of survival of the fittest," and that this self-described human barnacle was nothing more than a "nerveless, soulless, brainless, eyeless polyp" that should crawl back into its shell. [15]

The diatribes of Barnacle and Brown added spice to dry reading, but they hardly affected Robinson's campaign strategy and the ultimate outcome. Through September and October, Robinson criss-crossed the state making political speeches in small towns on the high plains, in bustling cities like Denver, and as far west as the Ute country, a trip that involved some danger. Part of the time he traveled with Jenkins, who had become his good friend and political mentor. As the electoral season reached its climax, Robinson finally made his way back to the mining country that comprised his home and base. He spoke in Chihuahua on October 27, Kokomo on October 18, Robinson on October 29, Red Cliff on October 30, and Breckenridge on November 1. [16]

The meeting at Robinson must have been the highlight of the campaign. D. J. Chadwick, chairman of the Republican Central Committee for Summit County, introduced Robinson to "the greatest ovation ever given to any candidate for public office" from the "hundreds of boys in blue" and other voters in Ten Mile, wrote the *Daily Herald.* Then Robinson made a "forcible speech" for about twenty minutes, followed by remarks from H. H. Eddy of Chihuahua, who was a candidate for the state senate, and Melvin Edwards of Red Cliff, a candidate for the legislature. After their talks, John W. Jenkins "dealt down with sledge hammer blows the heresies of the democratic party." [17]

The election went well for the Republicans. While the national ticket headed by James A. Garfield eked out a narrow victory, the Colorado slate led by Pitkin and Robinson claimed an easy win. While Pitkin turned to making what little preparation he needed to continue as governor, Robinson may have begun planning to run for the United States Senate, whose members were then chosen by state legislatures. Barely a few days after the November election, former Democratic congressman Thomas M. Patterson, when asked what Republicans might run for the office, replied that "Governor Routt, Governor Tabor, Senator Teller, Judge Bowen, and Governor-Elect Robinson" had all "enlisted for the honors." Although Patterson was hardly a disinterested observer, he suggested that Robinson had made his recent election "a mere entering wedge" in his quest for a Senate seat, "the mecca of his ambition." [18]

But if Robinson intended to run, he still kept his own counsel, although his activities did nothing to dispel the suggestion that he had set his sights on Washington. In mid-November, he hosted a post-election

ROBINSON, COLORADO. A Ten Miler gazes wistfully at the town, mine, and smelter complex that George B. Robinson developed at the foot of Sheep Mountain. Courtesy Colorado Historical Society.

party at the splendid Windsor Hotel in Denver, and his guests comprised a who's who of Colorado Republicans. There were senators Hill and Teller, who did not let their growing personal and political enmity prevent them from attending; plus Judge Bowen of Pueblo, many members of the bench and bar, a substantial delegation of newspapermen to insure the gala of adequate publicity, and of course, William Gilpin, the grand old man of the Grand Old Party. Throughout the evening, congratulatory speeches and festive toasts punctuated the amiable conversation between determined rivals, and Robinson basked in the limelight, his political career well launched, and perhaps that senate seat within grasp, just as the rumors insisted. He must have thought that his rising star, already shining so brightly in this constellation of notables, still had far to ascend before reaching its zenith. [19]

On Friday, November 19, Robinson returned in triumph to Leadville.

He spent the weekend over his store, relaxing with friends and looking into business matters neglected over the past few weeks. Then he heard disturbing news from Ten Mile, news so disquieting that he may have wondered if his achievements were about to collapse like a house of cards.

One problem involved a storm of complaints from his miners over the high-handed treatment they had allegedly received at the hands of Brown. Robinson could not be sure what had happened, but it seemed that while he was away, Brown had ordered the men to take their meals at the mine and buy all their goods from the firm of Ralph and Bergerman, who had opened a mercantile house in town. Brown had allegedly intimated that anyone who refused would be discharged. The miners had grumbled over this dictate, and when John Evans, the popular foreman, had refused to fire anyone who defied the order, reports had surfaced that he had been or was about to be fired by Brown.

Far worse than this internal quarrel was the external threat posed by John W. Jacque. His suit in the Breckenridge court had gone to trial that summer, and on September 27, the jury had rendered its verdict: nine men in favor of Jacque, three men in favor of Robinson, a split that may have reflected sentiments in Ten Mile. That verdict had settled nothing. The case remained pending in Breckenridge, and Jacque's future course remained unknown. Yet speculation was rampant that Jacque was through with the courts and that he had decided to seize the Smuggler by force. Not surprisingly, tension and tempers were rising when Robinson set out for Ten Mile on Monday, November 22.

No sooner had Robinson arrived in the valley than he received a visit from a group of miners led by James T. Stewart, the captain and chairman of the Committee To Wait Upon Governor Robinson. Stewart explained that Brown had endeavored "to coerce them in private affairs." He had ordered them to eat at the boardinghouse against their wishes, and he had demanded that they trade with Ralph and Bergerman, a firm in which Brown had a financial interest. As he was using his position to line his own pockets at the miners' expense, Stewart and company urged Robinson to remove Brown as general manager.

Robinson reacted cooly. He told Stewart that as a trustee of the Robinson Company, he could take no action immediately and could not remove Brown unless the allegations could be proved. He recommended, however, that Stewart and his men investigate the relations that existed between Brown and the firm of Ralph and Bergerman, and he promised to discharge Brown if the accusations could be sustained.

Robinson had taken a middle ground in an effort to buy time, but after he returned to Leadville that night, events took an unexpected though perhaps not unpredictable turn. Exactly what happened is to some extent conjecture because of the question of whom to believe. According to the *Daily Herald*, Robinson's miners held a meeting that night and resolved to confront Ralph and Bergerman in force to determine the truth about their alleged agreement with Brown. Another day passed, but about nine o'clock on Tuesday night the steady tramp of a large body of men resounded in town, and people rushed to their windows to see a reported one hundred men, armed with guns and clubs, marching up Palmer Street toward Ralph and Bergerman's store. There they stopped, and several men with Winchester rifles went inside, where they "confronted" Bergerman, who had to face the miners all by himself, since his partner, Ralph, fearing the worst, had fled at the sound of the approaching men.

According to the *Herald*, the leaders called upon Bergerman "to tell the true inwardness of the relations existing between the firm and Mr. Brown." And "with paled face and trembling knees," Bergerman gave them the story they wanted to hear: Brown was to receive 5 percent of the profits in return for using his influence to have the miners buy at the store. When the anxious men waiting outside heard this, "their rage knew no bounds," reported the *Herald*; "they wanted to burn the store, and only with difficulty did the leaders talk them out of it." No damage was done, and Bergerman went free, shaken but unharmed.

But the miners were not through for the night. Even though Bergerman's admission might have been enough to oust Brown, the enraged men burst out of control and started en masse for Brown's house near the mine. When they arrived, they pushed their way in and searched the structure, but they failed to find Brown, who had decamped in time. Well he did, said the *Herald*, because "in the excitement of the moment he would certainly have been made to ornament some convenient post or tree."[20]

On Thursday, November 25, when this account appeared in the columns of the *Herald*, it created consternation in the mind of James T. Stewart. He promptly wrote the paper charging that its "editorial grossly misrepresents" the entire sequence of events, and as captain and chairman of the committee he would "talk from the card." Stewart confirmed that he and several others had confronted Robinson with the charge that Brown had worked out an arrangement with Ralph and Bergerman, one of several firms that Brown had apparently approached. Robinson had replied that if true, he would suspend Brown and recommend his dismissal to the board of directors. With this commitment in hand, Stewart claimed that he and several others went "not in anger or with the intention of gutting the store . . . but simply to get a confirmation of the charge, Ralph and Bergerman being known to all of us to be our friends and champions on all occasions." Ralph met them in the store, Bergerman arrived a few minutes later without "fear and trembling" as the *Herald* had claimed, and they confirmed that Brown had proposed that he receive a share of the profits in return for making the miners trade at the store or be discharged. The firm had refused the offer, however; and in fact, said Stewart, Brown had since tried to direct trade away from Ralph and Bergerman. Hearing this report, the miners dispersed and did not go to Brown's house. "We started out with the intention of getting rid of Mr. Brown as manager, on account of his attempt to coerce the men to his pecuniary advantage," wrote Stewart, "and that being accomplished, we quietly dispersed."[21]

Although Stewart denied the charge that the miners had degenerated into an unruly mob bent on destruction and lynch law, his letter to the editor did not appear in print until Saturday, November 27. From Tuesday night on, tensions increased in Robinson and Leadville, and no doubt some people in both towns feared a repetition of the virulent Chrysolite strike that had convulsed Leadville that summer, a strike that may have been precipitated by Keyes to cover gutting the mine, a strike that Robinson, Keyes and other Roberts-connected individuals played key roles in crushing. But even if feeling ran high in Robinson, Brown was not in so much danger of lynching that he could not return at week's end. For several days the press debated whether or not he would be succeeded by George Daly, who was then running the Little Chief, Chrysolite, and other mines floated by Roberts. Daly was known as an implacable foe of labor. When asked, however, Daly denied that he had been offered the position by Robinson, said that he did not want it, and claimed that his present engagements were such that he could not accept the job even if tendered. Yet reports insisted that either Roberts or Robinson had chosen Daly to take over.

While no one could be sure about Daly, it was certain that Brown was through. Whether or not Robinson accepted his denial that he had used his position to line his pockets, whether or not Robinson sided with Stewart and the miners, or whether or not Roberts and Robinson had decided to replace Brown for other reasons, all were questions beside the point. The feeling against Brown was so strong that he could not continue, whatever the truth. Toward the end of the week he resigned, and on Saturday, November 27, 1880, Robinson rode over to Ten Mile with T. J. White, one of the bookkeepers, to review the corporate accounts and make what changes were necessary to pave the way for new management. [22]

Saturday the twenty-seventh was a cold day. Several inches of snow covered the frozen ground, and it seemed as if another hard winter lay in the offing. When Robinson and White arrived, they went directly to the general manager's house, where they got down to business with Brown. As they moved from subject to subject, they inevitably came to the question of Jacque and his lawsuits. The disquieting rumors that Jacque intended to seize the Smuggler had been mounting for weeks, and although Jacque had done nothing overt, tension remained high at the mine, and the whole Brown morass had done nothing to mitigate fears. Yet the struggle with Jacque now seemed to be on the verge of resolution. Robinson said that he intended to go to Leadville that night to meet with Jacque and settle the dispute. He asked Brown if he thought that $75,000 was enough to make a poor man comfortable, or so said Brown about eight months later.

About four o'clock in the afternoon, however, as the long shadows crept down from the mountains, word arrived that several armed men, identities unknown, had been seen lurking nearby. They were thought to be working for Jacque. Robinson hurried over to the mine to ask Martin Warner, the chief engineer, if he had any good men to put on guard. Robinson wanted four people, but finally concluded that two would do. Warner recommended that John Williams be stationed at the No. 1 drift in the incline and Frank Brown at the tunnel mouth. Robinson concurred and told Warner to have them at the smelter by six o'clock. He would be there to arm them.

Tension at the mine mounted as the bright afternoon drifted on into the early evening darkness. Warner went to the smelter at six o'clock only to find that there must have been a misunderstanding. Robinson did not appear. Rather than wait more than a few minutes, he walked over to Brown's house. There he spoke with Robinson, who suddenly found there were no guns to be had. Either they were at the mine, or they had been stolen by the men who had stormed Brown's house on Tuesday night. But Robinson repeated the instructions that he wanted Williams and Frank Brown to stand guard at the tunnel mouth, and he told Warner to get weapons from John Evans, the foreman, who had been reinstated (or perhaps not fired at all). Warner hurried off into the darkness. It was now a little after 6:30 P.M. [23]

Just about this time, Louis Richard Roy, the guard at the engine-house, saw several armed men appear in the gloom. When they drew within sixty feet, he recognized two. He commanded them to halt, then

MINERS AND GUARDS AT THE ROBINSON MINE. Although apparently taken in the late 1880s, this photograph shows the baggy clothes, soft hats, and candle stuck in the hat brim that were characteristic of the early Ten Mile miner. Courtesy Recen Family Collection.

asked their names. When they refused, Roy walked up where he recognized two others—James Stewart and Henry Knuckols. Roy asked what they were doing. Knuckols replied that they had come "for the purpose of getting the mine for Captain Jacque." They asked Roy to help, and when he refused, Knuckols replied that if Roy would change his mind, he could assure him of at least $5 per day in wages. More than that, they had come to help a poor man against a rich one. Roy stated that he had been hired by the Robinson Company and no one could go down in the workings unless they worked for the firm. Knuckols asked how the company had found out that they intended to jump the mine that night. Roy replied that he did not know. And Knuckols added that they had just come from the mouth of the tunnel, found the door locked, and concluded their plans were known. [24]

Among the men who saw this conversation was Fred Hermann, who was also on guard in the enginehouse. After Knuckols and the other armed men departed, word of the encounter passed to Sam Davis, the foreman on duty. Davis reacted quickly, no doubt thinking that Knuckols and his associates would soon return to force the entrance. Davis gave Hermann a gun and a few candles and told him to go to the mouth of the tunnel and, if anyone tried to break in, to shoot them. Hermann rushed off to his new station. It was now almost seven o'clock. [25]

While Hermann and Davis spoke hurriedly, Patrick Gillin—Patsy Gillin, as he was known—the miner who had lost his money in the collapse of the Merchants' and Miners' Bank, was trudging up the mine path on his way to work. About half way there, he met five armed men, but he failed to recognize any and continued nonchalantly along, completely unaware of the feverish response prompted by these men who were apparently walking away toward town. A little farther on, Gillin met Evans, James Stewart, and his brother Pete Stewart, but kept on toward the mine, where he was halted by Lon Roy. Roy asked Gillin if he had seen any armed men walking down the hill. Gillin said yes. Then Roy told him they were Captain Jacque's men and he supposed they were heading down to the tunnel mouth.

Once inside the mine, Gillin met Davis. Mincing no words in the crisis, Davis told Gillin to go to the tunnel house, gave him a .44 calibre Winchester rifle, and told Gillin to "use it." With a few candles to provide a flickering light, Gillin hurried down through the workings. When he arrived at the inside door to the tunnel, he found Hermann on guard. It was nearly seven o'clock. The seconds now ticked away inexorably, though ever so slowly for two panicky men guarding a bolted door they thought might be forced any moment by a larger group of armed men. And perhaps twenty minutes after Gillin arrived, they saw three forms, possibly four, come over the top of the tunnel. Hermann whispered to Gillin that if the men made any bad breaks, they would shoot. And as the party approached, one of the figures split off and walked toward the tunnel house. [26]

At seven o'clock, oblivious to this frantic activity, Robinson, White, and Brown were still huddled together in the general manager's house when they heard the shrill sound of the mine engine pierce the darkness outside. Robinson remarked that they had done enough work for one day and that more were to follow. They stood up and decided to walk over to the Robinson Hotel for a cup of tea. Warner had just left. They put on their coats and stepped out into the cold darkness. Robinson took the lead. They tramped along single file through the deep snow, and Robinson led the way down the tunnel trail, which was the shortest route to town. Brown opined that they had better take the main trail—he did not say why—but Robinson failed to hear or to heed, and continued along. It was now a few minutes after seven o'clock. Gillin and Hermann huddled behind the locked door in the tunnel, and as the minutes ticked by, they suddenly saw three or four shadowy forms approach in the darkness, and as the figures came nearer the tunnel house, one of them—George B. Robinson—broke off to the right. White followed to see why. Brown kept back in the distance. [27]

Robinson had apparently decided to check if the door to the tunnel was locked and to be sure that Frank Brown was on duty inside. He entered the tunnel house, followed by a still-puzzled White, unsure of what Robinson intended to do. White stumbled around in the darkness, then steadied himself, one hand on an ore car, the other on one of the wooden walls. Then he saw someone, apparently Robinson, light a match. Twenty-five feet away inside the tunnel, on the other side of the inner door, crouched Gillin and Hermann. They heard the sound of one man, perhaps more, enter the tunnel house—Captain Jacque's men?—and then one of them shook the door hard as if he was trying to get in.

"What do you want?" shouted Gillin.

"Nothing," came the reply from Robinson.

But Gillin failed to hear or recognize the boss.

"Get out of this then," shouted Gillin—and cracked off a shot from his Winchester.

Robinson sank to the floor of the tunnel house. He moaned a few times. Brown ran up to the outside door just as a stunned White burst out, told him to save himself and get help in town. And they raced off through the snow. [28]

Inside, Gillin gingerly approached the tunnel door. He heard someone, probably White, shout, "He is shot," but after that he heard nothing (or so he said later). Then he drew back and told Hermann to wait while he went to find Evans so that they could go out to see if anyone had been hurt. The first man Gillin met, however, was Ed Cassidy, the night watchman. Gillin said he thought he had shot someone. Then he found Evans and told him he had shot someone. Evans asked if he was afraid. Gillin replied not unless it was some innocent person. Then Gillin went back to find Cassidy, who now said he thought no one had been shot badly, perhaps only scratched on the back. Finally, the panic-stricken Gillin hurried back to his post at the tunnel mouth. [29]

That was Gillin's story, but Hermann gave a somewhat different account of this sequence of events. After Gillin cracked off that single shot, Hermann heard moans and a voice mourning "O my God, boys, what do you shoot me for. . . . O Dear, O Dear, am I to die here without any help." Gillin drew back into the tunnel, "Don't mention my name!" he begged Hermann, and then rushed off into the workings, leaving Hermann to stand guard alone with an obviously wounded man on the other side of the door. Before long, however, Cassidy and a few other men arrived to stand guard in force, and after a while, they heard sounds outside and thought that someone was stealing a body. They would not know who had been shot for another tense hour. [30]

In the meantime, White and Brown raced down the tunnel trail to Robinson. They hurried first to the house of Justice of the Peace Morehouse where they found George W. Chase, the constable and deputy sheriff on duty. White hollered. Chase opened the door. "Robinson is shot!" blurted White. "What, not George B.!" replied the incredulous Chase. But White could not be denied. While Brown scared up a horse and started for Leadville, White and Chase hurried back up the hill toward the tunnel house, a brave act here in the darkness where armed men waited ready to shoot on sight. On the way, they bumped into Warner, told him what had happened, and all three plunged on together.

There at the tunnel house they threw caution to the Ten Mile winds. They entered the building and heard a groan, someone struck a match, and by that flickering light in the cold darkness, they saw Robinson lying by the right side of the door. Oblivious to the nervous gunners waiting a few feet away, they lifted Robinson off that incarnadine floor, carried him down over the snow to the hotel he had built only a few months before, and laid him on a bed. Robinson was conscious, and as he held Warner's hand, he asked, "Do you think Brown would do that?" Warner thought he meant Frank Brown, who was supposed to be on duty in the tunnel (but who had never reached his post). Then Robinson looked at his blood-stained clothes and asked Chase, "George, what do you think of this?" But Chase fumbled for something to say: "I can tell you better after you tell me what you think." "I don't want any arrests made," said Robinson. [31]

Someone went for the local physicians, a Dr. Ming, who lived in the hotel, and a Dr. O'Connor, who resided a mile away in Kokomo. As they began to examine Robinson, stop the bleeding, and administer an opiate to kill the pain, the news of the shooting reached A. J. Streeter, the mayor. About eight o'clock he dispatched a telegram asking W. N. Burdick, Robinson's personal physician in Leadville, to come at once. It was this message that notified the outside world of the shooting. Burdick packed his bags and rode off into the cold, wintry night. Somewhere on the dark trail he must have passed Brown whipping his horse toward the carbonate camp, but whether the two spoke in passing remains unknown. And in Leadville people began to gather near the telegraph office, particularly the men who had helped break the strike some six months before. But as they gathered, not knowing what to expect, more than five tense hours elapsed before a second message came from Ten Mile.

Burdick arrived in Robinson about ten o'clock. He found the lieutenant governor-elect still conscious and examined him with a probe. Burdick found four wounds, and it was assumed that Gillin's bullet had shattered on a doornail before hitting Robinson. Burdick found two wounds above the hipbone and two below. Of the four, Burdick concluded that two were superficial, but he was certain that at least one and probably two had entered the.body cavity. Ominously, Robinson had a partial paralysis of the right leg. His pulse was 68. [32]

Brown, meanwhile, had arrived in Leadville about 9: 30 to find himself besieged with people asking questions about the shooting. But Brown had little truck with them. Apparently thinking that Robinson had been the victim of Jacque's men, or that the miners in camp had turned to further violence, he rushed to the hardware store, ordered arms of all sorts, and then dashed over to the sheriff's office for assistance.

By eleven o'clock many prominent people in Leadville had begun gathering at the Clarendon Hotel. When Brown appeared, he told the crowd his version of what happened. About a week ago, he said, a group of miners had met to demand his dismissal; later, a second meeting had demanded that he leave the camp. He referred to the articles in the *Daily Herald* and *Chronicle*, which had covered the controversy. Only then did he give his version of the shooting, noting that after Robinson had said, "It's only me, boys," back had come the angry reply "Shoot the son of a b . . . . , anyway," a statement not corroborated by anyone else. Fifteen minutes later, Brown said, he had lit out for Leadville, not only at the request of local merchants but also because someone had burglarized his house two days before and stolen fifteen Winchester rifles. [33]

George Daly now came to the fore. He suggested that an armed party be sent to Robinson forthwith, and others agreed because the business community was "generally unarmed and therefore not likely to be able to suppress any general outbreak." And ominously, no news had arrived in the past two hours. Finally, Daly claimed that Robinson had been "ruthlessly shot down" on his own property, and that it was probable that "a mob was in force at Robinson's Camp"; a posse should be organized, to go there, he said, protect the mine, and "put down a riot if found to exist." That brought an enthusiastic response. The crowd chose Daly captain of the relief effort, but organizing a large company took time, and finally at one o'clock in the morning, after five interminable hours without fresh news, a second telegram arrived from Ten Mile. Robinson still lived, and with that report, Daly's company decided to go to bed. [34]

The second telegram, however, brought more incorrect information that seemed to support the contentions of Brown and Daly. Whoever wrote the telegram speculated that Robinson had been shot not from inside the mine but from outside, possibly by a shotgun or by several rifles or pistols. No one could believe that a single bullet fired from the tunnel could penetrate a door two inches thick and inflict multiple wounds. The telegram also said that Robinson's physicians had termed his condition "dangerous" although he might recover, and he was reported to be resting easier and "quite cheerful at midnight." [35]

Whatever uncertainties raced through Leadville, they were no different from the crosscurrents reverberating through Ten Mile. Many people from Kokomo and Recen walked over to Robinson to find out what had happened and what were Robinson's prospects for recovery. Everyone speculated about the real cause of the shooting. And the guards at the mine kept a more careful vigil, lest Captain Jacque's men return in force, though as the dark early morning hours passed, it became ever more apparent that the danger had passed, riots had not broken out, and no one's property seemed threatened by destruction. The real drama had become the imponderable question—would George B. Robinson survive?

Throughout the night, Burdick remained at Robinson's side, and at five o'clock in the morning, Robinson woke from his sleep. He passed some bloody urine, and his heart pulsation had increased to 80, both ominous signs. But he was conscious, the opiates kept him relatively free of pain, and later in the morning and on into the afternoon, he managed to conduct some business. He met with Daly, who had hurried over from Leadville, he exonerated James C. Brown from any wrongdoing in the Ralph and Bergerman affair, and when told who had shot him, he absolved Gillin from blame on the grounds that he had fired only because he thought the claim jumpers had entered the tunnel house. [36]

Throughout Sunday, telegrams hummed across the wires between Kokomo and Leadville. At 10:40 A.M., Dick Allen sent a mixed message saying that the weapon used was a shotgun, which had given Robinson four wounds, and he had suffered intense pain in the night but was resting a little easier now. "The smelter is running successfully," telegraphed Allen, "the governor is game, and will come out all right." It was hopeful news that eased some people's anxiety. But later in the day Allen had to report that Robinson had "had a severe hemorrage from the

bladder . . . the wounds are serious but not necessarily fatal at present."
At 4:23 in the afternoon S. D. Prescott sent word that Robinson was
"quite weak." And a few hours later in the evening J. T. Herrick telegraphed even more ominous news: "Robinson is in a very dangerous
condition. He will probably die."[37]

Burdick saw Robinson from time to time throughout Sunday, but
there was little he could do. By noon Robinson's pulse rate had increased
to 120 and decreased in force. A general prostration and weakness inten-
sified all afternoon. Robinson napped for ten to fifteen minutes at a time.
By eight o'clock in the evening, twenty-five hours after the shooting,
Burdick found him "without pulsation," and gave him the first of a series
of stimulants. And it was about this time that Robinson uttered his last
words. From nine o'clock on, Burdick stayed at Robinson's side. He was
semiconscious until three o'clock in the morning, but his life was ebbing,
and about 6:45 on the morning of Monday, November 29, he slipped
away. Daly sent the news to Leadville. [38]

The shock of Robinson's death reverberated around the state. Newspaper after newspaper ran special stories that groped for the unknown
truth about the shooting, and all published special tributes to Robinson
for what he had achieved in his brief career. The *Daily Herald* headlined
its coverage in great capitals: HE SLEEPS. The *Rocky Mountain News*
gracefully observed that he had been prematurely "called from the
realms of time." And the editors best summarized his pre-Colorado life
when they wrote that "of his early career, we know little or nothing."
Robinson had always kept his own counsel. [39]

But as these tributes went to press, there was still grim business at
hand in Robinson. That morning, Monday, the twenty-ninth, Morehouse
and Streeter, the chief legal authorities in town, ordered a full investigation. In the post-mortem examination, Burdick found that the two upper
wounds in Robinson's hip were superficial, as he had thought Saturday
night. Not so the other two. One bullet fragment had passed through the
bone and carried several pieces through to the back of the body, per-
forating Robinson's intestines. The other bullet fragment had lodged itself in the fourth vertebra, causing the partial paralysis of the right leg.
Robinson had died, said Burdick, of the perforated intestines and the
spinal injury. The same gloomy day, Morehouse convened an inquest
into the shooting. All the principals testified except J. C. Brown, who had
apparently not returned from Leadville. On the basis of this testimony,
the coroner's jury exonerated the unhappy Gillin from "all criminal intent" even though he had "fired hastily and without due consideration."
The ultimate verdict? Accidental shooting.

Now began the long, hard journey back to Michigan. About one o'clock that Monday, I. N. Rogers, an undertaker from Leadville, claimed the body, and escorted by the Summit Lodge of the International Order of Odd Fellows, he brought the remains to his rooms in Leadville for embalming. All the next day, while expressions of regret flowed here and there, and huge memorials appeared in the newspapers, people began to gather in front of Rogers' offices, so many that the police had to be called to keep order. At two o'clock on Tuesday afternoon, the funeral arrangements completed, Rogers opened the doors to allow the throng to view Robinson as he lay in state under a catafalque decorated by the American flag draped in mourning. The *Daily Herald* estimated that seven thousand people filed past in the next few hours, a figure that seems exaggerated. Then toward dusk began the funeral service, and after that, just before six o'clock in the evening, the pallbearers placed Robinson's casket aboard a special South Park train. Now accompanied by members of Leadville's paramilitary organizations, Robinson began his last journey east, a trip ironically delayed by a snowstorm that stopped the funeral train between Buena Vista and Kenosha Pass.

That night citizens of Ten Mile gathered in various places to pay tribute. In the town of Robinson, Albert Arents chaired a meeting complete with a peal from the bells that Robinson had bought for the local church. At a huge gathering held in Kokomo, Fernando H. Sutherland, the physician turned mineowner, called a meeting together, Judge John S. Wheeler presided, and with Cassius M. Coe of the *Summit County Times* acting as secretary, they formally expressed their admiration and regret, which were forwarded to Robinson's family. [40]

Later that night, Robinson's train broke through the snowstorm in South Park and descended Platte Canyon to the high plains. When it steamed into Denver at ten o'clock in the morning, Governor Pitkin and Mayor Sopris were there to lead the official mourning party. All state offices had been closed, a huge crowd lined the sidewalks, and many other people stood on cars along the sidetracks, even on the roofs of nearby buildings, to glimpse the occasion. Then a second, more elaborate funeral procession wound its way up Larimer Street to the Armory, with Denver's fraternal and paramilitary organizations providing an escort. Robinson again lay in state, viewed by an estimated eight thousand people. [41]

Then began the final leg of the journey. The next morning the pallbearers carried Robinson to a train bound east for Michigan. His political confidant Jenkins, Secretary of State Meldrum, and two other men formed the brief entourage that would accompany the body to Kalamazoo and Plainwell. Robinson's old mentor, Lucious B. Kendall, joined them in Chicago. Once in Kalamazoo, Robinson lay in state for a third time, but then the remains were taken a few miles north to Plainwell. And here gathered his family, friends, and associates: his mother, Mrs. Forbes; his fiancée, Miss Norman; his old mentor Kendall; his good friend Jenkins; his associate Roberts; and many others. On Tuesday, December 8, George B. Robinson was laid to rest in the family plot on the crest of a knoll in the cemetery at Plainwell. [42]

CHAPTER 7

Slaughter of Geese

IF the arrival of spring had brought bright hopes and heady optimism for the Robinson Company, then the onset of winter offered little more than gnawing uncertainty and pervasive gloom. The Robinson shooting numbed Ten Milers almost as much as the bone-chilling cold, the incessant litigation with the intractable Jacque appeared to defy resolution, and doubts even surrounded the management and ownership of the great mine itself. About the only good news that seemed to lift sullen spirits in Ten Mile was the imminent completion of the Rio Grande line from Leadville, which would smash the frustrating logjam posed by the inadequate transportation system.

In the aftermath of Robinson's shooting, confusion reigned at the mine on Sheep Mountain. John Evans, the foreman, took charge, temporarily, and saw to it that security was increased in case Captain Jacque should redouble his effort to seize the Smuggler (if indeed he had intended to do so that fateful Saturday night). Yet Evans was no more than an interim manager, and rumors circulated anew that George Daly planned to take charge. One report even claimed that before he died, Robinson had asked Daly to become general manager and that Roberts had confirmed the appointment.

Whatever the truth of Daly's original denials, he now agreed to take over. Yet his path to control was uncertain. Owing to Robinson's funeral he could not return to Ten Mile until December 1, 1880, and when he arrived, Evans refused to recognize Daly's authority on the grounds that

152

Robinson had placed him in charge. Another day passed before this impasse could be resolved, but by the end of the week, Daly had taken the reins. He replaced Evans with Joe McDonald, late of the Little Chief mine in Leadville, and he announced new plans to increase the output and work force. [1]

But while Roberts and Daly pushed forward, they still had to face two vexing issues. One was the Robinson estate, which presumably went to Robinson's mother, Mary V. Forbes, since he had died intestate. This did not inhibit operations per se since the Robinson firm was a body corporate, but it did affect control of the enterprise because the estate held the overwhelming majority of capital stock. The other problem was the unyielding effort of Jacque to wrest what he thought was his rightful one-half of the Smuggler.

Whatever Jacque had intended to do on that lamentable November 27, by early December he seemed resolved to pursue his quest strictly in court. While his one case continued in Breckenridge, he decided to bring another suit in federal court, but before doing that—perhaps to raise money or spread the risk—he sold to three other individuals one-half of his share for $25,000, and they joined him in the new lawsuit. Jacque's attorneys also contacted Daly, who was not so intransigent as Robinson had been. On December 13, Daly agreed that Jacque could have his attorneys visit the Smuggler, appoint a "disinterested person" to monitor ore removed, and send in experts to study the claim; but only on condition that "no attempt peaceful or otherwise" be made to take possession. Jacque agreed, stating that he had "no designs to take such possession." And speculation increased that the two sides would reach an out-of-court settlement that would "lift the mine from litigation," said the *Rocky Mountain News*, and allow it to "perform its mission in building up Colorado as the great mining center of the continent." [2]

While Jacque's representatives pursued their investigation, Mary V. Forbes arrived in Colorado to lay claim to her son's estate. Accompanied by her brother, she went to Denver, made various arrangements, and then journeyed to Leadville. The Lake County Court had appointed George W. Trimble, a Leadville banker, the interim administrator, but on December 17, Judge A. K. Updegraff relieved Trimble and appointed Mrs. Forbes, Lucious B. Kendall, and Job A. Cooper, cashier of the German National Bank in Denver, the three coadministrators. The court fixed the bond at $1,500,000, which Cooper advanced because Judge Updegraff ruled that the estate would be granted in Colorado, thus requiring a resident of the state to be involved.

After a brief sojourn in Leadville, Mrs. Forbes set out for Ten Mile,

THOMAS EWING. Though less controversial than his predecessors, Ewing's conduct in managing the Robinson mine was certainly the most questionable. From O. L. Baskin & Company, *History of the Arkansas Valley.*

where she arrived on December 18, three weeks after the shooting. She and her brother probably took rooms at the Robinson Hotel, but wherever they stayed, they had to endure a disturbance that broke out at eleven o'clock that night when the guards at the mine opened fire and sprayed some two hundred bullets into camp. For ten minutes projectiles "went whistling over the town like a flock of bees," accompanied by the incessant shriek of the mine whistle that "joined in the concert." A few people reportedly had close calls, including a Mrs. Stowall, who saw her bedpost shattered while she was sitting a foot away. This was not the first time the trigger-happy guards had blazed away in the night, and many condemned the indiscriminate shooting. But why it took place at all was the real mystery. Some said that Daly had ordered the fusillade in order to frighten Mrs. Forbes into selling her stock for less than she should. [3]

But now ostensibly in control of the estate, Mrs. Forbes moved quickly to sell her shares in the Robinson Company, and it seems likely that John W. Jenkins served as an intermediary. Since at least 1874 he had been an associate of Wilson Waddingham, a western cattleman, land baron, and venture capitalist, who had investments in Colorado, and the suspicion is strong that Jenkins brought Waddingham and Mrs. Forbes together. Also entering the negotiations was Thomas Ewing, a veteran mining man about forty-three years old, who may have been negotiating with Robinson before the shooting. If so, talks continued with Mrs. Forbes, and on February 21, 1881, two months after her visit to Ten Mile, Ewing and Waddingham bought three-quarters of the stock and took control of the company. [4]

But if Mrs. Forbes thought she had her money free and clear, then she was wrong. For one thing, she was a defendant in Jacque's suit pending in federal court, and as if one lawsuit were not enough, she fell afoul of another in Summit County. Mrs. Forbes, Kendall, and Cooper had all assumed that Lake County had jurisdiction over the estate because Robinson had made his home in Leadville, but no sooner had the sale to Ewing and Waddingham been completed than Adam L. Shock, probate judge of Summit County, appointed the Ten Mile physician and miner Fernando H. Sutherland administrator of the estate. The reason? Robinson had moved his legal residence to Ten Mile shortly before he was shot. When Mrs. Forbes, Kendall, and Cooper tried to take the money from the mine sale, they found themselves blocked. Yet the Summit County Court did not take this action until March 28, 1881, more than a month after the sale to Ewing and Waddingham, and more than three months after the award of the Lake County Court—and one wonders why?

All this did was lead to more legal proceedings before a second Summit County judge, William A. Guyselman. On May 6, Mrs. Forbes, Kendall, and Cooper filed a petition claiming that the award made by the Lake County Court was valid and the award made to Sutherland had been obtained by fraud and was therefore void. But Guyselman disagreed. On June 14 he ruled that Robinson had resided in Summit County at the time of his death; while "it would have been a pleasurable duty for the court to have appointed the legal heir and next of kin" the administrator, the time for Mrs. Forbes to have filed her claim had passed, and the court saw no choice except to appoint Sutherland. Therefore, the judge dismissed Mrs. Forbes petition and ordered her and the other administrators to turn over $150,000 to Sutherland, although they could hold the remainder, subject to the court's order. [5]

Meanwhile, Daly kept operations going as smoothly as anyone might have expected. He installed new machinery in the mine and the smelter, and put down new tracks for ore cars running from the new adit to the reduction works. Then as winter grew worse, production declined. The "lawyers, experts, surveyors, etc." preparing for Jacque's suit also disrupted mining, though perhaps not as much as Daly contended. Day after day he shipped an average of thirty tons of ore to the Robinson and La Plata smelters, and good reports continued to come from below ground, where the ore body was reported to be three feet wide and still running more than 100 ounces of silver per ton.

Yet the Robinson smelter did not fare well. Daly and Arents drew shipments from the White Quail, Aftermath, Climax, Gilpin, and Forest, and while this was fine, the fact was that the Robinson's ores were "rebellious" or "refractory," meaning that they had too little lead and too much sulfur to be a good vehicle for collecting the silver. Daly had to buy lead-bearing carbonates from the White Quail and Aftermath, as well as low-grade base bullion in Leadville. But with the new railroad connections, he opened negotiations with smelters in Pueblo and Kansas City in hope of expanding his options and increasing returns.

The stock itself, listed on the New York Mining Stock Exchange, fluctuated with the news. After Robinson's death, the price churned in a narrow range between $8.25 and $9.00 per share, although in January it touched a low of $6.00 before gradually rising to about $9.50 per share in March. Each report of litigation, ore shipments, and capital improvements affected the price, yet the shares were generally described as "quiet and weak," and except for the impending Jacque trial, they commanded little attention. That was hardly true, however, for other companies floated by Roberts, notably Horace Tabor's Little Pittsburg Consolidated Mining Company, which collapsed with reports that the mine had been gutted and the ore exhausted. [6]

Once Ewing and Waddingham took control, changes in management followed. Roberts resigned as president, although the enterprise remained identified with him. The presidency devolved upon Brayton Ives, president of the New York Stock Exchange. Lucious B. Kendall took his seat as vice-president, presumably to represent Mrs. Forbes, and that summer he made at least one journey to Ten Mile to work on the estate. Stephen V. ("Deacon") White, president of the New York Mining Stock Exchange, continued as corporate treasurer; James K. Selleck, a state senator from New Jersey, became secretary; and Ewing replaced Daly as the head of all operations in Colorado.

Once Ewing took charge, he increased production, although his success reflected Daly's work and the warming spring weather. By April he had boosted output to eighty tons per day, by far the largest in Ten Mile. And he had other good news to announce. Daly's search for a better smelting contract, coupled with new railroad service, had enabled the company to sign an agreement with the Boston and Colorado Smelting

Company, whose plant at Argo, outside Denver, used a technology that could not only treat sulfides but also demanded an ore low in lead. By the end of April, Ewing had shipped two thousand tons to Argo, and some predicted the mine would yield "an immense product of ore" because the drifts and stopes could produce "an almost unlimited amount" of mineral. [7]

Trading in the stock picked up in May. Nearly 5,000 shares changed hands in the first week when the price fluctuated between $8 and $9. By mid-month, the weekly trading volume had risen to 6,550 shares and the price to $10.75. In the midst of the surge, however, the editors of the *Engineering and Mining Journal* took note of enterprises associated with Roberts, particularly the State Line mines in Nevada. They warned that there were "few investors in the East who had not had a taste of the financial management of the present controllers of the State Line mines, and fewer still who desire to renew their experience with it."

Yet this warning had little impact on the Robinson Company. When Ewing reported that production had increased to 120 tons per day, the price of the shares advanced to $11 apiece. Once again, the *E&MJ* reiterated its warning about enterprises associated with Roberts, particularly the State Line in which "never were purchases made on so little information and so much faith." But if others entertained such forebodings about the Robinson, their fears were apparently laid to rest when Brayton Ives visited Ten Mile and expressed his pleasure with both the mine and the management. Even so, the month of May saw the first break in the price of the State Line and the Iron Silver, and the normally conservative, circumspect *E&MJ* went so far as to castigate Roberts by name. [8]

Despite the collapse of the State Line and Iron Silver, to say nothing of the Little Pittsburg, Chrysolite, and Little Chief, the prospects of the Robinson Company seemed propitious. In early June the *E&MJ* printed a telegram from Ewing saying that ore shipped to the Argo and other smelters amounted to $100,000, the firm's surplus had increased to $140,000, and the enterprise had declared its third dividend, this one for $50,000 payable on June 15. Even more good news came with the announcement that Otto H. Hahn, another highly respected metallurgist of European origin, had agreed to succeed Arents at the company's smelter. Right into June, the stock continued strong, with the price holding between $10 and $11 per share. [9]

Yet even so, by June the *Engineering and Mining Journal* was beginning to cast an ever more wary eye. That month Ewing released the usual breathtaking report about the steady advance of the prospecting drifts, the increasing production at the smelting plant, and the new

10,000-ton contract with the Argo works. But when Ewing joined in the praise of the State Line, the *E&MJ* warned that his accolades should hardly be thought of as "disinterested." And the editors added that "all who sincerely wish to foster a legitimate mining business will do well to discourage the Roberts' plan of selling stocks."

But this caveat had no influence. In June, Ewing gave a special tour to a Colorado newspaper reporter, an account the *E&MJ* reprinted. The reporter noted the hurried efforts to fill the 10,000-ton contract, but more than that, his enthusiastic pen proclaimed that the mine looked splendid, the ore reserves amounted to 30,000 tons worth $100 each— $3 million—the miners discovered more ore with greater value at depth, development only seemed to increase the ore in sight, the mine would pay dividends for years to come, even extra quarterlies, and Ewing told the reporter that in all his experience, he had never seen an ore body so uniform in thickness and grade.

This was the most glowing report yet published on the fantastic wealth of the Robinson mine, and the editors of the *E&MJ* leaped to the attack. "This is another one of Roberts' mines," they charged on June 18. While they conceded that it was a good property, they warned that the stock was "selling much too high," in part because the mineral was "very refractory and expensive to work." They also cautioned that it was "a safe rule to discount superintendents' reports," and claimed "good authority" for stating that the Robinson mine did not have anything that approached $2 million in net ore values, let alone the $3 million that Ewing had indicated. What was more, "good and disinterested authority" believed that Captain Jacque had a viable claim against the company, one that would probably cost $250,000 to settle. And the editors thought that because the stock had received so much bolstering in the press, it was "evident that the insiders [were] working their way out." [10]

But the public took little notice of either the *E&MJ*'s warnings or the collapse of other firms sponsored by Roberts, perhaps because the mine reports continued to be spectacular and because the company officers took issue with the critics. James K. Selleck, the corporate secretary, who the *E&MJ* thought was "quite inexperienced in mining matters," replied that Roberts had never held more than one share of stock and that Ives had replaced him as president. The firm had purchased the Summit smelter for its own use, the mine had $3 million net value in sight, or very nearly that," and instead of bailing out, the insiders were "getting all of the stock that they can." S. V. White, the company treasurer, had now become one of the largest stockholders, and Wadding-ham, who had paid the Robinson heirs $1 million for 150,000 shares, held his interest as an investment, "not selling or caring to sell one share of it." Selleck denied what was undeniable—the ore was refractory—and he predicted that the mine would last another twenty-five years. To bulwark Selleck's remarks, White sent a public telegram to New York, saying that the ore reserves were "simply immense."[11]

The verbal jousting continued on into summer. On July 2, the *E&MJ* again denounced the State Line business as nothing more than "downright robbery" committed through "proper puffing and button-holing by a gang of blowers." Yet the charge had little effect on the Robinson. In came White's praise for the enterprise, the declaration of a fourth dividend for $50,000, and the assertion that even after this money was paid, the firm would still have another $76,000 in surplus.[12]

On it went all summer. In Ten Mile, Ewing developed a new level and announced the discovery of another rich body, and in late July he shipped five hundred tons and pronounced the new ore body as "opening magnificently" with assays of ninety ounces of silver per ton. The mine looked well throughout. Sales of stock jumped sharply from 1,000 or 1,200 to more than 6,000 shares per week. The price held steady about ten dollars. The firm announced its fifth dividend, another $50,000, payable on August 15, and reports circulated that Waddingham had assented to an out-of-court settlement with Jacque. With that heady news, the price of stock charged past twelve dollars per share on strong volume.[13]

And indeed the company and Mrs. Forbes had finally reached an agreement with Jacque. The first reports suggested that Jacque and his colleagues had agreed to accept between $150,000 and $200,000 to settle the dispute. A short time later the *E&MJ* put the exact figure at $160,000, and when the final payments were made that August, they brought to an end the bitter confrontation that had cost George B. Robinson his life. Yet there was a tragic sequel that very month when the news came from New Mexico that George Daly had been killed by Apaches, a death that seemed to perpetuate the pattern of tragedy surrounding so many principals in the Robinson drama.[14]

The settlement of the Jacque dispute was propitious, however, and with the approach of fall, the Robinson's stock grew very strong. Volume increased, the price rose to $13 per share, and the sky seemed the limit if the spectacular reports from Ten Mile could be believed. Yet the *E&MJ* continued its warnings. While the editors printed "the sensational reports" intentionally circulated to bolster the price, they stated bluntly that the ore reserves in sight did not justify the price; and when they published a report claiming that another large ore body had been struck in the 700-foot level, making the Robinson "the greatest mine in the West," they also warned that they had "excellent authority" for stating that this discovery was nothing more than finding the regular ore body where it had been expected. Furthermore, the company still had trouble in smelting a refractory ore. While the editors thought the property a good one, they opined that it would bring "disappointment to those who [bought] at figures which seem to be based on wild reports."[15]

Wild reports or not, the stock remained strong even though the State Line and other Roberts ventures had broken in price. The August figures from Ten Mile were fantastic as usual—Ewing had mined 2,257 tons worth $200,000, or nearly $90 each, the cost of mining was a mere $4.25 per ton, the ore in sight had increased to 40,000 tons, the vein still stood at eight to twenty feet thick, and extensive development continued. On September 1, the directors declared another $50,000 dividend, which would bring the total paid in less than a year to $425,000.

This did nothing except spur the Robinson stock to new heights. Even though there was troubling news that Ewing had closed the smelter because of the low percentage of lead in the ore, the firm announced that it had signed a new contract to sell the entire output to the Argo works. In mid-September, the weekly volume increased to 10,000 shares with a steady price of between $12.50 and $13 per share, and despite still another caveat from the *E&MJ* that the price was too high, the weekly volume rose to 12,440 shares and the price to a new high of $13.50. With that, the *E&MJ* could do nothing more than repeat its insistent warning, though this time couched in a sarcasm born of frustration. "The insiders," it said, "though believing in the stock, are kindly letting the public have some at the present prices, as they are taking a very handsome profit in doing so."[16]

On into October continued the boom. On October 1, the directors declared the regular monthly dividend of $50,000 and topped that with an extra payout of $50,000, which would bring the total to $525,000. Weekly sales of the stock rose sharply to 28,677, which pushed the price to a new high of $14.13 per share. The *E&MJ* sounded its usual warnings that it was "surmised by some of the brokers that there [was] some 'washing' being done," but hardly anyone paid much attention.

And on October 8, feeding the boom itself, the *E&MJ* republished an interview that had appeared in the Denver *Tribune*. Ewing bragged that when he had taken his position six months ago, the company had only 11,500 tons of ore in sight; now there were 75,000 tons. The firm had a lucrative contract with the Boston and Colorado Company and a second with the La Plata—contracts so good that the La Plata returns would pay all the mine's expenses, making the large receipts from the Argo nothing but profit. On he waxed: the ore averaged 100 ounces of silver per ton; the regular work force consisted of 80 men, although as many as 120 toiled at one time or another; the entire works had cost $200,000; development had revealed "a deep mine, a true fissure"; the ore did not have to be concentrated but could be shipped directly; the new power drills would reduce costs; and "not another mine in the West [could] show a similar body of equally rich ore." [17]

This interview enhanced the "very strong bull feeling" that prevailed toward the stock, notwithstanding the stream of jeremiads that flowed through the columns of the *E&MJ*. Except for a short-lived break to $12.25, the price held steady between $13 and $14 per share on heavy volume throughout the month; 23,360 shares traded in the third week of October alone, and there was even one brief advance above $14. Some price weakness appeared late in the month when rumors circulated that Roberts had been captured by Indians or Mexicans, but the report proved unfounded, though it gave the *E&MJ* another opportunity to philosophize that "if the value of the stock [was] based on George Roberts' welfare, and not on the mine, it [had] a poor bottom." [18]

November began with the usual spate of good news. The directors declared the usual monthly dividend of $50,000, as well as their second consecutive extra for $50,000. But then came the break. A tidal wave of selling engulfed the company on Monday, November 5. The stock opened at $12.75 per share, then plunged all day closing at $10.15, a 20 percent loss. While most of the damage had been done, the deluge continued all week, with the price eventually falling to $9.00 per share, a loss of nearly 30 percent of its value Monday morning. And the volume? 93,061 shares! The largest number ever traded in one week in the history of the New York Mining Stock Exchange! And at $9.00 per share, the price steadied—at least for two weeks. [19]

During the summer and fall of 1881, Brayton Ives had encouraged his friends to buy Robinson stock. Yet he must have read the incessant warnings in the *E&MJ*, and witnessed the collapse of other firms sponsored by Roberts. By October, Ives had begun to question the insatiable flow of good news that inundated his offices in New York. But he was cautious. He knew he was largely a figurehead president, and he hoped to avoid a direct investigation because of the potential embarrassment should anything be found amiss, and of course, he wanted true inside information about the prospects of the Robinson mine. The mysterious Waddingham may have felt the same way and talked matters over with Ives.

In late October or early November, shortly before the price broke,

Ives used an intermediary to quietly approach James D. Hague. A blue-blooded Bostonian, if ever there was one, Hague had spent his entire career in the minerals industry—copper mines in Michigan, a geological survey for the federal government, gold mines in California—he was known to be thorough, honest, reliable, and conservative. And very much in demand because of it. Ives asked Hague to make a personal examination of the Robinson mine, but Hague had other commitments. Yet he agreed to approach William Ashburner of San Francisco, a prominent mining engineer. Ives assented, and Ashburner accepted—he received a $1,000 fee in advance. But because of this delicate, circuitous approach, Ashburner had not received his full instructions when he started from San Francisco on Saturday, November 10. Hague told him to pick them up at the post office when he arrived in Denver. [20]

While Ashburner was en route to Denver, Hague sent him letters of introduction. From Ives came a letter to Ewing directing that Ashburner be admitted to inspect the property. To the Boston and Colorado Company came another letter asking them to let Ashburner examine the books that pertained to the Robinson shipments. And now Hague told Ashburner more fully what the investigation was for. Various "friends" desired "a confidential report on the present condition and prospects for the Robinson Mine; the amount and value of the ore in sight," and anything else "desirable for them to know in forming their opinions on the value of the stock." Hague also warned that he had received word "rather confidentially—therefore observe discretion"—that some of the Argo managers had recently bought large blocks of Robinson shares at higher prices than now prevailed. He also noted that "the sudden shrinkage of the stock" had prompted the investigation, and he added parenthetically that Ashburner should also check on the amount of ore sold to the Leadville smelters. Yet "the main question," wrote Hague, was "the present condition of the mine and the estimated value of the reserves." He urged Ashburner to "spare no pains in examining, measuring, sampling, and assaying to any extent that may be useful."

Hague went on. He presumed that Ashburner knew Ewing personally, and noted that Ewing was thought "to be largely interested" in Robinson stock. Thus, said Hague, since his friends desired the investigation to be "kept as confidentially as possible," Ashburner should address his report to "My Dear Sir" and enclose it inside another envelope addressed to Hague's offices at 18 Wall Street in New York. [21]

Though he had no idea of Hague's "friends," Ashburner went to the mine a week later and presented the letter from Ives. And much to Ashburner's shock, Ewing refused to recognize the authority of Ives! That should have made Ashburner deeply suspicious, but after a while, enough time for Ewing to contact New York, he decided to admit Ashburner "as he had nothing to conceal," wrote Ashburner later. Yet it appears that Ashburner, perhaps misled through Hague's talk of "friends" and his own amicable acquaintance with Ewing, allowed himself to talk much too freely about his purposes, and although he knew very little, he knew enough to make everything plain to Ewing.

But even if Ashburner had remained as silent as a stone wall, it is hard to believe that Ewing would not have guessed the underlying purpose of the examination. Yet even so, Ashburner might have done his job well. All he had to do, it seems, was go down in the workings and take ore samples—and that is precisely what he failed to do. When he arrived, he wrote later, he was "far from well," and when Ewing volunteered to provide samples to spare him the arduous work below ground, Ashburner accepted. So Ewing's samples were the ones that Ashburner had assayed, while Hague and his "friends" fretted in New York as the price of Robinson shares hovered precariously around $9. [22]

On or about November 24, Ashburner telegraphed Hague and mailed his report to the inscrutable "My Dear Sir." Aside from basic assumptions and intriguing details, the crux of the matter was that the mine had 55,350 tons of ore in reserve, and that after settling with the smelters, the net value would be $35.55 per ton, or $1,968,000. Ashburner noted that Ewing had given him every facility and had afforded him free access to the books, vouchers, and certificates from the smelting companies, while the mine impressed him as being so well managed and developed that there need be "no fear" but that the present shipments could be maintained. And it seems likely that Hague got the substance of this report to Ives and Waddingham shortly before the stock market opened on November 26, almost a year from the day when George B. Robinson was fatally wounded. [23]

Now came the deluge. Although the stock opened the session at $8.75, it sailed into a storm of selling. Within hours the price plunged $2.00 to $6.75 per share, and in the next two days it gyrated before sinking as low as $5.25 on November 29, a year to the day after Robinson's death. When contacted about the debacle, the corporate officers reported that Ewing had resigned; the interim manager, Mr. Stevens, had telegraphed that the outlook for the mine did not look encouraging; and when Ives himself had to face the press, he could do nothing more than concede that there had been "a good deal of pretty tall lying going on somewhere." That only caused more panicky selling the next day, when the stock plunged to a low of $3.75. And the volume for the week? 311,561 shares!

If the crash in the Robinson stock was not enough, even more bad news flowed in from the West. On November 30, Henry Wolcott, manager of the Argo smelter, told a reporter that his company had loaned the Robinson firm $90,000 to pay the last dividend, the enterprise still owed $30,000 over and above the ore shipped to Argo, and the Robinson firm had to pay still another $32,000 as its share of the settlement with Jacque. Even worse, a party coming from Ten Mile brought news that fifty miners, nearly the entire Robinson force, had been laid off, leaving only a small prospecting crew. Shipments would be drastically curtailed because all the valuable ore had been mined.

The Robinson now became the topic of heated debate. The Denver *Tribune* stated bluntly that "the failure of the mine in the face of recent favorable reports" would no doubt tend to destroy "what little confidence" the public still retained in the mining business and the people connected with it. And the editors of the *Engineering and Mining Journal* declared that if the majority of mining superintendents treated westerners the way they handled eastern investors, more than one of their charades would result "in a tree, a rope, and a man attached."[24]

Such hyperbole aside, on December 1, with the price of Robinson shares fluctuating around $4.25, having lost about 50 percent of their value in four days, Hague telegraphed Ashburner, who had now returned to San Francisco. Hague told him that Ewing had resigned and the new manager had reported that the mine's prospects did not look encouraging. Then he asked Ashburner if he thought his sampling had been sufficient to leave his "confidence unshaken." Hague wanted to know for the benefit of his friends who had bought at twice the present price on the receipt of Ashburner's telegram.

While Ashburner's reply has been lost, he must have cringed when he realized his disastrous error of omission. Yet telegrams and letters continued to crisscross the continent, and in due course Hague told Ashburner that his report had been widely read and just as widely criticized, even though everyone thought that it was "a straightforward, honest, and in every respect, so far as it goes, trustworthy statement." But, said Hague, he and his friends needed "a much further knowledge of the truth," favorable or otherwise. It appeared that Ashburner had been "the victim of a shameful imposition." A man who had been employed "to assist you did all he could to cheat you; and that what samples you took were replaced by better ones." He also told Ashburner that Wolcott had just sent a man to examine the mine, and on the basis of the report, Senator Nathaniel P. Hill, the principal owner of the Argo smelter, had sold his Robinson stock "at a large sacrifice," indicating that the unpropitious reports were "something more than idle rumor."

Hague continued. He noted that Ashburner had sent no diagram of the levels and stopes, and he observed that the upper five, worked-out levels had produced $1 million and all the dividends. If so, Hague asked, how could Ashburner predict that the three lower levels would produce twice as much unless the dimensions of the ore body were larger, or the value of the mineral higher, neither of which was the case, so far as he knew. Hague also pointed out that Ashburner's integrity seemed to demand a thorough examination; he would find his professional reputation seriously impaired by a misleading report based on trickery and deceit of which, some thought, Ashburner was the unsuspecting victim. Put in this position, Ashburner had little alternative except to reexamine the mine. When he arrived, wrote Hague, he would meet William N. Symington, a mining engineer who had joined the board of directors. [25]

Meanwhile, trading in Robinson stock remained strong in the face of the shocking recital of bad news. In the week of December 3, more than 244,000 shares changed hands as the price gyrated between $4.33 and $6.88 per share. On December 10, the *E&MJ* reprinted Ashburner's report to "My Dear Sir." It was "gratifying" to learn, wrote the editors, that "an expert" who commanded "confidence and integrity" had declared that the bottom had not gone out, but they added that it was "impossible to say" to what extent he had sampled the ore body. And they opined that "had the mine been worked without a market for the stock in view," Ashburner's assertion that the net reserves amounted to $1.9 million might have been "a fair assumption." But there appeared to be a stock deal in the working of the mine, efforts had been made to push the price to $20 per share, and the editors warned that when a mine manager was a large stockholder during a bull market, he could hardly resist the temptation to make the best showing possible. [26]

Through mid-December the Robinson stock made tidal waves in the market. Volume remained enormous; 358,000 shares traded in the second week of the month as the price swung wildly between $2.75 and $5.00 before ending the week at $3.85 per share. So many assertions and denials appeared in the press that the editors of the *E&MJ* pronounced the crosscurrents "positively bewildering." It was freely asserted that Ashburner had been tricked, and at last Ives let it be known that Ashburner had agreed to make a second examination. But that hardly steadied anyone's nerves. If anything, it seemed more disquieting.

In the third week of December, 247,000 shares changed hands as the price slumped to $1.90. The stock had lost about 80 percent of its value in scarcely a month. [27]

Ashburner could not return to Ten Mile until December 20, but once at the mine, he met Symington and a Mr. Palmer, who represented the Boston and Colorado Company. And now for the first time, Ashburner visited the lower levels. He and Symington took ore samples and had them assayed, they trudged through the workings on Christmas Day, and after this hurried, but intensive examination, they sent their separate reports to Ives.

And the news was grim. Ashburner reported that the ore body had been worked out above the sixth level, there was little left between the sixth and seventh levels—only about 600 tons with comparatively low values—and while there was still some hope for discovering new mineral on the eighth level, it seemed likely that daily shipments would cease in January or February.

Then he offered his personal reflections. It had been with feelings the nature of which he could hardly express that he made this assessment. He could scarcely comprehend how he had been deceived. Had he known the true nature of the investigation, he would never have taken the job. He had thought he could trust Ewing as one who enjoyed "the utmost confidence" of the company president, and he had not presumed "for an instant that the mine and its prospects would be misrepresented," or that any confidence that he placed in Ewing would be abused. But, said Ashburner, he had had to rely on Ewing because he was far from well. He could see now that Ewing had worked the mine "solely with a view of first deceiving and then robbing the public." And now, wrote Ashburner, nothing remained for him to say except that in November he had been conscientious, but his report was indeed an "exaggerated and misleading one, the result of misrepresentation and trickery" on Ewing's part. [28]

Aside from this personal recrimination, Ashburner returned his $1,000 fee to Hague, and only then did he learn about the mysterious circumstances surrounding his original investigation. Hague replied that the individual who had paid the fee was none other than Waddingham. When Ashburner had arrived on his first visit to Ten Mile, Waddingham's interest in the Robinson Company had been "comparatively small." He had increased it substantially, "with subsequent loss," owing to Ashburner's report, but in retrospect Waddingham thought that Ashburner's error was an honest one, and he refused to accept the $1,000.

In writing Hague, however, Ashburner apparently suggested that Ewing and Waddingham had acted in concert to swindle the public, and to this Hague took exception, at least to a degree. In the past few weeks, he wrote obliquely, he had learned more of Waddingham's operations. Yet Hague was philosophical. "There is no help in it now," he wrote, "The mistake is a bad one for all concerned." He was glad that Ashburner's reputation was "so well established" that no one would seek any reason to disparage "your honesty of purpose and your integrity of character." And Hague apologized to Ashburner for he had intended "a friendly act" in turning over a fee, only to have Ashburner wind up "in such a disagreeable affair."[29]

Such private comments aside, the recriminations reverberated through the press. The New York *Tribune* stated openly that "conspirators deceived Professor Ashburner" with salted assays. And when the editors of *Bullion* assessed the workings of the stock market over the past twelve-month, they averred that the year had seen the "slaughter of geese that laid golden eggs." And the logical conclusion was that investors had no rule for escaping the wiles of mining sharps. As a result, 1882 was opening with the flattest market seen in a long while.[30]

Yet in Ten Mile, the winding down of 1881 was more important for another matter—it marked the fast approaching end of the carbonate boom launched by the discoveries of Robinson, Sheddon, and Jones. In the years to come, historians would contend that the death of Robinson, the burning of Kokomo, and the collapse of the Robinson stock knocked the underpinnings out from under the industry and created a harder, less prosperous era. But this was not true. They were spectacular events, memorable tragedies, but they were coincidental benchmarks that only seemed to have a devastating impact on the mining industry. In actuality, by the end of 1881, the miners had largely exhausted the rich carbonate ores. They had never been as extensive as in Leadville, which was beginning to experience the dislocations caused by a shift in its own ores from rich carbonates to poorer sulfides. These problems would have appeared whether or not Patsy Gillin had shot George B. Robinson, whether or not Thomas Ewing and perhaps others had deceived a gullible public, and whether or not Kokomo had burned to the ground.

But few could deny that the past two years had seen a spectacular upsurge in output. While no one could give exact figures for Ten Mile, the Summit County returns as a whole revealed a remarkable increase from $309,000 in 1879 to $439,000 in 1880, and then a breathtaking leap to $2.6 million in 1881, thanks largely to the great performance of the

Robinson mine and solid production from the White Quail, Aftermath, and other properties. The year 1881, in fact, was the most spectacular that the county would see for more than a generation to come. [31]

The final sequel to the Robinson drama played on in the courts, as Mary V. Forbes struggled to wrest control of her son's estate. Despite the claims to jurisdiction advanced by the Summit County Court, the ultimate ruling was that Robinson had died a resident of Lake County, and so the final disposition of the estate remained in the hands of that court. Yet the matter dragged on until July 3, 1883, when Mrs. Forbes received the sum of $768,324.17. Two years before, however, the Leadville papers had announced that the estate amounted to $993,000. What accounted for the $225,000 difference? Where had the money gone? To Jacque? To attorney's fees? To administrative costs? To losses in stock speculation? Probably all accounted for something, particularly the settlement with Jacque, but whatever the truth, Mrs. Forbes lived out her final years in Michigan, where she died in 1902 at the age of 89. [32]

And Job A. Cooper, one of the co-executors? When he discharged his final duties, he probably thought that this episode in his life was behind him, but if so, he was wrong. In 1888 he ran for governor. He bested his rivals for the Republican nomination, and in a state that generally elected Republicans, he was a good bet to win election in November. But the campaign invective grew worse and worse, and in the middle of fall, a number of Democratic newspapers accused Cooper of taking the bulk of the money from the Robinson estate and sending Mrs. Forbes back to Michigan with nothing more than a train ticket. The *Rocky Mountain News,* which was still no friend of the Republicans, even ran a blunt cartoon underscored by the comment that "the Robinson estate was a good Job."

Such accusations of fraud produced the inevitable outcry from the Republican ranks, and newspaper reporters promptly trudged off to Leadville to look over the documents. After an examination of the record, which showed that Mrs. Forbes had received $768,000, newspapers across the state, even pro-Democratic organs, published accounts of the final settlement. And in the end the charges of stealing the Robinson estate hurt Cooper not at all. In fact, the flurry of charge and countercharge may have helped his chances, for in November the voters elected him governor of Colorado, an office that George B. Robinson might have held. And that seems to be the final assessment of Robinson's meteoric career—a handful of imponderable what-ifs and might-have-beens. [33]

CHAPTER 8

The Tide of Retrogression

As 1881 approached its end, the mines of Ten Mile were about to complete their most productive year to date. Boosted by the rising output of the spectacular Robinson mine, as well as lesser properties like the White Quail and Aftermath, the valley had emerged as one of Colorado's leading mineral producers. Though it shipped far less than Leadville, whose mines accounted for more than half the state's output, Ten Mile had surged past all others and seemed a fair bet to widen its margin. But that was before the gut-wrenching blows of fall—the inferno that destroyed much of Kokomo on October 13 and the shocking collapse of the Robinson Company a few weeks later. The future that once seemed as bright as the golden aspen of fall now seemed as stark as the bare branches of winter. [1]

As 1882 dawned, mining in Ten Mile still reeled from the thunderous collapse of the Robinson Company. As one charitable commentator put it, the Robinson had "suffered in reputation from mismanagement and overworking." The company had few miners, and water had drowned the lower workings. But the enterprise was far from through. The new management got the pumps going, found enough capital to resume development, and by summer the thud of blasting below ground and the crunch and shriek of machinery above signaled that the Robinson was back in production. Although the ore averaged only 45 or 50 ounces of silver per ton, hope still continued that mining would disclose a new bonanza.

Mining continued elsewhere on Sheep Mountain. The Idalia Com-

169

pany, Grey Eagle, and Ballarat all shipped for a time, but had to contend with spring freshets and drowned workings. Near the top of the mountain, Messrs. Hutchinson and Ryan drove a new incline into the Wheel of Fortune, replaced old machinery, and made steady shipments. The Graphic Mining Company sold a considerable amount of ore from the Crown Point, which seemed to be emerging as an important producer. And there was still hope, but little production, from the Michigan and Snow Bank.

The story was much the same on Elk Mountain. The Aftermath and the Milo passed into the hands of the American Mining and Smelting Company, a Chicago-based enterprise then expanding its smelter in Leadville into one of the largest in Colorado. The White Quail, still controlled by capital in Philadelphia, continued to ship ore, but only until late in the year when operations ceased. One commentator explained obliquely that "through mismanagement the profits of the mine were absorbed in developments or otherwise expended." Exactly what happened was judiciously left unsaid, but the results were obvious. The Recen brothers and a bank in Leadville attached the property for nonpayment of debts. At the lesser properties on Elk Mountain, miners continued working the Raven and Eagle, the Badger and Little Ida, but they were operated through the Milo, Aftermath, and White Quail to conserve capital and fight the water problem.

There was much less work on Jacque Mountain this year. The Recen brothers developed the Queen of the West, where they mined some rich streaks of galena and black sulphurets. By the end of the year, they had three shafts along with 400 feet of drifts and 100 feet of crosscuts. While this hardly compared to the Robinson or White Quail, it made the Queen of the West the largest mine on Jacque Mountain. A distant second was the Mayflower, where a feud between the owners retarded operations.

Across the valley mining continued among the spectacular crags of the Ten Mile Range. The Maximus and the Bernadotte, both owned by the Colorado Land and Mineral Company, sent some very rich ore to the smelters, but overall production was comparatively small. Prospecting remained vigorous on the rocky slopes of Fletcher Peak and other grey spires, but the Ten Mile Range hardly rivaled even the declining output of Sheep, Elk, and Jacque mountains.

Ten Mile saw other subtle, but important, changes this year. Lessees took over more and more mines, which was generally a sign of falling production and declining grades of ore. The mines also shipped less carbonates and more sulfides. Into Ten Mile came the first concentration mills to crush and concentrate lower grades of ore prior to shipment. Donald Doncaster opened one, Thomas Greer converted his smelter into a mill, and that left the White Quail works as the only smelter in Ten Mile. But as before, it operated only sporadically. William McNair built a plant for his Vulcan furnace, which apparently drew its heat from burning coal gas, but he had little success. Most mining companies in Ten Mile sold their ore and concentrates to smelters in Leadville or Denver. [2]

Despite the decline, the year closed with decent results. The Robinson had shipped $315,000 worth of ore and concentrates; the mines above Kokomo-Recen another $470,000; and the smelting works in the district, about $238,000—a grand total of $1,023,000. This was slightly more than 90 percent of the county's production of $1,107,000. While this was comparable to the production of Clear Creek and Gilpin counties, it ranked far behind Lake County, where the Leadville mines produced nearly $15,300,000, almost two-thirds of the state's output. [3]

By early 1883, the boom had given way to a sense of déjà vu, to a sense of what-ifs and might-have-beens. As winter slipped by, a feeling of uncertainty, even anxiety, seemed to pervade life in Ten Mile. And the *Ten Mile News* seemed to catch the quiet desperations of the day. In March the editors reported that the Felicia Grace had gone back into production, the Nettie B. had shipped several carloads of ore to the smelters, and the Reconstruction expected to commence operations in April. Yet against this optimism had to be set the more pessimistic news that the Aftermath had shut down, the Robinson had sued several employees for stealing ore, and in another case Judge Shepard had ruled in favor of the owners in a suit filed against them for nonpayment of wages—a decision the editors denounced as "contemptible" as the district had seen "too much bilking of poor miners." About the only good news was that the price of mines and mining claims had fallen, and commonsense seemed to be "asserting its sway," which suggested that Ten Mile could look forward "to a new era of prosperity." [4]

As the year unfolded, the Robinson mine attracted more than its share of attention. The huge surface plant dominated the landscape at the base of Sheep Mountain, and hope never ended that the mine would come back into bonanza. Trading in the stock remained high; yet the price rarely topped one dollar per share, and gradually slumped to eighty cents on heavy volume. Lessees took over the mining, guards remained posted at all the portals—probably to prevent the lessees from fighting among themselves or stealing ore—and reports still told of drilling, blasting, new machinery, and other improvements, but not much bo-

nanza ore. When the company held its annual meeting, it revealed that
the ore shipped averaged scarcely $18 per ton. After that, the stock
price slumped to as low as sixty-two cents per share. [5]

In March 1883, the Robinson Company leased the property to Thomas
Greer. He continued operations by subleasing to others, shipping the
ores to his plant for concentrating, and then selling the concentrates to
the Argo smelter. Later, Greer began building a mill at the mine, and
operations appeared more promising as spring progressed. There were
signs of better ore, sixty-five men toiled in the workings, and by June,
Greer had increased shipments to eighty tons per day. But this optimism
receded as the month wore along. The spring runoff overwhelmed the
pumps and flooded the lower workings. The new concentration machinery failed to live up to expectations, and Greer continued to ship
what ore he could to his mill at Kokomo. But this apparently brought
little profit. Greer went to New York to talk the company into revising the
lease. When the word spread, the price of the stock fell to fifty-three
cents per share.

During the summer Greer gave up his lease, and William Gleason
took over. No stranger to Ten Mile, he was the foreman of the Greer
concentrator and held several leases throughout the district. Like Greer,
Gleason worked the mine largely through subleasers, perhaps a dozen in
all, who did pretty much what they pleased, according to the *Ten Mile
News*. Nobody—or at least nobody in public—really seemed to know
how much ore was coming from the workings. Not surprisingly, the
price of stock dropped to thirty-eight cents per share toward the end of
the year.

Even though the Robinson mine resembled little more than a shadow
of its famous old self, Sheep Mountain continued to attract much attention. James Stewart leased the Giant this year. Ryan and Hutchinson
blocked out several large ore bodies in the Wheel of Fortune. The owners of the Grey Eagle spent some $6,000 to $7,000, a relatively modest
sum of money, to explore and develop the mine. The Forest, Nettie B.,
and Snow Bank all shipped some ore. But perhaps the best producer this
year was the Crown Point, which became one of the largest shippers in
the valley with ores averaging a surprising $100 per ton.

The mines north of Sheep Mountain had a far more difficult time than
in years past. On Elk Mountain, the Fisher bank and the Recen brothers
kept the White Quail tied up with attachments, but even after these
matters were resolved, there was little production from a mine that had
once bid fair to rival the Robinson, and then after Gleason and J. B.
Lovell, the lessees, got the property into limited production, back came

the Recens with another attachment. The American Mining and Smelting Company allowed lessees to take over the Aftermath and Milo,
which struggled along, producing a fair grade of ore averaging 25 ounces
of silver and 25 percent lead per ton.

The situation was even worse farther north. On Jacque Mountain
miners shipped a few ores from the Ida L., Bledsoe, and Delmonico, but
from the chief property, the Queen of the West, came far less mineral
than in 1882 because the Recen brothers struck large pockets of sulphurets. The situation was even grimmer on Copper Mountain, where
the Reconstruction and Storm King shipped next to nothing. [6]

But 1883 seemed to be the year that mines in the Ten Mile Range
attracted more attention than in the past. The most notable were the
Maximus and the Bernadotte, located near the summit of Fletcher Peak
just over the range on the east, or Blue River, side. Although the company had developed the mines before, it had found little rich ore—just
enough to keep going. In April, however, came reports of a rich strike—
silver-bearing ore along with gold in narrow veins. By summer the enterprise had some forty-five men on its payroll. They took out ore running as much as $700 to $1,000 per ton. And from August until October,
when the driving snows and numbing winds closed in, the firm kept its
crews hard at work mining the narrow veins, hand sorting the rock,
packing the ore into canvas bags, and using jack trains to haul it down to
Kokomo-Recen. [7]

The excitement at the Maximus and Bernadotte sparked more intensive work on this airy summit. Miners set to work on the Golden Chord,
Nova Scotia, Nova Scotia No. 2, Smuggler, Pilgrim, and Pilgrim's Progress. By mid-fall, everyone was shipping something and it was said that a
good miner could make four dollars to six dollars per day by securing
a lease. The *Ten Mile News* proclaimed there were "many veins on
Fletcher Mountain as good as those of the Maximus and Bernadotte,"
and it required "only a little money and some knowledge of mining to
make several of them pay." Perhaps so, but Tim Foley, who had operated
mines in Ten Mile and Leadville for years, told a *News* reporter that he
doubted any properties on Fletcher Mountain would return a profit, because the mineral lay in narrow fissure veins, and working them required
"ability of no mean order," which Foley thought was "almost entirely
wanting" in Ten Mile. Perhaps Foley was right. The high winds and severe cold ended mining there in mid-fall, and a suit over contested
ground between the Maximus and Nova Scotia No. 2 only added to problems. In fact, litigation and other matters kept the Maximus closed for
the next four years. [8]

By the end of 1883, leasing and concentrating had become the order of the day. All the major mines in the district had passed into the hands of lessees. Although a few companies and individuals operated directly, they were relatively small producers, if that. A substantial percentage of the ore now went to the concentrating mills owned by Greer, Doncaster, and others. There were few carbonates left. The year also saw a number of the old placers reworked, some no doubt for gold, others to mine the pockets of the Denver South Park and Pacific Railway, which had begun building through Ten Mile.

No one could deny the ongoing decline. "Ten Mile district does not show the life it possessed two years ago," wrote one observer. "Almost every branch of mining is at a standstill, with a future equally dark." The ores shipped had comparatively little silver. What made them attractive was the iron and lead that was essential in smelting. That was the saving grace that staved off a collapse. [9]

Public recriminations, however, went hand in hand with the district's decline. "Most of our mine managers have come here without the least bit of experience in their business," lamented the *Ten Mile News* that fall. "They have learned their trade, if they have learned it at all, at the expense of the camp. Men have run mines here who didn't know porphyry from sandstone, who couldn't run a drift to save their souls or timber a shaft without having it cave in on them." But the mills had to shoulder their share of the blame. "There is one thing against us," complained the *News*. "We have no concentrating works of sufficient magnitude to do justice to our ores." Successful plants in California, Montana, and Arizona cost anywhere from $50,000 to $100,000, but the most expensive in Ten Mile, the Greer, had cost no more than $8,000, and the results showed. "It is needless to say," opined the editors, "that such small concerns cannot do any close work as plants which cost ten times as much. You cannot expect a $50.00 bronco to do the work of a $500.00 thoroughbred." The *Summit County Journal* agreed. What Ten Mile needed, said the editors, was "a careful, thorough system of dressing devised by scientific minds and carried into use by practical hands." [10]

The onset of winter brought the usual problems. The hard freeze and the deep snow curtailed operations everywhere. Not surprisingly, the long, lonely vigil through these months, coupled with the waning industry, induced discouragement. The *Summit County Journal* caught these feelings well in February 1884 when the editors lamented that "Ten Mile, once the second producing mineral section in Colorado, has dwindled down to almost nothing. The great Robinson mine is remembered only as something that was." [11]

Spring brought the perennial revival of hope. A little mining had gone on all winter, and on March 1, the *Summit County Herald* claimed that Sheep Mountain had not played out. The Nettie B. had just shipped some ore to Leadville, and it seemed that the site of old Kokomo would become more valuable for mining than town building. A few miners had hauled new machinery up the slopes of Jacque Mountain, and reports circulated that William Gleason would soon begin driving an adit from Kokomo Gulch into the depths of Elk Mountain to reduce operating costs and tap veins thought to be far underground. And the editors chided local miners who had rushed off for the new boom in the Coeur d'Alene region of Idaho, and noted that some men might find the old placers in McNulty Gulch more profitable to work. [12]

But the fortunes of Ten Mile had still drifted down to their lowest ebb since the rush began, and the *Herald* was philosophical about it. The editors conceded that the Kokomo fire had ruined many businessmen, contributed to the present "stagnation," and given the district "a decidedly black eye," but no mining district in Colorado, they thought, had suffered such "disaster and drawback" as Ten Mile and still bounced back. There had been problems of course—"the questionable manipulations" of the Robinson Company, the joint stock enterprises formed to market property in many instances "secured by fraud," the closing of the Elk Mountain mines even though "most all mining men" agreed that a second contact was to be found, and the attempt to run smelters "some of which never turned a wheel," and others which "may as well have not done so."

Yet there was still hope. New discoveries presaged a new era. Ten Mile seemed to be "speedily and readily coming to the front as a safe and sure region for the prospector and investor to make their stake." Development in the past few weeks was the "guarantee of the statement." All the district required was "work—steady, unflinching, continuous work," and along with it "the money wherewith to prosecute the work." But there was the rub—the lack of investment capital. [13]

Despite the *Herald's* promotions, mining in 1884 got off to a slower start than usual. The snow hampered operations for weeks on end. Some owners brought in special crews to shovel away the drifts, but even when some properties resumed mining, the district did not have enough cars to ship what production it had. Everything seemed to be worse than before. The editors of the *Herald*, however much they might have tried to boom the district, could not deny that "high grade ores are the rare exception." And miners who refused to accept the prevalence of complex, low-grade sulfides lived mostly on hopes, mining what ore they could to keep going. "Hopes are believed justly entertained as to the future of the Triangle on Sheep Mountain," went one report in April. There were "encouraging prospects" for the Mary Lode on Bartlett Mountain ran another report. And perchance a few miners struck a pocket of rich ore as did the owners of the Felicia Grace. [14]

As summer approached, the snows persisted. "The impassibility" of the roads disrupted mining through May, and the drifts remained so deep that toward the end of June the *Summit County Journal* predicted that the townspeople could have a "snow-balling match" on the Fourth of July right in the heart of Kokomo-Recen. But once the snow and ice melted, miners gave more attention than usual to the old placers. Some men re-worked Clinton Gulch, where they found some "exceedingly rich dirt." Phil Foote, Thomas Gillin, and others leased the old Stetthauer Placer and reportedly took some $300 in gold from a cubic yard of earth—"no snibe but an actual reality," said the *Herald*—and one assay purported that the placer still held as much as thirty ounces of gold per ton. In fact, Summit County's production of alluvial gold more than doubled this year to $205,000, more than it had been since the early 1860s. [15]

As 1884 wound down to its end, few could deny that the year had been unprosperous. There had been shipments from this mine and that, but only the Robinson, Felicia Grace, and a couple of others had produced much. Lower prices for silver and lead had hindered production, to say nothing of the heavy late snows, and a coal miners' strike, which ham-pered the industry indirectly. Nor could it be denied that people were steadily leaving the valley, some for the season, but others for good. The *Herald* claimed that two miners left daily, and if that kept up for a couple of months, there would soon be "nothing but a geographical point to mark the spot where Kokomo-Recen once was." The *Summit County Journal* remembered that a few years ago Robinson and Kokomo had been "promising towns," Frisco "would take no denial," Montezuma and Chihuahua "were rivals," but beginning in 1880, "a steady retrograde movement" had developed, and Breckenridge alone had "stemmed the tide of retrogression. [16]

The year 1885 seemed to be a repetition of 1884. January arrived in the midst of the usual snowstorms that buried Ten Mile, retarded pro-duction, disrupted rail service, and kept most people cooped up in their homes. But the *Summit County Journal* reported "new and valuable strikes . . . in the old workings of the Robinson," that the Last Chance had "come to the front with a good find of high grade ore," and the Felicia Grace had realized "more to its owners than they had dared to hope for a few months ago." Shipments had picked up, probably reflecting higher prices for silver and lead, and prompting the Rio Grande Railway to keep open its line from Leadville. At some mines "the welcome sound of the hoisting engines" rumbled day and night, and weekly shipments reportedly aggregated about 100 tons of ore and concentrates. This was fine, but it was hardly the stuff of booms. Yet the perennially optimistic editors trusted that "the shipping of ore will soon revivify the camp."

As spring arrived, these hopes persisted, but revitalization remained nothing more than a will-o'-the-wisp. By June ore cars again rumbled over the rails on Fremont Pass. The price of lead continued to rise, giving some boost to mining, and this year the cool, crisp weather of fall persisted longer than usual, only a light snow fell in December, and what mines remained in operation kept shipping longer than usual. "There has never been a winter in this section," claimed the *Summit County Journal*, "wherein the work of nonproducing mines and the development of prospects has continued as steadily as it has at present." With this good fortune, production for the year reached about $750,000, half of Summit County's output, yet that was only a fraction of Leadville's $9,600,000 or Colorado's overall $21,600,000. [17]

Such aggregate figures aside, what was it like for a "typical" mine in Ten Mile during this time? Charles J. Moore, a local mining man, revealed some data when he investigated the Queen of the West in December of 1885. Since making their first shipment on October 13, 1881, the day that Kokomo burned, the Recen brothers had developed their property as best they could. They assembled two log cabins that could house as many as forty men, and with a work force toiling ten hours per day, they sunk three shafts, drove three adits, and developed crosscuts on six different levels. Yet the Recens' resources and the mine's wealth never allowed the brothers to work around the clock, and to lower costs, they eventually began coordinating operations with the adjacent Mayflower. By December 1885, the Recens had shipped more than 2,800 tons of ore mined from pay streaks averaging two and one-half feet in width. This brought a gross return of $165,000, or a little more than $59 per ton, virtually all the value in silver, along with a miniscule amount in gold and lead. But after deducting about $21 per ton for shipping and smelting, this left the Recens with a net return of about $39 per ton or $109,000 in all, and from that they had to deduct another $5 per ton, which was the cost of mining and interest. This was a modest-sized operation, but one that provided excellent returns to the Recens. [18]

The mild winter of 1885–1886 along with the rising price of metals allowed some miners to keep going. The Snow Bank remained in production. So did the White Quail worked by Wilfley and Lovell. And the Felicia Grace shipped two ore cars per week. The lessees running the Wheel of

Fortune installed new machinery that brought an instantaneous reward when they struck a good body of high-grade ore. After that came the announcement that the Wheel would repay its debts, give miners their back wages, and begin working on a profitable basis. Even the Robinson had good news—a 5 percent dividend for its stockholders—and the superintendent, Charles J. Moore, reported that the enterprise would soon take control of all mining itself. [19]

Moore seemed to be leading a renaissance. Then thirty-two years old, a New Jersey native who had grown up in Kansas, where he had clerked in a grocery store, Moore had worked at the Robinson mine through all its vicissitudes since 1879. Now he was superintendent, testimony that for some, Ten Mile provided some upward mobility. Early in 1886, when Moore returned from the annual meeting in New York, hopes ran high that the mine had begun a more prosperous era. Although he had reduced production, his crews had advanced the main incline, and he expected to cut out a new station at the 1,600-foot level. The incline was still in ore, and although the deposit was now only two feet wide, shipments still averaged twenty tons daily.

Yet the Robinson mine still labored under a star-crossed sky. In September, Moore was struck down by "paralysis of the brain"—either a brain tumor or a stroke. From mid-month on, he was unconscious, but he did not slip away until the last of October. He left a wife and child, as well as his family back in Kansas, when "the eternal destroyer" carried him off "at the threshold of what was supposed to be a long life of usefulness." [20]

As now seemed usual for Ten Mile, whatever optimism prevailed in the spring smoldered along through summer, and then flickered away in the fall only to be succeeded by another spark of hope in winter. That October of 1886, a reporter for the *Summit County Journal* came over from Breckenridge to visit Kokomo-Recen, "the sole metropolis" of Ten Mile. In alighting from the passenger car, he wrote, he caught a glimpse of the worst part of town. The old smelter buildings were in "a wretched, tumble-down condition," the roofs were caving in, the smokestacks were falling over, and the fences had been blown down. Between the railroad depot and the town, where five years before there had been scores of "homes of happy families," now there were very few people, the windows were "boarded up or broken in, sidewalks all gone, paling fences all total wrecks, etc." Only in the center block on the main street of Recen was there any visible sign of the old life, but even so, "the evidence of departed greatness" was painfully evident.

Yet this reporter repeated the perpetual hope that a revival would come. The mines surrounding the town were still numerous and their output "not only large and steady but profitable." They would "yet redeem Kokomo-Recen and make its name in the world as one of the great mining centers in the state." Many miners felt this way, too. W. E. Musgrove, the superintendent of the Robinson mine during its heyday, still lived in Kokomo, "the picture of good health and good living." There also was Arthur Redman Wilfley, the "civil engineer," who was interested in the concentrating works near town. When Kokomo was "cleared of the wreckage of mistaken enterprises," thought this reporter, it would enjoy "a permanent and brilliant future."[21]

But this was by no means apparent in mid-1887. In May, when a second correspondent for the *Journal* paid "a flying visit" to the "little metropolis of Ten Mile," his report reflected the depressed conditions. In the heart of Kokomo the "half worn down buildings" acted like "a wet blanket on visitors" and elsewhere the scores of wrecked structures looked even more disheartening. But there was still hope. "Some of the finest men in the county" made their homes here, and in the vicinity were "some of the most profitable mines in the state," although a number had been drowned by surface water. That, of course, was an old story. [22]

There was some good news this year, although not much. The Recen brothers incorporated their mine as the Queen of the West Mining Company and obtained an infusion of capital from Robert S. Brookings, a prosperous St. Louis merchant who would one day endow both Washington University and the Brookings Institution. Yet the Queen of the West shipped little or no ore in 1887, nor did the Crown Point, Grey Eagle, Nettie B., Wheel of Fortune, and a host of lesser properties. The Felicia Grace, Last Chance, and Nova Scotia No. 2 did, but their production was negligible. The Robinson declined to reveal its output, yet it was considerably less than the $175,000 shipped by companies that kept their production confidential. The year, however, was a good one for the White Quail, leased by Wilfley and his partners. Probably because of the high prices the smelters paid for lead-bearing minerals, the White Quail shipped $135,000 in ore and concentrates. That accounted for about 20 percent of the county's production, and the shy, reticent Wilfley seemed to be emerging as one of the leading miners in Ten Mile. [23]

The year also saw the approximate completion of the first systematic study of the district's geology. Underway for almost a decade, this work had experienced its own vicissitudes. The drama had played out on a crooked axis stretching from Washington, D.C. to Denver, Leadville, and Ten Mile. The principal actor was Samuel F. Emmons, or "Frank"

Emmons, as he was called, a man who had made his mark as one of the nation's leading geologists.

Emmons was a blue-blood if ever there was one. He came from a well-connected family in Massachusetts, studied at Harvard University, and then went on to the École des Mines in Paris and the Royal Mining Academy at Freiberg, Saxony. Later he joined the Fortieth Parallel Survey, where he made his reputation. When Congress created the United States Geological Survey in 1879, Clarence King, the first director, appointed Emmons chief of the Rocky Mountain Division. By this time the Leadville boom had struck full force, and King and his associates decided that Emmons should make a thorough geological study to complement others planned for Virginia City and Eureka, Nevada. [24]

Emmons was an incongruous figure in the mining camps. Outwardly he might have been anybody. Thirty-eight years old now, he was "tall, spare, rather harsh featured but distinguished looking," remembered Mary Hallock Foote, who got to know him well because the geologists camped in the woods behind the Foote cabin in Leadville (where they corraled many a home-cooked meal). Emmons had "a somewhat hawklike profile, deficient in chin, black hair, marked eyebrows, an open-air color on his thin cheekbones." And he was "always good natured, always imperturbable," although he was struggling along with an unhappy marriage. There the similarities ended. When in Leadville, he wore riding clothes of Indian-tanned white buckskin made by his London tailor. That made him conspicuous. He was also devoted to Turkish baths and Russian cigarettes. And though he had a few business interests on the side—like a preposterous plan to launch a national cattle trust—he was worlds apart from the silver-struck boomers. His interests were "wholly scientific and theoretical," remembered Mrs. Foote, and for an eminent geologist, "he was as fond of people as he was of rocks." [25]

When Emmons took charge in August 1879, he led a diverse group of scientists. W. F. Hillebrand, the chemist, hailed from the Sandwich Islands. Ernest Jacob, one of the assistant geologists, came from Ireland via the Royal School of Mines in London. Whitman Cross, the other assistant geologist, hailed from Massachusetts but had graduated with distinction from the University of Leipzig. Others then on board, or who would soon join the division, came from Brazil, France, Germany, Scotland, and Switzerland, as well as the United States. It was a truly international team that sought to bring the best thinking available to the study of central Colorado. [26]

Leadville came first. Emmons wasted little time in getting his men into the field to begin studying the bustling mining district still on the crest of its remarkable boom. The scientists spent much of the fall camped near the Footes' cabin above town, and from there they studied the geological features, mapped the ground, examined the workings below, and took ore samples to be assayed. Even after the first snows ended the fieldwork, Emmons resolved to forge ahead with "a winter's campaign in the mines." Throughout these long, frigid months, he and his men continued developing data for a book that would eventually become a landmark in the field of economic geology.

As Emmons expanded his fieldwork, he and his men worked their way up the east fork of the Arkansas River toward Fremont Pass, and once again the historical dynamic of the region was about to repeat—the logic of events in Leadville were about to spill into Ten Mile. Emmons eventually decided that to define his studies of Leadville, he needed more precise information on the geology of other mining districts. It was this quest that brought him into the mountains near Kokomo in the summer of 1880. And so the first systematic study of the geology and mining industry of Ten Mile devolved in an offhanded way from the systematic, searching work on Leadville.

By September, Emmons had established a Ten Mile team consisting of Cross and Jacob, the assistant geologists; A. D. Wilson, the topographer; and Arthur Lakes, a young mining engineer who seemed to be a jack-of-all-trades. They established a work camp on Sheep Mountain, and by the end of the month, said Emmons, Cross "had traced the serpentine boulders to their source and found many interesting and complicated phenomena connected with the porphyritic eruptions." When Emmons joined his colleagues, his "first occupation" was "to catalogue and take chips from the rocks already collected." Yet the scientists had only this month of September, for Emmons knew that "the season would probably not admit of much geologizing among these high peaks." That made it imperative to curtail the survey, for "months could easily have been spent, when only weeks could be given."

Although Emmons decided to exclude everything that did not have a direct bearing on the study of Leadville, this proved impossible—the Ten Mile project took on a life of its own. Emmons himself began discussing the intrinsic features of "the famous Robinson, Wheel of Fortune, and White Quail mines." But the season was against them. In late September "a most unprecedented snowstorm" brought the study "to an abrupt termination." Unlike previous storms, "the snow lay without melting sensibly," a crust formed every night, and the animals could no longer forage. One that wandered away was thought to be stolen. Emmons switched his men to underground work, but after two days they quit for the year, although Jacob made several quick trips to Ten Mile that fall. [27]

The Ten Mile study now ran into one problem after another. Funds were tight, and Emmons had to give top priority to pushing the work on Leadville. Then the comptroller in Washington ruled that the government would not pay room and board at a hotel for more than thirty days at a time, a decision that Emmons claimed put "a practical prohibition on the work of mining geology." Whatever hopes he held for Ten Mile in 1881, his division could do little more than devote about six weeks time, mostly in September, to studying the topography and geology, although this was enough to bring the map very near to completion. [28]

It was much the same story in 1882. Emmons knew he had yet to make a systematic study of the geology and the mines, although he thought such work would take only two or three months in the field. After that, the chemists would analyze the ore samples. As late as August, when Emmons got Jacob and several others to Ten Mile, he thought he could finish the survey by the end of the year. But against his hopes was the effort of his new boss, John Wesley Powell, to hold down costs.

In late August, Emmons toured the various mining districts (partly by using free passes offered to mining men attending the annual meetings of the American Institute of Mining Engineers). He sent Cross to help Jacob finish the geological study that now appeared to be more complicated than they had anticipated. And after hiring several new assistants, he went to Robinson, where he spent much of September examining the geology and the mines, directing corrections to the map, and obtaining plats of the underground workings from surveyors in Leadville.

The work went forward under less than optimal living conditions. Because of his tight financial constraints, Emmons lodged his men at the Robinson Hotel, which they all found "far less agreeable" than camping—as they were crowded together, three or four in a room, "which was far from clean," and "the food was of poor quality and badly cooked." The financial situation was even worse, embarrassing really. As Powell suggested, Emmons tried paying for board in rations, but given the current price of provisions, he found the survey ration would yield only fifty cents per day per man. That would hardly pay board. Emmons wrote Powell that he would have preferred to pay his team's expenses out of his own pocket.

By the end of September, however, Emmons found the geology clearly taking shape in his mind. He remembered that two years before, his first glance had given him the impression that Ten Mile's geology was extremely simple. But now he found the valley so "unexpectedly interesting" and "intensely complicated" that he thought it important to provide as much detail as possible. Yet the season did not cooperate. The high altitude, the foot of snow that covered the ground, and the blinding snowstorms hamstrung research. There was also a dearth of adequate personnel. Emmons and Cross had to leave in late September, and one of the replacements, a Swiss scientist, spoke English so poorly he had to be transferred. To find a replacement, Emmons turned to a local mining engineer, Victor G. Hills, who was willing to work at the "moderate compensation" of five dollars per day because he wanted to prepare a map for his own use. [29]

The task of completing the fieldwork now fell largely to Jacob and Hills. While Jacob focused on geology, Hills began a complete triangulation of the district from a baseline measured on the railroad near Robinson. Working closely with his assistant, Arthur Redman Wilfley, Hills ran stadia lines to all the important mines and other significant features in the valley. Emmons grew increasingly annoyed that Jacob and Hills were taking so much time, although he conceded that because of the small pay, he had agreed that Hills could do his research at intervals in his own business. In December, Emmons finally wrote Hills to finish the fieldwork as fast as possible. Jacob, however, did not complete his geological study until January 1883, and because of further corrections, Hills could not deliver the map until the end of the month. [30]

Other members of the survey had studied Ten Mile in Denver. By November, most of the rock samples had arrived for Cross and Hillebrand to begin their microscopic and chemical analyses. But even in Denver there were delays, at least one "owing to the imperfection of the platinum apparatus obtained at great expense in England." Once Jacob and Hills completed their research, the mapmakers finally took over. Yet not until March 1883 could Emmons send the first copy to an engraver in New York. Throughout this time the Ten Mile project struggled forward in the long shadow cast by the massive study of Leadville, and also had to contend for time and money with lesser mining areas like Golden and Silver Cliff. Ten Mile stood far from top priority, no doubt because of its decline as an ore producer, although statements to that effect never appeared in Emmons' letters to Powell. [31]

Despite the innumerable delays, by the spring of 1883, Emmons thought the Ten Mile study would soon be published. The fieldwork seemed virtually complete, the laboratory analyses were approaching an end, and the map was nearly ready. But money remained so tight that

Emmons did not have enough to carry any project to completion. Work on Ten Mile ground to a halt for months on end. At last in October, with the research nearly complete, he began writing the report. Yet he made little progress and still hoped to get some up-to-date reports on conditions in Ten Mile, particularly at the Robinson mine. [32]

The Ten Mile study now seemed to grind on without direction. In August 1884, Emmons reported that except for Jacob's detailed geological notes, the material for the report was all in hand; the monograph would be short; and he would take up the writing once he finished the Leadville study. Yet he completed nothing that year. Emmons and his men did a little research on Ten Mile in 1885 and more in 1886. But still, no Ten Mile report. In fact, none on any of the districts under study. In July 1886, Emmons confessed he was discouraged. The study nearest completion was the huge monograph on Leadville—he was correcting the page proofs—but Ten Mile and the others still languished; and owing to the press of work at the Government Printing Office, Emmons concluded that it was "useless to attempt to prophecy the date of their publication." [33]

So the work continued in its desultory way. Cross made some "final" studies of the rocks, there were a few more alterations to the map, and in October 1886, Emmons visited Ten Mile not so much to engage in any systematic investigation, but more to observe certain points bearing upon the theory of ore deposits. Once back in Washington, he again turned to writing the report, now that the Leadville monograph had been published. By June 1887, he had carried the study to an advanced stage along with the monograph on Silver Cliff, but "for various reasons," he noted, it was "not possible to foresee exactly at what time they will be ready for publication." [34]

Emmons could not know that the Ten Mile monograph was many years away from the printing press. And perhaps it was just as well. As 1887 drew to a close, the low-grade ores and hard-to-reduce sulfides had brought the industry to a virtual standstill. The time had long passed when his survey might have helped the miners in Ten Mile—there was little demand for a study ironically developed as the district declined. Yet one man undoubtedly benefitted from doing research for the monograph. This was Arthur Redman Wilfley, who had run some of the stadia lines with Jacob and Hills.

Wilfley had arrived in the boom, when the mines seemed a good bet to rival their famous counterparts in Leadville. He had witnessed the storied events at Robinson, the euphoric coming of the railroad, and the tragic burning of Kokomo. Perhaps he should have left, like so many

ARTHUR REDMAN WILFLEY. By the late 1880s, Wilfley had emerged as the most important miner in Ten Mile, but his most significant achievements still lay ahead. Courtesy Jay E. Niebur.

others, as life in the valley floundered in an ocean of low-grade sulfides. Yet there was the paradox: Wilfley prospered as mining in Ten Mile sank farther and farther into the doldrums.

Very little will ever be known about Wilfley's formative years, but it seems clear that he came from humble origins. He was born at Maryville, Missouri, in 1860, the middle child in the eleven born to Redman and Maria Wilfley. A veteran of the Mexican War, Redman was a none-too-successful miller with a penchant for wanderlust and martial glory. The Wilfleys always seemed to be on the move, and Arthur received a scanty education. His most important learning came in the various mills that Redman owned and operated. While still a boy, Arthur obtained considerable experience with machinery and engineering.

Wilfley might never have come to the Rocky Mountains except for the Leadville boom. In 1878, the feverish news of silver strikes at Leadville burst over the nation. Their hopes sparked, Redman and Maria packed their belongings and moved west with Arthur, now eighteen, and the younger children. Arthur rode the rails in an open flatcar to guard the sawmill boiler the Wilfleys intended to set up at Leadville. They would make their living that way while they searched for rich claims. This was by no means a novel strategy. Many individuals made a living at one business or another while they looked for the big bonanza on the side. George B. Robinson was just one example.

By the time he arrived in Leadville, age and circumstance had wrought the physique and character that Arthur Redman Wilfley would bear through life. He was about average in build; he had no really distinguishing physical characteristics; he might have been anyone. But there the similarities ended. If Redman was boisterous, hard-living, even dissolute on occasion, then his son Arthur was much the opposite. He neither smoke, nor drank, nor danced, nor played cards—not because he had any moral or religious objections, but because he thought they wasted time. Wilfley had a Calvinist devotion to work. He was also quiet and shy, perhaps even taciturn, and he was about to begin suffering from chronic chest pains caused by a congenital heart condition.

As planned, the Wilfleys went first to Leadville, but they found the competition ferocious, and coupled with that was the breathtaking news from Ten Mile, which was boomed as another Leadville. Before the year was out, they set their sights on Kokomo, and that was where the census taker found them in 1880. By now, however, they had turned from sawmilling to mining, not as mineowners or managers but as hard-rock miners who trudged up the mountainsides at dawn, toiled in the darkness by day, and drifted down the steep trails, exhausted, at twilight. What happened to the sawmill enterprise is a matter of conjecture.

From the outset, Arthur Redman Wilfley was not the typical hard-rock miner. As time permitted—mostly his single day off on weekends—he prospected on the peaks that loomed above Kokomo. He was particularly attracted to Fletcher Peak, the gnarled gray spire that towered over the valley east of town. By the end of 1881, he had staked his first claims, some above timberline, which he worked as best he could, living in a crude rock shelter that he built under an overhang.

Throughout 1882, Wilfley began spending less and less time as a hard-rock miner and more and more as an entrepreneur. He formed a number of partnerships for prospecting and mining, particularly on the shoulders of Pacific Peak, another spire on the east side of the valley. He also studied assaying with J. C. Staats, the chemist at the Kokomo smelter and a lessee of the Robinson mine. Even more significant, Wilfley struck up a friendship with Victor G. Hills, who took a special interest in him. After Wilfley attended to business by day, he studied in Hills' office by night. It was through Hills that Wilfley began working with Emmons' team on the Ten Mile survey. [35]

All this bore fruit in 1883. For a man whose formal education was so rudimentary, Wilfley made such rapid progress under Hills' tutelage that in February he passed the examination to become a deputy mineral surveyor. Then, in March, the two men formed a partnership as "civil and mining engineers" who did "all branches of engineering."

Over the next year Wilfley surveyed claims in Iron Mask Gulch and on Mayflower Hill, Fletcher Mountain, and Pacific Peak. He also located, bought, and sold what claims he could. All in all he made a fair income, but Ten Mile's steady decline had the inevitable consequences. For one, Wilfley's family moved back to Missouri, although Redman began coming out summers to work for Arthur. For another, in 1884, Hills and Wilfley dissolved their partnership when Hills decided to relocate in Pueblo, where he became an ore buyer. Wilfley then abandoned his own work as a surveyor to take a job as the superintendent or foreman at the White Quail mine. [36]

By this time the White Quail enterprise had fallen on hard times. Though long the largest producer on Elk Mountain, the firm's prospects had dwindled since the glory days of the district. The company had apparently gone belly up, and the assets, mostly the mine and surface buildings, had come into the hands of George R. Snowden, an attorney in Philadelphia. In 1884, he leased the mine to William Gleason of Leadville and J. B. Lovell of Denver (the former business manager of the White Quail Company). In May 1885, however, Gleason stepped aside, and Wilfley and Lovell took control of the lease.

Lovell recognized that the White Quail needed many capital improvements. One was a new adit to reduce the cost of mining. Another was a new mill, because the current plant, located in the old smelter buildings, was not much use. That summer Lovell persuaded Snowden and his associates to extend the lease two years, until August 1887, and reduce their share of the net smelter returns to 20 percent. In return, Wilfley and Lovell agreed to invest $5,000 to lower the incline track, retimber the workings as needed, and drive the new adit from Searle Gulch.

This arrangement, however, said nothing about a new mill. Instead, Lovell agreed to invest the $5,000 to develop the mine, while Wilfley formed a partnership with Henry D. Clark and David D. Colcord, two well-known mining men in Ten Mile, to build a mill that would concentrate the ores shipped from the White Quail and other mines. This left Wilfley so strapped for cash that he had to lease several other mines in Ten Mile to keep going. [37]

By 1886, Wilfley and his partners had completed the new mill, but not the new adit. It went forward very slowly. The prices of silver and lead declined, the returns from the mine did not pay the expected costs of driving, and Wilfley had to contend with his painful heart condition and manage his other business ventures. Wilfley and Lovell also had their differences, particularly when Wilfley began to pay himself a salary against the written terms of the partnership agreement that specified that Wilfley's work was to be free.

Far more important than these problems were the almost perpetual negotiations that Lovell conducted with Snowden to extend and modify the lease. The Philadelphians were reluctant to do so, but always caved in. They had little choice except see the mine close. This was particularly true in 1887, when Wilfley and Lovell estimated the cost of completing the adit at $20,000, and Lovell used this figure to persuade Snowden and his colleagues to plow back all their returns into one-half the construction costs and extend the lease another two years. This agreement nearly fell through when Snowden learned that Wilfley had located the adit in his name only. The Philadelphians were irate. But Lovell managed to renegotiate the contract, with the result that the White Quail Company took control of the adit, while the lease was extended another two years until June 1891.

As they drove the adit deep into Elk Mountain, they quietly approached the owners of adjacent mines, notably Henry I. Higgins, president of the American Mining and Smelting Company. Higgins was so discouraged by the valley's prospects that he wrote he would consider "any proposition" for a lease. As a result, Wilfley and Lovell took over the Climax and Aftermath, which could be mined through the adit. Lovell encouraged this strategy. He wrote Wilfley that they "had better secure all the intervening property through which the tunnel is to be driven and to do this *at once.*"

By 1887, Wilfley had clearly made his mark in Ten Mile. Even though he owned none of the mines on Elk Mountain and only a share of the mill, the whole complex was coming to be known as "the Wilfley mine." Yet some people thought that Wilfley was "crazy" to spend so much money driving an adit that would eventually revert to the White Quail Company. But Wilfley was never one to take counsel from naysayers. While he drew a grim picture for Lovell and Snowden (and nearly everyone else)—an endless recital of hard rock, low-grade sulfides, and poor prices for metal—he painted a far more optimistic portrait for his mentor, Hills. In July 1887, Wilfley wrote that he thought the mine would "positively net $1,500,000.00."[38]

Wilfley's personal life was also taking a different tack. He took a fashion to Ethel Thomas of Robinson, perhaps the daughter of Mr. and Mrs.

Thomas who had hosted that splendid New Year's party so long ago, it seemed, in 1881. But Ethel's family forced her to break off the romance. Early in 1886, however, Wilfley met Addie Farnham, a new arrival from Tenant's Harbor, Maine. Addie had ostensibly come to Kokomo to teach school and live with her aunt, Kate Colcord, the wife of one of Wilfley's business partners. In June, Wilfley proposed a marriage, but Addie refused, apparently because of someone back in Maine. Wilfley persisted, however, and finally Addie accepted. To have a church wedding, they went over to Leadville, where they were married on November 23, 1886. And just for this occasion, Wilfley spent seventy-five dollars on a new suit, by family tradition the only one he ever bought.

Once married, Wilfley resumed his work—or overwork—in the minerals industry. At one time or another he leased nearly all the mines that once figured so prominently in the carbonate boom—the Snow Bank, the Forest, the Nettie B., even the Robinson. When their output was combined with that of the White Quail, Aftermath, and Climax leases, it seems that through much of 1886, 1887, and 1888, Wilfley and his various partners were mining, milling, and shipping much of Ten Mile's production. Yet Wilfley's heart condition and his overworking created havoc with his health—not the best situation for man expecting his first child, as Arthur and Addie were in 1887.

Besides the birth of a daughter, May, this year proved to be a significant one in Wilfley's career. Once the Philadelphians extended the lease until June 1891, Wilfley gave much more of his attention to driving the adit from Searle Gulch. This required capital, and despite the substantial ore shipments made in 1887, Wilfley found himself in serious financial straits as winter approached. The adit was now a thousand feet into the depths of Elk Mountain; it had already cost $15,000, which was far more than the original estimate; and it was nowhere near completion. Wilfley concluded that he needed another $11,000 to finish the job. Lovell was so discouraged that he wanted to quit the lease. Only Wilfley, it seems, remained hopeful.

Wilfley did what he had to in order to raise the money. Somewhat in desperation, he approached Mary A. Clark, the mother of Henry D. Clark, his partner in the Wilfley mill. She agreed to loan Wilfley the money he needed, but only in return for a share in the profits in the Aftermath and White Quail leases and from the adit itself. It was a stiff price to pay, but Wilfley had no other choice.

With this new infusion of capital, Wilfley pressed forward with greater resolve. At Lovell's insistence, he bought new machinery to expedite drilling, but this only added to costs. To augment his cash flow, Wilfley mined more ores than perhaps he should have (it retarded the advance of the adit). But through the late winter and on into the spring and summer, Wilfley drove himself and his miners and did what he could to meet the deadline set for September. Yet September came and went with the adit still unfinished. Wilfley's crews struggled on through autumn, and finally in December 1888, they broke through to the White Quail workings far underground. They may have celebrated the completion of this arduous project, but not Wilfley, for that was not the Wilfley way. He merely noted in his books that the final cost had come to $28,567, of which he had invested $17,725 and the White Quail Company another $10,842.

But if Wilfley eschewed celebration, he wasted no time in exploiting the ore body. After dissolving some of his older partnerships, he formed a new one with Ethan E. Byron. A Ten Mile miner originally from Maine, Byron had won Wilfley's confidence by serving as foreman in the latter stages of the adit project. The two men got along well, and in the first seven months they operated the White Quail, Wilfley netted $25,000 in profits.

Wilfley, however, still owned only a small portion of the Wilfley mine—a few minor claims with Henry D. Clark—but with profits coming from the adit, he clearly saw the possibility of consolidating all the important properties on Elk Mountain. In April 1889, he took a one-year option on the Aftermath, Climax, and Milo, owned by the American Mining and Smelting Company. The same month he bought a half interest in the Avalanche, Modern Science, Onward, Viligia, Silver Bullion, and other claims. Then in November he bought out Clark, and in December he acquired a fifty-six acre placer at the foot of Searle Gulch so as to obtain a clear title to the land on which stood the Wilfley mill and the portal of the adit.

Wilfley was hardly through. In April 1890, he exercised his option to purchase the Aftermath, Climax, and all other claims owned by the American Company. But his major effort involved the White Quail itself. Silver prices rose sharply in 1890 owing to the passage of the Sherman Silver Purchase Act. Snowden and the Philadelphians probably saw this as an opportune time to sell, for the value of the mine had risen with the price of silver. Wilfley opened negotiations with Snowden, and in the early summer, Wilfley paid $50,000 for the entire stock of the White Quail Company. Then he bought Lovell's share of the lease for another $20,000. By July 1890, Wilfley controlled the properties that had borne his name for several years.

By this time, however, Wilfley no longer made his home in Ten Mile. His success had helped keep the valley alive, but his efforts did little to revitalize the boom. Kokomo, Recen, Robinson, and the other camps continued to decline, and they were no place for a prosperous mining man to raise a family. Arthur and Addie were expecting again in 1889. With the adit complete, that spring they decided to relocate in Denver, a standard practice for successful mining men, but they stayed in Kokomo until Addie gave birth to their second child, a son named George, that August. But even if he now lived in Denver, Wilfley never severed his connections with Ten Mile. He remained intimately associated with the fortunes of the district while he managed from afar through Ethan E. Byron. [39]

Not content with the status quo, Wilfley and Byron kept looking for new ways to increase their returns from the White Quail. This meant that they had to do something about complex, low-grade sulfides. About this time Wilfley and Byron heard of the Austin process of pyritic smelting, a method designed to use very little fuel—only enough to raise the sulfides to the point of combustion, after which they would burn, thus furnishing the heat required for their own reduction. [40]

Among the first enterprises to adopt the Austin process was the Bi-Metallic Smelting Company of Leadville. Controlled by a group of well-known mining men that included David H. Moffat, Jr., and Eben Smith, as well as James C. Wigginton, who had worked briefly in Ten Mile during the boom, the Bi-Metallic firm had remodeled the defunct La Plata smelter and gone into business in 1891. So far as anyone knew, the enterprise was successful.

Late in 1891, Wilfley and Byron learned that the Austin patents were controlled in Colorado by the Union Mining and Smelting Company. Besides Austin, who resided afar, the chief figure in this enterprise was Thomas F. Walsh, an Irishman who had prospered in Leadville in much the same way that Wilfley had prospered in Ten Mile. Wilfley and Walsh probably knew one another because they had offices two doors apart in the Boston Building in Denver. Unknown to Wilfley and Byron, however, just about this time Austin wrote Walsh that they should try "to acquire interests in mining properties above everything else."

Common objectives went hand in hand. By March the two parties had agreed to organize the Summit Mining and Smelting Company to build a pyritic smelter near Kokomo. If the plant was successful, Wilfley and Byron would convey a one-half interest in the White Quail Company to the new firm in return for one-half its capital stock. The Summit Company would take over the leases that Walsh and Austin had acquired near Kokomo, and they in turn would receive the other half of the capital stock.

Construction began immediately. Walsh supervised most of the build-

INGOTS AT THE SUMMIT SMELTER. Built by Wilfley and his associates in the early 1890s, the plant never lived up to expectations because of faulty technology, complex ore, and low prices for metal. Harry H. Buckwalter photographer, courtesy Colorado Historical Society.

ing of this the first smelter constructed in Ten Mile in nearly a decade. The Rio Grande Railway ran a spur into the plant, and once the track was in place, Wilfley began shipping ore. Walsh hired Albert I. Goodell, an experienced smelterman, to run the plant, and in September, they began a series of trial runs on Wilfley's ore. The tests convinced Wilfley and Byron that the plant could reduce the ores from Elk Mountain, and in November they closed the deal with Walsh and Austin. The Summit Company was reorganized. Wilfley became president, Walsh vice-president, and Byron treasurer and assistant general manager. Unknown to Wilfley and Byron, however, it was just at this time that Austin wrote Walsh that he thought that "much ingenuity" had been shown in the construction of the Leadville and Kokomo smelters, but they were not what he would have built *"for the particular problem in hand."* The trouble, wrote Austin, was that the ore was "either too low in values, too zinky, or too fine."

Although the new plant had cost $60,000, no sooner had Wilfley and Byron closed the deal than operations went sour. The smelter ran profitably in October and November, but it posted a loss for December. Silver was falling in price, and that was one reason, an ominous one. Wilfley thought that he could convert the losses to profits through the economies of scale. He increased production at the mine, mill, and smelter, but throughout the winter, he could show nothing but red ink— losses at the smelter, losses at the White Quail, and losses at the Robinson, Bledsoe, and Iron Mask leases acquired from Walsh and Austin. Because the losses were small, Wilfley hoped that increasing production would eliminate them, but nothing worked, in part because of the continuing fall in silver prices. Finally, in May 1893, scarcely six months after taking the smelter, Wilfley and his associates declared it a failure.

By good luck, however, the Summit Company had expanded operations elsewhere. In September 1892, Wilfley had set out for the booming camps of Fremont and Hayden Placer, located west of Colorado Springs. Intrigued by the prospects of what would soon become Cripple Creek, a fabulous gold-mining area, Wilfley persuaded his partners to buy three claims for the Summit firm and agreed to loan the company the money it needed. This proved to be a good investment, for the Summit Company earned $45,000 from these mines in the first six months of 1893. [41]

Wilfley was by no means the only miner in Ten Mile during these years. Other men tried just as hard in hope of striking a rich ore body, lowering costs, or keep going on the chance that the price of silver and lead might rise enough to bring their marginal properties into production. Yet throughout the late 1880s and early 1890s, all the principal mines remained in the hands of lessees until Wilfley himself broke the pattern when he acquired the White Quail.

During these years the Breckenridge newspapers offered flashes of information like the bits and pieces that once filled the columns of the Ten Mile papers. In 1887, for example, the editors reported that "the boys" leasing the Grand Union mine on Chalk Mountain had readied for shipping three carloads of ore averaging eighty ounces of silver per ton. The White Quail concentrator ran as usual "to the benefit of the owners and the community." Mr. Wilson of the Enterprise mine had encountered a fine streak of mineral that promised to turn out well. On Fletcher Mountain, the Callahan brothers had hired a dozen men and were jacking some very high-grade ore down to Kokomo. And after a four-year hiatus, the Maximus had come back into production under a group of lessees. [42]

But aside from the Wilfley mine, it could not be denied that the industry produced very little. In 1888, the Delphos mine shipped nearly $100,000 in ore and concentrates, but its nearest rival, the Queen of the West, sent less than $50,000, partly because the Recens were ensnarled in a legal thicket over loan payments to Robert S. Brookings and his silent partner, Samuel Cupples. The Felicia Grace and the Nova Scotia Boy shipped less than $20,000 each, while the Wheel of Fortune, Nettie B., Colonel Sellers, and Crown Point shipped nothing at all. The Robinson kept its output confidential, but whatever it was, it was anything but spectacular.

The story was very much the same in 1889 and 1890. While Wilfley continued shipping substantial amounts of ore from Elk Mountain, there was comparatively little production from most other mines. The Queen of the West had a modest output. The Robinson declined to reveal its production, as was the company's practice now, but its output for both years combined was probably no more than $125,000. Perhaps the most important new producer was the Delphos, which had a spectacular year in 1889 when it produced more than $200,000 while owned and managed by Wilfley and Mary A. Clark. This good record continued into 1890, when the mine shipped more than $150,000. [43]

One important change in Ten Mile during these years was the appointment of Jesse F. McDonald as superintendent of the Robinson mine. A native of Ashtabula, Ohio, where he was born in 1858, McDonald had grown up in Pennsylvania. At an early age, he displayed a penchant for engineering, and in 1879, he headed for Leadville, where tradition says he arrived with nothing more than a coin for breakfast money. But McDonald never starved. He got a job as a chainman for a survey party, and after that, he rose fast. He became first a mining engineer and then a mine manager, and that brought him to the attention of the Robinson Company, which hired him in the late 1880s. [44]

Before spending more money on development, McDonald sought a new evaluation of the mine. He approached two well-known men in Leadville: Henry E. Wood, proprietor of a highly regarded sampling agency, and Philip Argall, a portly, young British mining engineer making a large reputation for himself. When Wood and Argall examined the Robinson in February 1889, they were none-too-impressed. Over the years, they said, the lessees had "practically exhausted" the shipping ores in the old workings, and were now mining into the deep limestone in search of new ore bodies. The most·favorable statement that Wood and Argall could make was that the mine had "a first-class double-tracked tunnel" driven into the mountainside from the old smelter buildings.

The mine had been developed in three chutes, none of them in very good shape or holding much promise. At the No. 1 Chute, the workings had caved in, and water had risen. Wood and Argall were informed, however, that the chute still contained "large quantities of high grade ore." At the No. 2 Chute, the shipping ore had been "largely worked out," but Wood and Argall were "confident" that it held about 100,000 tons averaging about fifteen ounces of silver each, all of which could be concentrated and shipped. At the No. 3 Chute, which the lessees had developed on their own, the ore was mostly low-grade, holding about twenty-two ounces of silver per ton. Wood and Argall had little positive to say about the surrounding claims, although there were indications of a large chute of low-grade ore in the Big Giant.

Despite this discouraging assessment, Wood and Argall ended their report with guarded optimism. The leasing system in vogue for the past four years, they said, had prevented any systematic development and left the property "in an unfavorable condition." Only "a vigorous development policy" could offer the hope of finding new ore bodies. Wood and Argall recommended just such a plan. If the enterprise followed their suggestions and built a 100-ton concentrator to treat the ore in sight and the rock on the mine dump, the Robinson would yield a profit of about two dollars per ton. [45]

Aside from the annual predictions of a revival, the coming of the 1890s brought little to stem the decline. The first half of 1891 went fairly well, but then came a stunning setback in October when fire destroyed the Wilfley mill. That curtailed shipments immediately, for Ten Mile had no other concentrator. The price of silver also fell below $1.00 an ounce, putting more pressure on miners. Despite these problems, the White Quail produced nearly $100,000, and other mines perhaps as much as $250,000, but this was the lowest output since the rush began.

Yet hope continued. "Never has the New Year dawned upon us more auspiciously," proclaimed one resident of Kokomo on the eve of 1892. The district was "never more prosperous" and would soon rival Aspen and Leadville. But 1892 brought little change. The heavy snows retarded mining as always. There were reports of people leaving for Creede and Cripple Creek. But aside from an increase in production at the White Quail, a rise no doubt influenced by the construction of the Summit smelter, the mines shipped little more than they had the year before; and as 1892 ended, disastrous days loomed unforeseen just over the horizon. [46]

And so another year had come and gone, and in pretty much the same fashion. Hopes in the spring, increasing production in summer and fall, and discouragement come winter, when reality indicated that output had fallen. The cycle seemed as endless as the slow but steady decline. Yet mining, however central, was only one aspect of life in Ten Mile. There were social, political, and religious endeavors as well, to say nothing of business ventures besides mining, which to a large degree mirrored the vicissitudes of mining itself.

CHAPTER 9

Until Gabriel Sounds His Horn

IF Ten Mile had suffered from one shock—in George B. Robinson's death—as 1880 came to a close, then it sustained two even harder blows as the year 1881 drifted down to its end. And what a bitter end that was! The burning of Kokomo, followed hard by the collapse of the Robinson Company, had done far more to numb the valley than the sudden demise of its most famous miner. No matter how startling Robinson's shooting had been, his mining company endured, a steady employer bent on expansion. But as the winter of 1881 descended on Ten Mile, the flames of October had turned homes and businesses into charred embers and wind-blown ashes, and after that, the closing of the Robinson mine threw many men out of work, no one knew for how long.

Despite these misfortunes, few people in Ten Mile seemed ready to quit. The mines were about to complete their most prosperous year, and the future still looked remarkably bright. Kokomo would be rebuilt, and perhaps the Robinson Company might stage a renaissance.

After the devastating fire of October 13, the Rio Grande Railway and the Recen brothers stepped to the fore. Within days the railroad offered to carry building materials from Leadville to Kokomo at no cost to buyers, and the Recens broadcast their offer to give lots to anyone who would erect a building worth more than $300, begin construction within thirty days, and complete the work in a reasonable time. Many individuals took advantage of the offers. That October, the Summit County *Times*, the United States Post Office, the merchants J. N. Harder and

197

Thomas Latta, as well as the mining engineer Victor G. Hills, all decided to cast their lots in Recen. Others, however, chose to relocate to Robinson, and a few decided that it was time to quit Ten Mile for good.

As the snows descended over the valley, the sawmills whirred anew, hammers cracked through the chilly air, and the frames of new homes and businesses rose where there had been nothing but open space. In parceling out lots, the Recens did very much what Amos Smith had done two years before at Kokomo—they chose the business and commercial areas, and they reserved a site for the Odd Fellows, a second for a church, a third for the Masons, and so forth. Some individuals, businessmen in particular, wanted specific sites; so in spite of the offer of free lots, some people paid for a desired location.

There were two ironies in reconstruction, however. The Recen brothers expected their community to be known as Recen, but the people who moved there preferred the name Kokomo. The Post Office failed to change its address, mail came addressed to Kokomo, and so the town acquired the hybrid name of Kokomo-Recen, or remained known simply as Kokomo, even though Mr. Smith's town had ceased to exist. The same thing happened to the main thoroughfare; in Recen, it was technically Pollock Avenue, named after the old pioneer William P. Pollock, but because the street was a continuation of Ten Mile Avenue in old Kokomo, it remained known as Ten Mile Avenue.

By the spring of 1882, the bustling town resembled something of the old Kokomo on the hillside above. The one- and two-story business structures, generally built on long narrow lots measuring 25 by 100 feet, faced Ten Mile Avenue, their tall narrow windows and doors cut in a facade highlighted by fancy cornices on false fronts. Down the streets ran long wooden boardwalks. A few had railings, but most did not. Houses were set back on the sidestreets or built on the mountain slopes. Most were one-story buildings—some log, some frame, some clapboard over logs—but in any case they had few rooms. Poorer people used newspapers for insulation and wallpaper, while the more prosperous had wallpaper itself. Some homeowners eventually planted small plots of grass surrounded by low picket fences, but others had nothing more than a boardwalk set across the front. And if a house nestled on a hillside, as so many did, it offered boys and girls a chance to go sledding from the doorsteps during the winter. Out back, many houses still had platforms where women could stand above the drifts to hang clothes. [1]

Kokomo was not the only Ten Mile town to feed the flames of destruction. Scarcely six months later on April 27, 1882, a fire broke out in Wheeler. Again, the exact origin was never determined, but about 3:30

AN ORE SLEIGH. Though best known in Ten Mile's early development, ore sleighs were used well into the twentieth century. William Creamer photographer, courtesy Alice R. Work.

on Thursday afternoon, people on the street sniffed the pungent smell of woodsmoke, and moments later they saw orange flames and black smoke burst through the upper windows of the building next to the post office. The alarm rang out and volunteers rushed to the scene, but Wheeler had no fire fighting equipment. People hurried to save whatever they could. A whole cluster of buildings "went like a flash," said one commentator. The frantic efforts of several persons finally stemmed the flames, and the only casualty was Mrs. Wheeler's badly sprained ankle. Yet gone to charred embers that night were Judge Wheeler's store, billiard hall, and blacksmith shop, as well as the post office, milk house, and office building. The headline of a Kokomo newspaper summed up the story:

FIRE AT WHEELER

The Little Gem in the Ten Mile Valley Almost Obliterated

Like many people in Kokomo, Judge Wheeler decided to rebuild. He had some insurance, but to begin immediately, he went to Ordean's Summit County Bank, where he borrowed $1,500, paying a whopping interest charge of 2 percent per month. Wheeler hurried to reestablish his enterprises, but he never recovered. A year later, in June 1883, when the judge was unable to pay the debt and interest charges, the bank foreclosed, and in July, Wheeler's property was auctioned off at the Kokomo post office. [2]

The burning of Wheeler was by no means the last flirtation that Ten Mile had with the flames of destruction. The new Kokomo-Recen had a brief dalliance with disaster. In the evening darkness of October 6, 1883, an arsonist placed a cigar box filled with paper and matches against the wall of a wagon shop. Once ignited, the flames licked their way through the dry wood and might have engulfed the whole town. But nearby, the printers at the *Summit County News* chanced to be working late into the night. They discovered the fire, rushed out, and extinguished the blaze before it could spread. In next week's paper, published two years to the day after the Kokomo conflagration, the editors took note that the town had barely avoided "wholesale murder" done "at the hands of an incendiary." Many people might have been caught in bed asleep. The culprit, however, was not apprehended. [3]

While no one knows what motives smoldered in the heart of this arsonist, what seems certain is that alcohol ignited much of the violence that plagued Ten Mile. Many fights and shootings took place at the ubiquitous saloons where John Barleycorn flowed in abundance. Most men had ready access to firearms, and large numbers of lonely miners had little to do but drink in their off-hours. Discharging firearms at night became a popular pastime in Robinson. A shoot-out that November 1880 was only one of the worst offenses. In one of the saloons both shootists— one of them drunk—emptied their guns at close range, narrowly missing a little girl. One wonders what role alcohol may have played that December in the fusillade that greeted Mrs. Forbes and nearly killed Mrs. Stowall.

Yet Kokomo was hardly different. The same year Charley Norton, the proprietor of the Senate Saloon in Breckenridge, and his friend Patsey Thornton went drinking in Kokomo. Norton got drunk, developed a violent quarrel with another patron, and when the city marshall arrived to quell the disturbance, Norton allegedly shot the marshall. A crowd seized Norton and Thornton, threats of lynching spread through town, and for a time rumors insisted that Norton had in fact been hung. [4]

Police officials were hardly immune from assault. In June 1881, Al Huggins, described as "a well-known desperado of the Ten Mile," and Kokomo's ex-marshall Phillip G. Foote, called "not a bad character except when under the influence of liquor," both got drunk at a saloon in Kokomo and started firing their revolvers. When Huggins saw Donald Doncaster, the mayor of Recen, walking along the street, Huggins fired but missed. Thomas Brown, the policeman, ran up, but when he tried to quiet Huggins, all he received were "the vilest epithets" before Huggins shot him in the chest. Brown collapsed in the street, Huggins and Foote fled to Recen. Marshall Sutton of Kokomo then assembled a posse that went to Recen. When Huggins resisted arrest, someone shot him in the face with a shotgun. Sutton's posse took both men back to Kokomo. That afternoon, a vigilence committee formed to take action, particularly because Brown was a popular man, his fate uncertain. To avoid a possible lynching, Sutton hurried his prisoners to Robinson and put them on the train for Leadville. Foote escaped en route, and although Brown was thought to be mortally wounded, he did recover, which was fortunate for Huggins, who had to stand trial only for assault and battery with intent to kill. [5]

The shooting of Brown was hardly the final vestige of violence in Kokomo. In October 1882, Michael B. Marshall shot one Moran in self-defense. "Nice place, this Kokomo!" thundered the Breckenridge *Daily Journal*. Later that year in December, two other men—one a miner, the other an "ex-saloonist"—had a "shooting interview" in which both men were shot, one seriously. Two years later on an August night in 1884, a would-be assassin exploded some giant powder in front of the store owned by P. Y. Thomas the merchant. The blast shattered the front window, but failed to detonate the powder inside where Thomas and his family were sleeping. The *Summit County Journal* denounced the crime as "the most dastardly outrage ever perpetrated in a civilized town," as the Thomases might have been "hurled into infinity." But like the arsonist who had torched the wagon shop, this criminal escaped, despite a $200 reward.

Sudden violence also lurked outside the towns. In December 1881, Samuel Ogden, a prospector who lived near Robinson, told about Jack

Peters and Jerry Gallegher, two miners with a claim on Sheep Mountain. Although they had signed an agreement, it failed to work out, ostensibly because Gallegher drank too much. After a time they dissolved the partnership, but Gallegher must have felt aggrieved, for one night, "his brian inflamed with drink," he broke into Peters' cabin, set fire to the bed, and forced Peters to flee with nothing more than his night clothes. Peters escaped with no further assault on his life or his dignity, but Gallegher was ultimately forced to leave the valley. [6]

Not so lucky was Henry Bridenthal, a miner from Bedford, Pennsylvania. He worked at the Maximus mine on Fletcher Mountain until about March 1884, when he died under mysterious circumstances. After his body was found in the snow, debate ensued over his fate: had he been caught up in a snowslide outside his cabin? Or had a mysterious assailant killed him first? The authorities ultimately decided that Bridenthal had been murdered, and a $200 reward was posted for information, but that brought little result. The crime was never resolved, and the murderer escaped an appointment with Jack Ketch. [7]

Ten Mile also had its share of fisticuffs, larceny, and robbery. In July 1881, two drunks got into a particularly brutal fight outside a saloon in Robinson, and two years later in 1883, a court in town sentenced John Powers to twenty days in jail for stealing chickens. Far more serious was a crime committed against Captain John W. Jacque. In the summer of 1883, he was riding alone from Kokomo to Frisco when he was accosted by three road agents. They made his horse jump, and he was thrown to the ground and knocked unconscious. When Jacque revived, he found the trio had stolen his money and other possessions; the only thing they missed was his watch. The newspapers blamed the railroads, because their building contractors had hired disreputable people, but that must have brought little solace to Jacque, and the highwaymen were never apprehended. [8]

Claim disputes could still lead to violence. In June 1885, Frank Dougherty, Jack Mathews, and others apparently jumped the Crown Point mine owned by Judge Luther M. Goddard and others. The night watchman, J. Mercer, whom the company owed a reported $3,000, asked the management in Denver for instructions. When he received the vague reply to protect the property, Mercer told the alleged jumpers that he would start shooting in ten minutes unless they left. When they failed to depart, he proved as good as his word. The first victim was Dougherty, who was shot through the hip. Several miners brought him down the mountainside on a sled, but he lingered only a few hours, "suffering great agony" before he died. Mercer was charged with manslaughter. [9]

Aside from crime, tragedy struck through negligence, carelessness, or simply bad luck. In October 1881 a Rio Grande train steaming down Fremont Pass to Robinson lost its brakes and ran wild before the tracks parted throwing the locomotive off the rails, crushing the engineer, and injuring the brakeman so seriously that he was not expected to live. This was the worst that year on the Blue River Extension, a line poorly built and prone to accident.

The snow itself could be murderous. In January 1883 an avalanche near Frisco killed Fred Plate; not until July were his remains recovered and shipped back to Iowa. Three years later in January 1886 came an even worse tragedy when three men, Lawrence Braschke, a railroader; Peter Hanchon; and one McWilliams were killed in a Ten Mile snowslide. [10]

Illness and disease presented special problems. Georgia Burns, who lived in Robinson, remembered years later that "it was impossible to get a nurse in the camp and the only doctor was usually off on a drunk." Chloe, a black woman who sang in one of the local saloons, sometimes doubled as a nurse, at least for the Burns family. Ten Mile also witnessed the usual number of infant deaths, like the passing of Georgia's brother Harry, who apparently died of blood poisoning. Early in 1883, Ten Mile experienced a smallpox scare. There was talk of demanding compulsory vaccination and quarantine, but no epidemic developed. The most notable victims were a physician named Mellor and a male nurse, both of whom recovered. More dangerous than smallpox was pneumonia; several deaths in 1883 prompted the *Ten Mile News* to admonish everyone who felt the symptoms to consult a physician at once. "Delay is fatal." As a case in point the *News* reported that a miner named Dougan had died of pneumonia leaving a family back in Virginia. [11]

What seems remarkable is that some people thought that Ten Mile might be a good place to recover from disease—in this case, tuberculosis, which might be cured by the fresh air and dry climate. One person with this hope was Harry Learned, an artist, who was probably the cousin of William Gleason, the mining man. Though born in Scotland, Learned had emigrated to New York, where he did theatrical paintings, but contracted the disease and decided to leave for the Rocky Mountains in hope of a cure, which he apparently found. He spent eighteen years in Ten Mile, painting many Colorado scenes, including some of the district. [12]

Ten Mile also had its share of racial and ethnic tensions. In 1883 a worried Breckenridge *Daily Journal* reported that "celestials"—meaning Chinese—had arrived to work in the placer mines. This portended trouble. The Chinese were generally outcasts in the West, because they toiled for lower wages and allegedly displaced white labor, thus creating a vehement animosity that occasionally culminated in race riots and lynch law. No Chinese apparently came to Ten Mile, though there was apprehension. Yet Ten Mile did have a small number of blacks. Chloe and her daughter (last names unknown) arrived as early as December 1880. More blacks came as construction workers three years later for the Denver South Park and Pacific Railroad. The South Park also brought in gangs of Irish and Italians, who lived in their separate enclaves as did the blacks. More than once the tensions, misunderstandings, and prejudice of the day led to vicious fist fights and savage beatings. [13]

Life in Ten Mile, however, was by no means one of sickness and prejudice, violence and tragedy. Those phenomena captured the attention of the newspapers. There were also happy times like the New Year parties hosted by the Gowenlocks, the Thomases, and the Merry Mountaineers, and the summer festivities sponsored by Judge Wheeler. In June 1881, he ran a spectacular advertisement in the local newspapers: *"Fourth of July Celebration,"* proclaimed the headline. Below this the judge announced that Wheeler would celebrate "that greatest event in the history of the world"—the Declaration of Independence—with "orations, addresses, music, etc."

Wheeler's festivities drew ever more press as the day approached. The Breckenridge *Daily Journal* predicted the celebration would "probably be the most successful one which has ever taken place in the county." Besides prominent speakers, the judge had "everything of the best in the line of refreshments," the grounds were the finest available, and the groves of pine were "as beautiful as can be seen in any section of the mountains." The *Journal* predicted an especially large turnout from Kokomo and Robinson because those towns had made no special arrangements to celebrate independence. As the day neared, the *Journal* proclaimed in the unabashed patriotism of the day that Wheeler would see "a first-class, old fashioned Fourth of July time. The eagle will flap his wings and scream from crags a mile high, and the cheers from many throats will echo from rock to rock for miles away."

This inaugural celebration created something of a Ten Mile tradition. Even though Wheeler was still rebuilding from the fire in 1882 and suffered financial reverses in 1883, he continued his gala. If nothing else, it was good business. By 1883, the festivities had expanded to include

A VICTORIAN HOME IN RECEN. This spare structure was high class in Ten Mile. Bill Graff, who built the White Quail smelter and owned part of the Queen of the West mine, stands with the horse at left. Henry Recen with the black and white dog is on the boardwalk next to Graff. Daniel Recen sits in the cart at right. The others are unidentified. One of the Recens probably owned the house. Courtesy Recen Family Collection.

sporting events. The Robinson Mine challenged the County Seat "to play a match" of baseball. The organizers scheduled a horse race as well, although it had to be postponed two days because of bad weather. [14]

Affairs like this were annual celebrations only. On a week-to-week basis, the newspapers offered Ten Milers as much entertainment as they did news and advertising. Kokomo had obtained the valley's first newspaper when Coe and Macready established the *Summit County Times* in 1879, but they were hardly destined to enjoy a monopoly. In 1880 they began to compete with themselves when they launched the Robinson *Tribune*. Not long after came the *Ten Mile News*, the *Summit County Herald*, and the *Ten Mile Circular*. Not all Ten Milers devoted themselves to local papers, however. Some people preferred Leadville publications like the *Daily Herald*, the *Chronicle*, or the *Democrat*. Still others bought county newspapers like the Breckenridge *Daily Journal* or Redcliff's *Eagle River Shaft*.

For awhile, Coe and Macready had the best of the struggle with their *Summit County Times*, but after the Kokomo fire, they lost momentum. They took out a loan from the Bank of Leadville to obtain the capital needed to rebuild, and they came under fire from the Breckenridge *Daily Journal*, which decried the *Times*' masthead claiming the paper was published at a higher altitude than any other in the world. In the fall of 1882, Coe and Macready did away with this, much to the satisfaction of the *Journal*, which crowed that the *Times* had "at last stepped down from its perch of 'highest altitude, etc.' About time—after Robinson's *Tribune* had looked down upon it for more than a year."[15]

The change in the masthead, however, may have signalled deeper problems. Coe and Macready were unable to repay their loan, perhaps because the declining economy of Ten Mile could not support several newspapers. In September 1882, the Bank of Leadville took possession of the *Times* and put Edwin G. Hogan in charge. This was evidently an interim arrangement, however, for Hogan and J. S. Swan, the county assessor, bought the business later that fall.[16]

They had little success, however. In December, when they abruptly ceased publication, the *Journal* wondered if the *Times* had not "climbed the golden stairs." Before long, it became apparent that Hogan and Swan had gone the way of Coe and Macready. In late December the *Journal* bewailed that the *Times* "departed this life, aged three years." From the *Eagle River Shaft* rose the lament that "one by one the roses fade," and the editors intoned that they would "sadly miss the many bright gems of unique grammar that appeared in its columns the last weeks of its tender life." Not to be outdone, the *Ten Mile News* observed that through "a powerful effort" by Hogan and Swan, "the corpse was resurrected to enjoy a posthumous existence," but now it had "sought solace in the tomb in which it will abide until Gabriel sounds his horn. . . ."

Yet even the *Ten Mile News* was in precarious straits. Another weekly founded in Kokomo in 1881, it had run steadily for two years, but no sooner had the *Times* gone to await Gabriel's call than the *Daily Journal* noted that the *News* seemed intent on "camping upon the trail of the Coe and Macready outfit." It was "a question of who would starve first." The declining population of Ten Mile could still support one newspaper, thought the editors, but there was no room for three—the *News*, the Robinson *Tribune*, and the *Summit County Herald*.[17]

In fact, all three starved at once. The *Ten Mile News* missed three weeks in January, then resumed publication until July, when it appeared on a half-sheet instead of four full pages. "Like a well-flavored fat oyster," chortled the *Daily Journal,* the *News* "comes to us again on the half shell." That signalled the approaching end; the *News* went to press for the last time that summer. The Robinson *Tribune* went the same way. Coe and Macready lost control about the time they lost out on the *Times.* By February 1883, J. S. Swan had emerged as editor and proprietor, but he had sold out to Frank M. Woods, who had run the *Ten Mile Circular.* He had no luck either, and by July the *Tribune* had also gone to await Gabriel's call. [18]

That left only the *Summit County Herald.* The failure of the *Ten Mile News* and the Robinson *Tribune* probably extended its lease on life, but it still went through rapid changes in ownership. In January 1884, the editors announced that for a time the *Herald* would appear on a half sheet, an ominous sign. Soon it began to appear in irregular fashion. The editors tried to stimulate interest with a series of articles on mining frauds, and in the spring they cut the annual subscription rate to two dollars in hope of increasing circulation. But nothing could revive the *Herald*'s fortunes. Long before the end of 1884, it had gone to press for the last time. [19]

The failure of the *Herald* and its rivals reflected the excessive competition and the declining fortunes of Ten Mile, and when these newspapers went out of business, no others rushed in to fill the vacuum. In fact, there was none. The Leadville papers had frequently run stories about Ten Mile, and the Breckenridge *Daily Journal* had published a special feature known as "Ten Mile Riplets." So Ten Milers still had several newspapers to read, except when the snow cut off the trains.

As elsewhere in American society, Ten Milers divided along the standard political lines of the day, Republicans and Democrats. Some politicians were already veterans of Colorado's partisan strife when they arrived, notably William P. Pollock, Judge Wheeler, and Colonel John W. Jenkins. Still others had held office elsewhere—Benjamin H. Butcher had served a term in the West Virginia legislature, and James A. Clark had represented Baltimore in the Maryland House of Representatives. But they and others all shared one hope—to advance their political careers through a new electoral base in Ten Mile. [20]

Every year had its elections, and if the state and national campaigns of the even-numbered years did not provide enough opportunity, there were always the state, district, and local struggles that harnessed political energies in the so-called "off" years. And if George B. Robinson's election as lieutenant governor served as a glittering example of what an ambitious bonanza king might accomplish, then far more typical were the successes and failures that highlighted the off-year elections of 1881 when the politicians geared up their machines, such as they were, to contest local offices.

As early as June 1881, the Democratically-oriented *Summit County Times* stated that "the campaign of the present year promises to be an exceedingly lively one." Many candidates had entered the field, and several slates would "undoubtedly be smashed" before the parties held their nominating conventions. Nearly all others would be "completely wrecked" once the balloting began. By June, Ten Milers knew that at least a dozen men hoped to become county sheriff, and there was ample evidence that other offices such as county clerk and recorder would "be reached for like a ripe fig."[21]

After jousting for advantage during the summer, the politicians increased their activity as the county conventions approached in October, a scant month before the general election set for the first Tuesday in November. No matter how energetically any candidate campaigned, he was by no means certain of election even if he captured his party's nomination. There were no "safe seats" in Summit County. The Republicans and the Democrats were fairly evenly matched, which meant that most nominees faced a tough fight regardless of their persuasion.

In 1881, both parties planned to hold their county conventions in Kokomo, a reflection of Ten Mile's new prominence in the affairs of Summit County. The Democrats made plans to meet first, and on October 4, they set out for the Kokomo schoolhouse, although they might as well have gathered in Wheeler. County assessor Gannon and the editor of the *Daily Journal* almost failed to make it from Breckenridge to Kokomo because their coach broke down on the bad roads. Other delegates coming from Argentine, Swan, and more outlying camps made the accustomed stop to imbibe at Judge Wheeler's en route. They were soon joined by the Breckenridge delegates, and for a time it was feared that assessor Gannon was "apt to put a heavy tax upon the Wheeler pool table to get even with that institution for games lost." Once in Kokomo, the various delegations caucused, more often than not at one of the local saloons.

But caucusing and drinking aside, it was the convention that counted. At the appointed hour Judge Wheeler called the delegates to order. The selection of a candidate for district attorney was an early contest, and James A. Clark, the Kokomo attorney, was the convention's choice. Just before the balloting began, Benjamin H. Butcher introduced a motion to bind the delegates selected to attend the district convention in Leadville to Clark "so long as there was a chance for his nomination." This motion carried unanimously, and four days later in Leadville, Clark did indeed receive the Democratic nomination.

Other contests were real struggles. For county clerk and recorder, the delegates split over Judge Wheeler and James K. Parnell. When the ballots were counted, Judge Wheeler lost, despite his leading position in the Summit County Democracy. Another close contest involved the nomination for sheriff, which finally went to Dan Hanley of Kokomo, who was described as an individual noted for "his honesty, integrity and manliness." Then thirty-five years old, Hanley was a part owner and superintendent of the Washington mine on Sheep Mountain.

Ten Mile's Republicans were every bit as active as the Democrats. They nominated J. A. McCune, the mayor of Kokomo, as their candidate for county treasurer, and chose Colonel Jenkins as their candidate for district attorney in the fifth judicial district. Like Clark, however, Jenkins had to face another preliminary contest, but between the two conventions, the fire of October 13 swept through Kokomo. When the Republicans met a few days later in Leadville, they passed a resolution to "deeply sympathize with the businessmen of Kokomo for the grave misfortune that befell them," as well as the families who had been rendered homeless by the catastrophe. After that, the convention selected its final candidates, and Colonel Jenkins seemed on the verge of a political renaissance when the delegates chose him as the Republican candidate. In the few weeks that remained before the November election, Jenkins did his best in the race against Clark, but in the end Clark won by a scant 149 votes out of more than 8,600 ballots cast. [22]

Even though Jenkins lost this election, he was by no means ready to quit politics. The campaigns of 1882 offered him another chance. In September, he threw his hat in the ring, this time for the state legislature. His campaign, however, went badly. When the Republicans held their convention, they "broke up in a row," and virtually half the delegates walked out. The Summit County split may have reflected the deep statewide schism in the Republican ranks that year. Jenkins still managed to receive the nomination, but his chance for a political comeback was compromised when an independent Republican faction nominated its own candidate in the person of George B. Colby, the young attorney now serving as mayor of Kokomo.

Perhaps because they sensed a statewide victory with the Republicans so bitterly divided, the Democrats smoothly resolved any controversies within their ranks. That September, when they caucused in

Frisco at the call of Judge Wheeler, their convention sailed along steadily toward the harmonious nomination of strong candidates. The delegates chose Butcher to square off with Jenkins, and they picked Luther M. Goddard as their nominee for judge of the fifth judicial district.

It was predicted that the election would be close. Goddard and Butcher waged strong campaigns aided by the Republican split, while Jenkins saw his comeback plans dealt a wholly unexpected blow. While boarding a passenger car in Kokomo, he slipped and fell and broke his leg, an accident that put him out of the campaign but days before the election. When the votes were counted, Goddard won election as judge, while Butcher bested Jenkins by the narrow margin of eighty votes. Colby received ninety-three votes, which suggests that Jenkins might have won, had not a member of his own party siphoned off the decisive margin. That of course was symptomatic of the statewide contest, for the split in the Republican ranks allowed the Democratic candidate, James B. Grant, the Leadville smelter king, to squeak through to victory, giving the Democrats their first governor in Colorado's history.

An unhappy footnote to the campaign came in mid-November when Jenkins had to have his leg amputated just above the ankle. He lay in critical condition for days, with death expected at any hour, but he survived. Although he lived several more years, however, his political career was over. [23]

Still other political changes were coming to Ten Mile. In 1883 the legislature split off Eagle and Garfield counties, creating the modern boundaries. Later in the year, county elections came again, and this time the Republicans swept to victory. Their good fortune continued into 1884 when their Kokomo ticket swept the field. This, of course, dismayed the *Summit County Journal*, which bewailed the fact that Kokomo had suffered another calamity and would "wither like Jonah's gourd under twelve months of Republican blight." [24]

With their recent success, the political seas looked inviting to the now-unified Republicans as the fall campaigns of 1884 approached. The key race, so far as many Ten Milers were concerned, was the contest for the state senate seat representing Summit, Eagle, and Garfield counties. The incumbent was H. H. Eddy of Breckenridge, a Republican wheelhorse, but the Democrats fielded a strong candidate in Representative Butcher. He received the party's nomination at the convention in Red Cliff, but he faced a hard run. When the votes were counted in November, it appeared that Butcher had won a very close race. Yet Eddy levied the charge of voting irregularities in Garfield County. Before the issue could be resolved, Butcher took his seat in the state senate, but that was only until the solons could decide on the question of fraud. When they did, they voted along party lines to oust Butcher and reseat Eddy.

After 1885, Ten Milers played a lesser role in county politics, not because they were less interested, but because the declining fortunes of the minerals industry, and with it the falling population, made the valley a much smaller factor in political life. Moreover, most of the old mainline politicians left. Judge Wheeler moved back to Weld County in 1884. Butcher relocated about the same time. William P. Pollock resigned as county assessor in 1887 and returned gravely ill to Pennsylvania. And Colonel Jenkins' life ran out the same year. Ten Milers still campaigned for public office, but not to the extent they had in the bright days of the boom. [25]

Despite the steady decline through the 1880s, Ten Mile witnessed the coming of a second railroad. This one began building not so much because of a desire to tap the Ten Mile trade, but more out of the logic of the railroad wars and the wish to profit from the Leadville market. In the late 1870s, the struggle to garner the central Colorado trade had resulted in the Royal Gorge War between the Rio Grande and Santa Fe lines and in the thrust of the Denver South Park & Pacific toward Leadville. A temporary settlement came with the so-called Tripartite Agreement, the Treaty of Boston, and the Joint Operating Agreement. These pacts eliminated the Santa Fe from central Colorado, allowed the Rio Grande to build up the Arkansas Valley to Leadville (and from there to Ten Mile), and gave the South Park access to Leadville over the Rio Grande track from Buena Vista via the Joint Operating Agreement.

Except for keeping the Santa Fe out of the central Rockies, these agreements never proved entirely satisfactory. William Jackson Palmer and the Rio Grande feared they would lose the right to build westward to Gunnison, and this misgiving finally prompted Palmer to renounce that portion of the Joint Operating Agreement and begin building over Marshall Pass toward Gunnison. Meanwhile, the Union Pacific Railroad, controlled by the controversial financier Jay Gould, had acquired both the Colorado Central and the South Park railroads, making those lines more formidable competitors. As a result, friction increased between Palmer and Gould over the division of fees, costs, and profits on the Buena Vista–Leadville run. Even though the Joint Operating Agreement called for the Rio Grande and South Park to split the gross receipts equally, the Rio Grande got the lion's share of the freight traffic—75 percent in 1880 and more in 1881. Only the passenger traffic split evenly.

The vastly unequal division of freight inevitably led to change. The Rio Grande now claimed that it should get returns equal to the actual percentage, whereas the Union Pacific insisted upon the 50–50 division called for in the Joint Operating Agreement. The two lines negotiated in June and July 1881 in an effort to resolve the impasse, but both parties were far apart. On July 28, the Denver *Republican* wrote that "the spectre of war . . . over the Leadville business is increasing in size hourly and is liable to burst with disastrous effect soon." And burst it did in August when both roads cut their passenger rates from Denver so sharply that some people traveled at less than cost. The Union Pacific also announced that it would not pay its share of the costs and fees on the Buena Vista–Leadville line, and the Rio Grande retaliated by announcing that it would seek an injunction to prevent the Union Pacific from shipping over the track. This, said the *Republican*, would be "ruinous" to the Union Pacific and force the enterprise to build to Leadville through its subsidiary, the South Park. Shortly after, the Rio Grande went to court seeking payment of $350,000.

The Union Pacific now faced a major decision. If it wanted to tap the trade of Breckenridge, Ten Mile, and Leadville, it would have to construct its own line into the Blue River country and then around the mountains to Leadville. No small task. Yet if it decided to build, it could still choose from two gateways to Summit County: it could run track west from Georgetown over Loveland Pass, or it could put down rails from Como in South Park and cross 11,400-foot Boreas Pass into Breckenridge. The Union Pacific seriously considered the first alternative, but finally decided to have the South Park build from Como over Boreas Pass.

Dirt flew that summer as the South Park's crews began grading the roadbed from Como. By October, they had cleared the right-of-way through dense forest as far as the open summit of Boreas Pass. From there, they began grading the circuitous descent into Breckenridge, but by now winter had set in. The numbing cold, penetrating winds, and swirling blizzards defied the builders' efforts, and construction ground to a halt, a portent of the operating problems to come. During the winter the South Park signed contracts for rails and ties, then in April, the tracklayers began to hammer down rails on the segment from Como while the road graders pushed on through the snowdrifts and down the switchbacks to Breckenridge. After a frenetic summer of construction, the South Park ran its first trains to Breckenridge in September. Later that fall the builders hurried down the Blue River Valley to Dillon, and from there turned east, reaching another seven miles up the Snake River Valley to Keystone.

Winter again idled the construction crews, but the management of the Union Pacific and South Park used the time to plan and negotiate. For one, they settled the $350,000 lawsuit with the Rio Grande through an agreement by which they would pay $280,000 in return for the use of the Buena Vista–Leadville line under the terms of the Joint Operating Agreement. For another, they prepared to build a line from Dillon through Ten Mile Canyon to Leadville. To do this, the South Park contracted for rails and some 50,000 ties, many to be cut at Wheeler, and hoped to begin construction with the spring thaw. But as the snows melted, the South Park could not get construction into motion, apparently because the parent Union Pacific Company was rushing to finish the Oregon Short Line. Not until summer did the Union Pacific sign a contract with C. W. Collins & Company of Omaha to build the Dillon-Leadville extension at rates probably in the range of $20,000 to $32,000 per mile. And only then did Collins—Chester W. Collins, the brother-in-law of the Union Pacific's president, Sidney Dillon—begin allocating work to subcontractors. Despite the late start, the builders still hoped to finish the line to Leadville in sixty days, although one Denver newspaper remarked that such speed would require nine or ten thousand workers, far more than were at hand.

Construction, lawsuits, high-handed tactics, and alleged sabotage now went hand in hand as the South Park pressed forward. On August 3, the graders turned over the first ground near Dillon. The Leadville *Daily Herald* proclaimed a "RAILWAY WAR INEVITABLE" and predicted that it would be "the most bitter rail-war ever witnessed in this state." And no sooner had the first shovels of dirt flown near Dillon than the Rio Grande sent the Union Pacific notice that it intended to cancel the Joint Operating Agreement in six months, at the time specified by contract, February 6, 1884. Simultaneously, the Rio Grande apparently used a third party to obtain the right-of-way for a street railway up California Gulch outside Leadville, from which half the camp's shipments originated, and thus prevent the South Park from laying down ore in Denver at one dollar per ton, which it hoped to do. [26]

Undaunted, the South Park pushed on. Construction began at both ends of the route, and the Rio Grande, ironically, hauled supplies and equipment over Fremont Pass to build the Ten Mile section. Yet the South Park found both material and labor in short supply. Carlyle and Corrigan of Pueblo brought in an estimated 365 teams used on the Oregon Short Line, but laborers proved so hard to find that the Union Pacific recruited workers as far east as Omaha. More than one Colorado newspaper took note of a line in the Omaha *Herald* that reported the Union Pacific "hiring and forwarding to Colorado, all the able-bodied laborers to be had in this country to work on the new short cut to Leadville." The road offered trackmen $2.25 per day, rock men $2.50, but it subtracted a board of $5.00 per week, and at least some of the pay was in script redeemable only at stores specified by the railroad. But the South Park got the men it needed, Irishmen, Blacks, and Italians, who spoke little or no English. They came to Denver on special trains that ran right through to Leadville or Dillon.

Construction rolled along. The engineers went out to run surveys of the final path. One segment went over Izzard's Placer at Frisco, others followed the old stage routes. Workers streamed in by the trainload to bend their backs in this sweat-intensive task. By the middle of August the South Park had a thousand men on the job; by mid-September, 1,800. That month the *Summit County Journal* reported Ten Mile Canyon "swarming with men." Local contractors got some business, but more went to outsiders like J. D. Kilpatrick, who came with his teams and crews after working on the Oregon Short Line. Everyone talked of speed—"earnest haste," said the *Daily Herald;* "the greatest expedition," said Kilpatrick. [27]

Despite the emphasis on celerity, the South Park changed the route after construction began. The original surveys called for the Ten Mile extension to begin at Dillon, but the line decided to move the point of departure to a site known as Placer Junction, later renamed Dickey, three miles from Dillon. This not only saved time and track, but also offered an easier grade around the Ten Mile Range. From Dickey, the line would run to Frisco to pick up Ten Mile Creek, which it would follow to Wheeler. There the road would enter the narrows of Ten Mile Canyon and twist and turn for several miles before emerging into the more open valley at Recen. From Robinson, the line would wind its way up the switchbacks on Fremont Pass, and then swing down the east fork of the Arkansas River to Leadville. The grades would never exceed a maximum of 4.30 percent, but some curves, particularly on Fremont Pass, would run from fifteen to twenty degrees. When completed, the line would be 34.6 miles along.

The real problem, however, was not construction, but the right-of-way. With its track in place, the Rio Grande was ready to dispute the South Park's advance. From Fremont Pass to Dillon, the Rio Grande's track lay almost entirely on the west bank of Ten Mile Creek, and wherever it built, the South Park by law had to avoid coming closer than fifty feet to the centerline. This was easy to do near Dillon, but was virtually impossible in Ten Mile Canyon and Kokomo-Recen. And the Rio Grande people knew it. On August 27, with construction barely begun, the Rio Grande obtained a temporary injunction preventing the South Park from entering the Rio Grande's right-of-way throughout Summit County, as well as on the depot grounds at Robinson and at Summit Station (soon to be known as Climax) on Fremont Pass.

The South Park responded with its own lawsuit. The firm's lawyers contended that a federal law of 1875, which granted railways a right-of-way on federal lands, allowed the South Park to come within the Rio Grande's right-of-way; moreover, because the Joint Operating Agreement would terminate on February 6, 1884, and the construction season was so short, the South Park had to build now or suffer irreparable injury. Whatever the merits of their arguments, however, the South Park failed to persuade the court to dissolve the injunction. It remained in force. But this hardly daunted the line's management. They ignored the injunction and kept their crews on the job.

The battlelines were now drawn, legal and otherwise, and caught in the middle were the county authorities who were expected to uphold the law. Sheriff Dan Hanley obtained injunction notices to serve on South Park employees and arrest warrants for anyone who disobeyed the injunction. He was also reported as saying that Major James Evans, the South Park's chief engineer, would be the first one arrested should the road continue building. And the very next day, Hanley arrested Evans and his chief assistant. They promptly posted bail, however, and went back to work, although their arrest did halt construction in the Kokomo area where the South Park's crews had entered the Rio Grande's right-of-way. Yet grading and track laying continued elsewhere, and Hanley, working by himself, had a hard time serving notices and warrants on every worker.

As construction continued in Ten Mile, the Rio Grande lost a battle in Leadville. On September 5, the city council voted 8 to 7 to give the South Park a right-of-way within city limits. Although some people alleged "connivance" between officials of the Union Pacific and members of the city council, the vote stood. In an effort to halt work, the Rio Grande parked an engine across the point where the South Park intended to cross the Rio Grande tracks. That blocked construction for a time. In retaliation, the South Park graders may have vandalized portions of the Rio Grande line in Ten Mile Canyon. One newspaper later reported that the South Park had posted armed guards to prevent the Rio Grande men from tearing up its track.

Yet the South Park faced more problems than the Rio Grande. Disease riddled the construction crews. In September, the Summit County *Journal* noted "much sickness among the laborers employed on the extension through Ten Mile canyon." The Denver and Leadville newspapers published similar reports, including an interview with James Connors, a patient at the city poorhouse. He told of being hired in Kansas City by a "mancatcher" who deceived him about the work to be done in the Rockies, but who took two dollars in payment just the same. Connors also complained about being paid in script rather than cash and of not being able to get enough blankets for sleeping in the chilly mountain air. In another interview, Dr. Law, the Lake County physician, said that laborers were coming with false hopes "caused by the misrepresentations on the part of the Union Pacific." [28]

Besides disease, friction developed among the workers. They were a mixed lot: Irish, Italians, eastern Europeans, and blacks. Many of the Europeans spoke no English, but that probably mattered little compared to the racial and ethnic tensions that developed, particularly at the work camp near Chalk Ranch. About November 1, friction erupted into violence when a group of Italians allegedly attacked one of the blacks who had apparently wandered into the Italian enclave. They beat the man severely, and might have killed him, according to published accounts, but for a group of Irishmen, who dragged the Italians off. When two deputy sheriffs arrived to restore order, they arrested four Italians and hauled them off to Leadville.

The Italians faced special problems. Prejudice against them was strong. The newspapers usually referred to them as "dagos." Many who arrived in Leadville—probably penniless—slept in the dance halls or saloons until rousted out. Later they crammed into vacant houses in the worst parts of town. The *Herald*, for one, repeatedly characterized them as "dirty, crummy, greasy, lousy Italians . . . worse than Chinamen," which was very strong language. The Irish and the Italians did not get along well, and the friction between them may have been exacerbated by the contractors, many of whom were of Irish extraction.

Besides the tensions within the work force, the South Park had to contend with labor problems. Perhaps related to the ethnic frictions was a strike staged by Kilpatrick's Italian crews who claimed they had not been paid. Kilpatrick told them the money was on the way from Omaha, but that did little good. The strike slowed construction near Kokomo until the cash arrived. [29]

If these problems were not enough, the South Park also faced a struggle with the placer owners. During the carbonate boom, the placer ground had been all but abandoned, but as the South Park approached Kokomo, the nature of the terrain and the necessity of avoiding the Rio Grande's right-of-way required the line to lay track across much of this land. That gave the placer owners a chance to demand the best price. As early as September 1883, the *Summit County Journal* reported that the

BOUND FOR KOKOMO. This train stopped to take on water, possibly from the Solitude Tank at Wheeler Junction. Copper Mountain at right guards the entrance to Ten Mile Canyon. William Henry Jackson photographer, courtesy Colorado Historical Society.

owners "of some nonproductive placers" near Kokomo were "taking steps to secure an injunction restraining the South Park Railroad from passing over them." And the editors philosophized that this section of the country was "as well supplied with men of D.H. dispositions as any part of Uncle Sam's domain."

Once again, all parties coupled a struggle in court with a battle on site. The placer men sought injunctions and damages against the South Park, but that hardly mattered to the railroad, which kept grading toward Kokomo. Yet matters came to a head early in the winter. Although many of the placer miners lived in Breckenridge, in November they met on the Follett and Stetthauer claims to ascertain their value. Even though the ground was frozen and covered with snow, the results were astounding. The amount of fine and coarse gold in each claim "proved to be not only a surprise to the property owners themselves," reported the *Summit County Journal*, "but more so to many who had in their minds condemned years ago all property in the Ten Mile valley as being worthless for the purposes of washing gold."

But that hardly resolved the struggle. The placer miners had made the tests to bulwark their claims to damages, for by now the railroad construction crews had graded through the area "absolutely destroying the Follett claims and materially destroying the Stetthauer." When the courts decided the issue later that month, they awarded damages of $7,400 in the Follett suit and another $21,000 in the Stetthauer case— substantial amounts of money for worthless placer ground. Yet these awards did not settle the issue, because the South Park decided to appeal the decisions while it put down rails to Kokomo.

The prospect of violence loomed large as winter closed in. The Stetthauer people accused the South Park of planning "to throw their steel" over the placer at night. To prevent this, they hurriedly built a log fortification dubbed Fort Stetthauer. "The Kokomo War" was on. Meanwhile, the placer miners argued in court that Kilpatrick had pushed ahead in defiance of the court's injunction. Judge Luther M. Goddard agreed, although he was hardly a disinterested party since in private practice he represented the Rio Grande. Goddard ordered Kilpatrick arrested for contempt and had a special train dispatched from Leadville to corral the builders. When Marshall Foote of Kokomo, a man best known for hard drink and blunt action, tried to arrest Kilpatrick, a scuffle may have ensued in which Foote pistol-whipped Kilpatrick for allegedly resisting arrest. Tempers finally cooled before any real violence erupted, and as December wore on, the defenders of Fort Stetthauer huddled in their primitive fortress while the lawyers went back to court.

Just before Christmas, the dispute reached its climax. The South Park posted a $20,000 bond in the Stetthauer case while the two sides continued their litigation over the actual damages to be paid. The "gallant defenders" of Fort Stetthauer then evacuated their stronghold, and the South Park wasted little time in blowing it up. The *Summit County Journal* lamented that "the future historian will have no gallant defense to record of Fort Stetthauer in writing the history of these troublous times." And the editors later reported that the Stetthauer people agreed to accept $11,000 in a final settlement. [30]

By now the South Park had built through Ten Mile Canyon and was fast approaching Kokomo, where it would again challenge the Rio Grande's right-of-way. In hope of settling the dispute, Judge Moses Hallett had set up a three-man commission, one person representing each side and the third individual representing the court. In early December they made their report. The South Park had located about 1,800 feet of its line within the Rio Grande's right-of-way at Kokomo, although the South Park would be about fifteen feet above in terms of grade. The South Park could move its track outside of the line, but only at a significant increase in costs. The commission thus proposed a compromise that

AFTER THE KOKOMO WAR. A South Park trestle passes over the Rio Grande track east of Kokomo, which was then actually Recen, shown here in 1892. The Queen of the West Road runs like a swordslash up Jacque Mountain to the Recens' mine at the upper right. Courtesy Colorado Historical Society.

would add to the South Park's expenses, but still be less costly than moving the whole line outside the Rio Grande's right-of-way.

This proposal apparently satisfied the South Park, but the Rio Grande showed no inclination to go along, and the dispute continued into January, when the South Park took the initiative. With 200 men, the road began laying rails across the Rio Grande tracks, sidings, and depot ground in Robinson in order to make the connection with the rails coming up Ten Mile Canyon to Kokomo. When the news reached Leadville, the Rio Grande superintendent got up a special train of fifty armed men, and once in Robinson, set two mogul engines running back and forth across the South Park's tracks until the Rio Grande could get an injunction. But this final dispute was resolved a short time later when both railroads accepted the compromise. From a technical perspective the Rio Grande had won its point about the South Park building within the right-of-way, but as a practical matter, the compromise allowed the South Park to make its connection to Leadville. Finally, on February 5, 1884, the South Park ran its first train from Breckenridge to Leadville, just one day before the expiration of the Joint Operating Agreement.

Even though the South Park had completed its High Line around the mountains, it could not begin regular service. The snow, ice, and cold made sure of that, for the line did not have the snowplows and snowsheds to contend with the season. The road had to renegotiate with the Rio Grande to extend the Joint Operating Agreement until May. But so much snow fell on Boreas Pass and Ten Mile Canyon that winter that the South Park had to persuade the Rio Grande to reextend the agreement. Not until July had enough snow melted for the road to begin clearing and repairing its track, and it was not until September 30, 1884, that the South Park opened its highly publicized "Short Line to Leadville." True enough, the road cut twenty miles off the route and one hour off the time, and all for $12.50 one way. [31]

The High Line, however, did little to stem the decline of Ten Mile. Innumerable persons departed as the economy slumped. A few people rushed off in the Garfield County excitement of 1883, more in the Idaho stampede of 1884. Some of those leaving drew public notice, like Silas W. Nott, who relocated in Glenwood Springs after his stagecoaching enterprise failed, or Mrs. A. T. Moore, who removed to Leadville after she gave up the Bon Ton Hotel in Robinson, or William P. Pollock, who left for Pennsylvania after suffering a paralytic stroke. But except for private good-byes, most individuals drifted away without fanfare.

A census taken in 1885 pretty much told the story. Of the 2,040 people who lived in Summit County, virtually half lived in Breckenridge.

Next in population came Robinson with 367 people, Recen with 207. Kokomo had a mere 78 (as opposed to perhaps 1,000 five summers before), and Wheeler another 78.

Yet life in Ten Mile still seemed to go on much as it had before, just on a smaller scale. In March 1886, a Mr. Brown of Breckenridge escorted Miss Rennie, Miss Mueller, and Miss McCallum to a "ball" in Robinson, after which they returned from this apparently all-night affair on the morning train. In April a Mrs. Beach of Leadville lectured in hope of raising funds to establish a home in Colorado Springs for the state's "prodigal daughters." There was a meeting at the Robinson Town Hall to make plans for erecting a maypole in Union Square, although "the boys" would have to make their evening rounds on snowshoes if they hoped to hang baskets—six feet of snow still covered the ground. It was also predicted that the coming season would be "one of the greatest activity" in the building line. [32]

But even as life continued, few would deny that the scene was depressing. Ten Mile had fewer amenities now than ever before. Education was a case in point. Schoolteachers apparently proved hard to find. Wilfley's wife, Addie, did some teaching one year, and a Miss Fannie Remine another, but they had relatively few students. Mrs. James Doran taught briefly at the school run by Our Lady of the Snows Catholic Church in Robinson, but both church and school were plagued by financial problems, scarcely alleviated by fund raisers like the St. Patrick's Day Dance. It was no wonder that successful miners like Wilfley and McDonald moved their families to Leadville or Denver where their children could attend better schools.

Church life had never been strong in Ten Mile, and in the late 1880s even what little there was seemed to be waning. In 1886, Father Chapius of Our Lady of the Snows left Robinson to take a parish in Breckenridge. Reports circulated that a group of nuns was coming to take charge of a hospital and some Benedictines from Chicago to replace Chapius. No hospital appeared, but the church remained open into the early 1890s. Unlike the Catholics, the Protestants did not even have a church. Couples who wanted a church wedding had to look elsewhere. Wilfley and Addie Farnham went over to Leadville in 1886, while Charles Colcord, one of Wilfley's associates, and Josie Dowd, the postmistress of Kokomo, traveled to Breckenridge with a trainload of family and friends in 1887. [33]

By the late 1880s, Ten Mile had almost returned to the custom of itinerant preachers. In May 1887, for example, the Reverend J. B. Hewett traveled from Breckenridge to Robinson and Kokomo to conduct services. When he returned, he reported that he had founded a Union Church

DOWNTOWN RECEN. Passengers stand in front of a Rio Grande mixed train at the depot in Recen. The newly built schoolhouse, already a prominent landmark, sits on the hill at right. Courtesy Colorado Historical Society.

consisting of seven members: two Congregationalists, two Lutherans, two Baptists, and one United Methodist. This was "very creditable to Kokomo," praised the *Summit County Journal*, for it showed that Christians there had "common sense and charity enough to sink all sectarian differences for the common good of the community."[34]

As for business, Ten Mile no longer had any newspapers or banks, but a few enterprises still struggled along. J. H. Gleason ran the Palmer House Hotel in Robinson, no doubt trying to capitalize on the name of the famous hotel in Chicago. J. C. Morehouse sold real estate to all comers in Robinson, just as he had since the boom. Over in Kokomo, for two dollars a traveller could bed down at the Mountain House, or a shopper could buy from James W. Dowd, who had emerged as the chief merchant in Ten Mile. Long gone were Frank Ralph, Jacob Bergerman, and so many others. A host of saloons had also departed. There was still Nelson's, of course, and there was Carlson's, "a ball-toss" from Dowd's store, and no doubt there were others, but like the hotels, their number had dwindled.[35]

The saloons were also about to suffer from the temperance movement. In 1887 a Miss White came to Kokomo to lecture on the evils of demon rum. She apparently caused nary a stir. But four years later in 1891, Reverend Florida F. Passmore created a furor after he took charge of Father John Dyer's Methodist Church in Breckenridge. Passmore was a fanatic (some might have said deranged). From the outset, he used his position to insist the county authorities uphold the state law banning the sale of alcohol on Sundays and between midnight and 6:00 A.M. other days. He also took aim at the ever-present gambling that went on in saloons.

The authorities, however, were reluctant to take any action. Men like Sheriff Frank Brown thought the law unenforceable (they were right). Even the *Summit County Journal* decried "the silly laws placed at the disposal of any crank." But Passmore railed from the pulpit and stump with such force that Brown and his counterparts had little choice except close the saloons as the law prescribed, much to the dismay of miners who had trudged down from the hills for a Sunday in town. Overall, Brown and his men were unenthusiastic and not very effective, and that prompted Passmore to upbraid them in public.

Brown replied with a public letter written "in the name of the Godly and ungodly." He told Passmore that while he and his men were "enforcing the laws with your assistance and insistence," Passmore should look to his own shortcomings. Brown charged that Passmore had "caused more disturbance in this county than all the saloon men and gamblers put together." What was more, "never in the history of Kokomo [had] there been as many broken heads and blackened eyes" than the day when Passmore began interfering in community life. With all this, and the impossibility of enforcing the laws, why should he not arrest Passmore for disturbing the peace?

Brown's letter did little good. Passmore continued blasting away, virtually disrupting court with his thunderous oratories against demon rum, particularly when the courts found it difficult to convict, just as Brown and the *Journal* predicted.

Despite the fury of Passmore's crusade, the campaign might have petered out harmlessly, but in the midst of the uproar, events became ugly. Miners apparently baited Passmore whenever they could, but no one dared lay a hand on him because of his position and size—he was huge. On the night of August 17, 1891, someone dynamited the belfry of Father Dyer's church. The culprit was never apprehended; all the townspeople could do was to pass the hat to buy a new bell. And Passmore remained undeterred. He continued his assault, though with less and

MASONS OF TEN MILE. Corinthian Lodge No. 42 of Kokomo proudly claimed that it was the highest Masonic Lodge in the United States. Courtesy Recen Family Collection.

less influence. It was not until 1894, however, when he was hung in effigy, that he was recalled from Breckenridge. Two years later he was expelled from the ministry. [36]

Aside from Passmore, there were the usual light and dark events of life. In June 1888, the Corinthian Lodge No. 42 gave a grand ball at Anderson's Hall in Kokomo, the Sulphide Club held its usual meetings in town, and groups of people continued to travel from Ten Mile to Breckenridge or Leadville to have a night on the town, just as they had since the railroads arrived. On the dark side, however, John F. Kelley, the master of the railroad boarding train cut his throat at Climax in March 1892. No one knew why, and most people were shocked because he had always been such a genial companion. [37]

Even though Pollock, Wheeler, and Jenkins had now left the valley, Ten Milers still took an interest in politics. This was particularly true in 1887 when both the Democrats and the Republicans selected Kokomo-Recen for their county conventions. The Democrats gathered on the first Saturday in October. Wilfley and James W. Dowd (now a county commissioner) were among the representatives of Kokomo-Recen, John S.

Wheeler, Jr., among those from Wheeler, and old J. C. Morehouse among the group from Robinson. Ten Milers also obtained some nominations for office: H. M. Woodford of Robinson received the nod for county assessor, and George D. McDonald of Kokomo the pick for county surveyor. In the only spirited contest, R. R. Kirk of Breckenridge nosed out Daniel F. Callahan of Kokomo by one vote to obtain the nomination for sheriff.

This convention, however, had little real drama. There were no hard-fought struggles, no slanderous attacks on persons or policy, and no careers dashed. Not even any hard-drinking and gambling. The *Summit County Journal* noted rather prosaically that the gathering "was not attended with as many inconveniences as was thought it would be" (Kokomo-Recen was after all falling apart), and there was but a limited amount of whiskey and beer "sampled." The high point of the convention, it seems, was "a real good dinner" served by the Mountain House. And where "jovial" Gus Carlson, "although on the other side of the fence politically," was patronized by the delegates.

The Republicans held their convention the following Wednesday. It was also dull fare and drew little attention. But the delegates did select candidates, including Frank Brown of Kokomo, who was chosen to square off with the Democrat's Kirk in the contest for sheriff.

The campaigns that followed were equally bland. The pro-Democratic *Journal* tried to stimulate some thunder toward the end when it predicted the Republicans would hear "the most astounding clap . . . that ever surprised their ears." Yet as in most elections, the Democrats took some offices and the Republicans others, and there was little change in the direction of county life. Apparently, the only Ten Mile candidate to win election this year was Republican Brown, who defeated Democrat Kirk for sheriff. And as usual, Luther M. Goddard was reelected a judge in the Fifth Judicial District. [38]

Although the Republicans and the Democrats held sway through the late 1880s, important changes were coming in the 1890s, largely because of the steady decline of silver prices. They had broken below $1.00 an ounce for the first time in 1886 and continued to sink over the next few years. Although the passage of the Sherman Silver Purchase Act of 1890 boosted prices back above $1.00 an ounce, it also stimulated production, and prices slumped again in 1891. This erosion, combined with the agricultural distress, prompted the creation of the Populist or People's Party, a national political organization. The Populists advocated many fundamental changes in American society—the direct election of United States senators (still chosen by the legislatures), the secret ballot, the nationalization of the railroads and telegraph, and what appealed most to miners—the free and unlimited coinage of silver at the ratio of sixteen to one with gold. Since the federal government had fixed the value of gold at $20.00 an ounce, free coinage promised to raise the price of silver to $1.25 an ounce. Most silver miners embraced the proposal, as did many farmers because it promised to put an end to deflation, induce inflation, and allow farmers to use the higher prices for crops to pay off mortgages and other debts with cheaper dollars.

Whatever their interest in the overall program, populism attracted people in Ten Mile because it promised to raise silver prices. This meant profits and jobs, good times instead of bad, perhaps even a boom instead of the bust. In 1891 the populists placed several candidates on the ballot in Summit County. None of them won any office, but with the price of silver declining, the party only grew in strength. [39]

As 1892 dawned, the *Summit County Journal* published a sign of the changing political winds. On February 27, the editors ran a "Notice of Importance to the Miners and Businessmen of Summit County." It called for a meeting to be held at the Firemen's Hall in Breckenridge to consider "matters of vital importance," including the organization of what was termed "a silver league." What made the announcement so unusual was that it was signed by W. H. Brickle, chairman of the Republican County Central Committee, and his nominal opponent, C. L. Westerman, chairman of the Democratic County Central Committee. [40]

This meeting pointed to more direct political action. A month later, a group of miners and businessmen, mostly from Kokomo, organized the Consolidated Ten Mile Silver Club. Believing that "the free and unlimited coinage of silver" was "of paramount importance" to the district, state, and nation, they adopted a document that called for the coinage of silver equal with gold, denounced "the attempts . . . of Wall Street to dictate to Congress," and declared that both the Republican and Democratic parties were dominated by "the eastern gold bug to the detriment of the laboring masses." From that point forward "free silver" would be the club's "war cry." [41]

The men of Kokomo were by no means alone. A week later a group in Robinson organized another silver club that adopted similar resolutions. Both bodies were part of a broad-based movement swelling through the silver country. By the end of May, Colorado had nearly sixty silver clubs like those at Kokomo and Robinson. Colorado also had a growing Silver League, an ostensibly nonpartisan education organization like the one at Breckenridge. The Silver League, however, had an obvious political over-

THE SENATE SALOON. One of Ten Mile's ubiquitous watering holes, Whitney's Saloon sold Anheuser Busch Lager Beer, among other refreshments. Sumner Whitney, the proprietor, standing in front with the apron, later became a victim of Ten Mile's most notorious crime. Courtesy Recen Family Collection.

tone like the more forthright silver clubs. All these groups became larger and more influential each month as the price of silver deteriorated.

At the same time, cracks appeared in the ranks of the regular statewide parties. Republican senators Teller and Wolcott both denounced the Republican president, Benjamin Harrison, as "the most unrelenting enemy of free coinage in office." And in their county and state conventions, Colorado's Republicans and the Democrats adopted pro-silver platforms. Nationally, however, both parties chose hard-money men as presidential candidates. The Republicans renominated Harrison, while the Democrats picked former president Grover Cleveland.

Meanwhile, the Populist Party had held its national convention in Omaha, Nebraska, in early July. For president, the delegates nominated James B. Weaver of Iowa, a Civil War general and long-time politician of national stature. More important to miners, the Populists called for the free and unlimited coinage of silver at the ratio of sixteen to one with gold. While this was only one of several planks that Populists championed, it impressed the silver men from Colorado. That July, when the party held its state convention in Denver, the silver clubs and the Silver League, despite some misgivings, decided to support the Populist ticket. Davis Waite, former Democrat, former Republican, and now a newspaperman from Aspen, won the nomination for governor. That November mining districts like Ten Mile gave huge majorities to Populist candidates, and with the Republicans and the Democrats either split, moribund, or openly backing the Populists, the People's Party swept to victory. Weaver carried Colorado for the national ticket, Waite captured the governor's office, and the party won huge blocks of seats in the statehouse and senate. But how strong this party would be, given its internal divisions and limited issues, remained to be seen. One thing that seemed ominous was that Grover Cleveland and hard money had won nationwide. [42]

So 1892 came to an end on an ambivalent note. The price of silver continued to slip, hard money remained entrenched in Washington, and Governor-elect Waite bided his time until he took office. But it remained to be seen what he and his associates could do, and perceptive individuals must have realized that the crisis was national, if not international, in scope. In Ten Mile the Summit smelter continued to belch fire and smoke, dynamite blasts echoed across the valley, and train whistles sliced through the clear mountain air. And as winter came, the ice covered the streams, snow buried the towns, and the winds swirled off the summits, and the people who still lived there huddled in homes to ward off the chill and waited to see what the new year would bring.

CHAPTER 10

Making About Expenses

THE year 1893 began with doubt and fear. While friend and foe waited to see what the Populists could do, the price of silver continued to tumble through the winter and spring. Then on June 26 came the shock. The Herschell Committee of the British House of Commons announced its recommendation that Her Majesty's Mints in India cease the coinage of silver rupees. With that, the price of silver plunged worldwide. In the United States, it plummeted from eighty to sixty-four cents an ounce in a matter of hours, and in that sudden, swift fall, silver miners found everything—mines, ores, concentrates, bullion, and metal—worth 20 percent less than before. Chaos engulfed the industry. "Everything turned upside down," wrote one mineowner the day after the crash. [1]

The repercussions swept across the West. The smelters announced that they would accept no ores and concentrates. The mines and mills laid off workers, and the industry rumbled on through summer like a lumbering freight train fighting its own momentum. To keep going, some firms cut wages, only to prompt sporadic strikes and lockouts that increased the chaos. To make matters worse, the price of metal continued to slide. By September the silver industry had ground to a halt, and unemployed men stalked the streets in numbers unseen before.

Ten Mile was no exception. Jesse McDonald shut down the Robinson, Arthur Redman Wilfley closed the White Quail, and the Recens stopped work at the Queen of the West. So it went at lesser properties. The Wilfley and Robinson mills ceased crushing and shipping, and the railroads cut service as the smelters in Leadville, Pueblo, and Denver refused to accept any ore except on a special basis. Ten Mile had seen bad times before, but these were the worst since the late 1870s.

Not everyone suffered to the same degree. The crash did not catch Wilfley and his associates as badly as it might have. Because the smelter had failed that spring, he and his colleagues, Thomas Walsh and Ethan E. Byron, had already begun to retrench when silver plunged. They also had about $45,000 coming from the sale of the gold mines at Cripple Creek. Over the summer and fall, Wilfley continued his cleanup, then reduced operations to a minimal level to await developments.

Like others, Wilfley realized that mining had not ended forever. The only question was when and how the mines would reopen. Late that fall, while he waited for the price of silver to stabilize, he approached T. F. Evans and Fred G. Uthoff, the principal owners of the Kimberly mine and the Captain Evans lode, which were close by the White Quail. It seemed obvious to Wilfley that everyone could lower their mining costs and increase the air circulation and drainage capacity if they worked at least part of the mines jointly. As a result, in November 1893, Wilfley paid $1,200 for permission to use the Evans Tunnel to remove ore and waste rock at night. Even though most mines were still closed, he drove a short drift from the Kimberly workings across the Captain Evans lode into the Wilfley group. He would be ready when mining resumed.

By the end of the year, conditions became more settled. Silver steadied above sixty cents an ounce, and as confidence grew that the price would not plunge again, the mines, mills, and smelters began to reopen. But now there were changes. Marginal enterprises remained closed, reducing the number of jobs. The smelting companies had formed an association to boost reduction prices and formalize buying through a clearinghouse. Even more important, the minerals industry was forced to cut costs through labor-saving technology and lower wages. When they resumed operations, virtually all the mines, mills, and smelters compelled their employees to accept wage reductions of about 25 percent, which was roughly comparable to the fall in the price of silver. It was no coincidence that the 1890s would see the rise of virulent labor-management conflicts, which wracked the industry for years to come as miners and smelters sought to regain what they had lost in 1893.

The revival in Ten Mile (such as it was) followed the same course as in the rest of the industry. Among the first to get going was Wilfley. As the drifting snows buried the valley, his exploration crews struck a good deposit of low-grade iron sulfides bearing gold. The smelters had increased their demand for this type of ore for fluxing, and as a result, in

March 1894, Wilfley struck a good bargain with the Pueblo Ore Company, which would resell Wilfley's product to the Pueblo smelters. [2]

By summer, many mines in the district had reopened on one basis or another. Wilfley leased the White Quail to Frank Warner and the Aftermath to Emmett Farrell, and with shipments coming from here and there, Wilfley's associate Walsh reported that the Summit Company was "making about expenses." Elsewhere, the Nova Scotia Boy was getting underway, George Chase of Robinson was taking good pay from his placer in McNulty Gulch, and a Mr. Cramer was reported to be "tearing up Gold Hill" on a "veritable quartz quarry" that held some gold. In August, the *Summit County Journal* wrote that Kokomo's steadily increasing output required two freight trains a day to haul away the ore and concentrates. [3]

Such boosterism continued in the face of hard times. In September the *Journal* claimed that Kokomo led all mining towns except Leadville in ore shipments, which was certainly an exaggeration, yet some mines were undeniably coming back into production. Reports had it that the Queen of the West would resume shipping in the near future. Judge A. B. Colcord and his associates were building a concentrator to work ores from the Union group on Gold Hill—in fact, there seemed to be more interest in the east side of the valley than Ten Mile had seen in years. Production from the Washington mine was on the increase, and it was said that Wilfley could ship one thousand tons daily if the price of metal would rise, but that might have been said about a lot of mines. [4]

Much of the money needed to reopen the mines came from Ten Mile itself—from "capital stored up in muscle energy and experience," to quote one observer. Little money came into the district from outside (there had been comparatively little outside investment for years, it seems). As elsewhere, miners who could invest in labor-saving technology and ore-concentrating machinery did so. By the end of the year concentration had "become a very important factor in this district," wrote the *Journal.* Yet it could not be denied that although production had increased, it had not returned to even the low levels seen before the silver crash. Though a reporter claimed that everyone had confidence in the district except the absentee landowners, the editors had to concede that there were more miners than work. And Ten Mile's most knowledgeable miner, Arthur Redman Wilfley, tried to sell out at the end of the year. But no one would buy his mines, at least not at the price he wanted. [5]

The approach of spring 1895 brought the usual revival. On Elk Mountain, Captain Evans resumed work on the Kimberly group, where his large force would "no doubt" produce two hundred tons daily this year, and Mr. Kimberly himself was about to break ground for a concentrating plant. George T. McDonald, the new foreman at the White Quail, also had the Colonel Sellers under his control, shipping seventy-five tons of ore daily. On Jacque Mountain, the Queen of the West, now said to be *the* high-grade property in Ten Mile, was shipping mineral worth more than one hundred dollars per ton. And in Searle Gulch, the Wilfley mill kept "incessantly grinding away" to produce concentrates that reportedly brought premium prices. [6]

The mines on the heavily timbered hills along the east side of the valley sparked even more interest this year than last. A. B. Colcord pushed ahead "with the determination worthy of a Trojan," said one report. Henry Moyer, the South Park agent at Kokomo, located a good claim of gold quartz, and it was said that many mines would go on a paying basis once the snow cleared. It was no surprise that demand for Gold Hill property increased dramatically. Even the old placers in McNulty and Mayflower gulches attracted new interest. Both Charles J. Senter and George W. Chase, among others, set to work near the head of McNulty Gulch, which lay at the foot of Bartlett Peak.

More mines came into production as summer approached. On Elk Mountain, David D. Colcord leased the Uthoff group, while P. R. Arnold took charge of the Washington and told one reporter that it would become a large shipper once the roads improved. (They were quagmires as usual.) Over on Sheep Mountain, new lessees bent their backs on the Columbine and the Wheel of Fortune, which was still a producer after all these years. And as usual, Jesse McDonald kept the Robinson shipping what he could, largely through the sweat of lessees. The Robinson seemed to have an inexhaustible supply of low-grade ores; while it did not produce much (apparently), it always produced something.

Some Ten Milers invested what little capital they had in new machinery and exploration, and a few found a seller's market for certain classes of ore. One commentator wrote that Ten Mile had the most desirable fluxing ore in Colorado, and it had prompted "lively competition" between the Leadville plants and the valley smelters. The Union Smelting Company of Leadville, for example, sent Fred S. Follett to tour the district in search of contracts, while the aggressive Pueblo Smelting and Refining Company struck deals with the Colonel Sellers, Evans, and Washington mines. There were no idle teams in Ten Mile. Everything in the district was in harness, wrote a reporter, who saw "no likelihood of poor business" for the rest of the year, and predicted that there would be more mining this summer than in the history of the district. [7]

The year 1895 also witnessed a major change in the Summit Mining and Smelting Company. Walsh had lost interest in Ten Mile. He was now preoccupied in developing mines near Rico, Ouray, and Silverton with various investors, including Lucious B. Kendall, George B. Robinson's old mentor. Walsh hoped to sell his interest in the Summit Company for $50,000, and Wilfley and Byron were happy to oblige, though not for that figure. After months of negotiation, they bought out Walsh in such a way that when they took control, Wilfley and Byron each owned five-twelfths of the stock and Isaac N. Turner, the new superintendent, the remaining two-twelfths. The sale, however, did not include the smelter. Walsh wanted to buy that, but not for another year could the miners reach an agreement by which Walsh paid $1,500 for the machinery, which he eventually used at a new plant in the San Juan Mountains. [8]

Wilfley also remained in contact with Frank Emmons, who still hoped the Geological Survey would publish his study of Ten Mile. Emmons continued to make occasional trips to the valley, where he spoke with Wilfley, and revised his monograph. He always thought it was near publication, but the project still languished, and not until 1898, nearly twenty years after Emmons began the work, did the Survey finally send it to press. By this time, silver mining in Ten Mile had long since passed its peak. Emmons' monograph, however, would serve as the basis of all future studies. [9]

Because of the depressed price of silver, Ten Mile continued to be a hotbed of Populist sentiment. In 1894 every drummer traveling through Kokomo was said to be "a political stump speaker" for the cause of free coinage. It was also predicted that Davis Waite, the Populist governor, would receive "a big rousing majority" in Kokomo come the November election. But that remained to be seen. The coalition that elected Waite had fallen apart for a host of reasons, not the least of which was his position that allowed the Western Federation of Miners to best the mine-owners in a bitter strike at Cripple Creek, as well as the derision heaped on him for various programs including a scheme to mint dollars in Mexico—"fandango dollars," the critics jeered. But more than anything else, Waite had to run against hard times. People in Colorado were worse off in 1894 than in 1892. He faced no easy road to reelection, even though the Republicans nominated a little known judge, A. W. McIntire, as their candidate. [10]

Politics in Ten Mile and Summit County moved along apace with the rest of Colorado. The Republicans and the Populists, and probably the Democrats, all held their county conventions this year in Dillon. When the Populists met, A. B. Colcord headed the delegation from Kokomo, and Charles J. Senter the group from Robinson, and when the Republicans gathered, George W. Chase of Robinson took an active part. What seemed so unusual this year was that the normally boisterous Democrats were very quiescent, perhaps because so many had joined the Populist ranks. The *Summit County Journal* claimed that "Democrats are so scarce they have to get a representative from the twin party to prevent being eternally lost."

By September, the fall campaign was in full swing. A. B. Colcord, the Populist leader in Ten Mile, entertained many candidates, such as Congressman Lafe Pence, who gave a speech that "like a flashlight focused on the dark doings of the Republican Party." But that sentiment ignored the fact that a number of Republicans and Democrats doubled as Populist candidates. This reflected the drive for free coinage, the growing split in the Populist ranks, and a measure of return to political orthodoxy. Women were particularly active in the election this year, as Colorado had just given them the vote. A Mrs. Marble, for example, stumped Ten Mile for the Republicans, while Lillian Colcord did more "missionary work" for the Populists than any other person in the county, according to the *Journal*. And as a sign of the times, this once pro-Democratic paper called on the voters to give their "united support" to the People's Party. The history of both the Republican and Democratic parties, said the editors, precluded "even the hope of monetary or other reforms," as both were "the tools of corporations, rings and trusts."[11]

But statewide, Populism had run its course. That November, the Populists picked up huge majorities in Ten Mile and other mining districts, but Waite lost to McIntire, and the party lost ground everywhere outside the mining country. While free coinage and Populism were far from dead, they had taken a hard blow. As 1895 began, "the redeemers," as these Republicans were called, prepared to take charge of the state again.[12]

Although the political complexion of Ten Mile changed in the 1890s, many other aspects of life did not, notably transportation. In August 1891, the *Journal* reported that the bridges between Frisco and Robinson were in "frightful condition." The editors implored the county commissioners to look into the matter, but they did nothing of consequence. A year later, "that most wretched apology for the county road" near Breckenridge allowed a team to plunge over an embankment, injuring two prominent county residents. And in October 1894, the *Journal's* Kokomo letter lamented that "good roads are a subject unknown to the people of this district." It had "the worst roads in the world."

Traveling by rail was easier, but not without problems, particularly on the South Park. In October 1894, the line removed the ramshackle car it used as a depot in Kokomo, leaving "nothing less than the broad canopy of heaven" to protect the traveling public, said one writer. But a month later the South Park began building "a palatial depot." Aside from the lack of shelter, engines and cars occasionally overturned, particularly after the spring runoff weakened the roadbed. Snowslides, which occurred often in Ten Mile Canyon, sometimes blocked the track for days at a time. Henry A. Recen, Jr., who grew up in the valley, remembered that it was often more convenient to travel by ski than by rail between Ten Mile and Breckenridge. And death still rode the iron horse. In December 1894, the Oddfellows of Kokomo assembled to bury Swen Peterson, the South Park section boss, who had been killed by a train on Boreas Pass. [13]

What few businesses Ten Mile still had managed to hold their own through the mid-1890s. J. W. Dowd remained as the leading merchant and continued to mix business with politics—he became the Kokomo city treasurer after the Populists swept to victory in 1895. As for lodging, a Mrs. McKenna was reported to be "thoroughly furnishing and refitting" the Miner's Home Hotel, where travelers could now find first-class accommodations. Not to be outdone, N. P. Anderson began grading a site for an addition to his inn. Ten Mile still had saloons and billiard parlors, though far less than during the boom. [14]

But the valley still had few public services. In May 1895 one man complained that it was "sad to state" that Kokomo had no fire protection, although the town probably had less need for that then than ever before, but a more pressing problem was the water supply, which became a political issue. The Populist mayor, D. J. Humphrey, pronounced the situation "grave" and worthy of "weighty consideration," and the city council began debating whether it should issue bonds to construct waterworks or wait until there was enough money in the town treasury. There was also talk of building an electric light plant. Ten Mile, however, still had no telephone service, nor would it for another decade.

Crime seemed to be much less of a problem now than ever before. There were fewer people, perhaps one-tenth the number of the late 1870s. The boomtown mentality had long since come to an end, and far fewer miners walked the streets with nothing to do in off-hours. If some persons still drank, gambled, and shot billiards, the populace was still too small to support the number of saloons and dance houses that had flourished more than a decade before. Yet many men still went armed. In August 1894, the *Journal's* Kokomo correspondent declared that "the city dads should arrest each and every walking arsenal. No need for shooting irons in these peaceable times." [15]

Yet the 1890s saw the most violent crime in Ten Mile's history. It began in Breckenridge on the night of August 11, 1898, when four men broke into the Denver Hotel to steal a bankroll from a local clothier. When someone's gun discharged, the robbers hurriedly changed plans and burst into the bar, where they took watches, stickpins, and money from the bartender and patrons. Then they escaped in the darkness, taking a steep trail over the mountains, where they hid in a small cabin nestled in a place near Kokomo known as Robbers Roost.

The next day, the county sheriff sent his deputy, Ernest Conrad of Breckenridge, over to Kokomo to investigate. Once there, Conrad deputized a well-known saloonkeeper, Sumner Whitney, and that afternoon the two men set off for Robbers Roost. After a time, they came across the small cabin and went in. There they found Dick Bryant, Dick Manley, "Broken Nose" Reilly, and their leader "Pug" Ryan, all men with unsavory reputations. Ryan apparently convinced the deputies that nothing was wrong, and the two left. Once outside, however, they changed their minds and returned. When Conrad asked to see what was under some blankets, the cabin exploded in gunfire. Conrad was killed instantly. Whitney, Bryant, and Manley were seriously wounded. Reilly and Ryan escaped in the melee. The shots attracted attention in Kokomo, and more men rushed to the blood-spattered cabin, where they found the dead and dying. They captured Reilly a short time later, but Ryan made good his escape.

The shock numbed Summit County. Bryant died before the day was out. A special train hurried Whitney and Manley to a hospital in Leadville, but their wounds were fatal. Before they died, however, both identified Ryan as the ringleader of the gang. In the meantime, Reilly sat in the Kokomo jail, but before long, the authorities spirited him away to Breckenridge to avoid an appointment with Judge Lynch, so enraged was the populace. Ryan, however, remained at large until 1902, when police in Seattle, Washington, arrested a tramp who claimed he was J. C. Moore, a local resident. After the authorities noticed the word "pug" tattooed on an arm, they deduced they had captured Ryan. Once extradited to Colorado (and recaptured after escaping from the Leadville jail), Ryan was convicted of murder and sentenced to life imprisonment at the State Penitentiary in Canon City. He died there in 1932. [16]

Crimes such as this, however shocking, were an aberration from the normal path of life. Far more typical were the clubs, sports, and celebrations that offered a welcome counterpoint to the business of mining and the press of hard times. The Knights of Columbus occasionally held a

SKIERS AT THE KOKOMO DEPOT. Although not known as a tourist center, Ten Mile did attract occasional skiers like these dressed in their outdoor best about 1910. In the 1970s, Copper Mountain emerged as one of Colorado's best downhill ski areas. William Creamer photographer, courtesy Alice R. Work.

bazaar. The I–X–L Social Club sponsored dances, and once in awhile, the Oddfellows put on a play. Ten Mile also had organizations like the Porcupine Club, which apparently brought in political speakers, and associations like the Sulphide Club, which mixed business with pleasure. The major political parties, of course, were as much social as political. [17]

What also excited people were sports. James W. Dowd received considerable press when he bought a string of racers, which were said to excel "any horseflesh" ever brought into Ten Mile; his steeds, "the scions of noble sires," won many a race. But the sport of kings was for only the few. Bicycles were for the many. In the mid-1890s the national bicycle craze engulfed Ten Mile. One group of enthusiasts pedaled twenty-eight miles to Soda Springs one Sunday in May 1895. And as elsewhere in America, baseball was "all the rage." Ten Mile boasted a

STUDENTS IN TEN MILE. Students and sled posed with teacher William
Creamer, possibly at the Robinson schoolhouse, about 1900. Unlike most
teachers, Creamer remained in Ten Mile for nearly twenty years. Courtesy
Alice R. Work.

number of teams like the Lilliput Club and the Wilfley Nine, managed by
John Wilfley "the coacher." Less energetic Ten Milers enjoyed an annual
trip to the Peach Festival in Grand Junction. [18]

The Fourth of July was still a celebrated event. Wheeler had now lost
out as a major site of festivities, but that made little difference. Cele-
brants went either to Kokomo or Breckenridge. Kokomo's celebration in
1895 was probably typical. The Elk Mountain Blues and the Kokomo
Reds played a well-attended game of baseball that ended in a 4–4 tie.
Small boys, "noisy, bumptious, grinning, shouting," said the *Journal*, ran
all over town setting off firecrackers and exploding their largest ones
near the obese. That evening the Kokomo Dancing Club hosted a grand
ball attended by seventy-five couples, who danced to the music of Gallagher's Orchestra until "Old Sol" snuck over the summit of Peak 10 with
the first rays of dawn. "The only noticeable lack of patriotism," frowned

the *Journal* "was the ascent of old glory." It did not wave over Kokomo because the town did not have a flag—"a shame and a disgrace," intoned the editors.

Education was still less than it might have been. The Kokomo schoolhouse remained in operation under a number of teachers who spent one or two years in Ten Mile. And people in Kokomo, few of whom had any advanced education, took great pride in the young who attended the State Normal School at Greeley. Miss Gussie Warner, as well as Dan and Charley Turner, the sons of Isaac N. Turner of the Wilfley mine, drew considerable publicity when they came and went at semesters.

As for religion, there was little change from the 1880s. Catholics could still worship at Our Lady of the Snows, but the parish was on its last legs. Protestants still waited for traveling preachers, mostly from Breckenridge, who came at night and sometimes on weekends. Ten Mile also had a few religious organizations, such as the Amheath M.E. Church group that gave a New England dinner in November 1894 in hope of raising money. And there were fraternal organizations like the Masons and the Knights of Columbus. Couples who wanted to be married in church still had to go to Breckenridge, Leadville, or Denver, but Judge Colcord could tie the knot in Ten Mile, as he did for some who wished to elope.

Kokomo also drew special business on Sunday, particularly from Leadville after the city council closed the saloons on the sabbath. Some people took the train under the guise of business, a few claimed they wanted to attend church, but most said they did not like "a puritan Sunday." They wanted to enjoy "the many little diversions which tend to make Sunday a poor man's holiday"—in other words, a few quaffs in one of the town's saloons. Many of Kokomo's "wicked business men," intoned the pious *Journal*, counted silver dollars till Monday morning. [19]

To some degree, this practice resembled another that developed in the midst of the great strike that convulsed Leadville in 1896 and 1897 when the Western Federation of Miners struck for higher wages and shorter hours. During the long, tense months, as the national guard patrolled the city, and miners shifted as best they could, some union men went to Kokomo to find work. There were few jobs, however, and this strategy was largely unsuccessful. Otherwise, Ten Mile was unaffected by the strike. If any union organizers arrived, their efforts went nowhere. As always, Ten Mile remained non-union. [20]

During the 1890s the hard times and floundering prices of lead and silver led many miners to search for new methods that might lower costs and increase recovery. Among them was Ten Mile's leading miner, Arthur Redman Wilfley.

MODEST QUARTERS. Even in the early twentieth century, newspapers served as insulation and wallpaper in some of Ten Mile's homes. William Creamer photographer, courtesy Alice R. Work.

Wilfley had no formal education in engineering. He was a mining engineer by practice and experience, not by college training, but the nineteenth century was less particular about academic credentials than the twentieth century would be. From his mines at Kokomo, he could see vast tonnages of complex low-grade ores which held silver, lead, copper, iron, zinc, and gold—ores that could not be mined and processed because the costs exceeded the value of the metals. What could he do to convert these essentially worthless ores into valuable minerals?

Wilfley's long experience in milling had given him a broad knowledge of ore concentration. He had used different vanners, jigs, bumping tables, and other ore-dressing machines that depended largely upon different specific gravities to separate the valuable from the worthless constituents. These devices worked well if the specific gravities were disparate, but not if they were similar, as they were in silver-bearing iron, lead, and zinc sulfides. (It was no coincidence that miners in Ten Mile belonged to the Sulphide Club.)

Even before the silver crash, Wilfley had tried to improve the concentrators then available. After installing various machines in his Kokomo mill, he conducted experiments in hope of processing "large bodies of lower grade ore that had never been treated before," as he later remembered. Yet his early study was sporadic and unsystematic. What was more, business came first. Then in 1893, Wilfley and his wife, Addie, visited the Columbian Exposition in Chicago, and there he saw a German concentrating table with a new design—a vanner with a transversely inclined surface. This gave him a new idea. That winter, as the minerals industry sat in the doldrums, Wilfley conducted more experiments at his Kokomo mill. He worked on through the next year, then early in 1895—the date is obscure—he first "placed a long riffle on the percussion type of transversely inclined table," he said. This was the basis for what became known as the Wilfley Table. He pushed ahead with more experiments, and in May 1895, he built a small-scale prototype which he tested over the summer months. When this unit proved successful in concentrating his complex low-grade ores, he had C. J. ("Bud") Estabrook, the foreman at the mill, build a full-scale model.

Despite the success of this first working unit, Wilfley was still a long way from a commercial model. Up to this time, he had kept his experiments secret from even his closest associates, but now he told his brother John, his partner A. B. Colcord, and others. Together, they experimented over the next year. They built models in various sizes, recorded data, tried various numbers of riffles on the table surface, and tested construction materials. By July 1896, after more than a year's effort, Wilfley and his associates had developed a production model. It was twelve feet long, five feet wide, and covered by linoleum with the riffles attached in an uneven line to the transversely inclined surface; a motor gave the table a characteristic head motion. Wilfley also had a captive market for the first five production units—his own mill at Kokomo.

But Wilfley was first and foremost a businessman, and with silver production hobbled by low prices, he hoped to sell tables throughout the industry. After building three more units at Kokomo, he made his first sales. He sold one unit to the Puzzle mill in Breckenridge, where the table received considerable publicity; a second to the Gold Mining and Milling Company, which operated the famous Mary Murphy mine near Romley; and the third to the Robinson mill, now managed by A. B. Colcord. The success of these units in working complex low-grade sulfides

THE WILFLEY TABLE. Developed at Kokomo in the 1890s, the Wilfley Table was still an important piece of ore-dressing machinery almost a century later. Courtesy Jay E. Niebur.

sparked interest and orders, and by midsummer it was clear that Wilfley could tap a ready market.

Kokomo, however, was hardly a manufacturing center, nor was it likely to become one. Almost immediately, Wilfley looked to Denver. Convinced that his table held enormous promise (and profits), he rented a building on Market Street, and by September he was in production. He sold more units to the Mary Murphy mine and the Puzzle mill, other well-known firms bought at least one table, and by the end of the year Wilfley had sold thirty-eight units of his No. 1 model at the standard price of $450, a relatively small price to pay for an important piece of equipment.

Wilfley, however, was lax in seeking a patent. He had no experience in such matters and thought it "a waste of time." Perhaps for that reason, he was less than careful. In the patent application, his attorney described only one riffle on the table surface, on the grounds that "one tapered riffle was as good as a thousand." Perhaps so, but it would take Wilfley more than ten years in court to prove it.

After his first success, Wilfley wasted little time in improving the table. When he opened his factory in Denver, he also took space in Henry Wood's new ore-testing offices nearby. Wood had known Wilfley for years, and he allowed Wilfley to conduct experiments through which he developed larger tables that increased recovery and smaller ones that could be used in laboratories. Wood, however, declined Wilfley's offer to allow him to buy one-half the patent rights.

Even more important, Wilfley came into contact with the Mine and Smelter Supply Company, the creation of Eben Smith, David H. Moffat, Jr., and others who had important connections in all the major mining camps, notably Leadville and Cripple Creek. Late in 1896, Wilfley and the Supply Company signed a five-year marketing agreement. Wilfley agreed to manufacture tables and sell them throughout Colorado; his brother John would sell the tables in Kansas and Missouri (homes of major lead industries); and the Supply Company would market the table throughout the rest of the country. Not content to stop here, Wilfley eventually sold the international rights to the Wilfley Ore Concentrator Syndicate.

Wilfley now expanded operations. He tried to market the table in Central City and Black Hawk, the state's oldest mining areas, but the results were disappointing. He had better success, however, in South Park and still more in booming Cripple Creek. Wilfley's marketing style was to install the table, put it through a series of trial runs, and use the results to convince the owners to buy the product. Sometimes, however, he built entire mills, a strategy that worked particularly well at Cripple Creek. When he built such mills, Wilfley generally took in partners like Wood to spread the risk; the mining company took an option to buy the plant if it proved successful, which it invariably did. Wilfley also promoted the table by giving small models to mining schools. While his brother John did not fare so well in Kansas and Missouri, the Supply Company enjoyed phenomenal success in western mining districts, and as orders for the table mounted, Wilfley had to move his factory to larger quarters, not once but twice in the late 1890s.

Despite the spectacular growth, Wilfley by no means enjoyed a monopoly. Selling concentrators was a lucrative business, and other firms were quick to enter the market, many with tables that infringed on Wilfley's patent. The Hallett Table, Cammett Concentrator, Woodbury Concentrator, Overstrom Table, Dunham Concentrator, Deister Table, New Standard Concentrator, Lodwic Table, and Card Table, were just a few of the alleged imitations. Anything but a humorous man to begin with, Wilfley was hardly amused at the success of his rivals. To protect

A CLOTHESLINE PORCH. The original caption reads: "Stood on this to hang up clothes when the snow was deep." William Creamer photographer, courtesy Alice R. Work.

his interests, he sought new patents and went to court, but he had to pay dearly in time and money to lodge so many lawsuits.

In July 1899, he brought suit against the Denver Engineering Works Company, which was manufacturing the Cammett Table, ostensibly invented by one of Wilfley's former employees, Ira A. Cammett. When the case went to trial in 1901, it produced some remarkable testimony, including A. B. Colcord's claim that Wilfley "stole" the invention from him. What was critical, however, was that the U.S. Circuit Court upheld Wilfley's contentions and established the validity of his original patent. Before the final decree, however, the judge announced his findings to both parties; as a result, Wilfley and the Engineering Company signed an agreement by which Wilfley granted the firm a license to sell its version of the Wilfley Table.

This case, *Wilfley v. Denver Engineering Works Company*, set both the precedent and the pattern for Wilfley's assault on those who infringed on his patents. For more than a decade, until 1914, he would have his attorneys sue, the cases would generally go to court, and the judge's decision in Wilfley's favor would become known before the final decree. Wilfley would then negotiate an agreement by which the competitor acceded to the court's decision, paid Wilfley a fee, and in turn received a license to manufacture and sell its particular concentrating table.

For a man with a bad heart, Wilfley led an exceptionally busy life. In the late 1890s he tried to develop a copper mine in Arizona, but failed miserably. Through his brother Charles, he invested heavily in the Denver Savings Bank only to lose a huge sum of money through fraud. By the early 1900s, however, he was devoting more and more time to invention. If he no longer manufactured tables at Kokomo, he used the mine and mill as a full-scale laboratory. He invented a moving hearth furnace for roasting. He developed several slime tables to recover gold and other metals from the tailings from the Wilfley table. He even worked on a sand pump. Yet these devices enjoyed relatively little commercial success because of their relatively high operational costs.

Such intensive work took its toll. Wilfley's health broke down several times. To recuperate, he took a number of extended vacations in southern California, which was now becoming a third home to go with his places in Denver and Kokomo. His fragile health, however, finally compelled him to sell the table manufacturing business to the Supply Company. [21]

As the 1890s passed, Wilfley spent less and less time in Ten Mile, and that might have been said about a great many others. Although some mines continued to ship, the general trend in production was down. People moved away one by one. Some went to Leadville, others to Breckenridge, and still more to Denver. A good many probably headed "back home," wherever that might have been. Only a few, like James Dowd, Nels Anderson, and Ethan E. Byron, found enough to keep them in Ten Mile, but as ore production continued to fall, these men seemed more and more like exceptions. And as the twentieth century dawned, this slow drift toward oblivion seemed likely to continue, though for how long no one knew.

CHAPTER 11

Rising Like the Phoenix

THE dawn of the new century sparked euphoric celebrations in many a quarter, but it brought only forebodings to Ten Mile. The population had drifted down to only a few hundred people. Robinson looked ever more like a ghost town, and Kokomo seemed only slightly behind. Those who remained struggled to make a living in the midst of what seemed like an endless supply of low-grade ore and capricious prices for metal. If well-known miners like Arthur Redman Wilfley and Jesse McDonald were making large reputations, they were doing it mostly elsewhere, not in Ten Mile. Although boosters never ceased to hail the return of good times, the valley's prospects seemed poor indeed, unless new technologies, higher prices for metal, or the discovery of new ore bodies could touch off a renaissance.

In the first years of the century, iron sulfides found a ready market in the smelters that needed iron for flux. Jesse McDonald, still operating through lessees, shipped enough to make a profit of $2,500 to $5,000 per month for the Robinson Company. Ethan E. Byron kept the Wilfley properties going and even took a lease on the Kimberly group. The Uthoff and the Michigan both ran steadily, and Wilfley's former superintendent, Isaac N. Turner, leased the Queen of the West from the Recen brothers.

Other mines had their ups and downs. The Maximus, Bledsoe, Wintergreen, and Snow Bank worked sporadically. The Colonel Sellers closed for a time, because the miners refused to toil without pay, and

Peter Breene, the Irishman who had once been state treasurer and lieutenant governor, blasted a new shaft so near his old mine, the Colonel
Sellers, that the new owner, a Mrs. Marshall, obtained an injunction to
shut him down for allegedly taking her ore. The Reconstruction on
Copper Mountain, which had been closed for as long as anyone remembered, reopened under the hand of John Goff, and after lying idle for
nearly twenty years, the Free America created a sensation when a gold
discovery pushed it to the forefront of Ten Mile's producers. [1]

In the midst of this work, however, the Robinson suddenly closed its
doors, turning the camp into a ghost town. Then in July 1900, the owners brought in Frank Bulkley, a well-known mining engineer, to examine
the property, as well as the nearby Eldorado. Bulkley found that after
years of operation, the main adit extended three thousand feet into
Sheep Mountain, the shafts aggregated three thousand feet deep, and
the workings consisted of "several thousand linear feet" of levels, in-
clines, upraises, and stopes. Despite such extensive mining, Bulkley estimated that the No. 1 chute still held 50,000 tons of low-grade ore; the
No. 2 chute, 100,000 tons (corroborating the findings made by Wood and
Argall in 1889); and the No. 3 chute, Jessie Ore Chute, and Denver City
lode claims, an unspecified tonnage. Bulkley thought the Eldorado had
another 50,000 tons. He was very optimistic, particularly because the
price of base metals had risen, while freight and smelting costs had
fallen. Although the Robinson had already produced $5 million, most of it
in the early 1880s, "only a comparatively small part" had been developed. The mine was "one of the great possibilities," and he predicted
that its future might rival its past.

Bulkley was not a man to let opportunity slip. He and several associates obtained an option and organized a new firm, the Robinson Consolidated Mining & Smelting Company. "Big Mining Deal at Robinson,"
headlined the *Summit County Journal* when the enterprise exercised its
option. And it was. The editors estimated the sale price at $600,000.
Who controlled the new firm is hard to say, but it was probably Bulkley
and his intimates, although he later said the directors included four men
from the old Robinson Company and four from the Boston Gold-Copper
Company of Leadville, which had been buying ore from the Robinson and
Washington mines. Whatever the internal mechanics, the directorate
glittered with the names of bankers and brokers from prestigious firms
in Boston, Providence, and New York. [2]

After Bulkley made a second investigation in May 1901, the company
published a promotional pamphlet. Ironically, in view of the shocking collapse of the Robinson Company in 1881, Bulkley noted that stock prices

could fluctuate violently "by reason of shrewd manipulation," and that sometimes "the fortunes of numberless men and women, sometimes representing the accumulation of years, [had] been swept away in a single day." Then he began his pitch. Although millions had been lost in railroads, farm mortgages, eastern industrials, and other investments, mining by contrast had steadily advanced. The great figures in mining and finance, like John D. Rockefeller, were quietly buying copper as well as gold and silver mines.

Bulkley wished to present "a proposition of unquestioned merit." The new company had bought the Robinson group and the Washington mine along with the rights to use the Loder pyritic smelting process. Although the Robinson had produced more than $6 million (which was $1 million more than he had noted the previous year), there were now "exposed and in sight" not less than 400,000 tons of low-grade ore and several miles of underground workings. Bulkley's plan was to erect a pyritic smelter—*THIS IS A SMELTING PROPOSITION*," he declared— thus it carried "none of the risks of the ordinary mining venture." The tonnage in the mine was "practically unlimited," every day the enterprise could smelt 500 tons at a profit of $2 each, perhaps more, and the firm would "doubtless" pay dividends for years to come, like the Homestake Mining Company. This was "not a stock jobbing scheme," he emphasized, but "a straight legitimate proposition."

Then came the ultimate pitch. "For the purpose of providing capital to build the smelter," wrote Bulkley, "a limited amount" of treasury stock would be sold. The firm would earn not less than 10 percent and probably nearer 20 percent on its capitalization of $1.5 million. Those who bought would make "an absolutely safe and exceptionally profitable investment."[3]

How much stock Bulkley sold is a matter of conjecture, but he sold at least enough to get going. By the end of the summer of 1901 he had reopened the mine and begun building the smelter. In September, the Breckenridge *Bulletin* reported that Robinson was "on the boom." Dilapidated buildings that had gone begging six weeks before now had owners and occupants. There was not a vacant building in camp, renovation had become the order of the day, and housing was tight. "Beds are at a premium," warned the editors, "so bring your blankets when you come." Yet the boom had its negative side. "Fistic encounters" were frequent, reported the paper, and it offered the usual lament that the roads were in "horrible shape." Some things never changed.

By the end of September came reports that the new Robinson was "rising like the phoenix from its ashes." A nearly deserted village two months ago, the town now had two hundred people, not all newcomers to Ten Mile. William Kutzleb, the mayor, had mined in the valley for years. And James Dowd, who launched a branch of "his big Kokomo institution," had merchandised in the valley for nearly two decades. Robinson now had two thriving hotels and a boardinghouse, four saloons, and of course, the one church that was part of "the municipal paraphernalia." But the real interest centered on the new smelter, which was expected to provide the town with electricity as well as reduce ore. [4]

Yet reality soon arrived. The smelter did not begin operations on schedule, and after a time, published accounts said that the company planned only a 300-ton per day plant, as opposed to the 600 tons mentioned earlier. Whether this reflected the company's original objectives, problems in raising capital, or a more accurate assessment by the newspapers, is hard to say. But the fact is that while the Wilfley, Uthoff, Michigan, and other groups kept mining on limited schedules through winter, the Robinson complex did not begin operation. Jesse McDonald, H. M. Shepard, and a few old Leadville men organized the Ten Mile Leasing and Mining Company, but that was the only firm shipping ore from Sheep Mountain. And as spring came, it became obvious that the new Robinson Company would not prompt another boom. Even after the smelter blew in, the Robinson mine remained what it had been—a small producer. [5]

If iron sulfides had held the district together during the 1890s, then zinc sulfides kept the mines going in the early 1900s. The miners had long known about zinc, but had shipped little ore because of the large penalties exacted by the smelting companies, none of whom had the technology needed to process zinc-bearing mineral. This changed, however, just before 1900 when some zinc shipments abroad stimulated several enterprises to introduce European technology. By the early twentieth century, miners in Colorado could sell zinc concentrates to some of the older smelters or to new plants at Canon City, Pueblo, and Denver, or as far away as Oklahoma. Metal prices also increased. From 1900 to 1907, silver fluctuated, but eventually rose from 62 to 68 cents an ounce; lead increased from 4.4 to 5.3 cents per pound; and zinc went from 4.4 to 5.9 cents per pound. [6]

Miners in Ten Mile took advantage as best they could. "The Uthoff keeps up its large daily output of some fifty tons," wrote the *Summit County Journal* in 1903. "Fifteen men are employed." The Michigan, Breene, and Wilfley mines were steady producers as well, while the Iron Mask, Snow Bank, and Queen of the West contributed their share, although they operated more sporadically, as did the mines on the east side of the valley. Some relatively new zinc-bearing properties, like the Boston mine in Mayflower Gulch, began to make a name for themselves, and a small mining camp known as Boston sprang to life. Larger mines like the Breene, Kimberly, and Wilfley built or expanded mills to incorporate the latest technology. But the Belt mine in Mayflower Gulch was "blown to atoms" after someone stuck seven or eight frozen sticks of dynamite into the coals to thaw. And there was excitement of a different sort in 1906 when the Robinson Company and several other firms passed into the hands of the International Mining Company, which promptly found a new ore body that created a sensation. [7]

If concentrating ores had become the technological order of the day, then consolidating mines became the economic norm. The trend, begun by Wilfley in the 1880s, had continued into the 1890s when various individuals had joined the Tiger, Nettie B., and other claims hard by old Kokomo, into what became known as the Uthoff group. The drive to consolidate persisted into the twentieth century, notably at the Robinson mine—first in 1901, with the union of the Robinson and the Washington, and later, in 1906, with the creation of the International Mining Company.

Consolidation was also coming again to the Wilfley properties, though not entirely for economic reasons. Ethan E. Byron had managed the Wilfley mine for years, and might well have continued, but in May 1905, he snagged his clothing on some machinery, and before anyone could turn off the power, he was crushed and battered so badly that he lived only a few days longer. Wilfley was out of town when he heard the news, but after the tragedy, he hurried back to Kokomo to manage operations himself. Yet he had no time for day-to-day work, and he knew the Byron heirs were either too young or unsuited to join the management. He also saw the possibility of consolidating operations with the adjacent Kimberly mine.

Wilfley approached the Kimberly Mines Company through an intermediary, and by January 1906, the two parties had reached an agreement, only to have it fall through at the last minute. Wilfley, however, was undaunted. Over the next few months he bought out the Byron heirs and increased his holdings in the Summit Company until he owned 83 percent of the outstanding stock. Then Wilfley resumed talks, but not until February 1907 could he sell his Elk Mountain properties to the newly organized Kimberly and Wilfley Mines Company for $162,000 (the *Summit County Journal* offered its "presumption" that the price was $500,000). Yet this "sale" was really more of a loan than anything else, for Wilfley was to receive his payment in monthly checks of principal and interest.

THE KIMBERLY-WILFLEY MINE AND MILL. During the twentieth century the complex operated profitably only when wartime brought high prices for metal. Courtesy Jay E. Niebur.

The plan, however, did not work out. The enterprise built a new mill, but because of litigation and other problems, the plant never operated. When lead and zinc prices plunged late in 1907 owing to an economic downturn, the Kimberly-Wilfley Company could not meet its payments. Wilfley agreed to reduce the purchase price to $125,000 to be paid at the rate of $7,500 per month with 5 percent interest on the unpaid balance. Yet even this proved a burden. In 1912 the enterprise went bankrupt and the property reverted to Wilfley. [8]

The tribulations of the Kimberly-Wilfley Company reflected the continuing problems in Ten Mile and throughout much of Colorado. The year 1907 began fairly well. In its Kokomo column of July, the *Summit County Journal* predicted "lively times for this old mining camp this season." Despite the falling prices for metal, ore shipments actually rose from $110,000 to $155,000, mostly in lead and zinc. The Uthoff, Michigan, and Queen of the West all produced something, so did some of the small mines in the Ten Mile Range, and the Breene and Wilfley mills kept pounding away. There was also spectacular news. "BIG STRIKE AT ROBINSON," headlined the *Journal* in July. After sinking a shaft more than 1,100 feet, H. M. Shepard announced that the International Company had struck, well to the northwest, what he thought was the main ore trend in the Robinson mine.

This euphoria was short-lived, however. By year-end the slump in metal prices had hit the industry hard. Most mines in Ten Mile closed, and from the $155,000 shipped in 1907, production plunged to $79,000 in 1908 and to $21,000 in 1909. It might have gone lower, but the International kept shipping lead-zinc sulfides until Shepard and his associates closed down in 1909 to develop the ore body and build a new mill. By the end of the year only the Michigan and the Queen of the West were in operation, and just barely. [9]

Over the next five years, however, Ten Mile went through another boom and bust that largely reflected the rise and fall in the prices of silver, lead, and zinc. In 1910, Shepard reopened the International; the Michigan, Roswell-Sprague, and Felicia Grace followed; and output soared to $180,000, more than it had been since 1905. And the editors of the *Journal* proclaimed that "Kokomo is still on the map." For the next four years, the output from the International carried Ten Mile, although sporadic shipments from the Mayflower, Michigan, Pearl, Queen of the West, Wintergreen, and even the Reconstruction made some contribution. The Kimberly-Wilfley group shipped virtually nothing. Yet Ten Mile's production still fell each year, and finally in 1914, it plunged to a new low of less than $14,000. With lower prices for metal, most of Ten Mile sat idle once more. [10]

Throughout these years, Robinson tottered on its last legs and might have collapsed except for the International Company. Even so, the town had to contend with fire. In June 1907, a blaze broke out at the Holmberg Kauffman Hotel. The flames leaped to the dry frame structures nearby. They proved easy prey, and before long, the fire had reduced virtually the entire business section to nothing more than embers. Gone were the hotel, a store, a saloon, and several unoccupied buildings, some dating back to 1879. And this was not the last fire in Robinson. In June 1916, a blaze broke out in a miner's cabin, spread up the east side of Main Street, and destroyed nine buildings. Seven families were burned out, and the flames consumed a boardinghouse for thirty-five men working at the Wilson mill. [11]

Not surprisingly, the population of Ten Mile gravitated toward Kokomo. In business, James W. Dowd operated the Ten Mile Mercantile Company until 1907, when John Colcord took over. P. R. Arnold sold meats and groceries, and both he and Dowd speculated in or managed mines on the side, though neither enjoyed anything that approached the success of the long-gone George B. Robinson. Mrs. M. A. Buffington ran the Mountain House; and Gus Anderson, the Clifton House, until Mrs. Anderson took over. Joe Bryant reportedly had the finest saloon in Ten Mile, but he had to compete with others, like J. E. Riley, who also served at least one term as mayor of Kokomo (or what was actually Recen).

More than in times past, women came to the forefront in business. Eva Carlson, and later May King, doubled as postmaster and proprietor of a candy and confectionary store. Mrs. Anna Swallow ran a similar shop, and a Mrs. J. F. Cooper taught music. Several women operated hotels and boardinghouses. Besides Mrs. Buffington and Mrs. Anderson, Mrs. R. De Barneure ran the Otis Hotel and doubled as "telephone agent," although Kokomo did not obtain service until 1906. A Mrs. C. Conwell also ran the Otis at one point, and later a restaurant and then a rooming house. While there is no proof, it seems likely that at least one of these "hotels" was a front for a brothel.

In politics, the People's Party faded away, and the Republicans and Democrats reasserted themselves. Women made their presence known here as well. Lula B. Hogan, Lillian Colcord, and a Mrs. Jones all won election as county superintendent of schools. But the greatest political success belonged to Jesse McDonald, who lived in Leadville despite his interests in Ten Mile. In 1902, he became the Republican candidate for lieutenant governor and was elected. In the gubernatorial race, however, the Democrat Alva Adams defeated the Republican James Peabody. Adams took office in January 1903, but days later, in what the pro-Democratic *Labor News* called the "Most Damnable Crime in American History," the Republican-controlled legislature voided Adams' election because of alleged voting irregularities. In the compromise that followed, Peabody took office, but resigned a day later in favor of McDonald, who served out the term. [12]

In these years of decline, Kokomo had no more amenities and social services than before. Public funds were so tight that in 1902 the townsfolk held a "grand ball" to raise money to keep up the Robinson and Kokomo cemeteries. The town did manage to get a physician in C. K. Osborne, but he stayed only a few years. Kokomo and the other towns still depended upon weekly visits from traveling preachers, except in the early 1900s when the Methodist Episcopal Church found a parson in a Reverend Knowles, but like Osborne's, his stay in Ten Mile was brief. Education provided the only constant in the person of William Creamer, who arrived in Kokomo in 1900. Although most teachers stayed no more than one or two years, Creamer remained as the teacher and principal at the single schoolhouse for eighteen years. Yet he rarely had more than ten students, and his salary hovered around $900 per year. Not surprisingly, he prospected and speculated in mining claims, but the big bonanza never came his way. [13]

Long before Creamer left, however, Kokomo looked undeniably forlorn. In April 1912, when Otis Archie King arrived with his wife and son to take charge of the Wilson mill, he found a place characterized by a sense of déjà vu. King remembered that he had slumbered over Fremont Pass in a "reverie" aboard a train of "dinky cars, drawn by an engine with an oversized smokestack" that resembled the woodburners of the 1870s. Then he was jolted awake by a conductor shouting "Ko-ko-mo, Ko-ko-mo" in stentorian tones. After "a wild scramble for baggage," King and his family stood on the boardwalk beside a frame building "called a depot," and from there, he took a quick glance at the town. Boardwalks still fronted the buildings, but he thought that the streets "of native soil, gravel, and rock lacked any suggestion from road commissioners." It seemed to King that most buildings had not been painted since they were put up in the 1880s, and he could see that the shingles had curled up and turned a dark brown from weather and age. The people, he thought, resembled the surroundings. "Even the old sour dough miners," he wrote, "stomping down the walks in their hobnail boots at the end of the

WILLIAM CREAMER'S LIVING ROOM. The furnishings reveal a typical turn-of-the-century home in Ten Mile. William Creamer photographer, courtesy Alice R. Work.

shift, with tin dinner buckets slung over their shoulders, seemed to blend with the surroundings, wrinkled and brown."[14]

King justifiably thought that Kokomo was about to turn into a ghost town, but what altered the decline was the onset of World War I in August 1914. Before long, the new demand for metals boosted prices. While gold held steady at $20 an ounce through government fiat, silver soared from 55 cents to $1.12 per ounce; lead doubled from 4 to 8 cents per pound; and zinc nearly tripled from 5 to more than 13 cents per pound. Ten Mile's production surged again. The Michigan and the Queen of the West went back into operation. Then in 1916, the Progress Mining and Milling Company reopened the Robinson and remodeled the Wilson mill with flotation equipment. From then on, the Robinson, Michigan, and Queen of the West ran steadily. The Uthoff, Felicia Grace, Colonel Sellers, Iron Mask, and Wilson worked on a sporadic basis, and so did the Wilfley. Ten Mile's output soared to a peak of $210,000 in 1917, more than in any year since 1905. [15]

As the conflict ended in 1918, however, the demand for metals subsided and prices fell back toward their prewar levels. While this may have been a return to normalcy, it dealt a devastating blow to miners who depended on silver, lead, and zinc. If the war had succored a dying industry, the peace administered the coup de grace. Ten Mile's output plunged to $126,000 in 1918 and to $65,000 in 1919. The Robinson, Felicia Grace, Snow Bank, Iron Mask, and Michigan-Uthoff (the two mines now worked in combination), all mined some ore, but with the collapse of Colorado's smelting industry, they had to ship ore and concentrates to Utah. In the early 1920s, the Ten Mile Mining and Dredging Company, in which the Recens held an interest, took some gold from the Eureka placer in McNulty Gulch. Although the cleanup amounted to little, it added to the valley's output, which rose in what seemed like one final gasp of production to $130,000 in 1922. Then output nose-dived to $25,000 in 1923. After that, the mines shipped little or nothing for nearly ten years. [16]

Yet the minerals industry in Ten Mile had not come to an end. Although the mines in the valley had closed, the previous decade had seen the unexpected development of a massive ore body that was destined to have profound ramifications not only for Ten Mile but also for the international mining industry.

No one knows for certain who discovered this deposit, or when, but most accounts point to Charles J. Senter, a Civil War soldier, Indian fighter, and wagon freighter. While Senter may have ventured into the valley in the mid-1870s, it seems certain that he joined the hundreds of boomers who stampeded from Leadville to Ten Mile in that cold winter of 1878 and 1879. Once the snow melted, Senter trudged to the head of McNulty Gulch, where he prospected on Bartlett Mountain. Here he found huge quantities of broken rock streaked with something that looked like graphite, and sometimes covered with a canary-yellow mineral that looked like yellow rust. In August 1879, Senter staked out three claims that he called the Gold Reef, perhaps because he thought his ship had come in—and in a sense, it had—but Senter's claims held little gold, and he never got rich. All he could do was hold on.

Time passed. In 1880, Antony Guyard, a French chemist, joined Frank Emmons' geological team to conduct the metallurgical studies of Leadville. While analyzing gneiss at one of the smelters, Guyard identified a metal known as molybdenum, a rare, scientific curiosity of little value. In retrospect it seems likely that the molybdenum came from a mine on Fremont Pass, but neither Emmons nor Guyard knew where. They expressed no further interest, and the finding lay buried in their scientific papers. For most of the 1880s, the dark mineral in Senter's claims and others nearby was frequently mistaken for graphite or galena. Although Senter built a log cabin that gave rise to a tiny community called Senterville, he spent his years living in Robinson, washing gold from McNulty Gulch, working various jobs, and writing occasional letters to the *Summit County Journal.* What kept him and others from selling their claims was the hope that they would strike the source of the gold that had washed down over the millennia forming the placers in McNulty Gulch. [17]

In the 1890s, assayers determined that the dark, graphite-like substance was molybdenite, a sulfide of molybdenum, and the canary-colored materials were molybdenum oxides. Yet any development was a losing proposition. While Ten Mile now had the requisite infrastructure, mining molybdenum was beside the point because the commercial market was virtually nil and the means to process the ore nonexistent. Most claim owners still hoped to find gold, and in 1902, Hugh Leal began driving what became known as the Leal Tunnel into the depths of Bartlett Mountain. About all he found was a huge quantity of worthless molybdenite, which he dumped on the mountainside.

So much molybdenum, however, sparked the interest of other men. One was E. G. Heckendorf of Denver, who owned a claim on Bartlett Mountain. Heckendorf was one of the first to learn that molybdenum could be used to harden and toughen steel, but he could not persuade anyone to invest. He also looked into the possibility of adapting the relatively new flotation process to recover the metal. So too did Otis Archie King. For some reason Senter had taken an interest in the diminutive, hard-driving boss of the Wilson mill, and King had begun looking for new opportunities as the Wilson ore body played out. In 1913, he shipped some molybdenite to Blackwell & Sons in Liverpool, England, and they gave him information on the metal, as well as an offer to buy at the rate of $1.75 per pound, or $3,500 per ton of concentrates. That put a new light on everything. The only problem, as King remembered years later, was that one ton would supply the world market for a year. [18]

King was not far from the truth. American steelmakers imported from three to ten tons of molybdenum per year, an almost negligible amount. Although the industry had studied many metals for use as alloys, it had devoted little attention to molybdenum, apparently because the sources were few and the supply uncertain. As Europe went to war in 1914, however, demand for molybdenum spurted in Britain and Russia, which needed the metal to manufacture armor plate. One response came from the Rocky Mountains. In 1915, King mined molybdenite from one of Senter's claims, processed the ore by flotation at the new mill built by the Pingrey Company, King's employer, and made the first commercial shipment from Ten Mile. [19]

While King's energy did not ignite a rush, it did spark a scramble for claims on Bartlett Mountain. Heckendorf took the lead, for he and several partners had already acquired more claims—some from Leal, some from Senter, some from others. Yet Heckendorf could not take control of the mountain. Senter retained some properties, King had options from Senter, the Pingrey Company owned more claims, and so did others, even John Beuffer, who still sold fresh eggs and produce from his farm on Fremont Pass.

Although Heckendorf acquired more claims than his rivals, he lacked the financial resources to develop a mine. In October 1916, however, he approached Max Schott, who had just opened an office in Denver for the American Metal Company, a huge diversified enterprise involved in many branches of the minerals industry. American Metal, or Amco, as it was sometimes called, was the American corner of an international triangle of closely related firms that also included Henry R. Merton & Company, which ran the English business from London, and the Metallgesellschaft (or Metal Company), which ran continental affairs from Frankfurt, Germany.

Schott investigated the claims on Bartlett Mountain, and in November 1916, he convinced Amco to take options on Heckendorf's properties. Although Amco took control within months, its officers and directors understandably saw developing a molybdenum mine as a high-risk venture. To spread the risk in the old Metallgesellschaft-Merton-Amco tradition, they formed a syndicate in which Heckendorf and his associates received 25 percent, Amco 7.5 percent, and the officers and directors of Amco the remaining 67.5 percent. Over the winter the syndicate raised $300,000 and the next summer began building a tramway, flotation mill, and housing for workers on the shoulders of Fremont Pass. Early in 1918, about the time that Schott and his colleagues put the mill into operation, the syndicate transferred the investment to the newly formed Climax Molybdenum Company, which took its name from the ramshackle depot built years before by the Denver South Park & Pacific Railway.

No sooner had the Climax Company come into being than it had to contend with a host of problems. After the United States entered the war, the federal government seized all German assets, including a substantial share of Amco (the British had already done the same with Merton & Company). In both cases the German share of the equity was eventually sold off, destroying the old Metallgesellschaft-Merton-Amco

CLIMAX STATION. Passengers wait for their train here on the summit of Fremont Pass sometime around 1900. Bartlett Mountain rises to the east above the station. The first molybdenum mining took place on Bartlett's southwest facing slopes a few years later. Courtesy Climax Molybdenum Company.

relation. Russia was knocked out of the war, eliminating sales there, and when peace came in November 1918, the molybdenum market evaporated. All the producers on Bartlett Mountain shut down, suffering the same fate as the silver, lead, and zinc miners. The molybdenum producers also fell into a bitter struggle among themselves over claims and water rights. Not until 1925, after much wrangling in the state and federal courts, did the Climax Molybdenum Company consolidate the great ore body on Bartlett Mountain.

By the mid-1920s, Ten Mile had a grim look and a bleak future. Climax had not shipped any concentrates since 1919. The Michigan-Snowbank-Uthoff group had closed in 1923, and mining throughout the valley seemed to have come to an end, perhaps for good. Old-timers like Wilfley were in the last stages of life, and just about everyone had moved on, except for a few who refused to quit, who clung to faint hopes amidst the dilapidated buildings that lined the unpaved streets and crumbling boardwalks. In November 1925, even the *Summit County Journal*, which always seemed willing to boom the district, had to concede that Kokomo looked like one of the familiar "ghost mining camps" seen throughout the Rockies. [20]

No matter how badly things looked, however, one man who harbored hopes for the future was Henry L. Brown, one of the chief figures in the Climax project. In 1924, he persuaded Amco that the old mines still held promise, and assured of financial support, he quietly negotiated with the major owners. As a result, by the end of 1925, Amco had acquired exploration leases for ten years on some 3.5 square miles of mining ground on Elk and Sheep mountains. As the snow descended over the unpainted buildings and crumbling shaft houses, Brown hired forty men to help him study the old workings, which had been closed in some cases for years.

In 1926, Amco brought in Basil Prescott, another mining engineer, to provide an independent report. After reviewing Brown's estimates of tonnage, grade, and costs, Prescott figured that if Amco built a mill with a capacity of two hundred tons per day, it might be able to make as much as three dollars per ton. But Prescott conceded the venture would be "a close proposition." Amco would be "terribly handicapped" because many mines had caved in, and no one had any mine maps or reliable information on the shape of the ore bodies. With few exceptions, wrote Prescott, the company would have to work "almost totally in the dark." Pessimism pervaded Prescott's report. Brown had blocked out so little ore that it was "premature" to finish a mill and begin operations. Emmons' folio was "not only inaccurate, but basically wrong"—the district's geology needed to be restudied completely. With the narrow profit margin expected, a slight decline in the price of metals would wipe out any profit, although a slight increase would vastly enhance the value of the ore. As for individual properties, the Robinson-Wilson group was more attractive than any other, but reopening would involve a large outlay of capital. The Uthoff appeared to have some unexplored areas, particularly in the old Nettie B., but Breene's Delaware group showed nothing encouraging. Whatever the output from these mines, the general result of the venture would be almost "entirely dependent" on the Kimberly-Wilfley group, which still possessed a large tonnage of low-grade ore that might be milled. As for money, Amco had already spent about $75,000 in exploration, but it would have to invest another $60,000 to complete the preliminary work and another $100,000 to equip a mill. Although Prescott was hopeful, he ended his report with an apology that his remarks were so "disappointing." [21]

Prescott's report had served its purpose. Amco decided that, given the current prices for metal, the ore in sight was insufficient for large-scale operations. The firm completed its cleanup in the Uthoff, Wilfley, and Kimberly tunnels, but decided not to reopen the mines. It gave up its leases and abandoned the project. [22]

Despite the shipments that Amco made from its cleanups, Ten Mile's output was so miniscule that there is no record of any production from 1923 to 1932 when someone shipped five tons of ore worth $613. Yet a few men clung doggedly to hope. In October 1934, another mining engineer, George W. Danehy, spent a week investigating the district, but after struggling with cave-ins and walls of ice, he submitted a report that resembled Prescott's. Danehy's report of huge tonnages of low-grade ores, however, was enough to convince another mining man, A. R. Rhine of Denver, that there might be a future, and he began quietly acquiring property on Elk and Sheep mountains. Even though prices were low, this was a brave effort—in August 1935, the *Engineering and Mining Journal* reported that Ten Mile was "virtually abandoned." [23]

Yet it was during the Great Depression of the 1930s that output in Ten Mile rose again, particularly after the Roosevelt administration devalued the dollar by increasing the price of gold from $20 to $35 an ounce. Walter W. Byron, son of Wilfley's old partner Ethan E. Byron, reopened the Delaware and did some development work on the Bledsoe. The Phillips Petroleum Company shipped some ore from the Gold Crest at the head of the Mayflower Gulch. Other mines, like the Boston, Wilfley, and Queen of the West, operated for at least brief intervals, and McNulty Placers, Inc., even did some dry land dredging for gold in McNulty Gulch. [24]

The frustrations of the men working the Gold Crest reflected the problems that miners faced in the 1930s. Because the property had been developed before, it already had a tramway and other machinery ready to be refitted and used. Two enterprising young men, Ben Parker and Ding Derringer, struck a deal with the owner and then found venture capital in Tulsa, Oklahoma, either from the Phillips Petroleum Company or men associated with it. When Parker took a job in Argentina, the management fell to James Boyd, a faculty member at the Colorado School of Mines (and later director of the U. S. Bureau of Mines and chairman of Copper Range Company). Boyd and his associates intended to drift along a vein of quartz that averaged from 1.5 to 2 ounces in gold per ton, a very rich ore. The vein, however, was only six inches wide. The hope was that it would eventually widen into a bonanza.

Boyd had to contend with all sorts of problems that made it seem like the 1860s. The mine was so high and remote that it was almost impossible to deliver machinery. The high altitude took its toll on miners. Avalanches were a constant threat in the winter, and more than once Boyd had to ski through deep snow to get to the mine. Managing from Golden also presented special frustrations. Boyd instructed his miners to drive a straight drift, but a mistaken survey caused them to create a dogleg, later explained as a feature designed to "keep out the wind." As mining progressed, it became obvious that the vein was not widening. When Parker returned from South America, he and Boyd decided that the Gold Crest was "deep enough." The investors were called together, and it was finally decided to close the mine despite an investment reported at $300,000. [25]

Given problems like these and the Depression itself, it was no surprise that the old mines in Ten Mile shipped so little ore. The largest production for any one of these years amounted to less than $26,000, in 1937, and the amount shipped exceeded 1,000 tons only in 1939. Much of this mining was apparently the assessment work the owners did to hold onto their property. In testimony to the depressed present and grim future, the railroads abandoned their track through Ten Mile in the late 1930s. The prospects for revival seemed nil. [26]

Not so at Climax, however. Even though the molybdenum mines had closed by 1920, the Climax Company chose Brainerd F. Phillipson, a young chemical engineer of magnetic personality, to help develop new markets. Phillipson conducted a promotional campaign that bore fruit when the automobile industry began to require molybdenum in much of the steel used in building cars. With that, and the development of additional markets, the demand for the metal rose sharply. Phillipson became president of Climax, and under his leadership output from Bartlett

Mountain soared from nothing in 1923 to 3.5 million pounds in 1929. This represented more than 90 percent of American and 80 percent of world consumption! Although production declined at the onset of the Depression, output rose almost ten-fold during the 1930s, reaching 26,875,000 pounds in 1940. To do this, however, Phillipson and his successor, Max Schott, had to enlarge all phases of the company's operations at Climax and build what amounted to a small company town on Fremont Pass. To a large degree, it was the spillover from Climax that kept Kokomo going. Fraternal organizations like the Masons drew new members, and the few bars, hotels, and shops that remained eked out a living that was just enough to sustain a tiny community. [27]

Kokomo might have poked along like this for years, but for the coming of World War II in September 1939. Even before the United States entered the conflict, the rising demand for lead and zinc boosted prices and sparked interest in the old mines. As early as 1940, with battles raging in Europe, Asia, and Africa, the new Wilfley Leasing Company used a $71,000 loan from the Reconstruction Finance Corporation to remodel the old Wilfley mill, install flotation equipment, and begin reworking the mine dump. A year later the enterprise reopened the mine. At the same time, A. R. Rhine and others found enough private capital to launch the Kokomo Metals Company. This firm took over the Washington and Hancock properties that Rhine had acquired in the depths of the Depression, renamed them the Lucky Strike group, and put them into operation. Yet Ten Mile's production for 1941 was still marginal—less than $21,000—although this was more than in any year except one since 1923.

Once the United States entered the battle in December 1941, demand for lead and zinc soared to unprecedented levels. With that, production surged in Ten Mile. The Wilfley Leasing Company began shipping steadily. So too did the Kokomo Metals Company, whose Lucky Strike mine leaped forward to become one of Colorado's leading producers of lead-zinc ore. Ten Mile's output soared to $215,000 in 1942, more than in any year since 1905.

Even so, miners found themselves handicapped by the deteriorating infrastructure. Without railroads, ores and concentrates had to be shipped by truck, which presented special problems because of bad roads. Reduction plants were now so few in Colorado that mining companies had to send their ore and concentrates to smelters as far away as Midvale, Utah, and Amarillo, Texas. And housing had deteriorated to such an extent that it was difficult for miners to find a place to live. Ultimately, in the summer of 1943, the Federal Public Housing Authority authorized the construction of several buildings, which when completed looked like concrete pillboxes plopped in the valley east of Kokomo. They provided shelter, if not aesthetics.

As the war continued, production in Ten Mile centered on four enterprises. The Wilfley Company continued shipping, although it abandoned flotation to send its ore directly to the Resurrection mill in Leadville. The Lucky Strike remained a large producer, and joining in were smaller mines like the Nettie B. Toward the end of 1943, J. Ben Ross and others organized the Kimberly-Kokomo Mines, Inc., which reopened the old Kimberly property and began shipping ore to the Golden Cycle mill at Colorado Springs. By the end of 1944, its shipments had surpassed those of the Lucky Strike as the largest from Ten Mile. Other changes were coming as well. The American Smelting and Refining Company, later to become ASARCO, bought the old Cole-Peterson tunnel, which it appropriately renamed the Victory; and in February 1944, ASARCO bought the Lucky Strike group. Although labor remained in short supply, production of lead and zinc, silver and gold, rose sharply from $215,000 in 1942 to about $700,000 in 1945—figures not seen since the 1880s.

Mining was not the whole story during these years. A. H. Koschmann of the United States Geological Survey brought in a team to restudy Ten Mile's geology, and the United States Bureau of Mines did some extensive diamond drilling, particularly along the Kimberly-Wilfley line. ASARCO also did a considerable amount of development work. These efforts revealed the presence of a fourth limestone horizon, located at greater depth than had ever been worked before. As the war ended in 1945, production from the mines looked bright, unless the nation sank back into depression as some predicted it would.

ASARCO's diamond drilling—30,000 feet of it—along with the studies and drilling of others, had revealed a huge ore body. To develop this deposit, the company placed what it now called its Kokomo unit in the hands of Sergei E. Zelenkov, a graduate of the Colorado School of Mines. As the postwar boom unfolded, Zelenkov brought in new technology ranging from drill bits to electrical equipment, and shipped ore by truck over Fremont Pass, first to the Resurrection mill and then to ASARCO's new Leadville milling unit. Even here in the mid-twentieth century winter still presented problems, for the trucks had to be specially designed with gas heaters to keep the ore from freezing en route.

Other firms kept mining as well, though none rivaled ASARCO. The Wilfley Leasing Company continued operations as the district's second producer until its output was surpassed by the Colonel Sellers, which had reopened in the postwar years. Smaller, more sporadic production came from the Nettie B., Queen of the West, and the Michigan-Snowbank group. Some firms installed machinery to rework the old dumps and tailings, notably the Wilfley Leasing Company, which ironically used the newest Wilfley tables to process the dumps at Wilfley's old mine. As a result of this activity, Ten Mile's output leaped to $4.6 million in 1948, the largest showing in the valley's history (though not perhaps in terms of constant dollars). The yield amounted to almost as much, $3.9 million, in 1949. Most of this production, of course, came from ASARCO's Kokomo unit, one of the largest lead-zinc mines in Colorado during the late 1940s.

Such mammoth production, however, was not to last. By early 1950, having shipped about 250,000 tons, Zelenkov found his ore reserves nearly depleted. He kept operations going through the first quarter, but on April 19, he closed the mine. The falling prices of lead and zinc also hindered the smaller producers. The Wilfley Leasing Company closed down, and so did most of the other shippers. Production for the year slumped to $1,160,000, much of it by ASARCO during the first quarter. [28]

Some miners tried to hang on. During the 1950s, Walter Byron leased the Colonel Sellers, Wilfley, Kimberly, and the Queen of the West. ASARCO did some diamond drilling; so did the Climax Molybdenum Company. Henry and Albert Recen, the sons of the town builders, mined the Silver Cloud; and the York Investment Company consolidated the Kimberly, Colonel Sellers, and the Michigan-Snowbank group; but production was negligible. With lower prices for metal and very low-grade, very deep ores, the economic conditions for mining in Ten Mile had passed again. Observations resembled those of the 1920s and 1930s. The Kokomo area was "almost inactive," wrote the Colorado Mining Association in 1952, and the next year came the report that mining in Ten Mile had "diminished to only a few scattered operations." Production reflected these comments. If the mines had shipped $1,160,000 in 1950, their output plunged like a rock tossed from a precipice to $10,000 in 1951, to $7,700 in 1952, and to virtually nothing at all in the next two years. Kokomo went back to its prewar condition, a marginal town that survived through moneys from Climax, now one of the world's greatest mines. [29]

The growth of the Climax mine had indeed been spectacular. The coming of World War II created an unprecedented demand for molybdenum just as it did for lead and zinc. Despite labor and material shortages, Climax responded with a remarkable increase in production. Although a slump came after the conflict ended, the postwar boom increased demand and prompted expansion until 1961, when the company

RUINS. By the early 1950s the wartime boom had turned to bust, the dilapidated buildings in Recen crumbled away, and the new housing built for miners during World War II stood closed at right. The railroad tracks had been torn up in the 1930s. M. J. Mattes Collection, courtesy Colorado Historical Society.

produced more than 49.2 million pounds of molybdenum mostly from the Climax mine.

Besides expanding operations at Bartlett Mountain and elsewhere, Climax became involved in significant corporate changes. It had always maintained a close relationship with the American Metal Company, which had gone on to spectacular achievements of its own in the United States and abroad. This association finally culminated on December 31, 1957, when the two firms united to form American Metal Climax, Inc.,

one of the world's largest and most diversified mining companies. From the time of its inception, the new enterprise tended to be known as AMAX, and eventually the company changed its corporate name to AMAX Inc. [30]

The continuing development on Bartlett Mountain now began to have a direct impact on the old mines and crumbling towns in Ten Mile. In the late 1950s, Climax began to lay broad plans to increase its mining capacity. So vast an undertaking, however, presented special problems, among them what to do with the tailings left over from milling the ore. After some study, the company's engineers concluded that the most feasible alternative was to use the entire Ten Mile valley for tailing impoundment. Top management concurred.

Before the enterprise could develop the tailings pond, however, it had to acquire virtually all of the Ten Mile valley. This not only included

private property, but also involved public property, a host of patented
mining claims of debatable ownership, and Forest Service lands that
could be obtained only through an exchange for lands desired by the Forest Service.

Climax Resident Manager E. J. Eisenach placed the responsibility for
this monumental task on the shoulders of A. J. Laing, the division attorney for western operations of the Climax Molybdenum Company.
The firm had already bought a large number of claims and acquired other
blocks of property through exchanges with the Forest Service. But there
was still much to do. Early on, Laing hired Robert W. Theobald, an attorney in Breckenridge, to examine titles and make abstracts of every
property in the valley. It also became obvious that to buy public property, the firm would have to disincorporate the last town remaining in
Ten Mile. This, of course, was what everyone called Kokomo, in actuality the town of Recen.

By this time Kokomo looked like a ghost town. No one lived in the
apartments built during World War II. Nearly all the old wooden buildings
were boarded and locked. Certainly no more than twelve to fifteen
people made their homes in the few structures still habitable. Most persons were miners at Climax, but among the others, Walter Byron served
as a county commissioner and his wife, Helen, as mayor. Bernadine
Joyce made a living as postmaster and doubled as cook at Phil Dougherty's Miner's Club, which housed a restaurant and bar that catered to
miners from Climax.

Much of the work on Kokomo was now assigned to Stanley Dempsey, a young attorney who joined the Climax Legal Department in 1964.
Following up on Theobald's work, Dempsey searched all the land records
to determine what interests AMAX still had to acquire. He found that
this included town lots, a number of mining claims, institutional property
like the Masonic Hall, and public property such as the streets, the water
system, the dilapidated town jail, even the land occupied by the public
school. As the weeks passed, the legal department determined who
owned every piece of property and then negotiated a purchase, frequently from the heirs of the original owners. In some cases, the firm's
tax manager, Harold Ballard, picked up tax titles from Summit County.

Obtaining the non-private property, however, involved far more than
negotiating a sale. To secure the Masonic Hall, Colorado law required
AMAX to work out a special arrangement in keeping with Masonic procedures for selling property. Dempsey worked with Ralph Barnett, who
was then head of the Lodge. To acquire the town and school district

property, AMAX found that it had to disincorporate both Kokomo and Recen. In the case of Kokomo, since it had no residents, the company obtained a judicial declaration of abandonment. But different procedures were required for the still-active town of Recen.

After studying Colorado law, Dempsey concluded that to accomplish the disincorporation of an active town, Recen would have to vote itself out of existence! This presented a number of uncertainties. As Recen would be only the first or second community to do this in the history of the state, there were few legal precedents. Yet it seemed to be the only way that AMAX could acquire the land, for the law prescribed that the streets would go to the private property owners on either side, and the other public property would be disposed of. Any funds remaining in the town treasury would be turned over to the school district.

The process of disincorporation moved slowly, but inexorably. Dempsey worked closely with Helen Byron, the mayor, and Peter Cosgriff, the town attorney. Both public officials and the few residents were amenable, and by mutual agreement, the town set election day, the first Tuesday in November 1965, as the date to vote on the proposal.

The day dawned very cold. Dempsey and Cosgriff (both of whom lived in Leadville) drove over to Recen to open the poll at the new school. All the voters cast their ballots before they went to work at the mine or after they came off shift in the afternoon, but the voting place remained open until 7:00 P.M. to comply with Colorado law. Shortly after seven o'clock, Dempsey and Cosgriff returned to Recen to watch the election judges open the ballot box and count the votes. The vote went in favor of disincorporation. The next day Dempsey and Cosgriff took the appropriate papers to the county courthouse in Breckenridge and filed a report with the Colorado secretary of state. Everything now went smoothly. AMAX acquired the streets of Recen, bought the other public assets from the school district, and razed the ramshackle buildings that remained. As a final detail, the county commissioners, sitting as a board of health, had the graves in the cemetery disinterred and the remains reburied in Breckenridge. Before long, the enterprise had consolidated its ownership of all the essential land in the Ten Mile district. What remained in the hands of others were the bordering Forest Service lands and a few claims and other property on the mountainsides.

Then the great project went forward. In the late 1960s and early 1970s, AMAX expanded its underground operations, developed the Climax open pit, augmented its milling capacity, and built the new tailing ponds. Over the years, as the tailings settled to the valley floor, they gradually buried the sites of Carbonateville, Robinson, Kokomo, and Recen. Mining had once brought them into being, and now, in a very unexpected way, mining brought them to an end. [31]

Aside from the unchanging facts of climate and geography, Ten Mile's first century had been shaped by essentially one force—the development of its natural resources, its minerals. This had not been constant or steady, but rather episodic and sequential, which in turn reflected the state of local and regional development, evolving technology, and the changing demand for gold, silver, and other metals. And crucial in that evolution was the role of California Gulch and Leadville, for in many respects what happened there provided the impetus for what happened in Ten Mile.

But there were other factors than minerals in the valley's development. Urbanization was an inherent part of both the western movement and nineteenth-century life. Mining was an essentially urban experience, and towns like Kokomo were islands of civilization in a sea of wilderness. Wagon and rail transportation were also elemental forces in western expansion, and so they were in Ten Mile, which was an important corridor on the road to Leadville.

Yet the key was mining, and the people who went to Ten Mile had colorful stories that illustrate many key themes in western mineral development. At first companies of adventurers, like the one headed by James McNulty, opened the district in that rush to snowdrifts in early 1860. Although the boom faded as the placers played out and the miners found it impossible to develop the silver lodes, nearly two decades later, the surge of development at Leadville spilled over into Ten Mile. That made it possible for some older miners and a newer generation of entrepreneurs—people like George B. Robinson, DeRobert Emmett, and Amos Smith—to finally develop the silver mines and launch more permanent settlements, though these still reflected the vicissitudes of mining. Then finally, in the early twentieth century, came the great era of massive, industrialized production as huge capital came in to develop the Climax molybdenum mine. Yet all during these years the two spirits or forces shaping the mining West lived side by side in Ten Mile: one was the independent free miner always looking for the big strike—he tended to live in Kokomo; the other was the industrial miner who worked for wages, never hoping or expecting to find the big bonanza—he tended to live in Robinson.

Regardless of time and goals, Ten Mile was a special place to be. Two miles above sea level, sandwiched between two high mountain ranges, and often buried by oceans of snow, it was a place to write home about.

THE CLIMAX MINE. Seen here in 1980, the mine had long since become the world's leading molybdenum producer. Courtesy Climax Molybdenum Company.

No one who went there forgot the experience. Yet what makes the Ten Mile story important is that it was a microcosm of life in the mining West. Over the years a few people made fortunes, others attained power and fame, some improved their lot in life, others eked out a living, and some went bust. The development of the Robinson mine had a national impact during its first bonanza years; and later, the development of the Wilfley Table and the Climax mine both had international ramifications that transcended Ten Mile.

Looked at another way, Ten Mile was part of the complex fabric of American development. Though its economy stemmed from mining, it was molded by the same social, economic, and political forces shaping the entire nation: baseball to biking, free silver to populism, immigration to ethnic prejudice, and temperance to women's rights. To the extent that those forces were part of the American pageant as it unfolded in the hundred years from 1860 to 1960, so too they underscored the Ten Mile story as it evolved in the district's first century of development.

Notes

The Bibliography has the full details of publication for the sources cited below.

Abbreviations

BDJ	Breckenridge *Daily Journal*
CHS	Colorado Historical Society
DPL	Denver Public Library
EMJ	*Engineering and Mining Journal*
FRCD	Federal Records Center, Denver
HU	Harvard University
LC	Library of Congress
LDH	Leadville *Daily Herald*
LWH	Leadville *Weekly Herald*
MSP	*Mining and Scientific Press*
NARS	National Archives and Records Service
RMN	*Rocky Mountain News*
SCJ	*Summit County Journal* (Breckenridge)

PROLOGUE.

1. Anne P. McNamara, "Archaeological Reconnaissance of the Climax Land Exchange," *Reports of the Laboratory of Public Archaeology*, no. 25 (December 1978); 10. This is a publication of Colorado State University, Fort Collins.

2. A. H. Koschmann and F. G. Wells, "Preliminary Report on the Kokomo Mining District, Colorado," *Colorado Scientific Society Proceedings*, 15, no. 2, 1946; and M. H. Bergendahl and A. H. Koschmann, *Ore Deposits of the Kokomo-Tenmile District*, U.S.G.S. Professional Paper 652.

273

3. S. R. Capps, *Pleistocene Geology of the Leadville District, Colorado*, U.S.G.S. Bulletin 386. B. S. Butler and John W. Vanderwilt, "The Climax Molybdenum Deposit of Colorado, with Section on History, Production, Metallurgy and Development by Charles W. Henderson," *Colorado Scientific Society Proceedings*, November 10, 1931.

4. Bruce E. Rippeteau, "A Colorado Book of the Dead," *Colorado Magazine*, 55 (Fall 1978): *passim*.

5. Charles W. Henderson, *Mining in Colorado: A History of Discovery, Development, and Production*, U.S.G.S. Professional Paper 138, 1–6.

6. Rodman Wilson Paul, *Mining Frontiers of the Far West, 1848–1880*, 109–114.

7. Ovando J. Hollister, *The Mines of Colorado*, 59–62; and Jerome C. Smiley, *History of Denver, with Outlines of the Earlier History of the Rocky Mountain Country*, 268.

8. Frank Fossett, *Colorado: Its Gold and Silver Mines, Farms and Stock Ranges, and Health and Pleasure Resorts. Tourist's Guide to the Rocky Mountains*, 2d ed., 119–225.

9. George E. Hyde, *Life of George Bent, Written from his Letters*, ed. by Savoie Lottinville, 107–109.

10. Fossett, *Colorado*, 122–25.

CHAPTER 1.   RESOLVED BY THE CLAIM HOLDERS

1. Hollister, *The Mines of Colorado, passim*.

2. Jerome C. Smiley, *History of Denver, passim*. Lyle W. Dorsett, *The Queen City: A History of Denver, passim*.

3. California Mining District Records, Box 1, Mining Districts Collection, CHS.

4. Duane A. Smith, *Horace Tabor: His Life and the Legend*, 15–20.

5. Hollister, *The Mines of Colorado*, 311–17. Don Griswold and Jean Griswold, *Carbonate Camp Called Leadville*, 2–4.

6. Records, Mining Districts Collection, CHS; Smith, *Horace Tabor*, 20–25.

7. J. W. to the editor, *Rocky Mountain Herald*, June 23, 1860; *The Western Mountaineer*, September 12, 1860.

8. Hollister, *The Mines of Colorado*, 115 and 327.

9. Diary of Mathew Sheriff, July 2, 1860, Sheriff Collection, CHS.

10. "A Tramp in the Mines," *Miners' Record, Tarryall Mines*, July 13, 1861. J. W. to the editor, *Rocky Mountain Herald*, June 23, 1860. Hollister, *The Mines of Colorado*, 328–330.

11. Diary of Mathew Sheriff, July 2, 1860, Sheriff Collection, CHS.

12. J. W. to the editor, *Rocky Mountain Herald*, June 23, 1860.

13. Hollister, *The Mines of Colorado*, 327 and 336.

14. William N. Byers, *Encyclopedia of Biography of Colorado* 1: 251–53.

15. "Rules and Regulations of the Washoe District," Box 4, Mining Districts Collection, CHS.

16. "Record of Claims on the Justice Silver Lode," Box 4, Mining Districts Collection, CHS.

17. "Rules and Regulations of the Washoe District," Box 4, Mining Districts Collection, CHS.

18. Daniel Ellis Connor, *A Confederate in the Gold Fields*, ed. Donald C. Berthrong, *passim*. A.D.R. to the editor, Breckenridge, October 18, 1860, in the *Western Mountaineer*, October 25, 1860.

19. U.S. Congress, House, Tenth Census Office Document, *United States Mining Laws* 14: 458.

20. Charles H. Shinn, *Mining Camps: A Study in American Frontier Government*, ed. by Rodman W. Paul, 277.

21. Diary of Edward Seymour, May, June, and July 1861, Seymour Collection, CHS.

22. Hollister, *The Mines of Colorado*, 327–31.

23. Sacramento Mining District Records, Book D, and California Mining District Records, Mining Districts Collection, CHS; Byers, "Scott J. Anthony," *Encyclopedia of Biography of Colorado*, 1: 251–53.

24. Hollister, *The Mines of Colorado*, 327–28.

25. Charles W. Henderson, *Mining in Colorado: A History of Discovery, Development and Production*, 1–9, 77, 88.

26. Testimony of Nathaniel P. Hill in U.S. House of Representatives, *Report of the Industrial Commission*, H. Doc. 181, 57th Cong., 1st sess., serial 4342, 12 (1901): 380. A. W. Hoyt, "Over the Plains to Colorado," 1–21. James E. Fell, Jr., *Ores to Metals: The Rocky Mountain Smelting Industry*, 6–10.

27. Hollister, *The Mines of Colorado*, 252–53; Henderson, *Mining in Colorado*, 32.

28. Pre-emption Certificate, Chalk Mountain Mining District, Bennett Seymour Collection, CHS.

29. Richard A. (Bob) Miller, *Fortune Built By Gun: The Joel Parker Whitney Story*, 1–16.

30. Joel Parker Whitney, *Reminiscences of a Sportsman*, *passim*; Clark C. Spence, "Robert Orchard Old and the British and Colorado Mining Bureau" (M.A. thesis, University of Colorado, 1951), 22–24.

31. Joseph E. King, *A Mine to Make a Mine: Financing the Colorado Mining Industry, 1859–1902*, 9–26.

32. Joel Parker Whitney, *Silver Mining Regions of Colorado, with Some Account of the Different Processes Now Being Introduced for Working the Gold Ores of That Territory*.

33. Archives, Commonwealth of Massachusetts; *RMN*, January 29, 1866; *Daily Miners' Register* (Black Hawk), April 14, 1867.

34. *Daily Miners' Register* (Black Hawk), July 11, 1866, October 20, 1866, and *passim*, 1866–1867.

35. Archives, Commonwealth of Massachusetts. Joel Parker Whitney, *Colorado, in the United States of America. Schedule of Ores Contributed by Sundry Persons to the Paris Universal Exposition of 1867. With Some Information About the Region and Its Resources*. Liston E. Leyendecker, "Colorado and the Paris Universal Exposition, 1867," *Colorado Magazine* 46 (Winter 1969): 1–15.

36. *Colorado Tribune* (Golden), July 8, 1868; Henderson, *Mining in Colorado*, 227.

37. Fossett, *Colorado*, 588; Letter, Breckenridge, Jan. 23, 1870, in *Colorado Tribune* (Golden), Feb. 3, 1870.

38. Hollister, *The Mines of Colorado*, 288–89.

39. Rodman W. Paul, *Mining Frontiers of the Far West*, 29–30.

40. *Mining Review* 8 (Nov. 1873):83. Fred Wilke et al. to Porter, Hodge, Barker, and Duggan, Anselm H. Barker Collection, CHS.

41. U.S. Congress, House, Tenth Census Office Document, *United States Mining Laws*, H. Document 13, pt. 14, serial set 2144, 47th Cong., 2d sess., 1882–1883, 14:479.

42. O. L. Baskin & Company, *History of the Arkansas Valley, Colorado*, 404–407.

43. Fossett, *Colorado*, 483–485.

44. Colorado, 1:149 and 2:353, Dun Records, HU. Fossett, *Colorado*, 481–485. Lode Book, Red Mountain District, Mining Districts Collection, CHS.

45. Interview with Henry A. Recen, CHS; newspaper clippings in the possession of Stanley Dempsey. Mary Ellen Gilliland, *Summit: A Gold Rush History of Summit County, Colorado*, 92–93.

46. Fossett, *Colorado*, 482.

47. Henderson, *Mining in Colorado*, 176 and 245.

CHAPTER 2.   FEVER HEAT

1. Hollister, *The Mines of Colorado*, 316–20; Samuel F. Emmons, *Geology and Mining Industry of Leadville, Colorado*, U.S.G.S. Monograph 12, 10.

2. Hollister, *The Mines of Colorado*, 318.

3. Henderson, *Mining in Colorado*, 133–35; Smith, *Horace Tabor*, 26, 37–38.

4. Fell, *Ores to Metals*, 70–80.

5. Fossett, *Colorado*, 407–408; Fell, *Ores to Metals*, 80–82.

6. Emmons, *Leadville*, 12; Griswold and Griswold, *Carbonate Camp*, 21–27.

7. Fell, *Ores to Metals*, 82–83.

8. *EMJ* 23 (March 1877):170, 25 (March 1878):221.

9. *MSP* 38 (April 1879):213, 230; Emmons *Leadville*, 14–15; Henderson, *Mining in Colorado*, 89; L. A. Kent, *Leadville. The City. Mines and Bullion Product. Personal Histories of Prominent Citizens. Facts and Figures Never Before Given to the Public, passim*.

10. Smith, *Horace Tabor*, 59–78.

11. O. L. Baskin & Company, *History of the Arkansas Valley, Colorado*, 409–410; *Portrait and Biographical Record of Kalamazoo, Allegan, and Van Buren Counties, Michigan*, 428–29; *History of Allegan and Barry Counties, Michigan*, 166; Edward Blair, *Leadville: Colorado's Magic City*, 30; *Leadville Weekly News*, March 3, 1880.

12. Smith, *Horace Tabor, passim*.

13. Testimony of West and Robinson in *Sarah Johnstone v. George B. Robinson*, Records of the United States Circuit Court, FRCD.

14. Testimony of West, *ibid.*

15. Testimony of Robinson, *ibid.*

16. *Ibid.*, and Fossett, *Colorado*, 493–94.

17. W. S. Keyes and J. B. Low, *Reports on the Mines of the Robinson Consolidated Mining Company of Ten Mile, Summit County, Colorado, 1879*. Stephen F. Smart, *Leadville, Ten Mile, Eagle River, Elk Mountain, Tin Cup, and All Other Noted Colorado Mining Camps.* . . .

18. U.S. Congress, House, Tenth Census Office Document, *United States Mining Laws*, H. Doc. 13, pt. 14, serial set 2144, 47th Cong., 2d sess., 1882–1883, 14:479–80.

19. O. L. Baskin & Company, *History of the Arkansas Valley*, 403–409; Smart, *Leadville, Ten Mile and Other Mining Camps.*

20. Fossett, *Colorado*, 494; letter from Leadville, February 8, 1879, John G. Vandemoer Collection, DPL.

21. Hall, *History of Colorado* 2:533. Clark, Root & Company, *First Annual City Directory of Leadville, and Business Directory of Carbonateville, Kokomo and Malta, for 1879*, 5–8.

22. Augustus A. Hayes, Jr., *New Colorado and the Santa Fe Trail*, 126.

23. Letter from Leadville, February 8, 1879, Vandemoer Collection, DPL.

24. Hall, *History of Colorado* 2:563; Clark, Root, *First Annual City Directory*, 16–19; *RMN*, June 20, 1880.

25. O. L. Baskin & Company, *History of the Arkansas Valley*, 395–96.

26. Clark, Root, *First Annual City Directory*, 16–19.

27. Unidentified newspaper clippings in the possession of Stanley Dempsey. Recen Interview, CHS.

28. O. L. Baskin & Company, *History of the Arkansas Valley*, 389.

29. *EMJ* 27 (Feb. 1879):115, 132.

30. *Ibid.*, 27 (March 1879):186.

31. *Ibid.*, 27 (Feb. 1879):132.

32. *Ibid.*, 27 (March 1879):206.

33. Reprinted in *EMJ* 27 (June 1879):411.

34. *EMJ* 27 (June 1879):411.

35. *Ibid.*, 27 (May 1879):339 and 27 (June 1879):411. Fossett, *Colorado*, 494.

36. *EMJ* 27 (June 1879):448.

37. Various legal documents, Office of the Secretary of State, Denver, Colorado. Clark, Root, *First Annual City Directory*, 13–16.

38. Various legal documents, Office of the Secretary of State, Denver, Colorado.

39. Recen Interview, CHS; various legal documents, Office of the Secretary of State, Denver, Colorado.

40. Hall, *History of Colorado* 2:565.

NOTES TO PAGES 59–79

CHAPTER 3.   NOTHING BUT MUSCLE

1. Fossett, *Colorado*, 481.

2. *EMJ* 27 (June 1879):411, 448.

3. Denver *Tribune*, April 5, 1879. Level Book, 1879, Box 2, Edward L. Berthoud Collection, CHS.

4. *EMJ* 27 (June 1879):448.

5. *Ibid.*, 28 (December 1879), 418.

6. Clark, Root, *First Annual City Directory*, 10; O. L. Baskin & Company, *History of the Arkansas Valley*, 390–91, 403–404; Robert A. Corregan and David F. Lingane, *Colorado Mining Directory*, 405–23.

7. Leadville *Reveille*, Dec. 12, 1879, printed in the *EMJ* 28 (Dec. 1879): 450. Kent, *Leadville*, 185—86.

8. Recen Interview, CHS.

9. O. L. Baskin & Company, *History of the Arkansas Valley*, 403–407.

10. Jay E. Niebur, in collaboration with James E. Fell, Jr., *Arthur Redman Wilfley*, 22–23.

11. *EMJ* 28 (June 1879):448.

12. O. L. Baskin & Company, *History of the Arkansas Valley*, 371, 405.

13. *EMJ* 28 (Dec. 1879):475.

14. Leadville *Weekly Herald*, June 26, 1880.

15. Fossett, *Colorado*, 501. Henderson, *Mining in Colorado*, 24. Henderson estimates Summit County's production as $252,351, a *decline* from his figure of $307,239 in 1878. As a decrease seems unlikely in view of the boom, we have chosen Fossett's figures as more accurate.

16. Fossett, *Colorado*, 493–501. Fell, *Ores to Metals*, 101.

17. *LWH*, Feb. 28, 1880.

18. *Ibid.*, May 15, 1880.

19. *Ibid.*, May 15, June 5, 1880. Burkey, "The Georgetown-Leadville Stage," 177–87.

20. *LWH*, May 15, 1880.

21. *Ibid.*, May 22, 1880.

22. *Ibid.*, May 22, 29, June 5, 26, 1880.

23. *Ibid.*, June 26, 1880. Fossett, *Colorado*, 498. Niebur, *Arthur Redman Wilfley*, 32. Kent, *Leadville*, 185–86.

24. Leadville *Daily Democrat*, September 16, 1880. O. L. Baskin & Company, *History of the Arkansas Valley*, 396, 404–405. *LWH*, Feb. 28, June 12, 26, 1880; *LDH*, Nov. 23, 1880; *EMJ* 30 (1880): *passim*. Fell, *Ores to Metals*, *passim*.

26. *EMJ* 31 (June 1881):430–31.

27. Henderson, *Mining in Colorado*, 235—36.

28. *RMN*, May 25, 1881, and *BDJ*, Dec. 2, 1882.

29. Henderson, *Mining in Colorado*, 237; New York *Mining Record*, April 16, 1881; *EMJ* 32 (Aug. 1881):125.

CHAPTER 4.   SURROUNDED BY PAYING MINES

1. Burkey, "The Georgetown-Leadville Stage," 177–187.
2. Fossett, *Colorado*, 494.
3. Clark, Root, *First Annual City Directory*, 3–28.
4. Charles S. Thomas, "The Pioneer Bar of Colorado," 202.
5. Clark, Root, *First Annual City Directory*, 3–28. *RMN*, Feb. 16, Oct. 16, 1879.
6. O. L. Baskin & Company, *History of the Arkansas Valley*, 408.
7. *Ibid.*, 400. *LDH*, November 2, 1880.
8. O. L. Baskin & Company, *History of the Arkansas Valley*, 405–11.
9. Burkey, "The Georgetown-Leadville Stage," 177–87.
10. *LWH*, June 26, 1880.
11. Niebur, *Arthur Redman Wilfley*, 23. Georgia Burns Hills, "Memories of a Pioneer Childhood," 32.
12. O. L. Baskin & Company, *History of the Arkansas Valley*, 399–414.
13. Athearn, *Rebel of the Rockies*, 93–100.
14. Telegram, Robert F. Weibrec to Joseph W. Gilluly, Leadville, July 21, 1880, Weibrec Collection, CHS. Denver and Rio Grande Railway, *Annual Report, 1880*, p. 25.
15. Telegram, Weibrec to Gilluly, Leadville, July 21, 1880; Palmer to Weibrec, New York, July 30 and August 10, 1880, Weibrec Collection, CHS.
16. See various documents signed by Weibrec, Robinson, and others, Weibrec Collection, CHS.
17. Telegram, Palmer to Weibrec, New York, August 10, 1880, Weibrec Collection, CHS; Ingersoll, *The Crest of the Continent*, p. 232.
18. Denver and Rio Grande Railway, *Annual Report*, 1880 and 1881; Time Card, Notebook #7, 1881, p. 1, Weibrec Collection, CHS.
19. Ingersoll, *The Crest of the Continent: A Record of a Summer's Ramble in the Rocky Mountains and Beyond*, 228–31.
20. *Summit County Times* (Kokomo), January 1, 1881.
21. Burkey, "The Georgetown-Leadville Stage," 177–87.
22. John L. Dyer, *The Snow-Shoe Itinerant*, 330–32.
23. *BDJ*, October 15, 1881.

CHAPTER 5.   THE MOST BRILLIANT PROSPECTS

1. Various testimony in *Johnstone v. Robinson*, FRCD.
2. Testimony of Caley in *Jacque v. Robinson and Musgrove*, FRCD.
3. Bill of complaint, *Jacque et al. v. Robinson and Forbes*, FRCD.
4. Reply, *Jacque et al. v. Robinson and Forbes*, FRCD.
5. Testimony of Caley in *Jacque v. Robinson and Musgrove*, FRCD.
6. Smith, *Horace Tabor*, 194–95.
7. Testimony of Caley in *Jacque v. Robinson and Musgrove*, FRCD.
8. Testimony of Caley in *Jacque v. Robinson and Musgrove*, FRCD. Opinion of Moses Hallett, *Leadville Mining Company v. Fitzgerald*, 4 Morr. Min. Rep. 381.

9. Testimony of Caley in *Jacque v. Robinson and Musgrove*, FRCD.

10. Testimony in *Johnstone v. Robinson*, FRCD.

11. Various testimony, *Johnstone v. Robinson*, FRCD.

12. Keyes and Lowe, *Reports on the Mines of the Robinson Consolidated Mining Company*.

13. Testimony of Caley in *Jacque v. Robinson and Musgrove*, FRCD.

14. Bill of Complaint, *Jacque et al. v. Robinson et al.*, FRCD.

15. Keyes and Lowe, *Reports on the Mines of the Robinson Consolidated Mining Company*.

16. Affidavits in *Johnstone v. Robinson*, FRCD.

17. Reply of Robinson Company in *Jacque et al. v. Robinson and Forbes*, FRCD.

18. Complaint in *Jacque v. Robinson and Musgrove*, FRCD.

19. Bill of Complaint, *Jacque et al. v. Robinson et al.*, FRCD.

20. *Pacific Coast Annual Mining Review and Stock Ledger*, 48–49.

21. California, vol. 17, p. 126, Dun Records, HBS.

22. *MSP* 36–39 (1878–1879): *passim*. King, *A Mine to Make a Mine*, 88–91.

23. California, vol. 17, p. 126, Dun Records, HBS; *Bullion*, November 15, 1879; King, *A Mine to Make a Mine*, 96–97.

24. Keyes and Low, *Reports on the Mines of the Robinson Consolidated Mining Company*.

25. *Bullion*, March 27, 1880.

26. *Ibid.*, November 15, 1879. *Mining Record*, January 17, March 20, 1880.

27. *LWH*, March 20, 1880. New York, vol. 414, pp. 336 and 342; vol. 416, pp. 100 a/101, 100 a/78, 100k, 100j, Dun Records, HBS. King, *A Mine to Make a Mine*, *passim*.

28. *LWH*, March 20, 27, April 3, 1880.

CHAPTER 6.   THE REALMS OF TIME

1. *LDH*, March 20, 1880.

2. *LWH*, March 20, April 3, April 20, 1880.

3. *Johnstone v. Robinson*, U.S. Circuit Court for Colorado, 12 Morr. Min. Reptr, 396.

4. *LDH*, October 21, 26, 1880.

5. Fossett, *Colorado*, 497–98.

6. *LDH*, June 26, 1880.

7. *LWH*, February 28, June 12, 1880. *Keyes and Arents v. Grant and Grant*, docket 613, FRCD.

8. *LWH*, February 28, June 12, 26, 1880; *LDH*, November 23, 1880. *EMJ*, 28 (1879) and 29 (1880): *passim*.

9. Leadville *Daily Democrat*, September 21, 1880. *LWH*, June 26, 1880. Hills, "Memoirs of a Pioneer Girlhood," *passim*.

10. *LDH*, October 23, 1880.

11. *Ibid.*, November 10, 1880.

12. *Ibid.*, August 28, 1880.

13. *Ibid.*; *RMN*, August 28, 1880.

14. Leadville *Daily Democrat*, September 16, 1880. *RMN*, October 3, 1880.

15. *LDH*, October 21, 1880.

16. *Ibid.*, October 26, 1880.

17. *Ibid.*, October 30, 1880.

18. *Ibid.*, November 9, 1880.

19. *Ibid.*, November 20, 1880.

20. *Ibid.*, November 25, 1880.

21. James T. Stewart to the editor, November 26, 1880, *LDH*, November 27, 1880.

22. *LDH*, November 28, 1880.

23. Testimony of Warner, published in *LDH*, December 1, 1880.

24. Testimony of Roy in *LDH*, December 1, 1880.

25. Testimony of Hermann in *LDH*.

26. Testimony of Gillin in *LDH*.

27. Testimony of White in *LDH*.

28. Testimony of White, Gillin, and Hermann in *LDH*.

29. Testimony of Gillin in *LDH*.

30. Testimony of Hermann in *LDH*.

31. Testimony of White, Chase, and Warner in *LDH*.

32. Testimony of Burdick in *LDH*.

33. *LDH*, November 28, 1880.

34. *LDH*, November 28, 1880.

35. *LDH*, November 30, 1880.

36. Testimony of Burdick in *LDH*.

37. *LDH*, November 30, 1880.

38. Testimony of Burdick in *LDH*, December 1, 1880.

39. See *LDH*, November 30, December 1, 1880, and *RMN*, November 30, December 1, 2, 1880.

40. *LDH*, December 1, 2, 1880. *RMN*, December 1, 2, 1880.

41. *RMN*, December 2, 3, 1880.

42. Kalamazoo *Gazette*, December 10, 1880.

CHAPTER 7.   SLAUGHTER OF GEESE

1. *LDH*, December 2, 3, 4, 1880.

2. Bill of Complaint, *Jacque et al v. Robinson et al*, FRCD. *RMN*, Dec. 17, 1880.

3. *LDH*, Dec. 21, 1880.

4. McCook Papers, CHS. O. L. Baskin & Company, *History of the Arkansas Valley*, 400–403.

5. *BDJ*, June 20, 1881.

6. *EMJ* 30 (Dec. 1880):367–68; 31 (Jan. 1881):67, 31 (Feb. 1881):97, 136, 148, 152; 31 (March 1881):166–69, 218.

7. *EMJ*, 31 (April 1881):270, 304.

8. *Ibid.*, 31 (May 1881):340–41, 356, 372.

9. *Ibid.*, 31 (June 1881):388, 393, 397.

10. *Ibid.*, 31 (June 1881):405, 413.

11. *Ibid.*, 429–30; *BDJ*, July 12, 1881.

12. *EMJ* 31 (June 1881):435; 32 (July 1881):9, 29; 32 (Aug. 1881):85.

13. *Ibid.*, 32 (July 1881):47, 59; 32 (Aug. 1881):92–94, 109–10.

14. *Ibid.*, 32 (Aug. 1881):109–10, 124–26. *Jacque et al. v. Robinson and Forbes*, FRCD.

15. *EMJ* 32 (Aug. 1881):126.

16. *Ibid.*, 32 (Sept. 1881):158, 172, 180, 189–91, 206.

17. *Ibid.*, 32 (Oct. 1881):242.

18. *Ibid.*, 32 (Oct. 1881):258, 264, 273, 290.

19. *Ibid.*, 32 (Nov. 1881):310, 327.

20. James D. Hague to N. J. Pettigru, New York, Nov. 7, 1881; Hague to William Ashburner, New York, Nov. 10, 1881, Hague Papers, HEH.

21. Hague to Ashburner, New York, Nov. 10, 1881, Hague Papers, HEH.

22. Hague to Ashburner, New York, Nov. 10, 1881, Hague Papers, HEH. Ashburner's Report, *EMJ* 32 (Dec. 1881):393–94. Ashburner to Brayton Ives, Denver, Dec. 26, 1881, in William N. Symington, "Report on the Quantity of the Ore in Sight in the Robinson Mine, Summit County, Colorado, Dec. 26, 1881."

23. *EMJ* 32 (Dec. 1881):393.

24. *Ibid.*, 32 (Dec. 1881):379.

25. Hague to Ashburner, New York, Dec. 13, 1881, HEH.

26. *EMJ* 32 (Dec. 1881):395.

27. *Ibid.*, 408, 421, 435–37.

28. Ashburner to Ives, Denver, Dec. 26, 1881, Hague Papers, HEH.

29. Hague to Ashburner, two letters, New York, Jan. 4, 1882, Hague Papers, HEH.

30. *Bullion*, Dec. 24, 1881; Jan. 9, 1882.

31. Henderson, *Mining in Colorado*, 245.

32. *BDJ*, June 20, Oct. 19, 1881. Leadville *Herald-Democrat*, Oct. 6, 1888.

33. Scrapbook #1, Job A. Cooper Collection, CHS.

CHAPTER 8.   THE TIDE OF RETROGRESSION

1. Henderson, *Mining in Colorado*, 99.

2. *BDJ*, Dec. 26, 1882. U.S. Department of the Treasury, Bureau of the Mint, Doc. No. 441, *Report of the Director of the Mint Upon the Statistics of the Production of the Precious Metals in the United States*, 554–58.

3. Henderson, *Mining in Colorado*, 90.

4. Quoted in Niebur, *Arthur Redman Wilfley*, 6–7.

5. *EMJ* 35 (1883): *passim.*

6. Henderson, *Mining in Colorado*, 238–39.

7. *SCJ*, Aug. 11, 18, Sept. 8, 15, 29, 1883.

8. *Ibid.*, Sept. 15, 29, Oct. 6, 13, 20, 27, 1883, and July 16, 1887.

9. Henderson, *Mining in Colorado*, 238.

10. *SCJ*, Sept. 15, Oct. 5, 20, 1883.

11. *Ibid.*, Oct. 6, Nov. 17, Dec. 15, 1883; Jan. 12, Feb. 26, 1884.

12. *Ibid.*, Feb. 26, March 1, 22, April 5, 1884.

13. *Ibid.*, March 29, 1884.

14. *Ibid.*, April 5, 12, 18, Aug. 2, 1884.

15. *Ibid.*, May 5, Aug. 2, 9, 1884; Feb. 28, 1885.

16. *Ibid.*, Nov. 15, Dec. 27, 1884; Jan. 3, 17, 1885.

17. *Ibid.*, Jan. 24, Feb. 7, 9, June 6, Dec. 30, 1885, Jan. 8, 1886. Henderson, *Mining in Colorado*, 91. The figures in the *Summit County Journal* vastly exceed those published by Henderson.

18. Charles J. Moore, "Report on the Queen of the West Mine, Summit County, Colorado," Jan. 9, 1886.

19. *SCJ*, March 10, 26, 1886.

20. *Ibid.*, March 26, April 2, Oct. 30, 1886.

21. *Ibid.*, Oct. 23, 1886.

22. *Ibid.*, May 28, 1887.

23. Incorporation records, Queen of the West Mining Company, Colorado State Archives, Denver. Hermann Hagedorn, *Brookings: A Biography. Report of the Director of the Mint . . . for the Calendar Year 1887*, 185–88.

24. Fell, *Ores to Metals*, 106. Samuel F. Emmons, *Geology and Mining Industry of Leadville, Colorado*, U.S.G.S. Monograph 12.

25. Rodman W. Paul, ed., *A Victorian Gentlewoman in the Far West: The Reminiscences of Mary Hallock Foote*, 180–82.

26. Emmons to King, Leadville, Jan. 3, 1880, and Denver, Oct. 4, 1880; Alfred M. Rogers to John Wesley Powell, Denver, June 15, 1883; Samuel F. Emmons Letterbook, 1879–1886, Record Group 57, NARS.

27. Emmons to King, Denver, Sept. 4, Oct. 4; and Leadville, Nov. 7, 1880, Emmons Letterbook, NARS.

28. Emmons to John Wesley Powell, Denver, June 22, 1881, and Washington, Aug. 5, 1882. Jacob Notebooks, Record Group 57, NARS.

29. Emmons to Powell, Washington, D.C., Aug. 15; Denver, Oct. 9, 1882, Emmons Letterbook, NARS.

30. Jacob, Notebook #18; Emmons to Powell, Denver, Oct. 9, Nov. 25, Dec. 8, 1882; Washington, D.C., Feb. 8, 1883, Emmons Letterbook, NARS. Niebur, *Arthur Redman Wilfley*, 23–24.

31. Emmons to Powell, Denver, Nov. 25, 1882; Washington, D.C., Feb. 8, 1883; Alfred M. Rogers to Julius Bien, Denver, March 9, 1883, Emmons Letterbook, NARS.

32. Emmons to Powell, New York, May 9, June 9, 1883; Washington, D.C., June 30, 1883; Emmons to Thomas Greer, Oct. 10, 1883, Emmons Letterbook, NARS.

33. Emmons to Powell, Denver, Aug. 22, 1884, and *passim*, 1881–July 1886, Emmons Letterbook, NARS.

34. Emmons to Powell, various letters, July 1886–June 30, 1887, Emmons Letterbook, NARS. The last quotation is in Emmons to Powell, Washington, D.C., June 30, 1887.

35. Niebur, *Arthur Redman Wilfley*, 8–24.

36. *Ten Mile News*, March 24, 1883.

37. Niebur, *Arthur Redman Wilfley*, 24–36.
38. Higgins, Lovell, and Wilfley are quoted in Niebur, *Arthur Redman Wilfley*, 38–39.
39. Niebur, *Arthur Redman Wilfley*, 33–56.
40. Fell, *Ores to Metals*, 209–11.
41. Niebur, *Arthur Redman Wilfley*, 56–59.
42. *SCJ*, July 16, Aug. 27, Sept. 10, Oct. 1, 1887.
43. *Report of the Director of the Mint, 1888*, 125–28; *1889*, 152–54; *1890*, 14–42; Niebur, *Arthur Redman Wilfley*, 43–44.
44. Newspaper clippings, DPL.
45. Henry E. Wood and Philip Argall, "Report on the Robinson Mine," 1889. Fell, *Ores to Metals*, 125, 181.
46. *SCJ*, Oct. 10, 1891; Jan. 2, 16, 1892; Feb. 6, 13, 1892. *Report of the Director of the Mint, 1891*, 175; *1892*, 130.

CHAPTER 9.   UNTIL GABRIEL SOUNDS HIS HORN

1. *BDJ*, Oct. 26, 1881. *RMN*, June 20, 1882.
2. *SCJ*, April 28, 1882. *BDJ*, June 19, 1883; Gilliland, *Summit*, 188–89.
3. *SCJ*, Oct. 13, 1883.
4. *BDJ*, July 22, 1880. *LDH*, Nov. 10, Dec. 21, 1880.
5. *BDJ*, June 17, 18, 1881; July 7, 12, 1881.
6. *BDJ*, Oct. 6, Dec. 9, 1882. *SCJ*, Sept. 6, 1884.
7. *RMN*, March 26, 1884. *SCJ*, April 5, 12, May 3, 1884.
8. *BDJ*, July 7, 1881; July 21, 1883. *SCJ*, Aug. 11, Sept. 1, 1883.
9. *SCJ*, June 13, 20, 1885.
10. *BDJ*, Oct. 8, 1881; July 7, 1883; March 17, 1886.
11. Hills, "Memories of a Pioneer Childhood." *BDJ*, Feb. 27, 28, 1883. *Ten Mile News*, March 24, 1883.
12. File card, Department of Material Culture, CHS.
13. Hills, "Memories of a Pioneer Childhood." *LDH*, Nov. 1, Dec. 5, 1883.
14. *BDJ*, June 11, 20, July 2, 1881.
15. *Ibid.*, Sept. 6, 15, 1882.
16. *Ibid.*, Nov. 11, Dec. 5, 6, 1882.
17. *Ibid.*, Dec. 26, 27, 28, 1882; Jan. 3, 10, April 3, 1883.
18. *Ibid.*, Jan. 29, July 6, 10, 1883.
19. *Ibid.*, Sept. 22, Nov. 17, Dec. 29, 1883; Jan. 12, May 3, 1884.
20. O. L. Baskin & Company, *History of the Arkansas Valley*, 399.
21. *BDJ*, June 28, 1881.
22. *Ibid.*, Oct. 1, 6, 9, 17, 18, 19, 26, Nov. 9, 1881.
23. *Ibid.*, Sept. 6, 12, Nov. 4, 15, 17, 1882. Denver *Republican*, Jan. 1, 1883.
24. Gunnison *Daily Review Press*, Feb. 19, 1883. *BDJ*, April 5, 1883. *SCJ*, Nov. 10, 1883, April 5, 1884. Niebur, *Arthur Redman Wilfley*, 9–12.
25. *SCJ*, Sept. 28, 1884; Feb. 26, 1887. *Summit County Times*, Nov. 1, 1884.

26. Poor, *Denver South Park & Pacific*, 238–39, 249–52; *SCJ*, Aug. 18, 1883; *BDJ*, Aug. 3, 1883.

27. *BDJ*, Aug. 3, 10, 1883; *SCJ*, Aug. 25, Sept. 1, 1883.

28. Poor, *Denver South Park & Pacific*, 252–54. *SCJ*, Sept. 1, 15, 29, 1883. Denver *Republican*, Sept. 11, 1883.

29. *LDH*, Nov. 1, Dec. 5, 1883. *SCJ*, Nov. 24, 1883.

30. *SCJ*, Sept. 22, Nov. 24, Dec. 1, 15, 22, 29, 1883.

31. Poor, *Denver South Park & Pacific*, 257–63. *SCJ*, Jan. 12, 1884.

32. *BDJ*, Jan. 8, March 18, April 16, May 1, 12, 1886.

33. *SCJ*, Dec. 21, 1885; March 26, May 21, Dec. 18, 1886; Sept. 10, 1887. Niebur, *Arthur Redman Wilfley*, 34, 45.

34. *SCJ*, May 14, June 4, July 9, 1887.

35. *SCJ*, Oct. 23, 1886. Denver & Rio Grande Railway, *Official Guide*, 1888.

36. *SCJ*, Aug. 1, 15, Sept. 5, Oct. 10, 1891, Feb. 6, 1892. Jim Ritter, "The Dynamiting of Father Dyer's Bell."

37. *SCJ*, July 9, 1887, June 16, 1888, March 5, 1892.

38. *Ibid.*, Oct. 8, Nov. 5,1887; Jan. 7, Feb. 25, 1888.

39. *Ibid.*, Nov. 7, 1891.

40. *Ibid.*, Feb. 27, 1892.

41. *Ibid.*, April 2, 1892.

42. *Ibid.*, April 9, 1892. James Edward Wright, *The Politics of Populism: Dissent in Colorado*, 135–58.

CHAPTER 10.   MAKING ABOUT EXPENSES

1. Ben Stanley Revett to John F. Campion, Denver, June 27, 1893, box 3, Campion Papers, University of Colorado.

2. Fell, *Ores to Metals*, 201–206. Niebur, *Arthur Redman Wilfley*, 61–62.

3. Thomas Walsh to David S. Wegg, Silverton, Colorado, July 10, 1894, Evelyn Walsh McLean Papers, Library of Congress, Washington, D.C. *SCJ*, Aug. 11, Sept. 1, 1894.

4. *SCJ*, Sept. 8, 29, 1894.

5. *Ibid.*, Oct. 20, Nov. 24, 1894. Niebur, *Arthur Redman Wilfley*, 61–62.

6. *SCJ*, March 16, 1895.

7. *Ibid.*, May 4, April and May, 1895, *passim*.

8. Niebur, *Arthur Redman Wilfley*, 64–65. Walsh to Wegg, Denver, Nov. 23, 1894; Ouray, August 6, 1895; Denver, March 18, 25, 1896, McLean Papers, LC.

9. Entries in Emmons' Diary, Aug. 31, Sept. 23, 1890, box 3; Samuel F. Emmons to Arthur Redman Wilfley, Leadville, Aug. 23, 1894, box 8, Emmons Collection, L.C.

10. *SCJ*, Sept. 8, 15, 1894.

11. *SCJ*, Sept. 1, 8, Oct. 6, 27, Nov. 3, 1893.

12. *Ibid.*, Nov. 10, 1894. Wright, *Populism*, 195.

13. *SCJ*, Aug. 15, 1891; July 2, 1892; Oct. 20, Nov. 17, Dec. 1, 1894; March 9, 1895.

14. *Ibid.*, Sept. 8, 1894; April 13, May 25, 1895.

15. *Ibid.*, May 4, 25, 1895; Aug. 25, 1894.

16. Gilliland, *Summit*, 280–88.

17. *SCJ*, Aug. 25, Sept. 29, 1894; June 8, 1895.

18. *Ibid.*, April 13, July 6, 1895.

19. *Ibid.*, Aug. 25, 1894, Jan. 12, May 25, July 6, 1895.

20. *Ibid.*, March 6, 1897.

21. Niebur, *Arthur Redman Wilfley*, 69–115, and *passim*.

CHAPTER 11.   RISING LIKE THE PHOENIX

1. *SCJ*, Aug. 18, 1900, Feb. 23, March 2, 9, April 6, June 15, 1901. Frank Bulkley, *Report on the Consolidated Robinson Mines*.

2. Frank Bulkley, "Report on the Robinson and Eldorado Mines and Log of Eldorado Shaft, 1900," unpublished report, Colorado School of Mines. *SCJ*, Dec. 8, 1900.

3. Bulkley, *Report on the Consolidated Robinson Mines*, 1901.

4. Breckenridge *Bulletin*, Sept. 14, 21, 1901.

5. *SCJ*, April 12, June 28, 1902.

6. Henderson, *Mining in Colorado*, 82, 245. Fell, *Ores to Metals*, 237–39.

7. *SCJ*, April 23, 1903, Aug. 25, 1903, April 16, 1904, June 2, Dec. 29, 1906.

8. Niebur, *Arthur Redman Wilfley*, 127–30. Kirby Thomas, "Report on Kimberly Mine, Kokomo, Colorado," unpublished report, 1907, with comments by George W. Danehy, 1935, Colorado School of Mines. Henderson, *Mining in Colorado*, 245. *SCJ*, Dec. 29, 1906.

9. *SCJ*, June 13, Aug. 31, 1907, and *passim*. M. H. Bergendahl and A. H. Koschmann, *Ore Deposits of the Kokomo-Tenmile District, Colorado*, Professional Paper 652, 5.

10. Henderson, *Mining in Colorado*, 245. Bergendahl and Koschmann, *Ore Deposits of the Kokomo-Tenmile District*, 5. *SCJ*, Dec. 3, 1910.

11. *SCJ*, June 22, 1907; June 10, 1916.

12. Wright, *Politics of Populism*, 245–47.

13. *SCJ*, July 12, 1902. *Colorado State Business Directory*, 1910 through 1915, *passim*.

14. Otis Archie King, *Gray Gold*, 13.

15. *SCJ*, June 10, Oct. 28, Dec. 30, 1916; March 3, 1917. Bergendahl and Koschmann, *Ore Deposits of the Kokomo-Tenmile District*, 5–7. Henderson, *Mining in Colorado*, 245. Niebur, *Arthur Redman Wilfley*, 130.

16. *SCJ*, Oct. 2, 1920. Bergendahl and Koschmann, *Ore Deposits of the Kokomo-Tenmile District*, 5–7. Henderson, *Mining in Colorado*, 245.

17. King, *Gray Gold*, 32–45. B. S. Butler and John W. Vanderwilt, "The Climax Molybdenum Deposit of Colorado with Section on History, Production, Metallurgy and Development by Charles W. Henderson," *Colorado Scientific Society Proceedings*, 12 (1931):316–17. *SCJ*, *passim*. Samuel F. Emmons to Clarence King, Leadville, Dec. 5, 1880, Emmons Letterbook, RG 57, NARS.

18. King, *Gray Gold*, 48–49. Butler and Vanderwilt, "The Climax Molybdenum Deposit," 316–17.

19. Butler and Vanderwilt, "The Climax Molybdenum Deposit," 316–17. Seymour S. Bernfeld in collaboration with Harold K. Hochschild, *A Short History of American Metal Climax, Inc.*

20. *SCJ*, Nov. 28, 1925.

21. Basil Prescott, "Report on the Kokomo Mining District, 1926."

22. Niebur, *Arthur Redman Wilfley*, 130.

23. *EMJ* 136 (Aug. 1935):399. George W. Danehy, "Report on the Mineral Deposits at Kokomo, Ten Mile District, Colorado," unpublished report, 1934, Colorado School of Mines.

24. Bergendahl and Koschmann, *Ore Deposits of the Kokomo Tenmile District, Colorado*, 5–7. *Colorado Mining Year Book*, 1933–1940, *passim*.

25. Interview with James Boyd.

26. Bergendahl and Koschmann, *Ore Deposits of the Kokomo Tenmile District, Colorado*, 5–7.

27. Bernfeld, *American Metal Climax*, 11. Butler and Vanderwilt, "The Climax Molybdenum Deposit of Colorado," 320.

28. Colorado Mining Association *Yearbooks*, 1940–1950. Bergendahl and Koschmann, *Ore Deposits of the Kokomo Tenmile District, Colorado*, 5–7. A. H. Koschmann and F. G. Wells, "Preliminary Report on the Kokomo Mining District, Colorado," 51–112. Sergei E. Zelenkov, "Mining Practice at the Kokomo Unit of the American Smelting and Refining Company," 13–16, 44.

29. Colorado Mining Association *Yearbooks*, 1950–54. *Denver Post*, Nov. 6, 1950. Bergendahl and Koschmann, *Ore Deposits of the Kokomo-Tenmile District*, 5–7.

30. Bernfeld, *American Metal Climax*, 12–13. Thomas R. Navin, *Copper Mining and Management*, 273–84.

31. Stanley Dempsey to James E. Fell, Jr., Sydney, Australia, Sept. 1981.

Bibliography

A. MANUSCRIPT AND ARCHIVAL MATERIAL

Anselm H. Barker Collection. Colorado Historical Society, Denver.

Edward L. Berthoud Collection. Colorado Historical Society, Denver.

John F. Campion Collection. University of Colorado, Boulder.

Colorado State Archives, Denver.

Commonwealth of Massachusetts Archives, Offices of the Secretary of State, Boston.

Job A. Cooper Collection. Colorado Historical Society, Denver.

Denver & Rio Grande Railway Collection. Colorado Historical Society, Denver.

R. G. Dun & Company Records. Harvard University Graduate School of Business Administration, Boston.

Samuel F. Emmons Collection. Library of Congress, Washington, D.C.

James D. Hague Papers. Henry E. Huntington Library and Art Gallery, San Marino, California.

James D. Hague Papers. Natural Resources Manuscript Group. Yale University, New Haven, Connecticut.

Edward M. McCook Collection. Colorado Historical Society, Denver.

Evelyn Walsh McLean Collection. Library of Congress, Washington, D.C.

Mining Districts Collection. Colorado Historical Society, Denver.

National Archives and Records Service
    Records of the U. S. Geological Survey, Record Group 57, Washington, D.C.

Records of the U. S. Circuit Court, Federal Records Center, Region 8, Denver.
John W. Jacque v. George B. Robinson and William Musgrove
John W. Jacque et al. v. George B. Robinson and Mary Forbes
Sarah Johnstone v. George B. Robinson
Winfield Scott Keyes and Albert Arents v. James B. Grant and James Grant
Edward Seymour Diary, Bennett Seymour Collection. Colorado Historical Society, Denver.
Mathew Sheriff Diary, Mathew Sheriff Collection. Colorado Historical Society, Denver.
John G. Vandemoer Collection. Denver Public Library, Denver.
Robert F. Weitbrec Collection. Colorado Historical Society, Denver.
Arthur Redman Wilfley Collection. University of Colorado, Boulder.

B. PUBLIC DOCUMENTS

Federal

Bergendahl, M. H., and A. H. Koschmann, *Ore Deposits of the Kokomo-Tenmile District*. U.S. Geological Survey Professional Paper no. 652. Washington, D.C.: Government Printing Office, 1971.
Capps, S. R. *Pleistocene Geology of the Leadville District, Colorado*. U.S. Geological Survey Bulletin no. 386. Washington, D.C.: Government Printing Office, 1909.
Emmons, Samuel F. *Geological Atlas, Tenmile District* U.S. Geological Survey *Special Folio* no. 48. Washington: Government Printing Office, 1898.
Emmons, Samuel F. *Geology and Mining Industry of Leadville, Colorado*. U.S. Geological Survey Monograph no. 12. Washington, D.C.: Government Printing Office, 1886.
Henderson, Charles W. *Mining in Colorado: A History of Discovery, Development and Production*. U.S. Geological Survey Professional Paper no. 138. Washington, D.C.: Government Printing Office, 1926.
U.S. Department of the Treasury, Bureau of the Mint. Doc. no. 441. *Report of the Director of the Mint upon the Statistics of the Production of the Precious Metals in the United States*. Washington, D.C.: Government Printing Office, 1883–1893. (Titles vary.)
U.S. Congress, House. *Report of the Industrial Commission on Trusts and Industrial Combinations*. H. Doc. 182, serial set 4343, 57th Cong., 1st sess., vol. 13, 1901.
U.S. Congress, House. *United States Mining Laws*. Tenth Census Office Document. H. Doc. 13, pt. 14, serial set 2144, 47th Cong., 2nd sess., 1882–1883, vol. 14.

State of Colorado

McNamara, Anne P. *Archaeological Reconnaissance of the Climax Land Exchange.* Report of the Laboratory of Public Archaeology no. 25. Fort Collins, Colo: December 1978.

C. BOOKS AND PAMPHLETS

Athearn, Robert G. *Rebel of the Rockies: A History of the Denver and Rio Grande Western Railroad.* New Haven: Yale University Press, 1962.
Bernfeld, Seymour S., in collaboration with Harold K. Hochschild, *A Short History of American Metal Climax, Inc.* Privately printed, 1962.
Blair, Edward. *Leadville: Colorado's Magic City.* Boulder, Colo.: Pruett Publishing Company, 1980.
Bulkley, Frank. *Report on the Consolidated Robinson Mines.* N.p., 1901.
Byers, William N. *Encyclopedia of Biography of Colorado.* Chicago: Century Publishing and Engraving Company, 1901.
Clark, Root & Company. *First Annual City Directory of Leadville, and Business Directory of Carbonateville, Kokomo and Malta, for 1879.* Denver: Daily Times Steam Printing House and Book Manufactory, 1879.
Colorado State Business Directory. N.p., 1910–15.
Connor, Daniel Ellis. *A Confederate in the Gold Fields.* Edited by Donald J. Berthrong. Norman: University of Oklahoma Press, 1970.
Corregan, Robert A., and David F. Lingane. *Colorado Mining Directory: Containing an Accurate Description of the Mines, Mining Properties and Mills, and the Mining, Milling, Smelting, Reducing, and Refining Companies and Corporation of Colorado.* Denver: Colorado Mine Directory Company, 1883.
Denver and Rio Grande Railroad. *Annual Reports.* N.p., various years.
Denver & Rio Grande Railway. *Official Guide.* N.p., 1888.
Dorsett, Lyle W. *The Queen City: A History of Denver.* Boulder, Colo.: Pruett Publishing Company, 1977.
Dyer, John L. *The Snow Shoe Itinerant. An Autobiography of the Rev. John L. Dyer, Familiarly Known as "Father Dyer," of the Colorado Conference, Methodist Episcopal Church.* Cincinnati: Cranston & Stowe, 1890.
Fell, James E., Jr. *Ores to Metals: The Rocky Mountain Smelting Industry.* Lincoln: University of Nebraska Press, 1980.
Foote, Mary Hallock. *A Victorian Gentlewoman in the Far West: The Reminiscences of Mary Hallock Foote.* Edited by Rodman Wilson Paul. San Marino, Calif. The Huntington Library, 1972.
Fossett, Frank. *Colorado: Its Gold and Silver Mines, Farms and Stock Ranges, and Health and Pleasure Resorts. Tourist's Guide to the Rocky Mountains.* 2d ed. New York: C. G. Crawford, 1880.

Gilliland, Mary Ellen. *Summit: A Gold Rush History of Summit County, Colorado.* Silverthorne, Colo.: Alpenrose Press, 1980.

Griswold, Don, and Jean Griswold. *Carbonate Camp Called Leadville.* Denver: University of Denver Press, 1951.

Hagedorn, Hermann. *Brookings: A Biography.* New York: The Macmillan Company, 1937.

Hall, Frank. *History of the State of Colorado.* 4 vols. Chicago: Blakely Printing Company, 1889–1895.

Hayes, Augustus A., Jr. *New Colorado and the Santa Fe Trail.* New York: Harper, 1880.

History of Allegan and Barry Counties, Michigan. N.p., n.d.

Hollister, Ovando J. *The Mines of Colorado.* Springfield, Mass.: Samuel Bowles & Company, 1867.

Hyde, George E. *Life of George Bent, Written from his Letters,* Edited by Savoie Lottinville. Norman: University of Oklahoma Press.

Ingersoll, Ernest. *The Crest of the Continent: A Record of a Summer's Ramble in the Rocky Mountains and Beyond.* Chicago: R. R. Donnelley and Sons, 1885.

Kent, L. A. *Leadville. The City. Mines and Bullion Product. Personal Histories of Prominent Citizens. Facts and Figures Never Before Given to the Public.* Denver: Daily Times Steam Printing Company and Blank Book Manufactory, 1880.

Keyes, W. S., and J. B. Low. *Reports on the Mines of the Robinson Consolidated Mining Company of Ten Mile, Summit County, Colorado, 1879.* N.p., n.d.

King, Joseph E. *A Mine to Make a Mine: Financing the Colorado Mining Industry, 1859–1902.* College Station: Texas A & M University Press, 1977.

King, Otis Archie. *Gray Gold.* Denver: Big Mountain Press, 1959.

Miller, Richard A. (Bob). *Fortune Built by Gun: The Joel Parker Whitney Story.* Walnut Grove, Calif.: Mansion Publishing Company, 1969.

Navin, Thomas R. *Copper Mining and Management.* Tucson: University of Arizona Press, 1978.

Niebur, Jay E., in collaboration with James E. Fell, Jr. *Arthur Redman Wilfley: Miner, Inventor, and Entrepreneur.* Denver: Colorado Historical Society, 1982.

O. L. Baskin & Company. *History of the Arkansas Valley, Colorado.* Chicago: O. L. Baskin & Company, 1881.

Pacific Coast Annual Mining Review and Stock Ledger. San Francisco: Francis and Ballantine, 1878.

Paul, Rodman Wilson. *Mining Frontiers of the Far West, 1848–1880.* New York: Holt, Rinehart and Winston, 1963.

Poor, M.C. *Denver South Park & Pacific: A History of the Denver South Park & Pacific Railroad and Allied Narrow Gauge Lines of the Colorado & Southern Railway.* Denver: World Press, 1949.

Portrait and Biographical Record of Kalamazoo, Allegan, and Van Buren Counties Michigan. N.p., n.d.

Shinn, Charles H. *Mining Camps: A Study in American Frontier Government.* Edited by Rodman W. Paul. Gloucester, Mass.: Peter Smith, 1970.

Smart, Stephen F. *Leadville, Ten Mile, Eagle River, Elk Mountain, Tin Cup, and All Other Noted Colorado Mining Camps. . . .* Kansas City, Mo.: Ramsey, Millett, and Hudson, 1879.

Smiley, Jerome C. *History of Denver, with Outlines of the Earlier History of the Rocky Mountain Country.* Denver: J. H. Williamson, 1903.

Smith, Duane. *Horace Tabor: His Life and the Legend.* Boulder, Colo.: Colorado Associated University Press, 1973.

Whitney, Joel Parker. *Colorado, in the United States of America. Schedule of Ores Contributed by Sundry Persons to the Paris Universal Exposition of 1867. With Some Information About the Region and Its Resources.* London: Cassell, Petter, and Galpin, 1867.

Whitney, Joel Parker. *Reminiscences of a Sportsman.* New York: Forest and Stream Publishing Company, 1906.

Whitney, Joel Parker. *Silver Mining Regions of Colorado, with Some Account of the Different Processes Now Being Introduced for Working the Gold Ores of That Territory.* New York: D. Van Nostrand, 1865.

Wright, James Edward. *The Politics of Populism: Dissent in Colorado.* New Haven: Yale University Press, 1974.

D.   ARTICLES

Burkey, Elmer R. "The Georgetown-Leadville Stage." *Colorado Magazine* 14 (Sept. 1937).

Butler, B. S., and John W. Vanderwilt. "The Climax Molybdenum Deposit of Colorado, with Section on History, Production, Metallurgy and Development by Charles W. Henderson," *Colorado Scientific Society Proceedings,* November 10, 1931.

Hills, Georgia Burns. "Memories of a Pioneer Childhood." *Colorado Magazine* 32 (Summer 1955).

Hoyt, A. W. "Over the Plains to Colorado." *Harper's New Monthly Magazine* 35 (June 1867).

Koschmann, A. H., and F. G. Wells. "Preliminary Report on the Kokomo Mining District, Colorado." *Colorado Scientific Society Proceedings* 15 (1946), no. 2.

Leyendecker, Liston E. "Colorado and the Paris Universal Exposition, 1867." *Colorado Magazine* 46 (Winter 1969).

Rippeteau, Bruce Estes. "A Colorado Book of the Dead." *Colorado Magazine* 55 (Fall 1978).

Thomas, Charles S. "The Pioneer Bar of Colorado." *Colorado Magazine* 1 (July 1924).

Zelenkov, Sergei E. "Mining Practice at the Kokomo Unit of the American Smelting and Refining Company." *Mines Magazine*, April 1951.

E.   PERIODICALS

Breckenridge Bulletin
Breckenridge *Daily Journal*
Bullion (New York)
Colorado Mining Yearbook, 1933–1955.
Colorado Transcript (Golden)
Colorado Tribune (Golden)
Daily Miners' Register (Black Hawk)
Denver *Republican*
Denver *Tribune*
Engineering and Mining Journal. New York: Scientific Publishing Company.
Georgetown *Mining Review*
Gunnison *Daily Review Press*
Kalamazoo *Gazette*
Leadville *Daily Democrat*
Leadville *Daily Herald*
Leadville *Daily Record*
Leadville *Weekly Herald*
Leadville *Weekly News*
Miners' Record, Tarryall Mines
Mining and Scientific Press. San Francisco: Dewey Publishing Company.
New York *Mining Record*
Rocky Mountain Herald (Denver)
Rocky Mountain News (Denver)
Summit County Journal
Summit County Times
Ten Miles News

F.   THESES AND DISSERTATIONS

Spence, Clark Christian. "Robert Orchard Old and the British and Colorado Mining Bureau." M.A. thesis, University of Colorado, 1951.

G.   UNPUBLISHED REPORTS

Bulkley, Frank. "Report on the Robinson and Eldorado Mines and Log of Eldorado Shaft, 1900." Colorado School of Mines, Golden.
Danehy, George W. "Report on the Mineral Deposits at Kokomo, Ten Mile District, Colorado," 1934. Colorado School of Mines, Golden.
Moore, Charles J. "Report on the Queen of the West Mine, Summit County, Colorado." January 9, 1886. Colorado School of Mines, Golden.

Prescott, Basil. "Report on the Kokomo Mining District, 1926." Colorado
    School of Mines, Golden.
Thomas, Kirby. "Report on Kimberly Mine, Kokomo, Colorado," 1907. Col-
    orado School of Mines, Golden.
Wood, Henry E., and Philip Argall. "Report on the Robinson Mine." 1889.
    Colorado School of Mines, Golden.

H. INTERVIEWS

Boyd, James. Conversations with Stanley Dempsey.
Fohr, Franz. Leadville, Colo., 1884. Bancroft Collection, University of Cali-
    fornia, Berkeley. Copy in Norlin Library, University of Colorado, Boulder.
Recen, Henry A. Colorado Historical Society, Denver.

Index

297